The
WARRIOR GENERALS

The WARRIOR GENERALS

WINNING THE BRITISH CIVIL WARS
1642–1652

MALCOLM WANKLYN

YALE UNIVERSITY PRESS
NEW HAVEN AND LONDON

For information about this and other Yale University Press publications, please contact:
U.S. Office: sales.press@yale.edu   www.yalebooks.com
Europe Office: sales @yaleup.co.uk   www.yaleup.co.uk

Set in Arno Pro by IDSUK (DataConnection) Ltd.
Printed in Great Britain by TJ International Ltd, Padstow, Cornwall

Library of Congress Cataloging-in-Publication Data

Wanklyn, Malcolm.
   The Warrior Generals: Winning the British Civil Wars, 1642–1652 / Malcolm Wanklyn.
      p. cm.
   Includes bibliographical references.
   ISBN 978-0-300-11308-2 (cloth : alk. paper)
      1.   Great Britain—History—Civil War, 1642–1649—Campaigns. 2.
Generals—Great Britain—History—17th century. 3.   Command of
troops—History—17th century. 4.   Generals—Great Britain—Biography. 5.
Great Britain—History—Civil War, 1642–1649—Biography.   I. Title.
   DA415.W328 2010
   942.06'2—dc22

                                                                    2010001906

A catalogue record for this book is available from the British Library.

10 9 8 7 6 5 4 3 2 1

Contents

Plates

Maps and Battle Plans

Maps

Battle Plans

Preface

It is part of human nature to look for parallels between events in the past and to draw analogies between them in the hope of discovering general rules that apply in all circumstances. In seeking to explain the victory of Parliament in the First English Civil War of 1642–6, the obvious analogy is with what happened on the other side of the Atlantic more than 200 years later. In the American Civil War the winning side possessed most of the industrial might and wealth of the United States of America and most of its population. The South was therefore living on borrowed time, and after four years, having consumed almost all its military resources, it ran out of steam, its armies collapsed and it surrendered. To historians from the last quarter of the nineteenth century onwards what was true of the South must also have been true of King Charles I and the royalists. Parliament enjoyed an almost unchallenged control over London and south-east England, the wealthiest and most populous part of Charles's three king-doms, together with most of the pre-war armaments industries. The king had what was left, the thinly populated, underdeveloped north and west. Such wealth as there was in those parts belonged to the great landowners, and this was finite rather than renewable, not the product of ongoing industry and commerce but merely riches accumulated over many generations. Therefore, if the king was to win, he had to win quickly. By the autumn of 1643 it was already too late. From then onwards defeat was inevitable.

However, it has been clear to me for a very long time that the climactic moment in the First Civil War occurred before the king ran out of resources. When Sir Thomas Fairfax won the decisive victory at Naseby on 14 June 1645, it was not against a poorly armed, ragged remnant of an army. Instead he had faced a well-equipped, well-fed force comprising infantry and cavalry of proven ability, which had just stormed and looted Leicester, a major enemy garrison. Superior numbers were an important factor in the battle's outcome, as they gave Sir Thomas a depth in reserves that the king's generals did not possess, but the royalists were only inferior in numbers because of a string of decisions taken in April and May which allowed units of divisional and corps strength to operate at a distance from the field army in South Wales and the West Country. Different decisions would have resulted in Prince Rupert having sufficient reserves to win the battle, but whether he would have done so is mere speculation. All that can be said with confidence is that if the royalists had had an extra 6,000–7,000 horse and foot on 14 June, they could not have fought a battle on the Northamptonshire wolds between Naseby and Sibbertoft. The landscape would not have permitted it.

There is also a crucial political dimension which seriously undermines any argument that resources are the be all and end all of any discussion about why Parliament won the First Civil War. Civil wars are normally fought by formal or informal coalitions. The resilience of such coalitions is as important for final victory as resources, and it is here that the analogy with the American Civil War breaks down. The Unionists had that resilience, the parliamentary coalition did not because of tensions between the war aims of the Independents on the one hand and the Scots and their English allies on the other. The coalition was already showing strong signs of falling apart in the winter of 1644–5, and it did so once the war was over, but it might well have disintegrated much earlier had the king and his military advisers avoided a battle for just a few more months. The royalist high command's mistake was to count its chickens before they were hatched. In the spring of 1645 it opted for an offensive rather than a defensive strategy in the mistaken belief that the quarrels between the enemy soldiers and the politicians which had accompanied the birth of the New Model Army would adversely affect its performance on the battlefield.

This is not to deny that resources were a highly important factor in the outcome of the so-called British Wars of 1642–52. I am firmly convinced that the demographic imbalance between the south and east of England and the north and west gave Parliament an important advantage from the start, and that as this was a finite resource it could well have rendered the royalist war effort unviable in the long run. However, it is fatuous even to imply, as some have done, that once they have explained the imbalance in resources between the two sides the reasons for Parliament's victory require no further discussion. Superior resources were only one of a number of reasons why the war was won to all intents and purposes in 1645, and not necessarily the most important. Another factor was the way in which the warring generals fought the campaigns and battles. It was not necessarily the most important factor, but it was of considerable significance at the very least and therefore worthy of serious consideration in its own right in both the First and Second Civil Wars and also in the Anglo-Irish and the Anglo-Scottish wars of 1649–52.

Thus, the purpose of this book is to examine the role of army commanders in achieving victory for Parliament in the wars fought in the British Isles between 1641 and 1652. As such it is complementary to my earlier work, most particularly *A Military History of the English Civil Wars* (with Frank Jones) and *Decisive Battles of the English Civil Wars*. The first focused very largely on strategy in the

First English Civil War, and for most of the time this was firmly under the control not of the army commanders but of their political masters, King Charles I and the two Houses of Parliament. The second focused on the art of writing about battles.

I would like to take this opportunity to thank my family, my colleagues and my friends in academic and non-academic life for their continued support. I would also like to express my thanks to the British Academy for assistance with the financial costs of the research for *Warrior Generals*; to the National Army Museum which has preserved the notes, notebooks and card indexes I compiled many years ago and gave to Brigadier Peter Young thinking I would never need them again; to Fr Tom Rock for his knowledge of the landscape of what is now south Dublin; to my colleagues Professors John Benson, John Buckley and Mike Dennis, and my former student Charles Singleton, for their humour and generosity; to the National Portrait Gallery, the National Trust, and Charles Singleton for permission to print illustrations of which they hold the copyright; and to Heather McCallum for her wise advice and encouragement at all stages of the book's writing and publication. Finally, I thank staff in the libraries and record offices who have helped me with my research, most particularly those in the Bodleian Library, Oxford, and the National Archives, Scotland, where old courtesies and traditional ways still survive, and at Birmingham Central Reference Library where they cling on by their fingertips. Long may such a noble learning culture survive!

Glossary

Military Terms and Concepts

Approach   Attacking a fortified town or castle by constructing parallel lines of trenches getting ever closer to the walls so that siege artillery can eventually pummel them at very short range.

Artillery Park   A term customarily used to indicate where the spare supplies and guns belonging to the artillery were located during a battle. The artillery park was well to the rear of the reserve line and was often defended by musketeers.

Battalion   Typically, a formation of 600 or so infantry taken from a single large regiment and central to the reforms of Prince Maurice of Nassau and Gustavus Adolphus.

Bridge of Boats   The seventeenth-century version of the Bailey bridge. Boats would be requisitioned, moored in a line across the river, and then covered with a walkway made out of planks.

Brigade   A formation made up of several regiments of cavalry or infantry.

Caracole   An early-modern cavalry tactic in which a mounted unit rode up to an enemy formation, fired its pistols and carbines and then rode back to its own lines to reload. The damage done to the enemy was likely to be light given the low muzzle velocity of most of the weapons with which cavalry were armed, and the risk that the enemy would get amongst the ranks of the attackers as they turned their backs in the final stage of the manoeuvre meant that this tactic had a very brief lifespan.

Carbine   A short-barrelled musket normally used by horse soldiers.

Case Shot   Canisters of thin metal filled with musket balls fired by field artillery.

Celtic Warfare   See **The Highland Charge**

Close Order   Charging cavalry achieved the greatest impact if they formed a compact body with knee contact between the troopers. However, close order was difficult to maintain unless charging over a flat landscape.

Colours   Every infantry or dragoon company and every troop of horse had its own colours in the form of a flag on a short pole. It provided a rallying point in battle and was carried by the third officer, the ensign or the cornet.

Combined Operations   The use of small or large units of infantry and cavalry to support one another in battle or on campaign.

Commanded Body   A body of musketeers or cavalrymen taken out of several regiments to perform a particular task.

Company   An infantry regiment would normally consist of between six and twelve companies. Each would be commanded by a captain or a field officer, either a major or a lieutenant colonel. The colonel's company would be commanded by a captain lieutenant.

Cuirassiers   Heavy cavalry typically clad in full armour down to the knees and armed with sword or lance and a brace of pistols or carbines.

Dead Ground   A feature in the landscape that provides an attacking force with cover from incoming fire.

Denying the Flank   Deploying an army prior to a battle in such a way that it could not be outflanked. This was done, typically, by making use of features in the landscape or by stationing units of infantry and/or cavalry on the flanks facing outwards.

Deployment   The way in which the army general or his subordinate generals of foot and horse positioned the various units of an army or a lesser force prior to the start of an engagement.

Doctrine   Rules of war of general application.

Dragoons   Mounted soldiers who normally fought on foot. They were armed with muskets or carbines.

Encounter Battles   Battles in which the two sides encountered one another by accident or where the general on one side perceived an advantage in not allowing the enemy general time to deploy his army in the conventional manner before attacking.

Enfilading Fire   Fire directed against a unit from the flank.

Fabian   Operations modelled on those of Quintus Fabius Cunctator, who deliberately avoided battle with Hannibal's larger army in the Second Punic War in the hope of wearing it down to such an extent that he could go onto the attack.

Fascines   Bundles of sticks bound up with rope that were used to fill up obstacles such as ditches prior to an infantry assault.

Field Artillery   Small-calibre artillery pieces firing cannonballs or case shot. As early as the First Battle of Newbury (20 September 1643) they were attached to individual infantry regiments.

Firelock Musket   The ancestor of the flintlock. The spark for igniting the gunpowder was produced by a flint striking a piece of steel, but flintlocks were expensive and easily broken. They tended to be used by regiments guarding the artillery train. It was less dangerous to have firelocks in close proximity to barrels of gunpowder than matchlocks.

Flying Army   A large force that had the ability to move rapidly across country. It was typically made up of mounted troops, with musketeers sometimes riding piggyback to supplement the firepower of the dragoons.

Foot   Another term for infantry. Their armour typically consisted of a helmet and back- and breast-plates. Their principal weapons were the musket and the pike, though most would carry a cheap sword for close-quarter fighting. Celtic warriors often carried a small shield or target.

Force (as, for example, in Balfour Force)   A useful twentieth-century term for describing a small ad hoc formation allotted a particular mission or task.

Harquebusiers   Medium cavalry typically clad in helmet, breast-plate and back-plate, and armed with the same weapons as cuirassiers.

Heavy Artillery   Large-calibre artillery pieces (e.g. culverins, demi-culverins, etc.) which accompanied the army on campaign. They were employed primarily in sieges to batter down enemy fortifications. However, they would play a prominent part in the barrage that normally preceded a battle.

The Highland Charge   A tactic said to have been devised by Alasdair McColla in the 1640s by which infantry armed with sword and buckler (a small round shield) charged the opposing infantry on foot.

Horse   Very frequently used as a synonym for cavalry, though dragoons were also horse.

Interior Lines   An advantage enjoyed by a defending force when being attacked from several different directions. Its commander, having the central position, could quickly concentrate his troops at a single location along his defensive perimeter and thus achieve local superiority over his attackers, with a good prospect of achieving a major tactical success.

Lancers   Heavy, medium or light cavalry armed with lances. Such units were only common in the Scottish armies.

Matchlock Musket   The basic infantry weapon which used gunpowder to fire a lead ball with a diameter of about a centimetre. The gunpowder was ignited by a slow-burning fuse called a match made of thick twine dipped in a fluid containing saltpetre and allowed to dry, which each musketeer had to carry into battle with him. Matchlocks were sturdier than firelocks and easier to make. They only had a single moving part, the match holder and trigger, the means by which the match was applied to the gunpowder in the pan. This was connected to the main charge in the barrel via a touch hole. In an infantry fight at close quarters, matchlocks were often upended and used as clubs.

Melee   A term used to describe two bodies of horse fighting at close quarters with sword and pistol. It was literally hand-to-hand combat on horseback.

Military Manuals   Generals had access to several types of military text. First there were those written in the Ancient World, which they might have used at school or university, Caesar's *Gallic Wars* being probably the most popular. Second, there were texts such as John Cruso's *Militarie Instructions for the Cavall'rie* (1632) and Roger Ward's *Animadversions of Warre* (1635), which were aimed at the junior officer and amateur soldier market and focused on army organisation, drill and the handling of small units. Third, there were texts written by contemporary generals that placed more emphasis on higher-level skills such as managing an army and military diplomacy, of which the most recent was Henri, Duc de Rohan's *The Complete Captain III: A Particular Treatise of Modern War*, translated by Captain John Cruso, and published by Cambridge University Press in 1640. Finally, there were texts that never attracted the attention of a printer but which may have circulated privately amongst interested parties, such as Will Legge's pre-war treatise that played to his then strength, the artillery.

Militia Regiments   The successors of the trained bands. They were raised from 1647 onwards in the English counties and were often full of former soldiers. They fought well at Worcester.

Musketeers   Brigaded with pikemen in infantry regiments, they were almost invariably deployed on the flanks of the body of pikes, which could serve as a refuge if they came under too much pressure from enemy cavalry. Musketeers were normally drawn up six ranks deep in open country. Their drill gave them the opportunity to deliver various types of barrage, but they usually only had the chance of firing once before their infantry formations came into direct contact with enemy infantry. However, behind hedges and walls the firepower of musketeers could be employed over a much longer period, as the cover gave them the chance to reload and fire a succession of barrages on command.

Muskets   The infantry firearm, which was muzzle loaded with a charge of gunpowder and a musket ball separated from it by a fabric wad. A rod was used to compress the gunpowder before the ball was inserted. Individually, muskets were highly inaccurate but they could be devastating if fired en masse at a range of fifty yards or less. In the New Model Army the ratio of musketeers to pikemen was two to one. There is only circumstantial evidence that other armies experimented with higher ratios, though it is possible that those which included garrison troops, like Charles I's at Naseby, did have a larger proportion of musketeers than was usually the case.

Oblique Order of Attack   Massing the bulk of the army against one flank of the enemy army so as to gain overwhelming local superiority and a quick victory before the enemy general can dispatch reinforcements.

Operations   Operations were the means by which strategy was put into effect. The conduct of operations was normally the responsibility of the army general, but the sovereign frequently exerted a measure of control ranging from written orders to having representatives on the general's Council of War. Operations is a concept rarely if ever used by military historians writing about any campaign earlier than the nineteenth century. Instead they tend to use strategy to cover both its aims and its execution.

Parole   A promise often made by prisoners taken in a battle or at the capture of a garrison that they would not take up arms again against those to whom they had surrendered.

Pikemen   Foot soldiers armed with pikes.

Pikes   Poles up to sixteen feet in length topped by a spear head. They could be used defensively to fend off cavalry or offensively against other formations of pikemen in the so-called 'push of pike', the aim being to cause their opponents to lose their footing, break and run. Occasionally, as at Adwalton Moor and Preston Bridge, the whole body would charge the enemy. In the New Model Army infantry regiments the ratio was one pikeman to two musketeers. When being attacked by cavalry, well-trained units would be able to form a hollow square within which their musketeers could shelter.

Pin (v.)   To deploy one's forces in such a manner that the enemy army was forced to remain in a position which put it at a grave tactical disadvantage.

Pistol   The typical missile weapon used by the cavalry, generally carried in pairs in holsters on either side of the saddle, but not on a belt around the trooper's waist as pistols had barrels a foot and a half in length. They were wheel-locks, which meant that the trooper did not have to carry match with him, but they were ineffective weapons with a low muzzle velocity, and their small-calibre bullets were rarely able to pierce body armour.

Regiment The principal cavalry and infantry formation often raised by a single individual who commanded it in battle and on campaign with the rank of colonel. Commissions were often granted for colonels to raise in excess of 1,000 infantry and 500 cavalry per regiment, but normally regiments were smaller even at the start of a campaign.

Sally A surprise attack made on besiegers by the besieged.

Standoff A defensive tactic by which an army general deployed his forces in such a position that the enemy general would be deterred from attacking them for fear of the casualties his formations were likely to sustain.

Strategy The overall objectives of a campaign or of a number of campaigns being fought in parallel. Strategy is normally determined by the sovereign before the campaign begins, and is conveyed to the army general in the form of a command. As the campaign progresses, however, it may be necessary to alter strategic objectives in response to changing circumstances.

Tactics The methods by which the army general set about inflicting defeat on the enemy in a confrontational situation, such as a battle, a siege or a standoff, or in a smaller encounter, such as the ambush of enemy units on the march or an attack on the villages where they were billeted.

Trained Bands Local defence forces made up of part-time soldiers, which first came into existence during Queen Elizabeth I's reign. A middle-sized English county would typically have 600 foot and 100 horse, which could be called upon by the lord lieutenant to put down civil unrest. Their military value in the Civil War, however, was limited, as they trained infrequently and trained-band soldiers could hire substitutes to serve in their stead. The City of London trained bands, originally six regiments but expanded to over twice that number in the first year of the war, constituted an exception. They trained regularly and were an important asset to Parliament at the First Battle of Newbury and at Cheriton, but their performance fell off during 1644 as the zealots were killed or volunteered for regular regiments.

Troop A cavalry regiment was made up of a number of troops ranging from two to as many as sixteen, though six to eight was the norm. Each troop would be commanded by a captain or a field officer, lieutenant colonel or major in royalist regiments, major in parliamentary ones. As in an infantry regiment the colonel's troop would be commanded by a captain lieutenant.

Wing A term used to describe formations on the left and right of an army drawn up to fight a battle. They were very largely made up of units of cavalry. However, the term was clearly used when a battle was not in the offing to describe a cavalry formation bigger than a brigade.

Topographical Terms

Champion Country   Open country without hedges, woods, etc.

Close   A small patch of ground enclosed by walls or hedges. Closes were often clustered around villages or hamlets, as at Church Speen and Naseby.

Commons   Land that was not cultivated, usually because of its low natural fertility and/or poor drainage. It was used for rough grazing and as a source of firewood.

Enclosures   Areas of agricultural land divided up into small fields or closes.

Fielden and Forest   A description of the topographical divisions of Warwickshire and Worcestershire. The south was open-field country (fielden). Much of the north and central part of the counties was woodland, formerly the Forests of Arden and Feckenham.

Lowland Heath   Open ground used for rough grazing. It was often covered to a greater or lesser extent by gorse and brambles, and parts might be poorly drained.

Meadow   An area of open land dedicated to the growing of grass for winter fodder. From the hay harvest until winter, meadows would be used as pasture land for grazing animals.

Open Fields   Areas of arable land often hundreds of acres in extent and cultivated using the strip system. Typically, a village's fields were cultivated on a three-field system of rotation with two growing crops and the other allowed to remain fallow to recover its natural fertility. There was little timber in open-field country, but the hedges dividing one village's land from another's, or dividing open grazing from common, were often formidable military obstacles.

Pass   A much wider concept than that which is in use today, namely any feature that narrowed an army's line of advance, such as a river crossing.

Ridge and Furrow   The typical physical appearance of open fields, where the parallel strips resembled a modern corrugated-iron roof. Ridge and furrow presented a major problem to units of foot and horse trying to move across it and still maintain formation.

Wolds   Areas of gently rolling agricultural land often at some elevation and away from river valleys. The High Cotswolds and the Northamptonshire Heights were typical wold country.

CHAPTER 1

The Generals

IT WAS the early afternoon of Thursday, 13 July 1643. Henry, Lord Wilmot, lieutenant general of cavalry in King Charles I's field army, sat on his horse on Morgan's Hill looking across a dip in the Wiltshire Downs. His orders when he left Oxford, the royalist headquarters, were simple and straightforward. He was to rescue the infantry and artillery of the army of the west under Sir Ralph Hopton, penned up in the town of Devizes for the past five days and very short of food and ammunition. However, blocking his way on Roundway Down, three miles short of the town, was a much larger parliamentary army commanded by Sir William Waller.

Behind Wilmot were three royalist cavalry brigades, in total some 1,800 officers and men. Two brigades, his own and Sir John Byron's, consisted of regiments which had fought well in earlier battles and skirmishes, but they were weary, having ridden forty miles in less than a day, and 'much lessened in the long march'. The third brigade under the earl of Crawford had not come so far, but it was even less ready to do battle. Waller's cavalry had ambushed it in a night engagement whilst it was on its way to Devizes with a supply of ammunition. Wilmot therefore placed Crawford's men in the reserve line. They were not to be employed 'until it should please God to renew their courage with our success'.[1]

Lack of numbers and tiredness were not the only problems. Wilmot's force also lacked firepower, as he had not brought any musketeers or field pieces with him. He had to get to Devizes quickly and might arrive too late if he kept to their slow pace. All he had was a small brass cannon carried in pieces on horseback whose sole purpose was to signal the arrival of the relief force. Wilmot obviously hoped that Hopton's men would join him, but it was not to be. The commanders of the western army could see nothing of what was happening on the downs to the north. Given Waller's reputation for subterfuge, the firing they could hear was probably a trick to tempt them into the open. Discretion was therefore the better part of valour. They would not leave the safety of their barricades until the situation clarified.[2]

Facing Wilmot on Roundway Down was a complete army comprising some 2,500 foot and 3,000 horse and dragoons, and a considerable number of artillery pieces.[3] At its head was Parliament's most consistently successful general, hailed as a second William the Conqueror by the London newspapers after winning a string of minor engagements from September 1642 onwards. Waller's cavalry were not only more numerous than Wilmot's, they were well rested. They also included Sir Arthur Haselrig's regiment clad in armour from head to knee, nicknamed the 'Lobsters' by their foe. The first large unit of heavy cavalry in Parliament's armies, they had done very well in a defensive role at the battle of Lansdown near Bath ten days earlier. Confidence was exceedingly high.[4] 'So sure was I of victory,' Waller claimed subsequently, 'that I wrote to Parliament to bid them to be at rest [i.e. not to worry] for that I would shortly send them an account of the numbers of the enemy taken and the numbers slain'.[5]

Sir William drew up his army in the conventional manner for battles fought in open country, with infantry in the centre and cavalry on the wings. They formed up on the last ridge of open country before the chalk downs of south

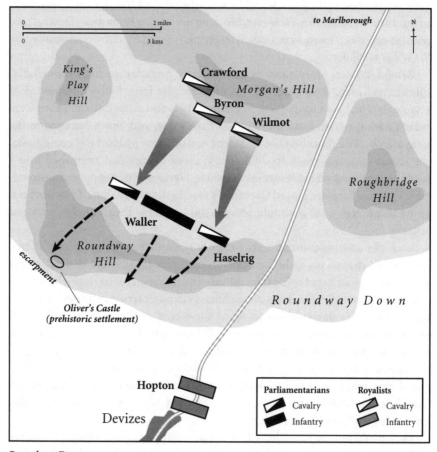

Roundway Down

Wiltshire gave way to the Vale of Pewsey and the wide-ranging sheep to the dairy cow straitened by its hedge-bounded pastures. There he intended to wait for the royalist cavalry to attack, confident in the strength of his position and the favour of the Lord. If the enemy decided to charge, they would have to pound up the slope losing momentum with every stride. To tempt them to do so he pushed forward a small body of cavalry from the right wing into the dip between his army and theirs to act as bait. As soon as the enemy attacked this vanguard, he probably intended Haselrig's Lobsters to charge them in the flank and put them to flight. The fighting would then be over to all intents and purposes. With another victory to his credit, and the most spectacular to date, Sir William could well find himself appointed commander-in-chief of Parliament's main field army, his superior the earl of Essex having lost favour because of his lack of success, his inactivity and his interminable complaints about being starved of resources.

Thus, in terms of both military muscle and battle preparedness, the odds were heavily stacked against the royalists. However, there was great urgency about their mission. If they did not fight (or fought and lost) the troops in Devizes would surrender within hours, thus depriving the king's army of 3,000 or so precious infantry. In addition, Wilmot almost certainly had a personal motive for fighting. It would give him the chance to show that he was a first-rate cavalry commander and not a pale shadow of Prince Rupert, the king's nephew. Therefore, taking personal charge of the right wing he prepared to give battle.

Wilmot's military career had been a switchback ride since returning from service on the Continent. He had fought bravely against the Scots in 1640 as second-in-command of the cavalry to the earl of Holland. However, at the outbreak of the First Civil War he was merely reinstated as commissary general. Prince Rupert was moved in over his head as General of Horse, whilst the post of lieutenant general was left vacant. According to Lord Clarendon, who hated Wilmot along with the rest of the king's young cavalry commanders, Rupert disliked him because he was ambitious, very experienced and popular with his men, and he was not in favour with the king.[6] To make matters worse, Wilmot had begun the war badly by avoiding a full-scale confrontation with the enemy at Dunsmore Heath in Warwickshire in September 1642. This caused some on the royalist side to question his courage. He nevertheless commanded the left wing of the king's horse at the battle of Edgehill, also in Warwickshire, on 23 October, and routed the enemy facing him, but rumours were circulating that his opponents had not been cavalry, but dragoons who were more accustomed to fighting on foot than on horseback. He had also failed to see off a formation of parliamentary horse on that wing, which had gone on to cause havoc, routing two of the king's five infantry brigades and turning what had been near certain victory into near defeat. Admittedly Wilmot had led a successful raid on Marlborough two months later. As a reward he received a peerage and the coveted rank of lieutenant general, but it was an easy victory over a rabble of newly raised men. However, it was a stroke of luck that Wilmot, not Rupert, was the most senior commander in town when news of what had happened at Devizes reached Oxford. The prince was thirty miles away to the north with the rest of the king's cavalry, acting as the flank guard for a small army marching down from Yorkshire escorting the queen and a much-needed consignment of gunpowder.

Wilmot began the battle of Roundway Down by ordering a commanded body of horse led by his major, Paul Smith, to draw their swords and charge the parliamentary vanguard. They were immediately successful in pushing the enemy back, but as the latter tried to make their way to the rear they fell foul of the remaining cavalry units on the right wing which Waller had deployed in large blocks just behind them and in close order six ranks deep. Seeing how much disruption this had caused, Wilmot charged with the rest of his brigade, probably catching Haselrig's Lobsters in the flank as they wheeled inwards to attack Paul Smith's men. Within minutes the entire parliamentary right wing was in flight, but Wilmot ordered his troopers not to pursue them. They were to regroup before switching their attention to the enemy units that were still on the battlefield.

The struggle on the other wing was more prolonged. Sir John Byron led forward his brigade at the trot, ordering his men not to fire their pistols until they were in amongst the enemy. Leaving a small party in reserve, Waller ordered his remaining horsemen forward, a sensible procedure in the circumstances, but they were either moving slowly or stationary when the royalists struck. A melee of some length then ensued, but efforts of the parliamentary reserve to intervene were thwarted by Crawford's brigade, which threatened them as they tried to move into a position to attack Byron's flank. In the end the entire enemy left wing also gave way and followed the right wing off the battlefield in the general direction of Bristol.

Waller's regiments of foot, which had been little more than spectators during the cavalry engagement, stood their ground for a while hoping that their horse were regrouping somewhere to the rear and would soon return to cover their retreat. This caused a stalemate. There was little that Wilmot's cavalry could do on their own against the firepower of massed ranks of trained musketeers protected by pikemen, and several troopers died when they ventured too close. However, the situation altered completely when the parliamentary infantry saw the infantry of the western army marching up the hill from Devizes. At this point the senior officers seem to have decided to shift for themselves. Mounting their horses they followed in the wake of the cavalry, urging their soldiers to follow them. If they did not do so, a massive barrage of enemy musket fire would tear holes in their ranks, break up their formation and allow Wilmot's horsemen to muscle their way in and cut them down where they stood.

The parliamentary infantry tried to make a fighting retreat westwards, their aim being to reach the Vale of Pewsey only two miles away where the hedges would give them protection against both enemy musket fire and enemy horsemen wielding swords. However, as they marched off the battlefield, they started to lose formation and then scattered completely when they tried to make their way down the steep escarpment separating the chalk from the clay. In such circumstances it is scarcely surprising that Wilmot's horsemen captured or killed almost all of them.

On this occasion, as one of Waller's captains Edward Harley eloquently put it, 'nothing hath been gained by us with multitudes'.[7] The royalist victory owed everything to the decisions taken by the two generals as to how to conduct the battle with the forces they had at their disposal. Waller's cavalry tactics were sound, and there is only second-hand evidence that Haselrig's heavy brigade attacked prematurely, their discipline overcome by religious zeal. It was also good practice for Waller to have deployed his cavalry in close order so that they could achieve the highest possible momentum in the charge, but he should have left sufficient gaps between various units for the vanguard to be able to get to the rear without causing disruption.

A much bigger mistake was not to make imaginative use of his regiments of foot. As Wilmot had no infantry with him, Waller could have deployed some of his musketeers in direct support of his cavalry. This was a very effective tactic for repelling a charge provided that the musketeers reserved their fire until the enemy were less than fifty yards away. Waller could also have detached commanded parties of musketeers and pikemen to attack the flank of Byron's brigade whilst it was locked in combat with his left wing. Sir William was an imaginative tactician, as he showed on numerous occasions off rather than on the battlefield, but if such an idea did come into his head, there was nothing he could have done about it. By that time he was in the thick of the cavalry engagement and unable to give orders to the rest of his army. Finally, by choosing Roundway Down as the place to fight, Waller showed overweening confidence in his ability to win, as the escarpment to his rear was a disaster waiting to happen should he suffer a setback.

Wilmot, on the other hand, used the few resources he had in exemplary fashion. His tactical plan, which entailed using his best men as shock troops whilst retaining a strong reserve, was extremely sound. Having few units to commit, his decision to lead the attack in person was equally sound. Given the strength of the enemy, his troops needed a heroic gesture from their commander if they were to perform at their best. There was no need for him to remain behind to manage the reserve. Crawford was to move forward when victory was assured as his men were still in a state of shock. However, as a skilled professional soldier he intervened when the left wing came under serious threat.

Next, having defeated the enemy facing him, Wilmot did not pursue them but ordered his cavalry to regroup ready to go to Sir John Byron's assistance, though in the event this proved unnecessary. Wilmot then turned his attention to the enemy infantry, but held his men back until Hopton's infantry arrived on the battlefield. Finally, when the enemy foot began to disintegrate as they moved off towards the escarpment, his cavalry were in position to take maximum advantage. As a result the pursuit stage of the battle was highly effective. When Waller left the west of England for London ten days later, he had no infantry with him and fewer than 500 cavalry.

The battle of Roundway Down was a relatively minor engagement in terms of the numbers involved, but the consequences were enormous. If Waller had won, he would have quickly overrun the south-west of England, which was to be the major source of all kinds of military resources for the king's armies for the next two years. In the second Newbury campaign fought in the autumn of 1644 at least half of the royalist troops came from those parts, and of the two major armies the king had in the field in May 1645 one was almost entirely made up of regiments raised in the south-west. In addition, royalist armies in 1644 and 1645 could not have taken the field without munitions brought in from abroad through ports like Bristol, Exeter and Dartmouth.

Roundway Down was not unique. The smaller army won at Preston in August 1648, in the battle which decided the Second English Civil War, and also at Rathmines in August 1649 and Dunbar in September 1650, victories that put Parliament's enemies firmly on the back foot for the rest of the wars in Ireland and Scotland respectively. The other side of the coin was that in many battles the stronger side, though victorious, failed to exploit its superiority in numbers as effectively as it ought to have done. This was the case in the First English Civil War at Cheriton (March 1644), Marston Moor (July 1644), Lostwithiel (August 1644) and Langport (July 1645), and at the Second Battle of Newbury (October 1644). Captain Edward Harley, then, was right when he wrote after Roundway Down that 'multitudes' did not invariably triumph. This he attributed to God, who liked to teach lessons to the over-confident and to show his power through 'exalting the humble and meek'.[8] But for God's will to be done, human instruments were required, namely the generals who commanded the armies. There were, of course, many men with the word 'general' in their title in the armies of the 1640s – heads of discrete departments like transport and intelligence, for example, and the commanders of cavalry, infantry and artillery (and often their deputies) – but it was the army commanders who had the power to win or lose a war in an afternoon, and they are the sole concern of this book.

The army commanders who fought in the British Isles between 1642 and 1652 were as diverse in their life experience as the characters in a stage play or a film, but they had two factors in common, their social origins and their gender. Almost without exception they came from the landed elite or the upper class – even out-and-out professionals like Edward Massey and George Monck, and the Scottish generals Alexander and David Leslie – and all were male. Although Queen Henrietta Maria described herself as the 'she generalissimo' in the summer of 1643 whilst accompanying the small army bringing munitions to Oxford from the north of England, the title was self-assumed. Her leadership was purely symbolic, as was that of female garrison commanders like Brilliana, Lady Harley, at Brampton Bryan in Herefordshire, and the countess of Derby at Lathom House in Lancashire.

There were army commanders, most particularly Oliver Cromwell and Prince Rupert, whom some of their contemporaries saw as heroes blessed by God and others as black-hearted villains in league with the Devil. There were great aristo-crats totally out of their depth like the first duke of Hamilton; officers who were fond of the bottle, such as George Goring and Henry Wilmot; but only one known cuckold, the earl of Essex. There were young men in their twenties like the Palatine princes Rupert and Maurice, and old men in their sixties like Sir Jacob Astley. There were friends driven apart by differences in allegiance such as Sir Ralph Hopton and Sir William Waller. There were men experienced in high military command before the wars began like the earls of Forth and Leven, and others totally lacking in pre-war military experience. In the latter category were the unlikely trio of the marquis of Newcastle, the bishop of Clogher and Oliver Cromwell. Some, despite being professionals, were over-promoted, like the Irish generals Garet Barry and Thomas Preston, but others rose rapidly and deserved to do so, such as Charles Gerard and Edward Massey. Most were fit in mind and body, but others were afflicted with a range of physical and mental ailments: Forth was deaf and subject to gout, Cromwell experienced recurring attacks of ague, whilst Sir Thomas Fairfax's manifold wounds seem to have affected his ability to put thoughts into words other than on the battlefield itself. There were those for whom their religion was of paramount importance, like Cromwell and Owen Roe O'Neill, and others who wore their religion lightly, like John Lambert (and many of the king's generals, according to their enemies).

Several died of disease whilst still in command, most particularly in Ireland, but the earl of Lindsey was the only one to die on the battlefield, and Prince Maurice the only one to be drowned at sea. Massey was the only former army commander to change sides, though Sir John Urry and George Monck had fought for the opposition at a more lowly rank. The careers of most commanders ended in dismissal, usually for not achieving the successes their political masters had expected of them. However, that was not necessarily the end. Some royalist generals like the marquis of Ormond and the first earl of Inchiquin in Ireland, and Monck and Prince Rupert in England, went on to become important servants of the state when Charles II regained his father's throne in 1660.

Two of the king's army commanders, Hamilton and the marquis of Montrose, were tried and executed after being taken prisoner, but none of Parliament's generals suffered the same fate after the Restoration of the monarchy in 1660. Essex and Lord Fairfax were dead. Sir Thomas Fairfax lived quietly at home protected by his powerful son-in-law, the duke of Buckingham, and by his success in raising the north against John Lambert, his former protégé, in the winter of 1659. Lambert, however, spent the last twenty years of his life in prison, whilst the corpse of Cromwell, removed from its resting place in Westminster Abbey, had manifold indignities inflicted upon it. The earl of Manchester was the only leading army commander to have fought for Parliament who held an important position post-1660, but that was at court, not in the armed services. The other parliamentary survivor, Sir William Waller, experienced the worst of both worlds. Imprisoned by Lord Protector Cromwell on suspicion of plotting against the Commonwealth regime, he was all but ignored after 1660, probably on account of his persistent and unfashionable Puritanism.

Officers of various ranks commanded armies in the field. In the case of the royalists, lord general was the highest position to which they could aspire and it was held successively by the earl of Lindsey, the earl of Forth, Prince Rupert and Jacob, Lord Astley. Their only superior was the king, who as generalissimo had absolute authority over all his officers. Only in exceptional circumstances did Charles act as army commander.[9] His place was at the summit of the chain of command presiding over the royalist Council of War, which distributed military resources, issued instructions to commanders at many levels, and settled disputes between them. It was also the forum in which army commanders, lesser officers and civilians discussed strategy, but with the king taking the final decision.

Through carefully worded commissions the king delegated to his army generals the power to command men, to grant commissions to lesser officers and to hold courts martial. The lord general's commission identified his rank as that of captain general, which gave him the right to send binding commands to generals of a lower rank, but the king might decide otherwise. Prince Rupert, General of Horse at the start of the First Civil War, took his orders only from the king. Charles's intention was probably to prevent friction between a self-opinionated and prickly member of the Royal Family and the aristocratic and equally prickly earl of Lindsey.[10] Instead, it may have helped to cause the hiatus in battlefield command, which almost lost the royalists the battle of Edgehill two months later.[11]

Similarly the king's say-so played a vital role if two generals of similar rank were to work together, as was the case with Rupert's expedition to relieve York in the spring of 1644. At that time the prince was the newly appointed commander of the king's army in Wales and the Welsh Marches, and as such he may have been junior to the marquis of Newcastle, who had been in effect captain general of the north of England for well over a year. However, the latter willingly accepted orders from the prince when he arrived at York because Rupert brought with him a letter from the king stating that he had conferred military authority on his nephew that was to all intents and purposes viceregal.[12] Similar authority was also enjoyed by generals in command of armies operating at some distance from the king's headquarters and cut off from easy communication with it, such as the marquis of Hertford in the west of England in 1642–3[13] and the marquis of Montrose in Scotland from July 1644 to early August 1645.[14] They were described in their commissions as lieutenant generals, but they were in practice captain generals.[15] At the other extreme were officers who were in command in their army general's absence, such as Major General Lord Byron, Rupert's deputy in the Welsh borderland for much of 1644, or those who were in charge of ad hoc assemblages of regiments like Wilmot at Roundway Down and Lord Goring in the West Country in 1645.

Parliament's practice was subtly different. The two Houses claimed the inalienable right to exercise the king's military prerogatives on the grounds that he was no longer competent to defend his people.[16] However, they delegated much of the detail, including issuing instructions to officers of all ranks and managing the day-to-day conduct of the war, to an executive committee, first the Committee of Safety and then the Committee of Both Kingdoms.[17] There was no generalissimo, though in 1642 the newly appointed captain general, the earl of Essex, was apparently keen to be appointed Constable of England with dictatorial powers in military matters including the right to negotiate with the king on Parliament's behalf. However, he failed to convince the two Houses that such an office was necessary.[18]

Essex therefore had to be content with the title of lord general, but as time passed this became an increasingly empty honour. He lost control of the north to Lord Fairfax in December 1642, and of East Anglia and adjacent counties to the earl of Manchester early in 1644. Both had commissions as lieutenant generals, but the powers Parliament conferred upon them were those of captain general.[19] The title of lord general, however, belonged to Essex until his resignation in April 1645.

The commanders of Parliament's provincial armies in the First Civil War other than Fairfax and Manchester held the rank of major general, the next step down in the hierarchy of command. This meant that they were subject to orders from the earl of Essex (though Waller in particular challenged the right of Essex to do so). In the Scottish army the earl of Leven, first appointed in 1639, clung onto the title of lord general until 1651, but did not exercise field command after 1645. His deputy, David Leslie, was therefore never more than lieutenant general, whereas the armies that Montrose defeated in the summer of 1645 at Auldearn, Alford and Kilsyth were under the command of major generals.

Parliament also appointed officers at the county or regional level who exercised an army general's powers but did not hold a substantive rank any higher than colonel. The most important of these were Sir John Meldrum and Sir William Brereton. Meldrum, a Scottish professional soldier, went to the north of England in June 1643 on Lord Fairfax's insistence that he needed a man in the Trent valley capable of knocking heads together. He remained in the north and the North Midlands for two years, leading ad hoc armies to victory at Montgomery and defeat at Newark, but died whilst storming Scarborough Castle as the First Civil War was drawing to a close.[20] Brereton had no such military experience, and like his friend Cromwell he rose slowly to a position of authority,[21] but by the beginning of 1646 he was in command of the siege of Chester with an army of several thousand men drawn from counties as far away as Warwickshire in one direction and Yorkshire in the other.[22]

Finally, a key feature of the fighting in all three of Charles I's kingdoms was the absence of a peacetime army. One very important consequence was that army generals were not already in post but ad hoc appointments. However, there was a conspicuous dearth of such talent in the aristocracy. Those members of the aristocracy who had some experience in Germany or the Netherlands had fought different types of war in different landscapes and had not commanded anything larger than a regiment. Such caveats also applied almost as much to the second pool of potential army generals, professional soldiers who had recently returned from the Continent. It is not therefore surprising that men who had no experience of campaigning often did as well in high command as those who had.

CHAPTER 2

The First Campaign of the English Civil War

THE OPENING MOVES

O PEN WARFARE broke out in England, the wealthiest and most populous of Charles I's three kingdoms, in the late summer of 1642 after five years of political turmoil that had afflicted both England and Scotland. Some of those who immediately took up arms on behalf of Parliament or the king had concerns about religion, civil liberties and social unrest. Others responded to pressures such as kinship and economic self-interest. The flashpoint was a fundamental issue of sovereignty, namely who should have ultimate control over the armed forces of the realm. In Scotland the king had just lost this right through determined action by a powerful body of opinion drummed into shape by the Presbyterian ministers and elders, and led by a powerful faction amongst the nobility. In England the matter had yet to be resolved, but the need to raise an army to suppress an uprising in Ireland brought the issue into stark relief. Traditionally the king had commanded the armed forces of the realm, but Parliament was making a bid for control. The king could not be trusted with an army. He would use it first to roll back the tide of reform in his other two kingdoms. Had not the Irish been encouraged to rebel by some of Charles's closest advisers (including Queen Henrietta Maria who was herself a Catholic)?

Charles's third kingdom had been comparatively peaceful since the suppression of the last uprising in 1603, but the Catholic majority had become increasingly alarmed by the violent and virulent anti-Catholic language of the king's opponents in the Lords and the Commons. If Parliament won the constitutional battle in England, the obvious inference was that the Catholics in Ireland would have a very hard time indeed, as the Irish Parliament was subordinate to the English one. Unless they took some action, they would find themselves forced to adopt an alien religion and an alien culture. In Ireland, then, the central issue was one of self-defence and self-determination, but as in England and Scotland it was also bound up with sovereignty. Security could only be achieved through weakening, even breaking, the links with English institutions, and this meant raising an army to resist an Anglo-Scottish invasion and to ensure that the Protestants living in Ireland were in no position to act as a fifth column.

The task of the army commander in all of this was to bring his sovereign's war aims to a successful conclusion. In an ideal world he would receive support in several key areas: first, sufficient delegated authority for his orders to be obeyed without question; second, sufficient military resources to carry out the strategy by which he was to accomplish his sovereign's desires; and third, such supplies as he needed to keep his army in good heart and up to strength for as long as the campaign lasted. Reality, however, was often painfully and frustratingly different. Immediate success was rare, and disillusion set in as the general came to see his sovereign's ambitions as overly optimistic and the sovereign lost patience with his general's inability to deliver military success on demand. The upshot was a vicious circle with the general achieving less and less, as the sovereign, determined not to send good money after bad, pushed resources in the direction of other generals who were making a better job of things or were more accomplished in covering up their mistakes. If outright sacking was politically embarrassing or dangerous, the sovereign would tend to compensate by interfering more and more in operational matters in the hope of rescuing something from the mess, whilst the general lapsed into despair as he saw his plans overruled and his reputation ruined in the eyes of his officers and men as pay, reinforcements and new military hardware became intermittent and then a mere trickle. In the end the general would lose his command, a scapegoat for all that had gone wrong, but his excited and enthusiastic successor would soon discover that he too was standing at the top of a slippery slope which led to disgrace and infamy.

The true nature of the relationship between army general and sovereign was neatly summed up by George Monck as follows:

> If he grow rich, he is traduced [defamed]. If he fail or prove unfortunate, he is contumnated [scorned], scandalised [libelled], and if the whole success answereth not their opinions who employ him, they will repine [complain], although the fault more often is caused by their neglect or wilfullness or by curbing the authority of the chief commanders too much; and people are always apt to judge of the general's actions rather by the event than by reason, so that it is hard for a man to take the command of an army and to keep his reputation until the end.[1]

Monck was also referring obliquely to the way in which the civilian viewed the military. Not only were civilians suspicious that soldiers were more interested in feathering their own nests than in fighting, they were also deaf to reasoned argument if everything did not go according to plan. However niggardly the military resources allotted to the army, however inclement the weather and however difficult the landscape over which the campaign was to be fought, only outright victory would satisfy them.

The field army that Parliament assembled at the start of the First English Civil War in the late summer of 1642 was as well resourced as was possible given the country's tiny arms industry,[2] and in this respect it was far superior to the

army the king was trying to raise. The rank and file were all volunteers. The officers of the rank of captain and above were either members of the aristocracy and
the landed gentry or professional officers, of whom there were shoals heading
for London in the summer of 1642 looking for employment in Ireland. The
infantry regiments were well armed with muskets and pikes, and differentiated
from one another by the facings of their uniforms: red for Denzil Holles's regiment, purple for Lord Brooke's, blue for Sir William Constable's, and so on. The
cavalry were apparently well mounted, but not that well equipped. Nathaniel
Fiennes, captain of a troop of horse at the battle of Edgehill, defended his
younger brother's absence on the grounds that he had persuaded him to ride to
Evesham the day before, 'for to take some arms that were come thither for such
of our men as wanted them'.[3]

Morale should have been good, as the rank and file were volunteers. For some
like Sergeant Nehemiah Wharton, who served in Denzil Holles's regiment, religious zeal and the belief that Parliament's cause was right with God were the key
factors,[4] but Wharton was not necessarily typical. Motives for joining the
colours were varied, particularly as the story spread around by the media was
that the war would be over in a trice. For those who had little in the way of
worldly goods and few prospects, the chance to plunder the houses of the king's
supporters and to live, however temporarily, on the fat of the land must have
been a powerful inducement, and even Holles's God-fearing regiment was not
immune to this kind of sentiment.[5]

The lord general the earl of Essex left London in a cloud of glory on
9 September 1642, cheered on his way by large crowds and by grandiloquent
speeches. He was to join his army,[6] which was assembling at Northampton, but
in the unsurpassable comment of John Morrill, 'from then onwards it was down-
hill all the way'.[7] Essex's principal reason for accepting the commission was
probably to defend the liberties of the subject, or rather those of the landowners
and rich merchants, against the king's penchant for absolute rule egged on by
evil advisers. The earl was not a radical in religious matters. He favoured the
Church being under Parliament's control rather than that of the king but does
not seem to have been keen on root and branch reform of the Church of
England. There was probably a personal tinge to his anti-royalism stemming
from the ways in which James I and Charles I had humiliated him on a number
of occasions, but he does not live up to the royalists' portrayal of him as the traitorous son of a traitor who had his eye on kingly power. His ambition was to
detach the king from his entourage and bring him back to London in a mood to
accept the role of constitutional monarch.[8]

The earl of Essex was probably in confident mood when he set out for the
Midlands. He accepted that a battle might be necessary, but hoped that it would
not. As with the king's various attempts to impose his will on his Scottish
subjects, Charles could well find it impossible to raise an army large enough to

The Midlands, 1642–1646

risk using it in combat. There was also the question of morale. So far the king's supporters had put up a very poor show. Essex's General of Horse, the earl of Bedford, had bottled the royalists of Somerset and Dorset up in Sherborne Castle; Portsmouth, the only royal arsenal in royal hands, was under siege; and a large brigade sent from London on Essex's orders had firmly rebuffed an attempt by the king's forces to occupy Coventry and the Central Midlands.

It is difficult to be enthusiastic about Robert Devereux, Third Earl of Essex. The keen-eyed, narrow-faced youth, who gazes out of the hunting scene portrait of Prince Henry painted in 1610, had taken on the well-padded figure of sedentary middle age. In woodcuts, Essex's square face with its pointed moustache is almost porcine, sloth and gluttony personified. As early as the spring of 1643 pen portraits of the earl written by royalists and parliamentarians alike homed in on the lack of urgency and the caution that characterised his generalship.[9] Underneath, however, was a solid core of resolution and determination that verged on the stoical, qualities that he was to display on the battlefield on several occasions during his stewardship of Parliament's main field army. He could also be brutal. Whereas in the spring of 1641 more radical members of the parliamentary coalition looked for some way of saving the life of the king's minister, the earl of Strafford, for Essex 'stone dead hath no fellow'. We only have Clarendon's word for the aphorism,[10] but it is not out of character. Although the earl spoke little, he did not hide his opinions when writing to or about people on his own side with whom he had differences.

Before setting out in early September, Essex promised Parliament that his life was at its disposal. There is little doubt that he meant it.[11] On the other hand, he was not 'an experienced and capable commander'.[12] His only experience of campaigning on land was four years in the Netherlands almost twenty years earlier where he had performed well, but only as a colonel of foot. At a more senior level of command he had shown little ability. He led an amphibious attack on Cadiz in 1625 but it had ended in farce with the English soldiers becoming incapacitated through drinking too much wine. They were quickly evacuated and the fleet withdrew covered in shame and without any booty, a most unsatisfactory comparison with the achievement of his father, the second earl of Essex, when he captured Cadiz almost thirty years earlier. As lieutenant general in the expedition against the Scots in 1639, Essex had shown some energy in garrisoning Carlisle and Berwick but this did not increase his experience of field command as there was no fighting.[13] His military reputation, however, was high, but it rested very firmly not on his but on his father's reputation and that of his ancestors as far back as the Wars of the Roses. Essex was also very popular with his troops, both officers and men. Others, however, already saw worrying signs of inactivity verging on lethargy in the fact that it took him a month to leave London for Northampton where he arrived on 9 September 1642,[14] but to be fair to the earl the troops which were gathering there were not yet a military force to be reckoned with. Indiscipline was rife, as evidenced by letters written by their commanders during the first week in September.[15]

The king's lord general, the earl of Lindsey, was half a generation older than the third earl of Essex and the last direct link with the glories of the Armada War. Although David Lloyd, writing in the 1660s, was probably wrong to claim that Lindsey had taken part in the second earl of Essex's attack on Cadiz, he had almost certainly witnessed Prince Maurice of Nassau's victory over the Spanish army at Nieuport in 1600. Like the third earl, Lindsey had commanded a regiment in the Netherlands in the 1620s, but all his subsequent commands had been at a senior level in the navy, apart from a brief spell as governor of Berwick in 1639.[16]

Lindsey's commission does not survive, but accounts of the autumn campaign suggest very strongly that he was unhappy as it only gave him absolute authority over the infantry and the artillery. Prince Rupert's commission put him on the same level of command as the lord general with regard to the horse,[17] but there is no evidence that Charles intended that Lindsey should merely be a figurehead with his field duties exercised by deputies.[18] However, by the same token, Rupert's authority over the cavalry and dragoons was real, not a fiction devised to overcome the embarrassment of a member of the Royal Family being ordered about by one of the king's subjects. The highly personal way in which Charles worded his letters to the prince shows that they cannot be the lord general's orders issued under the king's signature.[19] However, divided command in the field army did not become an issue until the second week in October at the earliest, as the two protagonists had other concerns. Rupert was absent from army headquarters for much of the time, leading parties of cavalry and dragoons into the 'no man's land' between the two armies,[20] whereas Lindsey was busy putting together a force capable of taking the field against the earl of Essex and defeating him.

The king's army was of a similar composition to Parliament's, though amongst the officers members of the landowning classes were far more numerous than the professionals. The rank and file were volunteers who enlisted for similar motives to those who fought for Parliament, but with loyalty to the Crown as an additional factor. Social deference to the lord of the manor may also have played a greater part as all the king's regiments were raised in the countryside, whilst most of Parliament's hailed from London, but Charles's army did not consist of thousands of poor peasants forced to fight by their feudal overlords.[21]

Fully a month before the earl of Essex reached Northampton, the king had established his headquarters at Nottingham.[22] However, although his supporters in the Midlands and the north quickly raised between 2,000 and 3,000 horse and dragoons, foot came in so slowly that Sir Jacob Astley, the general in command of the infantry, allegedly informed Charles that he had insufficient troops to stop the enemy taking him back to London with them if they appeared before the town in force.[23] Defending Nottingham was not the only problem. Regiments were being raised elsewhere in a wide arc stretching from Yorkshire and Lancashire through Wales and the Welsh borderland to Somerset and Dorset, but there were enemy forces athwart the most direct routes between many of the recruiting grounds and Nottingham.[24] In addition muskets and ammunition were in short supply. There was no arms industry in the areas controlled by the king's supporters, and what could be found in aristocratic houses and in the magazines of the county trained bands would only go so far. Imports were vital. Fortunately one ship carrying 3,000 weapons, 200 barrels of gunpowder and some field pieces had reached the Yorkshire coast in July, but some later ones failed to get through the naval blockade of north-east England instituted by the Royal Navy, which had sided with Parliament in the summer of 1642.[25]

By the second week in September the situation had eased slightly. Several new infantry regiments had reached Nottingham,[26] and considerable quantities of muskets, pikes and gunpowder were on their way south, having been shipped in from the Continent through Newcastle, the only major east coast port under royalist control.[27] Nevertheless the outlook remained gloomy. The enemy army gathering at Northampton was still far larger than the force Lindsey and Rupert had under their command, and there was no guarantee that the earl of Essex would not advance on Nottingham before they were ready. At this stage in the war he was showing every sign of being about to pounce. From mid-August onwards troops raised in Parliament's name had occupied the Central Midlands, the Fenlands and Oxford and its environs. In Kent cavalry raids led by Colonel Edwyn Sandys captured the leading royalists and secured all the principal towns for Parliament, whilst Portsmouth had surrendered to Sir William Waller.[28] To the king's military advisers there was no sense in remaining at Nottingham until the inevitable happened, or in advancing on Northampton in the hope of a miracle. Instead they must go in search of their missing regiments.

Essex's instructions from the Committee of Safety, approved by the two Houses of Parliament on 9, 16 and 21 September, gave him authority to do battle with the king's army, but not in such a way as to discourage Charles from throwing in the towel before the two armies came to blows. The first set of instructions was the most explicit. The lord general was 'to march with all forces you think fit' towards the king's headquarters, and to 'use your utmost endeavours by battle or otherwise to rescue His Majesty . . . from those desperate persons as are now about him'.[29] The second backtracked from the idea of a climactic battle. Essex was 'to advance his army towards the place where the king is as soon as conveniently so great a body can move', and present Charles with a petition begging him to replace his sword in its sheath and return to London. Backed up by the threat of force, the petition might be sufficient to persuade the king to give up before blood was shed. Moreover, the form of words used in the petition would allow abject surrender to appear as the gracious act of a loving monarch whose prime aim was to save his subjects from death and destruction. The final set of instructions attached to the copy of the petition sent to the lord general added nothing of substance to the first two, but by insisting that he should give the king time to reply before engaging him in battle they contributed materially towards the lacklustre campaign that followed.

A document appended to the instructions brought home to Essex the importance of not sticking his neck out. First, it ordered officers serving in the army who were MPs or peers to act as an ad hoc executive committee, which was 'to consult and advise touching such matters as concern the army'.[30] This meant that Essex still had the last word on tactical and operational matters, but he also knew that if he ignored the committee's advice and his decision turned out to be a poor one, he would be in trouble. Second, he was 'to observe such further directions and instructions you shall from time to time receive from both houses of Parliament'.[31] This was seemingly innocuous, but it was open-ended. So far his instructions had been strategic ones, but if he made any mistakes, they were likely to become much more precise. In such circumstances it was best not to be too proactive.

On 13 September, three days after Essex arrived at Northampton, the earl and his army set off towards Nottingham, only for spies to report that the king's army was on the march, destination unknown. Essex stopped his troops in their tracks and ordered them back to Northampton until the situation clarified, but there was another reason. The lawlessness of some of his infantry regiments had, if anything, increased, but in their defence it was argued that inflated prices in the Northampton area caused by the army's presence meant that ordinary soldiers could not afford to buy food. This was why they were deadening their hunger by 'liberating' deer and cattle from the lands of those whom they saw as Parliament's enemies. However, the soldiers had shown little discrimination, and attacks on the property of neutrals could easily turn neutrals into royalists. Such behaviour was also a threat to discipline. Soldiers might refuse to obey their officers' orders if given too much licence to attack the goods and possessions of their social superiors. Essex launched a two-pronged attack on the problem. He asked for more money to pay his men, and he also directed that the code of discipline approved by Parliament should be read at the head of every regiment. This made it clear to all that plunderers would be subject to the rigours of martial law.[32] However, evidence from later on in the campaign suggests that officers interpreted the ban on plundering very loosely, turning a blind eye to the ransacking of the houses of neutrals who happened to be Catholics.[33]

By the time the parliamentary army finally left Northampton on 19 September it was clear that the royalists were bound for Chester or Shrewsbury. Essex's first port of call was Coventry, solidly under parliamentary control since mid-August. From there he could either take the road to Chester via Lichfield and Nantwich used by people travelling to and from Ireland, or Watling Street (the present-day A5), which led directly to Shrewsbury. However, when he learned that the king was at Shrewsbury, he sidestepped to the south and made for Worcester instead. Probably the largest town in the Midlands in the mid seventeenth century, it was suitable to serve as the headquarters for an army which might soon be 30,000 strong. He had also learned that a single regiment of royalist horse commanded by Sir John Byron was likely to cross the parliamentary army's line of march. More important, it was escorting wagons carrying gold and silver plate voluntarily surrendered by Oxford colleges to help support the king's cause. Essex and his political masters firmly believed that, even if the king did manage to raise a sizeable army, he would not be able to keep it together for long because he did not have the money to pay his troops the wages he had promised. Converting plate into coin, however, might stave off mass desertion long enough for him to fight a battle, but if the convoy could be captured, the whole royalist war effort might collapse like a house of cards.

As the parliamentary army continued its march westwards, Essex learned that Byron had stopped at Worcester and was seemingly putting the city into a state of defence. As his regiment was far too small to serve as a garrison, he must be expecting reinforcements. Colonel John Brown, a Scottish professional soldier, suggested to Essex that his regiment of dragoons supported by a number of troops of horse should move on ahead to prevent supplies being brought into the city and to pin the enemy down until the rest of the army arrived to finish them off. The lord general agreed and the commanded party duly set off on 22 September, but four miles short of the city Brown and his officers decided to depart from their orders. Their force, they agreed, would be better employed crossing the bridge over the River Severn at Upton, eight miles to the south, linking up with locally raised infantry marching up from Gloucester, and then taking up a position to the west of Worcester where they could block Byron's safest route to Shrewsbury via Ludlow.

The cavalry and dragoons duly proceeded to Upton, where they crossed the Severn unopposed, but the Gloucester contingent had not arrived, distracted, it seems, by the rich pickings to be found in the house of the Catholic landowner Rowland Bartlett at Castle Morton between Tewkesbury and Malvern. Brown Force was too excited to wait and too keen on the job in hand to join them. Led ever onwards by the senior cavalry officer, Colonel Sandys, the conqueror of Kent, they marched north, their new objective being the bridge over the river Teme, which joined the Severn at Powick, three miles to the south of Worcester, and gave easy access to the road to Ludlow.[34] Prince Rupert, however, was riding to the rescue, leading a body of horse and dragoons which fortuitously was very similar in size and composition to Brown Force. Having marched overnight from Bridgnorth, he joined Byron on the morning of 23 September.[35] Rupert had no intention of defending the city. Instead his force was to provide additional protection for the convoy as it made for the safety of the hills of the Welsh borderland.

Brown Force had reached Powick the evening before. They spent the night in arms, but strangely failed to establish a presence on the far side of the bridge. Rupert, too, grasped the importance of the bridge at Powick, and positioned his troops in Wick Field directly in the path of any hostile move from the south against the convoy. Through the field passed the lane connecting Worcester with Upton, which then entered enclosures just short of the bridge.[36] The prince knew there was an enemy force in the vicinity, but had no idea how close it was, a reconnaissance party sent out before noon having failed to locate it. Happy that the convoy would soon be on its way, and that there was no enemy in the immediate vicinity, his officers and troopers dismounted, took off their armour, and stretched out in the sun. By mid-afternoon most were probably fast asleep. Rupert and his senior officers sat under the shade of a hawthorn bush somewhat nearer the bridge than their men, but the prince had taken precautions against a surprise attack by stationing a small party of dragoons at the point where the lane coming from the bridge left the enclosures and entered the field. Fortunately the remainder of the force were kept under tight control. They were not permitted to forage and were therefore ready to mount their horses quickly and move forward in orderly fashion should anything untoward happen. This was just as well as a man travelling from Worcester towards Upton had told the enemy exactly where they were.

Brown Force contained the most experienced body of horse in Essex's army, but that experience was in rounding up groups of confused and disorientated amateur soldiers, not in fighting regular troops. Sandys, however, considered that surprise would be as effective a weapon at Powick as it had been in Kent. Otherwise it is impossible to explain the disorganised and fragmented assault that followed with troopers charging the enemy in ones and twos as they emerged from the lane into Wick Field, even riding through their own scouts in their enthusiasm to get to grips with the enemy. They certainly gave Rupert's men little warning, but determined resistance by the royalist dragoons assisted by the prince and his companions gave the troopers time to deploy before counter-attacking. The parliamentary attack was also not helped by Colonel Sandys receiving a serious wound at the very start of the action, thus extinguishing the leadership from the front that was essential for success in shock tactics of that nature. The melee lasted some time, but as the minutes ticked by, cool discipline triumphed over exuberant disorder. Attacked in the front and the flank, most of the parliamentary troopers who had crossed Powick bridge found themselves trapped on the wrong side of the Teme. Rupert had won his first victory.[37]

Although the encounter near Powick was no more than a major skirmish, parliamentary casualties there were quite high and the immediate impact on the morale of the parliamentary army was considerable. Colonel Arthur Goodwin, writing to reassure his daughter Lady Wharton about what had happened, could not hide the facts. A colonel, a major and several captains had fallen into enemy hands, forty to fifty parliamentary soldiers were dead, and those who fled the scene caused such panic that Essex's men were in arms all night expecting a further attack. To make matters worse, Essex's own lifeguard, crammed with the sons of the parliamentary elite and students from the Inns of Court, misunderstood a command and fled to all points of the compass fearful that the enemy was upon them. In fact, Rupert was fifteen miles away on the other side of the Severn.[38] However, the adverse effect on the morale of the parliamentary cavalry may have been short-lived. The lifeguard and at least one of the troops of horse which had been at Powick bridge fought bravely at Edgehill a month later, and the very detailed account of the engagement in Wick Field published a week after Edgehill made no attempt to link it with the disappointing outcome of the battle.[39]

Wisely, Rupert made no attempt to pursue the enemy across the Teme. He did not know whether Brown Force was the vanguard of a much larger body of men and he was unable to see the survivors riding pell-mell towards Upton because the small rise on which Powick village stood hid their flight. He also did not change his mind about putting Worcester into a state of defence. Essex was approaching remorselessly from the east in overwhelming force, and there was no prospect of summoning up reinforcements, as the nearest major concentration of royalist troops was thirty miles to the north. Within hours of the engagement the bullion convoy with its reinforced escort was on its way westwards through Tenbury to Ludlow where it arrived forty-eight hours later.[40] Rupert ordered a night march, clearly thinking that Essex would be looking for quick revenge, but it was an unnecessary precaution. The lord general was content to occupy Worcester without losing any more men. He would then consider his next move, informed by the petition and its accompanying instructions which he received just before or just after arriving on the banks of the Severn.

Essex remained at Worcester for a month. Whilst there he sent a regiment of foot to strengthen Coventry's ability to withstand attack should the king decide to return eastwards, and another two to occupy Hereford with the aim of stopping forces being raised in south-east Wales from reaching Shrewsbury.[41] He also garrisoned Banbury with a fourth regiment. Finally, he sent a full brigade of foot to Kidderminster to guard the most likely line of advance towards Worcester, his intention being, it seems, to go to its support with the rest of the field army if the royalist army moved any farther south than Bridgnorth.[42] Containing the royalists was the name of the game, not advancing on Shrewsbury. The king's commanders quickly saw what was in Essex's mind, and were content. The longer Essex remained on the defensive, the stronger their army became as reinforcements arrived from Cheshire and north-east Wales.[43]

Why was Essex so inactive? What had happened to Brown Force rocked him back on his heels, but he was following Parliament's instructions to persevere with the political initiative. He therefore spent most of the time he was at Worcester trying to persuade the king to accept the petition and read its contents, but Charles played hard to get and put every obstacle in the way of receiving it. Another factor may have been that Essex felt he was too weak in mounted troops to take the offensive until the earl of Bedford arrived with his regiments of cavalry and dragoons, which had spent September and early October chasing the king's supporters from Somerset and Dorset. By the time they reached Worcester, advancing up the Severn valley towards Shrewsbury was no longer an option. The royalist army was on the move, but not in a southerly direction.[44]

On 10 October 1642 the royalist field army left Shrewsbury.[45] Thirteen days later the first major encounter of the English Civil Wars took place between the towns of Kineton and Banbury on the Warwickshire/Oxfordshire border. What is not surprising is the event itself, as the king was looking for an early battle and Essex's orders were to engage with the enemy as soon as Charles rejected the petition. What is surprising is that it took almost a fortnight for the routes taken by the two armies to converge, and this was largely due to Essex's decision to sit tight at Worcester.

Lack of intelligence concerning the movements of the enemy army was not the reason why it took the earl so long to respond.[46] In fact he had excellent intelligence, much of it obtained from an informant in the king's camp.[47] Essex knew several days in advance when the march would begin, and that it would be in the general direction of London.[48] He correctly interpreted the first stage down the Severn valley to Bridgnorth as a feint. He knew that the royalist army had divided on 13 October, with one corps passing to the west and south of Birmingham and the other to the north and east. He also knew that the enemy forces had come together again at Meriden Heath near Coventry on the 19th, and reasoned correctly that they would not besiege the town, as his army was close enough to mount a rapid relief expedition. When the royalists left Meriden, he knew that they were heading south towards the Thames valley, not east towards Watling Street, the fastest route to London for an army burdened with carriages, wagons and heavy artillery. Finally, he knew that the king's generals intended first to capture Banbury before moving on to Oxford,[49] but this was not his major concern. He had garrisoned Banbury some weeks earlier, and there would be plenty of time for him to march to the rescue provided that the royalists did not storm the town immediately or head straight for Oxford. Essex therefore directed his army's march towards Banbury. This was textbook stuff. Battles between besieging and relieving armies occurred time and time again in western and central Europe in the wars of the sixteenth and seventeenth centuries. Thus, it cannot have been a surprise that his scouts ran into the royalist rearguard in the Kineton area on the evening of 22 October and that the king's army stopped in its tracks and marched back towards him. Indeed, Essex may have been relieved not to have to pursue it any further given the logistical problems that were just becoming apparent – lack of provisions for man and beast and dwindling numbers as hunger and exhaustion took their toll.[50]

A second reason for delay was that for the first eight days of the king's march Essex was still waiting for a response to Parliament's petition, but surprisingly it took him two further days to get his army on the move after Charles finally rejected it. This does not sit easily with an earlier message to Parliament in which Essex claimed that his army was in an extreme state of readiness to seek out the king's forces and destroy them, or with his comment on 18 October that he had never thought that the king had any intention of responding positively to the petition and was merely playing for time.[51] Essex's officers and others subsequently blamed Philibert du Bois, deputy commander of the ordnance, for failing to requisition sufficient horses and oxen to pull the artillery train,[52] but Essex as army commander was ultimately responsible, having presumably approved the return to their owners of the draught animals requisitioned to pull the train from Northampton to Worcester. As it was, part of the train was not ready to leave Worcester until a day after the rest of the army. Its escort consisted of two infantry regiments and a full cavalry regiment commanded by Colonel John Hampden, probably the most famous of the king's leading opponents after Essex himself. They did not arrive in the vicinity of Edgehill until the fighting was under way. Drawing to a halt just short of Kineton, they spent the rest of the hours of daylight successfully fending off royalist cavalry intent on pillage and plunder.

This is not the only sign, or indeed the most important sign, of a major flaw in Essex's preparations. He should have given the highest priority to assembling the maximum number of men for what he and his political masters intended to be the first and last battle of the English Civil War, but he had not done so. In addition to the cavalry regiment with Hampden, several of his other troops of horse were scattered across the landscape of the South Midlands. Some were vainly trying to find where the fighting was taking place; others were on various missions or on garrison duty.[53] Of those that were close by, one at least failed to arrive whilst three others disintegrated as hordes of soldiers on horse and foot fleeing from the battlefield swept over them. To make matters worse, two infantry regiments additional to those placed in the Midlands' garrisons over the past month remained at Worcester, an unnecessary precaution. Essex's orders were to destroy the king's army, not to think in terms of a prolonged war. As a result, of the twenty regiments of foot that Essex could have had with him at Edgehill, eight were absent, as were at least ten troops of horse. Thus, the parliamentary army was much smaller than it ought to have been. Nevertheless, when Essex drew his army up on the morning of 23 October, covering the artillery train's line of march from Stratford-on-Avon, he may have hoped that the king's forces, which had spent the night in villages and hamlets to the north and east of Banbury, could not be assembled in time to fight a battle until the following day, and by that time Hampden's brigade would have arrived and also most, if not all, of the missing cavalry.

CHAPTER 3

Over by Winter? Edgehill and Turnham Green

T HE MARCHES of the king's army after leaving Shrewsbury seem to have been grounded in the belief that the earl of Essex would do nothing unless provoked. Writing from Wolverhampton on 17 October, the king expressed his amazement that Essex had been so inactive for so long. At first he expected 'daily a battle', now he thought that 'the rebels want either courage or strength to fight before they are forced'.[1] The encounter between the rearguard of his army and the vanguard of Essex's on the 22nd was therefore more of a shock to the royalist high command than it was to the earl. A reconnaissance party sent out early in the day had found no sign of the enemy, but this is not surprising. From Meriden onwards the countryside to the west of the line of march of the king's army was part of 'Forest Warwickshire', undulating and quite thickly wooded.

On the evening of 22 October the royalist soldiers were looking forward to a Sabbath day's rest after almost a fortnight marching from one end of the Midlands to the other.[2] The only exceptions were the officers and men of the train who were preparing their heavy artillery pieces for pulverising the defences of Banbury the following day.[3] Prince Rupert was all in favour of attacking the enemy vanguard immediately, but the king listened to the advice of others and decided to wait until he learned more about the whereabouts of their main body.[4] Rupert's next recommendation, however, received Charles's enthusiastic support. The army was to postpone the attack on Banbury. Instead it was to prepare for battle, with the Edgehill escarpment, visible for miles around, as its place of rendezvous.[5] What attracted the prince was the large tract of meadow ground stretching north from the base of the escarpment to within a mile of Kineton, an excellent place to fight a conventional battle when your cavalry are clearly superior to those of your opponent.[6]

Prior to the actual fighting there was a major readjustment in the royalist high command. The central figure was the earl of Lindsey, who resigned as lord general and received the king's permission to fight at the head of his own regiment. The various royalist sources for the battle are very clear about this. However, they tell overlapping but significantly different stories about how it all came about. The usual tale to be found in the history books is that Lindsey fell out with Prince Rupert in spectacular fashion on the morning of the battle over the way in which the infantry was to be deployed, with Lindsey favouring a tried and trusted Dutch model and Rupert a more modern formation copied from the Swedish army.[7] This is probably not how it happened, but it does make the important point that Lindsey suffered a massive affront to his pride and to his honour when the king failed to follow his advice.

A careful reading of the dramatic scene in *The History of the Rebellion* in which Lindsey poured out his heart to Sir Edward Hyde, the future Lord Clarendon, and the earl of Dorset in their lodgings some time during the night of 22–23 October shows that the lord general's grievance was twofold. The army was to be deployed 'in a form that he liked not' and the king had decided to abandon the Banbury project and fight a battle between Edgehill and Kineton 'without advising with him'.[8] However, it strains belief that the first decision took place on the eve of the battle. It was probably taken at Kenilworth some days earlier when the last infantry regiments arrived, and the king's commanders realised how poorly armed some of the foot soldiers were. The recommendation almost certainly came from Patrick Ruthven, Earl of Forth, who, having been in Swedish service, was well aware that their mode of deployment made more sense for a body of infantry with less than the normal complement of muske-teers.[9] Rupert only came into the picture much later, and it was indeed on his advice alone that the king ordered a battle to be fought on the meadowland between Edgehill and Kineton. Otherwise Charles would not have written as follows to the prince at four o'clock in the morning:

Nephew,
    I have given order as you have desired, so that I doubt not but all the foot and cannon will be at Edgehill betimes this morning where you will also find,
    Your loving uncle etc and faithful friend, Charles R.[10]

The parliamentary army deployed on a small rise in the ground just to the south of Kineton facing in the direction of the 300-foot-high escarpment of Edgehill. In the dip in between was the great meadow, a ragged rectangle some three miles broad and two miles deep. As was customary for battles fought in open country, the earl of Essex placed his musketeers and pikes in the centre, with the horse stationed to the left and right to protect their flanks and rear against cavalry attack. The main body of the infantry drew up in three large brigades each some 3,000 strong and containing three or four regiments which were capable of operating independently. The van and the middle brigades, those of Sir John Meldrum and Charles Essex, were in the front line. The third brigade, Thomas Ballard's, was somewhat to the rear of that of Charles Essex. This arrangement left a gap in the reserve line, which the brigade on the march from Stratford-on-Avon could fill when it arrived. As for the cavalry, more were stationed on the left than the right, as intelligence suggested (and rightly so) that Rupert would lead

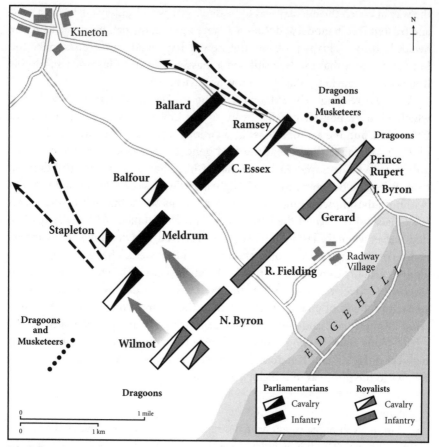

Edgehill

the royalist right wing into battle. Oddly, given its importance, the officer in command of the left wing was Sir James Ramsey, the lowest ranking of Essex's three cavalry generals.

Essex did not attack, possibly because he did not want to be known as the man who had ordered an armed assault on his king. Alternatively, by putting on a brave show clearly visible from Edgehill, he may have hoped to weaken the king's resolve, thus eliminating the need for a battle and the enormous bloodletting that would follow. However, precautions needed to be taken as the chances of the royalists not attacking were very slim.

The plan for seeing off Prince Rupert involved both cavalry and infantry, and must therefore have received Essex's approval.[11] Ramsey's wing was to remain stationary whilst the royalist formations would be disrupted by incoming fire as they gathered speed for the attack. Dragoons drawn up behind a hedge running parallel to their only line of advance, stiffened by musketeers from the reserve brigade, were to rake their right flank as they passed. When the royalists approached to within a hundred yards or so, they would encounter another heavy barrage from yet more musketeers positioned between Ramsey's squadrons, strengthened by case shot fired by the field artillery.[12] Finally, at point of contact they would encounter carbine and pistol fire from the parliamentary cavalry. By then the royalist formations should have fragmented with the momentum of their charge dissipated by the gaps in their ranks and the toing and froing of wounded and rider-less horses. It would then be a comparatively easy job for Ramsey's men to push them back at sword point in the melee and sweep them from the battlefield.

The plan for the parliamentary right wing was originally somewhat similar, with three regiments of cavalry, two in the front line and one behind, supported

South Central England and the South Midlands, 1642–1645

by the fire of artillery pieces, musketeers and dragoons.[13] However, after deployment, orders came for the right wing to be weakened as it looked as if almost the whole of the royalist cavalry was facing Sir James Ramsey. The cavalry would therefore be wasted if they remained where they were, and so one regiment, and possibly part of a second, moved into the reserve line covering the gap between the infantry brigades of Meldrum and Charles Essex. From that position the cavalry could charge between the infantry brigades if they required support in their fight with the enemy infantry, or else wheel to the left and assist Ramsey if the melee took longer to resolve than anticipated.[14] Elsewhere in the rear was the lord general's lifeguard, commanded by Sir Philip Stapleton, which was probably kept well out of the way because of what had happened after the engagement in Wick Field.[15] These decisions were to have a crucial effect on the shape of the battle as the result was that Essex's army now had a true cavalry reserve.

In the royalist army, the cavalry on both wings were drawn up in two parallel lines with Rupert commanding the right wing and Henry Wilmot the left. There were slightly more troopers under Rupert than under Wilmot, but the imbalance between the two wings was nowhere near as great as Essex and his officers had surmised.[16] The second line was to provide immediate support for the first if it got into trouble, but the gap between the two lines was big enough for regiments in the second line to wheel to left or right so as intervene elsewhere on the battlefield. The original intention was for the king's lifeguard of horse, some 300 strong, to take up a position well to the rear so as to be able to act as a reserve of last resort, but the troopers, fed up with being teased as the 'troop of show', persuaded the king that Prince Rupert needed their assistance. Rupert duly deployed them on the far right of the line of battle to protect his flank.[17] If they had remained in the rear, the battle might have ended very differently.[18]

The way in which the earl of Forth deployed the royalist infantry is uncertain other than that they were in a chequer-board formation. Bernard De Gomme's post-Restoration depiction of the line of battle has three brigades in the first line and two in support.[19] However, two contemporary accounts of the battle, one parliamentary and one royalist, describe the king's regiments of foot as being deployed in nine rather than five formations.[20] In addition, what De Gomme drew for posterity does not fit all the facts.[21]

Essex's battle plan fell apart within minutes of the first onset. After the preliminaries, a succession of salvos from the heavy artillery which inflicted little damage to either side, his troops drawn up on the wings faced a massed charge by the royalist first line of horse. On Ramsey's wing the cavalry's resolve weakened when royalist dragoons cleared the parliamentary musketeers from the hedges they were lining, thus eliminating half the supporting fire before it could come into play.[22] The cavalry may also have been surprised at the speed and determination of the royalist advance – not the sedate caracole practised in the Low Countries, but a full-blooded charge in close order, the culmination of which would be a violent collision, not a gentle peppering of pistol shot. Finally, the desertion of an entire troop to the enemy, led by the unfortunately named Sir Faithful Fortescue, must have been deeply disquieting.[23] In a panic Ramsey's men fired their pistols and carbines before the enemy came into range. The musketeers deployed between the squadrons of horse fired a volley as ordered, but the royalists swept onwards regardless. Within minutes of the two bodies of horse coming into contact, Ramsey and his regiments were quitting the battlefield in total disorder, and the following day Sir James was found wandering in some confusion near Uxbridge, only ten miles from London.[24]

At about the same time as the parliamentary left wing disintegrated, the four regiments of Charles Essex's infantry brigade also took to their heels without, it seems, coming into direct contact with enemy infantry. On the other wing Henry Wilmot's charge was as effective as Rupert's, and both his and Rupert's horsemen pursued the enemy horse and foot through Kineton and beyond. At almost the same moment the king's lifeguard of foot and Lord Lindsey's regiment led by Lindsey himself struck at the only formation left in Essex's front line, Sir John Meldrum's infantry brigade.[25]

However, within a very short space of time the parliamentary army had captured the initiative. First, the cavalry reserve commanded by the lieutenant general of horse, Sir William Balfour, an elderly professional soldier, charged into the centre of the king's infantry line. It took out at least two of the regiments and then attacked the royalist heavy artillery drawn up in front of Radway village, cutting down many of the king's cannoneers but failing to disable or carry off any of the cannon.[26] Second, Essex's lifeguard of horse charged into the exposed flank of Lindsey's regiments and stopped the assault on Meldrum's brigade in its tracks. The royalists then disengaged, fell back a short distance and began to regroup.[27] Third, the reserve infantry brigade took up the position in the front line vacated by the brigade that had fled the battlefield.[28]

The first of these manoeuvres probably involved Balfour doing something agreed in advance on the lord general's instructions or with his agreement.[29] The second was on the orders of the commander of the lifeguard without reference to a higher authority.[30] The third looks like Essex's own work, as some reports of the battle describe him as leading forward various units from the reserve line.[31]

The next stage of the battle, however, was certainly all Essex's work. He probably deduced from the way in which the two regiments hit by Balfour Force had disintegrated that the king's infantry brigades were potentially as brittle as that of Charles Essex. Moreover, the king's generals were likely to have used their best ones to attack Meldrum's brigade. The most effective way of building on success would therefore be to focus the forces that the lord general still had on the battlefield on overwhelming the earl of Lindsey's regiments, as this could well cause the rest of the enemy infantry to break and run. Using fresh troops from the reserve brigade, Balfour Force and the lifeguard, he attacked Lindsey's regiment and the royal lifeguard from all sides and, after a fierce fight in which they suffered very heavy casualties, forced them to fall back in some disorder towards Edgehill – leaving behind Lord Lindsey mortally wounded by a musket ball.[32]

What happened to most of the rest of the king's infantry is hidden from history, but there is no evidence that they went to the support of Lord Lindsey or that they were still on the battlefield at the end of the day. All that can be assumed is that they, too, fell back to the safety of the Edgehill escarpment during or immediately after the destruction of 'the king's two best regiments'. The only royalist infantry left on the battlefield as darkness fell were two formations on the extreme right of the line commanded by Charles Gerard. They had played little part in the fighting and had fallen back in good order on the artillery park, presumably when Gerard learnt what had happened a mile away to his left.[33]

Essex's response as the light left the sky was to redeploy his horse and foot so that they were ready to drive the last of the royalists from the artillery park, but the exhaustion of the parliamentary soldiers after several hours' fighting, a grave shortage of ammunition, and the return to royalist lines of some of the king's victorious cavalry, meant that the assault never took place.[34] Soon after 6.00 p.m. the royalist formations still facing the enemy followed their comrades and climbed up the Edgehill escarpment whose steepness protected them from further attack during the night.[35] They took with them their artillery pieces, which the enemy would otherwise have dragged away during the hours of darkness or early the following morning.

The earl of Essex's contribution towards the outcome of the battle is thus reasonably clear. Although most of his cavalry and dragoons and one of his three infantry brigades had performed very badly in the first quarter hour of the battle, he had deployed his army in such a manner that the units still remaining were able to move about the battlefield in support of one another. As a result the earl snatched a modest victory from the jaws of almost certain defeat, and he should get the credit. It is, however, unfair to pour scorn on his tactical plan for the left wing which led to the flight of a third of his army.[36] It needs to be put into context. Disrupting an enemy cavalry attack with gunfire worked well for Prince Rupert on one wing at the battle of Marston Moor in July 1644, and using dragoons drawn up behind a hedge line to fire into the flank of an enemy charge was a tactic used to good effect by Oliver Cromwell at Naseby a year later.[37]

In contrast, the way in which the royalist high command managed their army at Edgehill is an excellent example of how not to run a battle. The battle plan itself seems to have been a simple one.[38] The first-line cavalry on both wings were to sweep the enemy horse from the field, with the second line only providing support if the enemy stood their ground and seemed likely to win the melee.

The first upset came with the cavalry charge, when the second line on both wings followed the first line into the attack instead of waiting for the order to do so.

In the accounts of the engagement written some time after the battle, the commanders of the reserve line – Sir John Byron on the right wing and Lord Digby on the left – got the blame.[39] In Byron's case this may be unjust. Rupert failed to inform him that Sir Faithful Fortescue's troop would desert to the royalists as soon as battle commenced, and Fortescue's troopers had made things more difficult for themselves by not discarding their orange scarves, the sign that they were parliamentarians. As a result, when they tried to make their way around the flank of the royalist army at the time of Rupert's charge, they came under attack from the king's lifeguard. Seeing a skirmish to their right front, and thinking that it was a cunning move on Essex's part to capture the king who was now no longer protected by his lifeguard, Byron's men entered the fray and he and his troops routed Fortescue's men and then galloped off towards Kineton with the rest of the royalist right wing.[40]

There was no such excuse for the behaviour of the commander of the reserve on the left wing,[41] and not surprisingly Digby later claimed that he had not received orders to remain stationary when the first line charged.[42] However, the basic error was one of command and control. If Rupert and Wilmot had not put themselves at the head of the charge on their respective wings, they could have ordered their reserves to go to the assistance of the infantry and probably won a decisive victory.

The management of the infantry battle by the royalist high command was much, much worse. All the regiments other than Lord Lindsey's and Charles Gerard's appear to have done nothing beyond firing their muskets in the general direction of the enemy whilst watching the gory spectacle unroll in front of them.[43] This raises a fundamental question: who, if anyone, was in overall charge of the royalist infantry once the fighting had begun? If it was Lord Lindsey, as claimed by John Bellasis and Sir John Hinton,[44] he should have known better. A quarter of an hour into the battle there was a good case for putting himself at the head of his best regiments for a crack at what was probably the best enemy infantry formation still on the battlefield, but only if he knew that the enemy cavalry and Charles Essex's infantry brigade had already taken to their heels. If not, then it was not a considered move based on what had happened so far, but a vainglorious attempt to regain his lost honour and prestige. But whatever the circumstances, once the attack failed, he ought to have moved back to a position from which he could survey the whole of the infantry line in order to consider what to do next. Instead Lindsey remained with his regiment whilst it regrouped. As a result when Essex counter-attacked, Lindsey was incapable of exerting any further control over the course of the battle. The alternative scenario is unbelievable, but nevertheless possible. Lindsey did revert to the rank of colonel and thus relinquished responsibility for the overall conduct of the infantry battle,[45] but then the king either forgot to appoint a successor or else failed to realise that he needed somebody to give commands to the infantry as the fight developed.

What happened on the day after the battle is reasonably straightforward. With Hampden's brigade already at Kineton, and the prospect of another infantry regiment arriving from Coventry, Essex ought to have been keen to resume the battle, but the enemy would have to move first. Storming Edgehill was out of the question as it would be far too costly. The king, however, had no intention of returning to the battlefield in force. His infantry regiments were badly under strength and there were no reinforcements on the way, but as the hours passed confidence returned. Foot soldiers who had fled the battlefield were drifting back to their colours as they had no other choice. They were miles from home and the locals were unfriendly. Before evening, the royalist Council of War decided their army was strong enough to move back to the villages around Banbury where it had spent the night before the battle. This the enemy took to be the beginnings of an attack on Banbury itself, but instead of seeing it as an opportunity to finish the business, Essex ordered his army to set off in the opposite direction. They were to follow him to Warwick, the nearest friendly garrison, leaving the royalists free to continue their march.

What was Essex up to? If the royalists had fallen back towards the Welsh borderland, Warwick was the best place to be for intercepting them as they made for Bewdley bridge, the nearest crossing point over the Severn not in parliamentary hands. However, Essex's officers knew differently before they left Kineton.[46] Another possibility is that Essex was wary of fighting a second battle in open country because most of his cavalry had performed badly, but if so it is remarkable that he did not even try and keep in touch with the king's army. A more likely explanation is that he had temporarily lost his nerve.

The official report of the battle sent from the army to Parliament suggests that something unusual had happened. The army commander did not write it on the evening after, as was customary.[47] Instead he did nothing for nearly twenty-four hours and then left for Warwick without putting pen to paper. Worried that their political masters were waiting for news but also worried that they might be committing a breach of etiquette, six junior officers did the job for him.[48] The contents of the report are fascinating. The only mention of the earl's conduct in a letter several thousand words long is in the postscript. It is very brief and uses curious forms of words which suggest that the writers were hiding their embarrassment. The lord general was 'very well', and he had exposed himself to enemy fire in circumstances more dangerous 'than we could have wished', but that was all – nothing about his leadership role in the campaign or the battle. In addition, in the body of the letter there were some oblique criticisms of his generalship. The army took too long to leave Worcester; the enemy were allowed to leave on the afternoon following the battle without being harassed; and Essex had no operational plan on the 24th other than to rest the army for a few days. As for the future, 'we will God willing address ourselves to finish the work', but it is unclear if 'we' did or did not include the earl. All of this is in stark contrast to some later reports of the battle, which include some very positive remarks about Essex's personal bravery and the way in which he had conducted the battle, and nothing about the state of his health and his distressing propensity to take unnecessary personal risks. But what direct evidence is there about Essex's state of mind in the days following the battle?

The words of a royal herald sent by the king to Kineton on the day after the battle, as reported by Clarendon, suggest that something was wrong. As an honourable go-between, Sir William De Neve refused to provide the king and his advisers with information about the condition of the enemy army, but he did refer to 'much trouble and disorder in the faces of Essex and his principal officers'.[49] There is another piece of much more powerful evidence of Essex's distress, but its provenance is dubious. In the manuscript collection of a Staffordshire royalist family, the Levesons of Trentham, there is a letter seemingly written by Essex immediately after his arrival at Warwick, in which he makes a personal act of surrender to the king begging forgiveness for his numerous acts of treason. The immediate reaction is that the letter must be a forgery, but if so it is difficult to understand its author's objective. Nobody tried to use it to bring about the earl's downfall in his interminable disputes with a vociferous minority in the House of Commons, which began in the spring of 1643 and lasted until almost the end of his lord generalship. As a post-war forgery, the letter would have served no purpose whatsoever. Essex died in the autumn of 1646, and he had no direct heirs, either familial or political, to be embarrassed by such a bombshell.[50] On the other hand if it is genuine, why did not Essex destroy it once he came to his senses? But even if in the end the letter is set aside as totally at odds with Essex's unflinching commitment to Parliament's cause in good times and bad in 1643 and 1644, the decision to retreat to Warwick remains a puzzle, and such evidence as there is points to Essex's state of mind as being the root cause.

The second 'might have been' is much easier to resolve. Soon after the battle Prince Rupert suggested a lightning raid on London. Catching the enemy offguard with 3,000 horse and dragoons would cause panic and possibly a spontaneous royalist uprising, but the king preferred to stick with the cautious strategy agreed at Shrewsbury, a slow advance on the capital via Oxford and the Thames valley. His civilian advisers hardened Charles's resolve by arguing that the royalists' negotiating position was much stronger after Edgehill than before, and that slow, steady military pressure might bring Parliament to its senses. A second bloodbath, on the other hand, would be counter-productive, especially if it failed to achieve its objective. If this discussion had taken place on the day after the battle and the decision had gone in Rupert's favour, anything might have happened, as the capital was alive with rumours that the royalists had won an overwhelming victory. However, Rupert's diary makes it very clear that it took place four days later, by which time the mood in London had changed dramatically.[51] The army was alive and kicking, the local royalists had not stirred, and the city trained bands had put London in a state of defence.[52] In such circumstances a surprise attack with mounted troops alone would have been at best a complete waste of time, at worst a major humiliation.

One of the few people on the Council of War to support Rupert's proposed assault on London was the earl of Forth, who became lord general immediately after news arrived of Lord Lindsey's death.[53] Forth was the son of a Scottish laird. He was first commissioned as an infantry officer thirty-five or more years earlier, which means that he cannot have been much younger than Lindsey, though there is some uncertainty about the actual date of his birth. In Sweden's wars against Russia and Poland, and then in the Thirty Years' War (1618–48), he had risen steadily through the ranks, achieving at first regimental command, then the governorship of a succession of captured towns, and finally a senior field command, that of lieutenant general of cavalry. In the process he played a distinguished part in many sieges and battles, most notably in 1631 at Breitenfeld (near Leipzig) under Gustavus Adolphus, king of Sweden, and in 1634 at Nördlingen (Bavaria) under Bernhard of Saxe-Weimar. Forth returned to Scotland in the late 1630s where his garrison at Edinburgh Castle defied the Covenanters for seven months. In the end starvation forced his men to surrender, by which time Forth had scurvy, 'his legs swelled and many of his teeth fallen out'.[54]

Unsurprisingly, a man who had been comely and upright in his youth was battle-scarred by 1642. He was also subject to attacks of gout and was becoming increasingly deaf. Lord Clarendon described him three years later as 'dozed in his understanding, which had never been quick and vigorous'. Also, although full of integrity, he was 'illiterate to the greatest degree', and renowned for his heavy consumption of alcohol.[55] Nevertheless, Forth fought bravely on horseback as late as the Second Battle of Newbury in October 1644.[56]

At no time during his two-year spell as lord general did Forth have that overall authority in military matters which his predecessor had regarded as essential if he was to discharge his duties. He does not seem to have objected to Rupert retaining his autonomous position as General of Horse, or to the prince continuing to act as the king's principal military adviser. He also does not seem to have complained when Rupert usurped his role, as, for example, at the storming of Bristol in late July 1643, when the prince had almost the entire Oxford army under his command, some fourteen regiments of foot and both wings of horse.[57] Possibly, Forth was happy to act merely as chief of staff in the field army.[58] After all, he had held a similar position in the Swedish army, and he did not have that high aristocratic or royal background which expected untrammelled powers of command as a virtual birthright. However, when Forth became accustomed to his new role, he sometimes took an independent line, egged on by an anti-Rupert faction in the officer corps, who saw that the king respected the old general's opinions in military matters. This change can be inferred from Rupert's diary, which rarely passes anything but critical comments on Forth's conduct from the summer of 1643 onwards.

As the king's army approached Oxford, the earl of Essex sprang into action, probably on the receipt of instructions from Parliament that he must march to London as quickly as possible.[59] By the last day of October his army was in the Northampton area. There it joined Watling Street. It then moved none too rapidly to St Albans where it arrived five days later, but well before the king's army reached the outskirts of London Essex was encamped close to the capital.[60] He was also in contact with the London trained bands, and with regiments raised in the past three weeks to form another field army under the command of the earl of Warwick.

The second encounter between the two field armies took place just to the west of London on 12 November. A week earlier Essex had received the first command from his political masters that related to operational rather than strategic matters, and this was scarcely surprising given his indifferent performance in the campaign so far. To prevent marauding bands of enemy cavalry plundering the capital's western suburbs, he was to put the pass at Brentford (where a bridge carried what is now the A4 road over the River Bren) into a state of defence.[61] Essex duly sent two of his best regiments, those of Denzil Holles and Lord Brooke, but provided them with no cavalry support.[62] He also failed to put a senior officer in charge, probably because he did not anticipate a major attack on the pass by infantry. Later, when it became apparent that the king's entire army was approaching Brentford along the north bank of the Thames, he failed to see the danger and therefore did not send reinforcements. In other respects, however, Essex was operationally astute. He sent a brigade of horse and foot to Kingston on the other bank of the river that was large enough to deliver a flank attack on the royalist army as it passed. Its prime task, however, was to prevent the enemy using Kingston bridge to advance on London along the more open south bank of the river, if frustrated by the opposition it encountered in the small fields and narrow lanes that dominated the landscape on the north bank from Hounslow Heath eastwards.

For his confrontation with the king's army Essex chose the only area of open ground between Brentford and Hammersmith comprising Turnham Green, a small piece of lowland heath and an adjacent open field, also on the small side, belonging to the manor of Chiswick.[63] It was ideal for the purpose. The restricted space would make it very difficult for the royalist army to deploy, and if Essex had to order a retreat, the enclosed country between there and Hammersmith would make it easy for musketeers to protect his rearguard against enemy cavalry.[64] Finally, the flatness of the landscape meant that the king's commanders would not be able to see an outflanking movement that Essex planned through Acton to Hounslow Heath intended to cut off the royalists' retreat. However, the earl did not believe that a royalist attack was

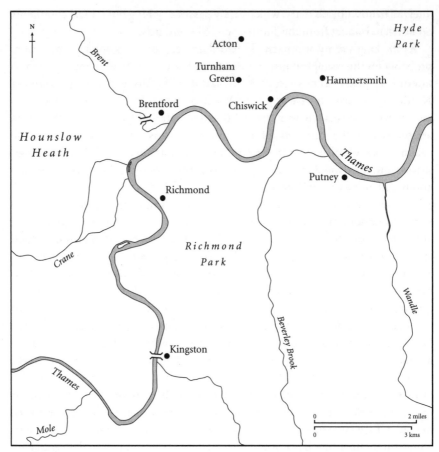

Turnham Green

imminent. Contacts between the politicians at Colnbrook between Slough and Hounslow meant that there was a strong chance of a truce.[65] He therefore took his seat in the House of Lords on the morning of 12 November, only to leave it almost immediately afterwards at the sound of distant gunfire.[66]

Under the cover of mist royalist cavalry patrols were testing the defences of Brentford. When these proved to be too firmly held for troops of horse to make any progress, Lord Forth sent in the infantry. The defenders of Brentford bridge put up stiff resistance, but superior numbers told in the end, as he brought regiment after regiment into play.[67] The parliamentarians sustained considerable casualties, mainly through drowning, but a new infantry formation eventually stopped the rot and covered the withdrawal of what was left of Holles's and Brooke's regiments from Brentford to Hammersmith.[68] The troops at Kingston, on the other hand, abandoned their positions without a fight on receiving orders that they were needed at Turnham Green. However, their roundabout march via Old London Bridge meant that they arrived too late in the day to take part in what turned out to be no more than a stand-off.[69]

Essex deployed his army on Turnham Green with the infantry in the centre in two lines, in the foremost of which field army and trained band regiments alternated. The cavalry were on the wings as usual, but he placed two strong regiments in front of the infantry to occupy ground, thus making it impossible for Rupert's horse to build up the necessary pace for delivering a devastating charge. The king's generals, forced to draw up their troops in an exceedingly cramped position, had only one offensive tactic available to them, head-on attack, but this was likely to be suicidal. They were facing thousands upon thousands of musketeers and also many artillery pieces. Their horse and foot would be shot down in droves before they reached the enemy line.[70]

The two armies faced one another for several hours, each waiting for the other to make the first move. Then, as evening approached, the royalists fell back across Brentford bridge without Essex making the slightest move to stop them, the intended outflanking movement via Acton having ended not long after it began, much to the anger of a particularly unwarlike MP, Bulstrode Whitelock, who had accompanied it. To make matters worse, Essex had made no arrangements for a pursuit.[71] The king's army therefore had an uninterrupted night's sleep on Hounslow Heath, and when Essex failed to attack at dawn, it crossed the Thames at Kingston and broke the bridge down behind it.[72] Essex's only response was to build a bridge of boats across the Thames at Putney so that his army could operate on the Surrey bank. When the king's army began to fall back in a westerly direction a few days later, he duly occupied Kingston, but that was all. On 19 November two MPs travelled there 'to desire him not to omit any opportunity in pursuing the king's forces according to his instructions',[73] but he did nothing until the risk of another confrontation had passed.

Falling back as far as Oxford, Forth and Prince Rupert placed their troops in winter quarters there and in the surrounding villages and market towns, but they left a large garrison at Reading despite the fact that the town was completely without fortifications.[74] By occupying Reading they would make it difficult for grain and other foodstuffs to reach the capital from Buckinghamshire by barges on the River Thames. The town could also serve as the launching pad for a new attack on London in the spring, when reinforcements should have arrived at Oxford from the west and the north.[75]

When Essex was sure that the king's army was no longer a threat, he occupied the country immediately to the east of Reading in force, whilst placing a small brigade at Aylesbury to guard a second route from Oxford to London over the Chiltern Hills. He did nothing of an offensive nature for the next five months, resisting as far as he was able the efforts of the Committee of Safety to use units of his army in minor operations at no great distance. He grudgingly allowed one of his cavalry colonels, Sir William Waller, to evict a party of royalists from

Farnham Castle, but he was slow in responding to cries for assistance from the
inhabitants of Marlborough, who were trying to put their town into a state of
defence. A mixed royalist brigade of cavalry and infantry from Oxford led by
Henry Wilmot overwhelmed them before help arrived, but on the return leg the
would-be rescuers gained their revenge by capturing Winchester and with it two
of the king's regiments of horse which had fought at Edgehill.[76]

Essex adopted a similar policy of extreme caution in the Lower Severn valley,
where he had left three regiments of foot and several troops of horse in his
hurried march to Edgehill. The garrisons at Hereford and Worcester were too
exposed. The area in which they were situated was royalist in sympathy, their
defences were in a poor state of repair, and if besieged they could not hope for
speedy relief. He therefore ordered the garrisons to withdraw to Gloucester and
Bristol, where the inhabitants were more positively inclined towards Parliament
and whose walls were in a better state to withstand a siege.[77] In the meantime the
earl took his ease in the king's apartments at Windsor Castle. He would wait for
spring before stirring, as was the custom in the campaigns he had fought on the
Continent. By then the roads would be dry enough to take the weight of his
artillery train and a new offensive could begin.

CHAPTER 4

Taking Stock, November
1642–April 1643

IN THE late summer of 1642 both sides expected the fighting to end in a matter of weeks,[1] but the first campaign had been inconclusive and the king and Parliament faced the daunting prospect of a lengthy war and all the human misery that would necessarily flow from it. However, Charles and his ministers did not hold Lord Forth and Prince Rupert responsible for what had happened and the diarchy remained in place. After all they had much to their credit. The military outlook was far rosier than it had been at Nottingham. The field army had driven the enemy army into the south-eastern corner of England and was well placed to renew the attack on London in the spring. Moreover, the generals could argue that the war might be over had the king listened to the advice they had given him after Edgehill. Others, however, had persuaded him to be cautious and the upshot had been the fiasco at Turnham Green, at best a complete waste of time, at worst a major political error which showed the enemy how small the king's army was compared with the forces they could bring into the field in times of emergency.[2]

However, the king's generals had their critics. The fiercest attack came from the poisonous pen of Lord Clarendon, who focused on this occasion on Prince Rupert. Rupert's failure to control the royalist cavalry had turned Edgehill from near certain victory into a desperate struggle for survival. However, although command and control was certainly an issue, it was a systemic one affecting the foot as well as the horse. Clarendon also accused Rupert of undermining an important peace initiative through his youthful enthusiasm. Whilst talks about a possible truce were taking place at Colnbrook on 12 November, the prince had led his cavalry in a foolhardy advance to Hounslow Heath without first consulting the king. There he encountered the enemy force defending Brentford and quickly got out of his depth. The rest of the king's army then had to go to his rescue and a major engagement ensued. This, and the sacking of the town that followed, derailed the peace process. Members of the two Houses of Parliament opposed to negotiations were able to win a majority by accusing the royalists of breaking the truce. However, this was all a pack of lies. Rupert slept at Egham on the night of the 11th–12th. The following morning, having received intelligence that the enemy had occupied Brentford in force, he visited the king at Colnbrook where he received orders to drive them out. Moreover, the king's infantry

The South-west of England and South Wales, 1642–1648

regiments received their orders to advance to Hounslow Heath well before dawn on the 11th, and arrived there earlier than the time Clarendon alleges Rupert sent to his uncle for help.[3] Moreover, the prospects for a negotiated peace at that point in time were unpropitious. Parliament treated the king's emissary in a most discourteous manner, and the terms on offer were almost as obnoxious as those Charles had rejected before the war began.[4]

Parliament's lord general was much more vulnerable. The fact of the matter was that Essex had not succeeded in furthering Parliament's war aims by one single iota. His generalship from Northampton onwards had been a sorry tale of missed opportunity after missed opportunity, from his failure to advance on Nottingham in September when the king's forces were at their weakest to his refusal to allow any harassment of the royal army as it fell back towards Oxford in mid-November. Essex's critics would have no truck with bad luck or the low cunning of the enemy. Instead they came up with a number of related points, which suggested that the lord general lacked the martial qualities needed for achieving a quick victory. First, he was in thrall to the clique of professional soldiers and old cronies on his general staff.[5] He and they were steeped in a military culture acquired from campaigning in the Low Countries where the enclosed landscape crisscrossed by numerous watercourses and dotted with powerful fortresses made for a form of warfare that was ponderous, immensely expensive in terms of military resources and almost invariably inconclusive.[6] In addition, some of Essex's junior officers who were professional soldiers had their own reasons for making the war drag on for as long as possible. Theirs was a precarious occupation in terms of financial rewards. They therefore needed time to fill their pockets either legitimately from the taxpayer in the pay they received or illegitimately through plunder and extortion.[7]

Second, whatever military operation Essex undertook, he always required an inordinate length of time to transform intentions into action. In the words of Henry Marten, commenting on the disappointments of the autumn campaign in a speech delivered in the House of Commons on 5 December 1642:

> all these miseries proceeded from his slowness [such] that we saw it was summer in Devonshire, summer in Yorkshire and only winter in Windsor . . . unless the lord general used more speed the kingdom would be ruined.

Thomas Hoyle was next. Also concerned that Essex's slowness would lose the war, he added a third criticism, carelessness.[8] This was more dangerous than lethargy. If he was merely slow to act, Essex might find it as difficult to lose the war as to win it (assuming that Marten's final point was a financial rather than a strategic one). If he was careless, he might lose it as readily as if he was unduly rash, and the events of the third and fourth weeks of October showed how carelessness could have led to calamity. The lord general had allowed the king's army to move unmolested across his front, gathering reinforcements as it went, and had then set off in pursuit with much of his army elsewhere because he had failed to plan for such a contingency.

Two consequences followed. In the first place, the true nature of Essex's relationship to the two Houses of Parliament was out in the open. The grandiloquent language that had accompanied his departure from London in September and returned very briefly with the capital's escape from fire and the sword seven weeks later was a sham. Well before the start of the new campaigning season, the moderate Denzil Holles, whilst drawing the attention of his colleagues in the Commons to the lawless behaviour of some of Essex's troops, reminded them that the earl was 'employed by them to preserve the liberty and property of the subject'.[9] The two Houses were without question Essex's political masters and his remit was to carry out their orders.

Second, as presaged in Henry Marten's speech, Essex's critics began to take an interest in other military commanders who showed signs of going for the enemy's jugular rather than conducting a slow and stately dance across the English countryside until the enemy ground to a halt through lack of supplies or sheer physical exhaustion. It is unlikely that their intention at this stage was to replace him as lord general or to reduce him to the role of a cipher or figure-head. In the winter of 1642–3, they probably wanted to do nothing more than to put fire in his belly or shame him into taking more vigorous action against the enemy.

Matters came to a head later in the winter when Essex reported to Parliament on the rundown state of his army. The only remedy in the short term was for the Lords and the Commons to go cap in hand to the wealthy city merchants and tradesmen for money,[10] but men who had cheerfully provided funds in September 1642 to enable Essex to lead a disciplined and contented army into the field now laid down conditions designed to cut costs. The earl was to disband his smaller regiments. Professional officers made redundant as a result were to be sent to the provinces where there was a dearth of experienced commanders, whilst the common soldiers were to fill up the ranks of the regiments that survived the cut. In future, regiments of foot should be 1,200 strong with 100 men in each company, whilst each troop of horse was to be 80 strong. In this way 'the excessive charge of paying more officers than are necessary may be avoided'. Finally, to prevent colonels making money on the side by claiming they had more men under arms than they actually had and pocketing the difference, an honest man was to be appointed in each regiment to keep the muster rolls up to date and pay only those soldiers who were on the roll.[11] Parliament accepted the demands and a number of regiments disappeared, but complaints about the expense of maintaining Essex's army continued. In his daily journal of House of Commons business, Sir Simon D'Ewes wrote as follows only a fortnight later:

> the men still at Windsor eating and drinking for four or five months last past consumed a mass of treasure without doing anything, to the dislike of all.[12]

Essex, however, was probably pleased at the promise of money to pay his troops, and not that unhappy with some downsizing, as he had already disbanded at least one infantry regiment which had fled from the battlefield at Edgehill without fighting. However, it is unlikely that he looked with favour on the citizens of London interfering with matters relating to military organisation.[13]

Another development that affected for good and for ill the ability of army commanders on both sides to carry out their masters' wishes was the provincial-isation of the war effort.[14] Living from hand to mouth on gifts, loans and what could be seized from enemy supporters was not a practicable way of running a war lasting longer than a single campaign. Establishing a proper wartime economy was essential to provide the steady flow of men and materials without which the sovereign's armies would wither on the vine. One way of enhancing this flow was to occupy as much territory as possible so that its wealth, its manpower and its manufacturing capability could be systematically exploited to further the war effort. However, guarding the geese that might lay golden eggs was not a job for the field army. New forces must be raised for this purpose, particularly if the enemy still had garrisons in the area. But provincial forces were potentially capable of doing much more than protecting their home territory. They could provide reinforcements for the main field army when required, and through their own campaigning they could also tie down enemy troops and supplies, but there were also a number of possible downsides to a development that would inevitably lead to a proliferation of armies. Provincial commands were competitors for centrally supplied resources. Provincial generals were rivals and potential successors. Provincial armies might require seed corn in the form of regular units from the field army to set them on their way. Finally, the lord generals might find their requests for reinforcements turned down if either the personal ambitions of the provincial commanders or the security of the home region were seen as being threatened.[15]

However, the earl of Essex on the one hand and the royalist military leadership on the other were to have strikingly different experiences of the impact of provincialisation on their ability to wage war. First, the chronology was very different. Provincialisation had no impact on Essex's running of the 1642 campaign. Regiments and brigades belonging to the field army which had overrun southern England in August and September did not remain there but rejoined the lord general before he left Worcester.[16] In October, Parliament toyed with the idea of making the earl of Pembroke general of the west, and commissioned the earl of Warwick, the commander of the fleet, to raise a second field army charged with defending London,[17] but neither proposal came to anything. Pembroke's commission was never issued and Warwick agreed early in 1643 to add his six new regiments of foot to Essex's army.[18] Only in Yorkshire did local requests that Ferdinando, Lord Fairfax, should command forces raised in the county meet with a positive response at Westminster.[19] However, the instructions issued to Fairfax two days before Edgehill were imprecise and amounted to little more than a request to keep the flag flying in the north in view of the 'good state of our affairs here'.[20]

During December, however, Lord Brooke became major general for the Central Midlands, Lord Grey of Wark major general of an Eastern Association to be run from Cambridge, and the earl of Stamford major general in Devon and Cornwall.[21] In early February, Sir William Waller received a similar commission covering the counties of mid Wessex and the Lower Severn valley, the so-called Western Association.[22] All were under Essex's overall command, but more ominously, on 3 December Lord Fairfax was commissioned as lieutenant general of the northern counties.[23] This made him to all intents and purposes independent of the earl. From then onwards his orders came from the Committee of

Safety,[24] and soldiers and politicians acknowledged his new status by describing him as lord general of the north.[25] Essex does not seem to have taken umbrage as he signed the commission within a day of receiving instructions from Parliament to do so. Presumably he and his supporters saw the counties beyond the River Trent as a subsidiary theatre, where vigorous campaigning by Fairfax might cause the king's officers to retain military resources in the north, which might otherwise be sent to strengthen the Oxford army. Thus, the lord general of the north would be indirectly assisting Essex in his task of winning the war for Parliament, not stealing his glory. The separateness of the northern theatre of war is also clearly shown in the instructions Fairfax received from the Committee of Safety in mid-April 1643 when Essex was in the final stages of preparations for an offensive in the Thames valley. He was to defend those parts of Yorkshire he held, to try and reconquer those he had lost, and to give such support as he could to his colleagues in Lancashire and Cheshire.[26] There was no mention of marching south with reinforcements for the field army.

In fact Lord Fairfax was not that successful in recruiting in Yorkshire, but from his power base in the towns of the West Riding he was holding his own against superior numbers, despite friction with Sir John Hotham who had a separate power base in the port of Hull and resented his authority. Essex asked Fairfax to appoint Hotham's son, Sir John Hotham junior, as his lieutenant general of horse, but the lord general of the north gave the position instead to his own son, Sir Thomas Fairfax. Young Hotham had to be content with a more limited jurisdiction outside Lord Fairfax's command, as lieutenant general of horse raised in Lincolnshire. This affront may have pushed the Hothams into taking the first step on the road towards changing sides.[27] However, relations between Lord Fairfax and the earl of Essex remained good and in the following year Fairfax raised no difficulties about his son receiving an emergency commission from the lord general of the south, which authorised him to take temporary command over forces in Cheshire, Lancashire and adjacent counties.[28]

The provincialisation of the royalist war effort occurred much earlier. At the end of June 1642 the earl of Newcastle received the king's command to garrison Newcastle, and then to consolidate royalist control over the counties of Northumberland, Durham, Cumberland and Westmorland.[29] On almost the same day the marquis of Hertford received similar orders to establish a strong royalist presence in the south-west of England and South Wales.[30] Finally, when the king's army left York for Nottingham in late July, Charles appointed the earl of Cumberland as his general in Yorkshire. All were actual or *de facto* lieutenant generals.

During the winter, as the earl of Cumberland had neither the competence nor the physical and mental stamina for high command, the earl of Newcastle took over Yorkshire and made York his army headquarters. After sending troops to occupy Newark, which was to become a vital staging post on the route along which resources would pass between York and Oxford, the king added Lincolnshire, Nottinghamshire and Derbyshire to Newcastle's generalship.[31] At about the same time Lord Capel received a lieutenant general's commission to command forces in North Wales and the adjacent English counties of Shropshire, Cheshire, Staffordshire and Worcestershire, whilst the king divided the marquis of Hertford's command by giving Lord Carbery responsibility for the three counties of south-west Wales, with Lord Herbert acting as Hertford's deputy in Glamorgan, Brecon and Radnor.[32]

The instructions that the royalist provincial generals received made it clear from the start that provincial interests or concerns were to be subordinate to the task of winning the war as quickly as possible. They were to send regiments to the field army as soon as they were complete, and also any additional military resources that came their way, and then to lead the rest of their troops to Oxford to support the attack on London. In September 1642 Hertford sent the king two or three regiments of infantry from south-east Wales, which joined the field army in Warwickshire before the battle of Edgehill.[33] Newcastle's contribution in terms of troops was less spectacular, but without the convoy of arms and ammunition sent south it is unlikely that the army could have done anything in the autumn campaign other than remain on the defensive.[34]

The commitment to increasing the size of the Oxford army was an ongoing one. The king wrote to Newcastle on three occasions in the closing weeks of 1642, ordering him to march south as soon as possible,[35] but priorities altered soon afterwards. The field army was running out of essential military supplies, most particularly gunpowder and muskets, and there was no way that such deficiencies could be supplied from the territory the king's supporters controlled in the South Midlands, Wales and the Welsh borderland. The queen, however, had purchased or otherwise acquired a large quantity of gunpowder, muskets and other war material on the Continent.[36] The original intention was for her to unload them at Newcastle or at a port in south-east England,[37] but in late January 1643 the king decided that Yorkshire was the best place for her to land. Newcastle was too far away and he had failed to establish a presence in the south-east. Moreover, the earl of Newcastle's army would be close by. However, he only controlled the central part of the county, the coast being dominated by parliamentary garrisons at Hull and Scarborough. There was another problem also. The overland route to Oxford would oblige Henrietta Maria and her wagon train to cross a band of country fifty miles wide controlled by enemy forces operating out of such garrisons as Derby, Coventry, Northampton and Warwick. The earl's new priority was therefore to cooperate with forces from Oxford and the Welsh Marches to ensure that the queen and her convoy reached its destination without incident before the start of the campaigning season.

Correspondence between the king's headquarters and Hertford's command is scantier, but two pieces of evidence, one dating from December 1642 and the other from March or April of the following year, show clearly that the forces Sir Ralph Hopton was raising in Cornwall also had instructions to join the field army, but they had 150 miles of hostile territory to cross.[38] They were also desperately short of cavalry despite the fact that Hopton found himself in Cornwall because in September 1642 it was the only place of refuge for the two troops of horse that the western royalists had raised in Somerset and Dorset to defend Sherborne Castle.[39] Lord Herbert received the same orders, but his regiments were ready too early. On their way to Oxford they received permission to have a crack at Gloucester, the only remaining enemy garrison on the River Severn.[40]

The king ordered the more mobile parts of the field army to help assist the provincial forces in their passage to Oxford. Thus, in January 1643 Rupert met the marquis of Hertford at Cirencester in the Cotswolds. The marquis had with him two regiments from west Wales raised too late to take part in the Edgehill campaign. Two months later the prince set out for the north, sweeping up hostile garrisons as he went. By that time the queen had landed safely at Bridlington in Yorkshire thanks to the protection afforded by the Dutch navy, but Rupert got no further than Lichfield. He successfully stormed the city after exploding a mine under its fortifications, but was then recalled.[41] In the summer Rupert's younger brother Prince Maurice helped Hertford escort the five Cornish infantry regiments from Devonshire into south-central England,[42] whilst in August Lords Capel and Herbert provided brigades of infantry to assist in the siege of Gloucester.[43] A month later Capel sent the newly raised Prince of Wales's regiment of foot, some 800 strong, to reinforce the royal army. It arrived just in time to fight in the First Battle of Newbury on 20 September, where it suffered heavy losses.[44] However, the actual raising of these new regiments required very little seed corn from the king's field army. Capel, for example, left Oxford for the Welsh borders in March 1643 accompanied by only eighty officers and men, whilst Captains Richard Bagot and Gervase Holles, who returned to Staffordshire and Nottinghamshire respectively in the winter of 1642–3 with commissions as colonels, only took their own companies back with them.[45]

Parliament in contrast weakened its field army during the winter of 1642–3 by sending quite large bodies of seasoned troops into the provinces to form nuclei around which new armies could form: they never returned. Of the three infantry regiments left stranded in the west by the march to Edgehill, one went to Exeter with the earl of Stamford,[46] another became part of Waller's army and surrendered at Roundway Down, whilst the third remained in garrison at Gloucester for the rest of the war.[47] In January 1642 when Lord Brooke left London for Warwick he took 400 foot with him, presumably his own regiment from the field army as it is never again mentioned in field army pay warrants.[48] Other units, primarily cavalry and dragoons, went to places as diverse as Yorkshire, Nottinghamshire, Cheshire, Lincolnshire and the Isle of Ely,[49] whilst Sir William Waller took with him in February 1643, or subsequently incorporated into his army, at least five of Essex's troops of horse including three troops belonging to Balfour's regiment, which had done so well at Edgehill.[50] The loss of infantry regiments was not yet a major problem, as the reservoir of potential foot soldiers in London and the south-east was far from empty, but the prospects for Essex's spring campaign were to be severely weakened by the loss of at least two and a half regiments of cavalry to the provincial commands,[51] especially as several new regiments of horse had joined the Oxford army by the beginning of April.[52]

Problems of divided command on the parliamentary side soon lessened. Some of the new major generalships proved to be very short-lived. The Cornish royalists decisively defeated Lord Stamford's army at the battle of Stratton in May. Subsequently what was left of his infantry helped defend Exeter, whilst his cavalry fled into Waller's territory and became part of his army.[53] With the surrender of Exeter in early September, Stamford's army disappeared for good. He then retired into private life but periodically caused a rumpus in Parliament by demanding his back pay and claiming that his officers had stabbed him in the back. Lord Brooke's command came apart even earlier when, after a hopeful start, a sniper's bullet fired from the spire of Lichfield Cathedral removed him permanently from the scene. It then took his successor, the earl of Denbigh, a whole year to put his army back together again.[54]

Sir William Waller and Lord Grey of Wark began rather better. Grey, assisted by Oliver Cromwell, recruited several thousand men in the eastern counties, but failed to develop the financial machinery for supporting them in the field. As a result the troops he led into the Thames valley in April to assist the earl of Essex faded away as the weeks passed. A second corps operating in south Lincolnshire under Cromwell's command had first pickings of the few resources that became available not only because they were closer to Cambridge but also because, rather than assisting the earl of Essex, they were protecting the northern frontier of the Association, which was under threat from the royalist garrison at Newark.[55]

Sir William Waller was more successful that the rest due to his single-mindedness, and his authoritarian attitude towards civilian administrators and more junior commanders alike.[56] By the time Essex took the field on 13 April 1643 he had cleared Wiltshire and Gloucestershire of royalists, and was about to invade Herefordshire. The fact that Sir William had faced enemy troop formations, which were either inexperienced or heavily outnumbered,[57] did not matter for those who saw his successes as a stick with which to beat the lord general. However, Waller's supporters, who would have liked to have given him command of a second national army independent of the earl of Essex's, failed to spot signs of the qualities they so despised in the lord general. They ignored the fact that Waller made a point of keeping well clear of large and experienced enemy formations. In February, for example, he scuttled back from Winchester to Farnham, his army base, when he discovered that Prince Rupert was in the vicinity.[58] He was also extremely wary of a similar-sized force to his own

commanded by Rupert's brother, Prince Maurice, which he encountered in the
Lower Severn valley in April and which managed to inflict a minor defeat upon
him in a running fight at Ripple near Tewkesbury.[59]

The royalist generals in the provinces also experienced mixed fortunes during
the winter and the early spring, but overall they did far better than their parliamentary equivalents. Lord Herbert lost his small army at Highnam near Gloucester in
March after a surprise attack from Sir William Waller, the rescue party from Oxford
under Lord Grandison having failed to arrive in time, but Herbert had raised
another army by late July.[60] Hertford was unable to set foot in the southern part of
his command between November 1642 and May 1643 because it was almost all
under enemy occupation. However, his deputy, Sir Ralph Hopton, was able to
galvanise the Cornish royalists into action and they managed to hold their own
against the increasingly large forces that Parliament sent against them, whereas the
earl of Newcastle's struggle with Lord Fairfax in Yorkshire swayed backwards and
forwards with the former's preponderance in resources being offset by Sir Thomas
Fairfax's excellence in commanding brigade-size operations.[61]

Lord Capel was the least successful royalist general. His newly commissioned
colonels made some progress in raising regiments, but he suffered a number of
military setbacks in the spring, mainly at the hands of the parliamentary
commander in Cheshire, Sir William Brereton. One cause was the depleted
condition of Capel's home territory, which the king's field army had swept clean
of volunteers prior to the Edgehill campaign. The local parliamentarians, on the
other hand, had either kept their heads down or used such resources as they had
to defend Manchester, only sending a company of dragoons and a few volunteers to join the earl of Essex's army for the Edgehill campaign. Second, the
orders Capel received from the king during the spring to undertake operations
outside his province, which he loyally obeyed, drained his command of troops,
thus giving Brereton in Cheshire the chance to seize the initiative. Nowhere in
the wars in the British Isles in the mid seventeenth century does the old proverb
'when the cat's away the mice will play' apply as well as it does to the fighting in
the north-west Midlands in 1643.[62] However, part of the problem lay in the fact
that Capel was an amateur soldier and that he lacked professional military
advice at an appropriate level. From February 1643 onwards the earl of
Newcastle had at his right hand General James King, who had fought in the
Thirty Years' War as a middle-ranking general like the earl of Forth,[63] whilst
Hopton had the support of a quiverful of officers with military experience, both
old and new.[64] However, access to military experience was not essential for
success. Honeyed words alone were apparently effective in south-west Wales
where Lord Carbery persuaded the towns of Pembrokeshire, which had
declared for Parliament in 1642, to make their peace with the king.[65]

CHAPTER 5

Parliament's Lost Opportunities, April–July 1643

THE 1643 campaigning season for the two field armies began in the early spring. For the first time in the war the earl of Essex was on the offensive, his objective to remove the threat to London by driving the king's forces from the Thames valley. For the past six weeks a truce had been in operation whilst peace negotiations took place at Oxford, but there was frenetic military activity elsewhere with minor battles being fought at Ripple, Hopton Heath, Middlewich, Whalley and Seacroft Moor.[1] When peace talks reached an impasse on 12 April, Parliament refused to renew the truce, and Essex's army immediately set off westwards, seemingly taking the king's generals by surprise, but impressions can be deceptive. Essex, reinvigorated by the criticism he had faced during the winter, may have been aiming to startle the enemy, but they were well aware that something was afoot. Sir Edward Nicholas, the king's principal secretary of state and spymaster-in-chief, wrote to Prince Rupert on 6 April observing that:

> There are preparations for all the earl of Essex's forces to march towards our quarters, and we hear this day that they are to begin to set forth . . . and from London we hear that Colonel Cromwell is to come from Cambridgeshire with 4,000 foot and horse to meet the earl in these parts.[2]

Why did Lord Forth not get his blow in first? The answer is that he was almost out of gunpowder, as the supplies the queen had brought from the Continent were still in the north. However, the king's Council of War did not take the threat from Essex very seriously, which is scarcely surprising given his record to date. It advised Rupert and Maurice that they would soon have to return to Oxford, but it did not stop the former's operations before Lichfield or the latter from continuing to play tag with Sir William Waller in the Lower Severn valley.[3] It also did not bother evacuating Reading and its garrison of six regiments of foot and at least one of horse which lay in the way of Essex's likeliest line of march.[4] If Reading was indeed his first target, the alertness of the garrison (which had skirmished with his forward units throughout the winter) would surely make him approach the town gingerly, thus providing the Council of War with plenty of time to assemble a relief force.

According to Clarendon there was much heated discussion in the Committee of Safety over whether to attack Reading or to go straight for Oxford.[5] Those members whose trust in God and the earl of Essex made them willing to risk their field army fighting a battle in the open fields of Oxfordshire lost the argument. Essex apparently sided with the majority, but, determined to make the odds in his favour as good as possible if a confrontation became unavoidable, ordered Waller and Lord Grey of Wark to join him. His big problem in a set-piece engagement was shortage of cavalry and their participation would improve the likelihood of success, as Waller would be able to bring at least 1,000 and Lord Grey probably 500 more. Essex also hoped that with Waller advancing on Oxford from one direction and him from the other, the king might take to his heels and so make a siege of the royalist headquarters unnecessary.[6]

On 15 April Essex duly set siege to Reading. A Council of War that convened the following day rejected the idea of storming the town, even though the royalists had done little to strengthen its defences. Instead it was to be starved into surrender.[7] Shortly after the siege commenced, the garrison commander let the royalist Council of War know that he was not as ready to face a blockade as he had let them believe. A relief expedition must therefore set out as quickly as possible and to that end Rupert and Maurice received orders to return immediately. They arrived on 22 and 24 April respectively,[8] only to find that their uncle was to join the relief expedition and that Lord Forth had already decided on the route it was to take.

The obvious route was along the south bank of the Thames. Reading was on that bank of the river, and much of the march from Oxford would be over open fields and commons where Rupert could make good use of his cavalry. John Gwynne blamed the failure to do so on treachery amongst the king's military advisers,[9] but his account of the pros and cons is not convincing, as the closer the royalists got to Reading the greater the problems posed by the landscape. If they veered well to the south of the Thames and approached Reading via the Bath road, they would encounter enclosures at Thatcham, where enemy infantry backed by artillery with cavalry in support could easily stop them in their tracks. If they took a more direct route following the line of the river, they would have to fight their way through the Goring gap, a narrow pass between the Chiltern Hills and the Berkshire Downs.

Forth's chosen approach via the north bank of the Thames should have the advantage of surprise as the woods cloaking the slopes of the Chiltern Hills would conceal the army's advance, but the relief of Reading from that direction depended on storming Caversham bridge, an even easier pass for Essex's army to defend than the Goring gap. However, Forth's plan of attack did not depend solely on the Oxford army crossing the river. At its approach the garrison was to make a sortie *en masse* towards Caversham. This should create sufficient confusion for them to disrupt the parliamentarian defences and rush the bridge before

The North of England, 1642–1648

the rest of the besieging force could intervene. All Forth had to do was capture or otherwise disable the guard post that Essex had placed on the Oxfordshire side of the bridge. However, the plan failed. The garrison did not attack when supposed to, as its acting commander, Richard Fielding, was in negotiations for the surrender of the town.[10] Also Essex had read Forth's mind. On 25 April the royalist infantry and dragoons found themselves facing not a guard post but a formidable defensive position centred on a large barn from which Essex's musketeers poured barrage after barrage into their ranks, causing heavy casualties. Forth did not persist. His men soon began to run out of gunpowder, and without gunpowder further assaults would be both suicidal and pointless.[11]

That night Richard Fielding managed to cross the river, bringing with him a copy of the terms that Essex had offered in return for immediate surrender. It can be inferred from Clarendon's description of Fielding's meeting with the king that Charles gave the document a cursory glance, seized on the fact that the garrison were not to become prisoners but to march away carrying their arms and ammunition with them, and gave his permission for it to be signed. On the 27th the Reading garrison duly abandoned their fortifications and joined the rest of the Oxford army near Abingdon.

Essex had captured Reading at minimal cost to his own men, but news of his generosity to the enemy aroused anger in London, particularly when he failed, as at Turnham Green, to follow up what had been an easy success. Editors of some London journals reminded their readers that in superficially similar circumstances Waller and Rupert had insisted on garrison soldiers becoming prisoners of war.[12] The lenient terms also meant that Rupert and Forth still had sufficient infantry to make a fight of it in the Thames valley, but the shortage of gunpowder was now more critical than ever, and there was serious talk of abandoning Oxford altogether and marching north to join the earl of Newcastle. After three or four days the severity of the military situation eased when it became obvious that Essex had no intention of immediately leaving Reading for points west. Forth then persuaded the king to allow him to bluff the enemy by setting up an armed camp at Culham, which Essex would have to assault whichever route he chose for his eventual advance on Oxford, as the forces at Culham could operate on either bank using Abingdon bridge.[13] The bluff worked. The royalist army remained at Culham for the next six weeks at first in some trepidation, but as time passed their eyes turned less and less frequently towards the Goring gap for signs of Essex's approach.

What held Essex back? The conventional explanation is his own given at the time, namely lack of supplies, most particularly money to pay his troops.[14] A more likely explanation is that, despite intelligence that the Oxford army was preparing to leave Oxford,[15] Essex feared defeat if he moved towards them. Lord Grey of Wark had arrived but without his horse which were with Oliver Cromwell, whereas Waller had marched off in a westerly direction and set siege

to Hereford. Without them a battle was out of the question.[16] The most important reason of all, however, was probably a political one, namely that Essex was
under orders from the Committee of Safety to remain where he was for the time
being.

The leading members of the committee, John Pym (King Pym to his
enemies), John Hampden, Lord Say and Sele, and the earl of Manchester, were
trying to open negotiations with the queen, and one of the carrots being dangled
before her was that Essex would not advance on Oxford until their emissary
returned from York. Not surprisingly she informed Charles that she would spin
out her discussions with the emissary for as long as possible.[17] This may explain
one of the oddities of the attacks on the earl of Essex in late April and the first
half of May: they were confined to the weekly journals, there was no criticism of
him in the Commons or the Lords. Persuading the queen to put pressure on
Charles to reopen negotiations may also explain the leniency of the terms for
the surrender of Reading.[18]

Essex also had every reason for thinking that the king's position at Oxford
would be ultimately untenable, as the earl had taken steps to prevent the queen's
ammunition leaving the north. Well before the siege of Reading he had sent
orders to his commanders in East Anglia and the East Midlands, Sir John Gell,
Lord Grey of Groby, Oliver Cromwell and Sir John Hotham junior, to join
forces to stop supplies that had reached Newark, the southernmost point of the
earl of Newcastle's command, from getting any further.[19] In the event these
commanders were to prove as much of a broken reed as Sir William Waller.

On 8 May the royalist commander in Leicestershire, Henry Hastings, set out
from Newark with forty wagons carrying 300 barrels of gunpowder and other
military supplies. Escorted by two regiments of foot and twenty-six troops of
horse, the wagons arrived at Banbury on 11 May without encountering any
opposition.[20] Cromwell and his fellow commanders were not even looking for
the enemy. Instead they spent several weeks bickering about the time and place
of their rendezvous. When they finally met at Grantham in Lincolnshire on the
9th, the royalist convoy was too far to the south to be intercepted.[21] The
escapade, however, was not as trouble-free politically for the royalists as it had
been operationally. Hastings's men believed they had a right to a share of the
convoy's contents, but they received a stern letter from Sir Edward Nicholas
written on the king's orders to the effect that for the moment they would have
to fend for themselves. The 500 muskets originally allotted to them were for the
infantry regiments at Culham, who would otherwise mutiny.[22] Nicholas was
almost certainly exaggerating, but there was discontent at Culham. A petition
got up by the field officers earlier in the month was a litany of complaints about
pay and conditions.[23]

The arrival of the munitions convoy and its escort did not make the king's
army strong enough to take the offensive, but it did allow for a further initiative

to bring provincial forces into the Thames valley theatre of war. On 19 May the
marquis of Hertford left Oxford with several regiments of horse.[24] His orders
were to raise troops in Wiltshire and Dorset and then to push further into south-
west England to fulfil the king's promise to provide the Cornish cavaliers with an
escort whenever they felt themselves strong enough to begin their eastwards
march.[25] Essex now ordered Sir William Waller to move his army from the Wye
valley into Somerset so as to prevent the two enemy brigades joining forces, but
once again Waller went his own way.[26] After a very brief tour of inspection of the
southern part of his command between 20 and 22 May, he marched his army off
in the opposite direction, sensing a royalist military vacuum. The king had sent
Prince Maurice back into the Severn valley with some cavalry regiments after the
failure to relieve Reading, but no sooner had he arrived than he received orders
to join Hertford in Wiltshire in case Waller tried to interrupt the marquis's
recruiting operations.[27] Waller, however, had his eyes on Worcester. Arriving
outside the city on 29 May, he tried to browbeat the garrison into surrender,[28]
but it was stronger than the one he had encountered at Hereford and much
better led, and the attempt failed.

Sir William's flagrant dereliction of duty enabled the marquis of Hertford and
Prince Maurice to move freely from Wiltshire into Dorset and so into west
Somerset as far as Chard, picking up recruits as they went. There they met the
Cornish regiments marching eastwards after tearing the heart out of the earl of
Stamford's army at Stratton near Bude in north Cornwall on 16 May. Sir Ralph
Hopton, the senior officer present, is often given the credit for the victory, but it
is apparent from his own account of the campaign that the strange decision to
attack the enemy position from four different directions was that of the Council
of War.[29] It would probably not have worked if the heavily outnumbered
Cornish had faced the whole of the earl's army, as he could have used interior
lines to throw his reserves against one assault or the other as occasion offered.
However, in reality the royalists won by profiting from their enemy's mistakes.
Stamford had tipped the odds in their favour. Believing that the royalists dare
not attack the hilltop position he had chosen, he allowed his cavalry regiments
to raid Bodmin instead and there was consequently nothing they could do
to help.[30]

After spending some time combining two brigades with different cultures
into a marching army, Hertford set out on the homeward leg bringing with him
at least eight new regiments of foot and some additional troops of horse,[31] but
blocking his way was Sir William Waller, who had at last arrived in Somerset.[32]
Destroying the royalist army of the west was now a much more difficult task
than it would have been in mid-May.[33] He was inferior to the enemy in foot, if
not in horse, and he only had himself to blame.

The royalist army of the west and Waller's army spent the last week of June and
the first fortnight of July sparring with one another along the Somerset/Wiltshire

border, with Waller gradually gaining the upper hand. The armies fought for the first time at Lansdown just to the north of Bath on 3 July. Sir William had chosen an excellent defensive position, which the Cornish infantry attacked head-on, suffering heavy casualties as a result, but overnight Waller withdrew into Bath, as he had probably intended to do from the start. For the royalists it had been a pyrrhic victory. Dispirited by the death in battle of the Cornish paladin Sir Bevil Grenville and by the explosion of a wagon-load of gunpowder early the following day, which killed several officers and badly wounded Sir Ralph Hopton, the army of the west staggered off in the general direction of Oxford, pursued by Waller's cavalry, but it did not disintegrate. Indeed the marquis of Hertford and Prince Maurice managed a successful fighting retreat to Devizes. Hopton and the infantry then barricaded themselves into the town whilst Maurice and Hertford rode off towards Oxford with the troops of horse in search of help.

Waller's conduct of the siege that followed was lacklustre. Devizes had no walls, its castle was in disrepair, and hedges, walls and buildings formed its only defences. Nevertheless assaults on the royalist positions invariably came to a halt when they encountered determined resistance, probably because Sir William thought storming the town would be unduly wasteful as the royalists were bound to surrender sooner or later.[34] There then followed the disaster on Roundway Down on 13 July.[35] Dwelling on what had happened in his memoirs written some years later, Sir William saw it as God's punishment for telling the world that his triumphs were solely due to his own qualities of generalship.[36] He must also have regretted allowing the enemy an eight-hour truce the day before the relief party arrived.[37] At the time, however, Waller and his supporters blamed the earl of Essex for not keeping an eye on what was going on at Oxford, and for not sending cavalry regiments to follow Wilmot as he rode towards Devizes. However, by mid-July the earl and his army were at Great Brickhill, thirty miles on the far side of the king's headquarters, and the intelligence he received from his scoutmaster general, Sir Samuel Luke, only mentioned Prince Maurice and Hertford's arrival. Luke's spies had completely failed to notice Wilmot's departure.[38]

In the meantime the campaign in the Thames valley had ground to a halt and the criticism began to build up a momentum. At first the focus was on Essex's lack of progress. In the words of one London journal, 'the glory of the taking of Reading may seem to be eclipsed by our staying so long there', whilst another warned that some people had begun 'deeply to condemn this slowness of motion'. Others cut to the quick: 'so little action hath been this week done in the army that much cannot [now] be expected . . . [as] nothing rideth on swifter wings than opportunity'. An intercepted royalist letter revealed the cost of delay: '. . . to speak the truth, had the earl of Essex hastened his advance towards us, 'tis very probable we had been mightily shaken if not shattered to pieces, yet we gather courage again'.[39] Keeping the love of his soldiers by not exposing them to the risk of mortal combat was more important in Essex's eyes than winning the war. Finally, the argument about squandered resources reappeared. Waller's campaigns were cheap. He had asked for little from Parliament or from London, drawing instead on the area where he was campaigning. Despite this he was almost invariably victorious. Essex's soldiers, on the other hand, were 'wholly idle' yet consumed valuable resources and taxation revenue. They, and by inference their officers, were unfit for purpose, in plain words they were useless.[40] However, the MPs and the peers did not take up the refrain even though the negotiations with the queen had ended inconclusively. They voted Essex a salary of £10,000 a year on 26 May, and a week later a letter from the speaker assured the lord general that he had the respect of the House of Commons despite the furore in the press.

> The great care and affection, with which your Excellency hath constantly proceeded in the management of this weighty and public affair, doth so far supersede all vain reports with vulgar censures. . . . With them [the MPs] they can make no impression. . . .[41]

This pledge of support owed much to a recent public relations exercise. Two weeks earlier Essex had travelled to London accompanied by his political advisers amongst the army officers, John Hampden, Arthur Goodwin and Sir Philip Stapleton, to explain in Parliament why he had not advanced on Oxford. Taking his seat in the House of Lords, a rare event since taking operational charge of the army the previous September, he stressed the serious impact of the failure to provide sufficient money to pay his soldiers' wages. If he had ordered them to advance, they would have mutinied. He also used the opportunity to lambaste the provincial commanders for allowing the munitions convoy to reach Oxford unscathed and to attack Waller for not joining him at Reading in April.[42] The speech was sufficient to open the coffers. Soon after he returned to the army, Essex received £25,000 with which to pay the troops their arrears.[43] Yet it was not until 6 June that he set out at last in the general direction of Oxford. Avoiding the easier routes along the banks of the Thames, which would have meant some kind of confrontation with the royalists camped at Culham, the parliamentary army moved slowly northwards. Four days later it took up quarters in and around Thame, a small market town situated in open country ten miles to the east of Oxford, but within easy reach of the woods and easily defensible passes of the Chiltern Hills should serious trouble threaten.[44]

The crablike scuttle into east Oxfordshire did not mean that the lord general felt any better prepared to fight a campaign. If anything he was worse prepared, but he needed to do something to fend off further criticism and also to get out of Reading where disease was now rampant.[45] He may also have been shamed into action by the plundering of north Buckinghamshire by royalist cavalry and dragoons. At Reading his troops had been too far away to do anything about it. At Thame he should be able to prevent it happening again.[46]

The advance to Thame is often seen as nothing more than a feeble gesture forced on the lord general by his political masters and by public opinion.[47] However, the cavalry imbalance between the two armies had eased now that five regiments were with Hertford and Prince Maurice in the West Country, and the royalists' first reaction was one of concern. On 9 June Lord Forth recommended to the king that the camp at Culham should be abandoned and the infantry used to defend the line of the River Cherwell, which ran due north from Oxford, and which Essex would have to cross in order to cut the army's line of retreat through Banbury towards the north of England. Probing attacks on royalist defences at Wheatley on 13 June and on 17 June at Islip caused some alarm, though neither was pressed home. In Prince Rupert's diary there is mention of renewed talk of abandoning Oxford, but the author claimed that it quickly ceased as 'the generality of the soldiers' were against it.[48]

By late June, however, Essex's army had lapsed once more into inactivity. A cavalry engagement with Prince Rupert at brigade level at Chalgrove just to the east of Oxford on the 18th had not gone too badly. The parliamentary horse fought well and only fell back because of pressure of numbers, but the death of John Hampden from wounds sustained in the encounter was potentially calamitous for the unity of the parliamentary cause. Although only a colonel of infantry, Hampden had the respect of all factions in the parliamentary coalition for his religious zeal, his political acumen and his longstanding commitment to the cause. He had also supported the lord general through thick and thin.[49]

Within days of Chalgrove Field a more adventurous royalist cavalry probe passed through the Chiltern barrier and raided villages on the reverse slope around High Wycombe.[50] At almost the same moment Essex's soldiers faced accusations of plundering civilians, and a speaker in the House of Commons passed the comment that the royalists were better at protecting Parliament's supporters than was Essex's army. The lord general immediately offered his resignation, and the MPs decided they had gone too far. For the moment he was indispensable, and they sent him a most abject apology on 29 June, claiming that they had not meant to reflect upon his honour. In the words of Sir Simon D'Ewes it was a 'low, unworthy and submissive way for a House of Commons to write, the word Excellency being used twelve several times in it', but 'our case at that time was so desperate it passed without a word deleted'.[51] Thinking that they had now gone too far in the opposite direction, the Commons turned a deaf ear to the lord general's renewed and increasingly frantic pleas for more financial assistance. These culminated in Essex's suggestion reported in the Commons on 11 July that the war should be decided by his and the king's armies coming together for a battle to end all battles, the outcome of which would surely show which side enjoyed God's favour.[52] This was not the cry of a desperate man, breathtaking in its naivety,[53] nor acknowledgement that he accepted the political programme of a majority grouping in the House of Lords which favoured making major concessions to the king to avoid outright defeat,[54] but a more visceral attempt to shock the Commons into grasping the serious-ness of the situation. The field army was visibly mouldering away through neglect. It would soon be incapable of defending Parliament, let alone going on the offensive against Parliament's enemies. The sentence may contain a touch of irony: surely the 'fiery spirits', many of whom were as religiously radical as they were militarily aggressive, would have the courage of their convictions and place the future of the army in God's hands.[55] The House's response was surprisingly muted, perhaps because it knew Essex was being ironical, perhaps because the arrival of his letter coincided almost exactly with news of Waller's defeat at Roundway Down. Nevertheless relations between the lord general and his political masters remained frigid for the rest of July and early August.[56]

The spat between Essex and the House of Commons did not cause a hiatus in military operations. The campaign rolled on in the same unspectacular manner. In early July Essex moved his army north to Great Brickhill, which was safe as it was close to the high ground that followed the line of the Chilterns. This was partly to provide more effective protection for north Buckinghamshire, where Prince Rupert's cavalry had been busy once more since Chalgrove Field.[57] However, Great Brickhill was also close to Watling Street, which Essex could use to good effect should the enemy threaten Northampton or Coventry, or should a second and much larger royalist munitions convoy (which was at Newark and accompanied by the queen) follow the same route as the first.[58] However, when Rupert moved from Buckingham to Daventry and so to Lutterworth in Leicestershire to provide protection for the convoy, Essex did not follow. It was far too dangerous to venture into the open-field country of the East Midlands. The queen had at least 1,000 cavalry with her and he would be outnumbered yet again.

Well before arriving at Great Brickhill, Essex knew that his army could not stop the munitions convoy's progress towards Oxford on its own. Disease, desertion, shortage of all manner of resources, pay weeks in arrears, heavy rain and minor military setbacks had all combined to sap both the army's morale and its military efficiency.[59] However, having issued orders for the East Midlands forces and Oliver Cromwell's corps of the Eastern Association army to converge on the Middle Trent valley, he was for a time confident that they would be able to stop, or at least delay, the convoy's advance. Before the end of May a force of 6,000 or so horse and dragoons from Lincolnshire and the North Midlands had assembled at Nottingham under the overall command of Lord Grey of Groby.[60] Immediately afterwards, however, Lord Fairfax ordered its commanders to join him in the West Riding of Yorkshire. His son, Sir Thomas Fairfax, had overrun the royalist garrison at Wakefield on 20 May, and the lord general of the north was expecting the earl of Newcastle to try and exact revenge, as his own forces were seriously outnumbered.[61] The commanders refused and Lord Fairfax protested, but the House of Commons' response was muted. Fairfax was to 'receive all encouragement' from the earl of Essex, an anodyne reply as the members knew that stopping the munitions convoy was the highest priority of all and that Essex had nothing else to spare.[62]

However, all was not well at Nottingham. The united front displayed by the contingent commanders of Grey Force in response to Lord Fairfax's orders to march into Yorkshire had evaporated. The reason appears to have been shortages of food and fodder caused by the presence of so large a body of troops in the Trent valley, and the plundering of the civilian population that had inevitably followed. The upshot was the arrest of Sir John Hotham the younger, the commander of the Lincolnshire horse. He had apparently threatened physically to assault Grey and Cromwell, but he was also suspected of treasonable correspondence with the queen. Essex considered that Grey's inexperience was a partial explanation for the quarrels and sent Sir John Meldrum, a highly experienced Scottish professional soldier, to replace him, but the results were disappointing.[63] After Meldrum's arrival, the flying army that had been Grey Force melted way. Hotham's contingent returned to Lincolnshire when their former commander escaped and made off in that direction. At about the same time Sir John Gell's Derbyshire cavalry and dragoons returned home. As a result, when the royalist troops at Newark took the initiative and threatened Nottingham, the only response Meldrum could make was to sit tight and wait for the enemy to lose patience, which they did by the end of the month.

The second convoy set out from Newark on 2 July. By then Meldrum had no more than 2,000 horse and foot left, the Nottinghamshire contingent and Cromwell's cavalry. All he could do was shadow the queen as she moved south, but he went no further than Dunsmore Heath between Rugby and Coventry for fear of being attacked by Prince Rupert's cavalry, which were quartered nearby.[64] With Prince Rupert about, there was, of course, no possibility of Meldrum and Essex joining forces but the queen feared they might, and the convoy therefore took a more westerly path than its predecessor, passing via Burton and Walsall to Kings Norton, just to the east of Birmingham, and so to Stratford-on-Avon.[65] Apart from a brief skirmish with local troops guarding the bridge over the Trent at Burton, the convoy's passage across the parliamentary-controlled Central Midlands was as trouble-free as that of Hastings two months earlier, and the king and queen met at Edgehill on 13 July at the very hour that Wilmot was destroying Waller's army at Roundway Down.[66]

Even though Prince Rupert, Lord Capel and Henry Hastings, now earl of Loughborough, had helped to swell the queen's escort at various points in her journey, the whole enterprise could not have succeeded without the military support provided by the king's general in the north. According to the earl of

Newcastle's wife, he gave the queen an escort of 7,000 horse and foot, which then became part of the Oxford army,[67] but this is only partly true. The force according to the queen herself was only just over 3,000 strong, and most of the cavalry returned home in or before January 1644. However, Newcastle had done all he could in the circumstances. Lord Fairfax still commanded a substantial army in the Leeds/Bradford area and the disaster at Wakefield had deprived the earl of Newcastle of many experienced officers and men, and significant quantities of military supplies. In addition the way in which Fairfax's son, Sir Thomas, had overrun a well-defended town showed he possessed military flair superior to that of Sir William Waller.[68] Whereas Waller won his victories by surprising enemy formations that were either outnumbered or largely made up of raw recruits, Sir Thomas Fairfax at Wakefield had defeated a force much larger than his own and consisting mainly of experienced soldiers who were well aware that an attack was imminent.

The earl of Newcastle led an invasion of the West Riding in mid-June, by which time the queen had arrived safely at Newark. Although his army was much larger than Lord Fairfax's in cavalry, most of his infantry were newly raised men, who were unlikely to perform as well as the veterans he had lost at Wakefield. Moreover, the Fairfaxes took up a position on Adwalton Moor near Bradford, which was surrounded by small fields and crisscrossed with ditches. The moorland was also pockmarked in places by spoil heaps and bell pits caused by coalmining, very hard-going for formations of horse and foot trying to keep close order as they moved forward to attack.

Initially, the parliamentary army did well, pushing the enemy back all along the line of battle, but Lord Fairfax committed his reserves too early in the engagement and there was nothing left to counter the royalists' desperate last fling, a pike charge against the lord general's infantry brigade, or the subsequent threat to the rear of the parliamentary position by Newcastle's cavalry reserves.[69] The parliamentary attack may also have lost momentum when Major Jeffries, who was in charge of Fairfax's train of artillery, refused to supply the Yorkshire and Lancashire musketeers with fresh supplies of gunpowder.[70] Possibly the Fairfaxes could have saved more of their army had there been any communication between them. Lord Fairfax's brigade fell back in good order, but Sir Thomas did not know it was doing so. The result was that his brigade came under attack from several directions and took to its heels. The royalist victory owed little to Newcastle or General James King. Instead it was a colonel of infantry who had ordered the pike charge, though King appears to have initiated the move against the enemy rear. According to Lady Newcastle, her husband and his military adviser seem to have gone happily into battle in a place where the landscape gave great advantage to the enemy without devising a tactical plan for overcoming it. Henry Slingsby, however, suggested that both armies were very keen to fight, and that the battle started when they blundered into one another.[71]

Between April and July 1643 Parliament's strategy had failed consistently on all major fronts. Although the capture of Reading had improved the security of London, the king's forces were still strong in the Thames valley and Oxford remained the king's headquarters. In the north and in the south-west Parliament's generals had lost thousands of square miles of territory. Admittedly there were some gains in the north-west of England and in Staffordshire, but Sir William Brereton's attempts to capture Chester and to invade North Wales had both failed.[72] The setbacks were not due to inappropriate or niggardly distribution of military resources. The principal cause was incompetent leadership by Stamford, Waller and to a lesser extent Lord Fairfax. As for the lord general, Essex, his biggest mistake had been not to advance on Oxford from Reading immediately after the town had surrendered, but, as argued above, it is highly likely that initially he was under orders from the parliamentary leadership to remain where he was. His reluctance to give the enemy a chance of catching his army in open country was also very wise. However, if he had been more active in raiding enemy quarters, he would have increased the king's insecurity and possibly caused him to be less keen to employ whole brigades of cavalry in the West Country under the marquis of Hertford, and this would have made Waller's task easier. Nevertheless, by doing almost nothing, the earl still had an army in being at the end of July.

The success of the king's cause in the spring and early summer owed little to Lord Forth. His plan to relieve Reading failed and his camp at Culham did not really deter the earl of Essex as the latter had no intention of attacking it.[73] The other royalist generals who had commanded armies or were to command armies in the future had enhanced their reputations, but their personal achievements are not that easy to determine. Hertford and Newcastle had done very well but for much of the time seem merely to have followed the advice of their Council of War. Wilmot's victory at Roundway Down was quite clearly his alone, even though Richard Atkyns entered a plea for Prince Maurice; but, the victory at Stratton was not Hopton's but a collective effort.[74] Nevertheless Maurice and Hopton had done enough to merit promotion, which followed in August and September respectively. Prince Rupert, moreover, was in the process of becoming something more than General of Horse. The king had made him commander-in-chief of the operation to protect the queen's convoy, with power to issue orders to both horse and foot. Hitherto he had only had such authority over cavalry and dragoons.

CHAPTER 6

The King on the Offensive

BRISTOL, GLOUCESTER AND THE FIRST BATTLE OF NEWBURY

NOT ONLY were the Parliament generals in the provinces responsible for losing vast tracts of countryside, but the fact that the king still had a field army in southern England in the summer of 1643 owed a great deal to the operational decisions they made that were not in the interests of the total war effort. The earl of Essex received nothing other than Lord Grey of Wark's corps of the Eastern Association army, a band of raw and ill-equipped tyros who melted away due to endemic disease and shortage of pay and provisions. In defence of Lords Fairfax and Stamford it can be argued that they were too far away and faced too much opposition from local royalists to be able to send reinforcements to the Thames valley theatre of war, but the personality clashes and worse affecting the parliamentary commanders in the East Midlands ruined Essex's plans to beat the earl of Forth and Prince Rupert into submission by starving them of gunpowder. His other plan, to combine Sir William Waller's army with his own to force the king from Oxford, had fallen foul of Waller's ambition for an independent command, his head turned by the epithet 'William the Conqueror' and the blandishments of the 'fiery spirits'. The first time he disobeyed Essex's orders he destroyed the best chance of making the king flee, the second time he prepared the way for the royalists to conquer the West Country.

The contrast with the conduct of the king's generals in the provinces is staggering. They loyally set about forwarding royalist war aims by occupying territory, raising troops, and doing everything they could to assist the Oxford army. As a result, when the sun broke through the clouds on 13 July 1643 with the arrival of the queen's convoy on the former battlefield of Edgehill and Henry Wilmot's victory at Roundway Down, Forth and Prince Rupert had the resources in terms of men and munitions to go onto the offensive. They themselves probably had between 8,000 and 10,000 men in arms. The western army, quartered at Bath after Roundway Down, was 4,000 or so strong, despite the losses it had sustained at Lansdown and in the march to Devizes. In addition, by mid-July 1643 Lords Capel and Herbert in Wales and the Marches could send them another 4,000 horse and foot as required.[1] Finally, several thousand of the earl of Newcastle's troops were in the Thames valley, having arrived there as escorts for the two great munitions convoys.[2] With such forces at his command the king could confidently have ordered an advance on London to coincide precisely with the time that divisions were appearing in the enemy coalition because of the setbacks sustained in the late spring and early summer campaigns. However, Charles then made what was probably the worst mistake of the Civil War phase of his reign by allowing Prince Rupert to use the Oxford army and the army of the west for an operation that was peripheral to his principal aim, to bring the war to a speedy conclusion, namely the capture of Bristol and Gloucester.

The most convincing argument in favour of the operation was that occupying Waller's bases, and thus making it impossible for him to reconstitute his army, was a useful way of keeping the two royalist armies busy until the rest of Newcastle's forces arrived. Charles was also probably led to believe that the operation would be a pushover. Colonel Nathaniel Fiennes, the governor of Bristol, though a convinced parliamentarian, lacked the mental stamina and the military know-how to conduct the effective defence of a city with a population not fully committed to the parliamentary cause and a garrison run down by Waller to provide troops for his army.[3] On the other hand the governor of Gloucester, Edward Massey, was a career soldier with no ideological commitment to Parliament and a father who had fought for the king. Even if the citizens of Gloucester were more zealous for the parliamentary cause than those of Bristol, Massey might be willing to change sides and bring the garrison with him.[4]

Prince Rupert probably pressed hard for the chance to command the operation. He was 'eager to wipe away the affront he had lately received before its walls', a reference to a failed attempt to overrun Bristol in March when he and his cavalry had lurked in the vicinity waiting for the chance to exploit an uprising of the citizens, which Fiennes discovered in the nick of time.[5] Even so, leaving royal honour aside, it is remarkable that the General of Horse rather than the lord general took charge of what was to all intents and purposes the entire Oxford army. Maybe the feeling was that it would require nothing more than a show of force for the two cities to return to their rightful allegiance. If so, there was a good argument for a member of the Royal Family being in charge, but the Prince of Wales and the Duke of York were too young and the king was busy with the festivities celebrating his wife's return. Rupert, a cradle Calvinist and a brave and bold general, was just the man for the job.

Another possibility is that Forth had opposed the expedition, but there is no contemporary record of a set-to in the king's Council of War. If there had been one, it is remarkable that Clarendon did not mention it given his remorseless antipathy towards the prince. However, this does not mean that there was not a dispute. Possibly Clarendon and Rupert were for once on the same side, with the former believing that the speedy surrender of Gloucester and Bristol would strengthen the hand of those members of the parliamentary coalition who favoured a negotiated peace, and the latter seeking to enhance his military reputation.[6] There is also the hint of a compromise hammered out in council in the king's letter to the prince written on 20 July, reminding him that the prime purpose of the expedition was not 'the taking of towns' but preventing Waller putting his army back together again.[7]

When Rupert received his uncle's letter, he was marching towards Gloucester, but on hearing that Waller had left Bristol he decided to attack the larger city instead.[8] The order of events suggests very strongly that he expected to capture it without any serious fighting. He began by deploying his army on the north side of the city in such a way as to make it appear larger than it was. Next he summoned the governor to surrender, but Fiennes replied that he could not in conscience do so 'till he were brought to more extremity'. At this point the enormity of the task facing Rupert became apparent and he and the rest of the royalist commanders spent the next few days discussing what to do next.

Like many other towns in the British Isles garrisoned in the wars of the mid seventeenth century, Bristol's medieval walls were not its first line of defence. Instead these formed a second line. Beyond the walls at a distance of between half a mile and a mile was a circuit of fortifications some five miles in length strengthened at intervals by forts. On the Gloucestershire side these comprised a ditch between six and eight feet wide and a wall between four and a half and six feet high, with the forts sited in such a way that almost every section of the wall could be subjected to intensive musket and artillery fire if it came under attack. The Somerset side had no forts but the River Avon provided part of the outer defence line with the equivalent of a moat, whilst a more formidable ditch and wall than that which was to be found on the Gloucestershire side protected the remainder.

With a garrison of between 2,000 and 3,000 infantry, the perimeter was not impossible to defend, and the fact that Bristol was on both banks of the river Avon also helped, as this made it more difficult for the attackers to exploit a breakthrough by moving troops from one side of the city defences to the other. The defenders, on the other hand, could take full advantage of interior lines to rush reinforcements to any danger spot using the bridges that lay within the city defences. Moreover, the open space between the outer circuit and the city walls made it easy for the garrison cavalry to attack any royalists who managed to get through the first line of defence.[9]

Prince Rupert's army drew up facing the Gloucestershire section of the outer defences, whilst the marquis of Hertford's army took up a position on the Somerset side. Rupert's engineers quickly discovered that undermining would be impossible, as the walls' foundations rested on hard rock.[10] Starving the city into surrendering, on the other hand, might take months, and so Rupert prevailed on Sir Ralph Hopton and Prince Maurice against their better judgement to agree to storm the city defences without first making a breach.[11] Rupert presumably hoped that the weak reply from the governor meant that he would use any kind of assault as an excuse for surrendering. The only other explanation for the tactically inept and highly wasteful attack that followed was that the prince had to capture the city quickly, as the earl of Essex might march to its relief or else threaten Oxford and thus scare the king into ordering Rupert to abandon the siege. Either reaction on Essex's part must have seemed unlikely given his general level of inactivity in the spring campaign, but according to the earl he did begin preparations for a relief expedition and the king may have got wind of them. However, there was no question of ordering Rupert to abandon the attempt. All Charles asked for was cavalry, which he understood to be of little use in attacking a town.[12]

The assault on Bristol, launched on 26 July, struck at six points in the outer defence line, presumably in the hope that the garrison commander would have difficulty in distinguishing full-scale assaults from feints. As it was, five got nowhere. On the Somerset side, one failed because of the lack of fascines to fill up the ditch, whilst the other two were not apparently pushed home with much verve and may indeed have been feints. This was not the case on the Gloucestershire side of the city where all three assaults were in deadly earnest. Two, those led by John Bellasis and Lord Grandison, were directly against forts, which, as Walter Slingsby, a professional soldier in the western army, wrote, were not fit 'to be taken by storm'. Not surprisingly, the approaches to the forts were full of dead bodies when the royalists withdrew.[13] The third only proved successful because of sensible forward planning by the commander, Henry Wentworth, and one stroke of good fortune.

Rupert had allowed the commanders of his divisions to devise their own tactical plans, and Wentworth decided to direct his assault against a section of the wall. After coming under intensive enfilading fire from the forts on either side as they broke cover, his troops assembled on a piece of dead ground immediately adjacent to the wall and ditch, which they crossed with ease. Luckily, the enemy cavalry did not attack until such time as the assault force had drawn up in formation in the space between the outer defences and the city wall and was ready to repel them. The royalist cavalry, however, were even later on the scene, and as a result some of the defenders of the outer ring were able to withdraw in good order into the city proper. Others, however, remained in their forts firing into the formations preparing for an assault on one of the city gates. When they attacked the royalists incurred yet more heavy losses before breaking through into the city proper. At that point the governor's nerve gave way and he agreed to surrender, but it had been a very tight-run thing. Rupert's troops were exhausted even though they had been supported in the final assault by musketeers from the western army, and it is unlikely that they would have had the spirit to fight their way through the narrow streets and storm the castle where the governor had prepared a last-ditch defence.

The two royalist armies had also lost many officers killed, including five colonels and probably well in excess of 500 musketeers and pikemen.[14] Nevertheless the king was very happy with Rupert's achievement. The royalists now held the second city in the kingdom. They had also acquired considerable quantities of military supplies, most particularly artillery pieces, and sufficient shipping to provide the king with the nucleus of a navy.[15] This bounty, together with the conquest of almost the whole of south-west England, improved the chances of a royalist victory in the long run, but the first and best chance of winning the war quickly by advancing on London when the parliamentary coalition was at its most friable had vanished.

Immediately after the capture of Bristol the king visited the city with the prime aim of deciding what the armies were to do next. The first decision, to remove the marquis of Hertford from the command of the western army, was almost certainly made by the king in consultation with Rupert before the expedition left Oxford.[16] According to Clarendon, Hertford and Prince Maurice had not worked well together, and the king wanted the marquis to be in his personal entourage because he valued his advice. All the other decisions, however, were a direct result of the losses sustained during the assault on Bristol. First, the western army was to remain as a separate entity under the command of Prince Maurice. His remit was to capture the four remaining large parliamentary garrisons in the south-west of England: Plymouth, Dartmouth, Exeter and Barnstaple. He was also to bring the Cornish regiments up to strength after the heavy losses they had sustained during July, and then to rejoin the rest of the king's forces in central southern England. Any sensible appraisal of Maurice's remit suggests November as the earliest possible date for his return, with the following spring as the more likely. It is also difficult to see any other way of providing for the security of the south-west. The Cornish were apparently restive on several counts ranging from fears for the safety of their homeland with Plymouth and Barnstaple still in enemy hands, to despair caused by the loss of their commanders, three of their five infantry colonels having been killed at Lansdown or Bristol.[17]

Second, at least six of the thirteen infantry regiments from the Oxford army had suffered such severe casualties that they remained at Bristol to give time for the sick and wounded to recover and for the gaps in the ranks to be filled by volunteers from the city and its environs. Hopton's account of this operation is a very positive one,[18] but packing existing formations with raw recruits had its dangers, as Forth and Rupert would discover at the battle of Newbury seven weeks later.

Third, it was not the right moment to order an advance on London, as the shortage of infantry could easily result in a re-run of Turnham Green and a revival of enemy morale. Instead the next target would be Gloucester, which after the fate of Bristol might surrender on demand.[19] The king duly went there in person to demand the city's surrender, but he received a dusty answer from two citizens, who had made no attempt to dress for the occasion or to devise suitable words for addressing a monarch. Charles then ordered a panel of experienced officers to undertake a thorough appraisal of the city's defences, and having heard their report the Council of War decided on a formal siege. The officers had apparently declared that Gloucester could be taken by approach in ten days provided the army received reinforcements from Oxford, Wales and the Marches.

The role of the army generals in the debate about the strategy for the Gloucester stage of the campaign appears to have been a limited one. Prince Rupert was present at both discussions. The writer of Rupert's diary claimed that he suggested an invasion of the Eastern Association as an alternative to besieging Gloucester, but we only have his word for it. According to Clarendon the Council of War was unanimous.[20] There is no evidence that Rupert suggested storming the town.[21] Not only would a repetition of the casualties incurred at Bristol cause another catastrophic decline in strength of the royalist infantry, but there was no possibility of over-running the defences without a breach having been made first. Gloucester relied on its town walls and these were far taller than Bristol's outer ring of defences. In normal circumstances seventeenth-century heavy artillery would have made mincemeat of the medieval masonry, but the town's governor Edward Massey had reinforced the walls with large baulks of earth, which immensely increased their strength.[22] In addition, although the enemy garrison at Gloucester was smaller, so was the length of the line it had to defend.

The earl of Forth was not present at the Council of War held at Bristol,[23] but this does not mean that he had not already given his opinion to the king prior to Charles's departure from Oxford.[24] Admittedly he and Sir Jacob Astley, the major general of infantry, were in overall charge of the siege, but Forth may not have been wildly enthusiastic about it. If he had been, Clarendon would surely have singled him out for blame for its failure. Clarendon's friend Lord Culpeper had pushed most strongly for the siege in the Council of War and this would have helped get Culpeper off the hook.[25] Clarendon could not blame Rupert, who had played little part in the siege, but this was not because Rupert disapproved of the operation. With his official rank of General of Horse, his services were needed elsewhere.[26]

The siege of Gloucester brought about a transformation in the fortunes of the earl of Essex. After the storming of Bristol he expected a royalist advance on London and had moved his army from Great Brickhill to Kingston-on-Thames so as to be ready to meet it. His mood was no brighter as the House of Commons was busy with legislation to allow Waller to raise a new army independent of the earl's control, a further humiliation. But in the middle of August the Committee of Safety, having discussed the dismal range of strategic options, decided that relieving Gloucester was easier than relieving Exeter, whilst threatening Oxford was to invite a catastrophic defeat.[27] The decision having been made, Essex had to be in charge, as he was the only general with an army, but it was to be strengthened by the addition of at least eight infantry regiments, five from the London trained bands selected by lot, another from the London garrison, and two regiments from Kent. His cavalry reinforcements included a regiment from Hampshire, another recently raised in London, and three other troops of horse probably also newly raised.[28] The rendezvous was to be at Brackley Heath on the borders of Oxfordshire and Northamptonshire where Lord Grey of Groby's regiment of horse joined the army.[29] There were no troops from the Eastern Association. What was left of Lord Grey of Wark's corps that had taken part in the siege of Reading expedition had retired to East Anglia to recruit, and Oliver Cromwell's corps was putting down a royalist uprising in Norfolk.[30] Thus Essex had far more infantry than he had had in Buckinghamshire in July, and also considerably more cavalry, though it is likely that Lord Grey of Groby's was the only new regiment with combat experience. Leaving Brackley Heath on 1 September, the army was in the vicinity of Gloucester five days later and relieved the city on the 8th, which was just as well as the garrison was down to its last three barrels of gunpowder.[31]

There is, however, very little evidence to indicate that the royalist Council of War saw Gloucester as a bait to tempt Parliament into fighting a climactic battle on grounds of the king's choosing, namely in the open country between Stow-on-the-Wold and the western edge of the Cotswolds where the royalist cavalry could be used to best advantage. Clarendon mentions this in passing, but it cannot have been any more than a remote possibility when the siege started. The king had not exaggerated when he informed the citizens of Gloucester that 'Waller was extinct and Essex cannot come'.[32] In addition, if Gloucester was bait, it took the royalist commanders a long time to do anything about springing the trap. The first sign that a battle in the Cotswolds was on the agenda is in a letter from the king to Rupert sent on 5 September. This suggests that it was first proposed on the 3rd, the day when Rupert left the siege works to join his cavalry in the Cotswolds having received intelligence that the relief force was passing to the north of Oxford. Charles informed his nephew that Forth was in favour of a battle and would see that the troops before Gloucester made their way up the Cotswold escarpment to join him. By then it was not too late to fight, but it takes two to tango. With his attention fixed on the relief of Gloucester, Essex sidestepped the royalist concentration on Birdlip Hill directly above the city and dived into the enclosed country of the Vale of Gloucester at Cheltenham, some miles to the north. The speed with which he had advanced across the Cotswolds probably caught the royalist high command by surprise, but at least they were quick enough for the infantry not to be caught in their trenches by the relieving army.

When Essex arrived at Gloucester, the king's army withdrew northwards across the High Cotswolds to the valley of the Warwickshire Avon, thus covering the approaches to Worcester and to the escape route from the Severn valley via Stratford, and so onto Watling Street by way of Daventry which Waller had used six weeks earlier. Essex shadowed the royalists as far as Tewkesbury, but his true intention was to reach safety in the Reading area by crossing the south Cotswolds into the Kennet valley and then proceeding to Newbury.[33] This was more risky as the army would mainly be marching through open country, but the route immediately gave it a twenty-mile lead over the royalists.

Essex and his troops set off for the safety of parliamentary-controlled territory on the morning of 15 September, and progress was very rapid. He had intended the first day's march to end at Cheltenham, but learning that a convoy carrying foodstuffs for the royalist army was quartering for the night at Cirencester, he decided to push on. Soon after midnight, his vanguard surprised the enemy in their beds, and the convoy's contents were speedily consumed by the soldiers or put away in their knapsacks for future use.[34] The following afternoon the army reached the temporary safety of enclosed country in north Wiltshire. By then the king's forces were in pursuit but the distance between the two armies had almost doubled.

Not only had the royalist generals been caught unawares by the direction of the enemy march, they had also doubted the accuracy of the first intelligence they received. Sir John Byron accused Prince Rupert, whilst the prince blamed Lord Forth and other members of the Council of War.[35] Nevertheless after much debate they decided late on the evening of 15 September that it might just be possible to catch Essex before he reached parliamentary-controlled territory, and the cavalry set off in hot pursuit over the open grasslands of the Cotswolds and the Berkshire Downs with Rupert at their head, whilst Forth and the king followed on behind with the infantry and the artillery.

The progress of Essex and his men through the clay lands of north Wiltshire was necessarily much slower than it had been over the Cotswolds, and the army took an entire day to cover the ten miles from Cricklade to Swindon, with the afternoon being set aside for an exceedingly premature thanksgiving service conducted by the army chaplains,[36] though it is possible that Essex gave his permission so as to allow time for the artillery train to catch up. As a result by the evening of 17 September the gap between the two armies had closed very significantly. Rupert's cavalry were at Stanford-in-the-Vale, only ten miles to the north-east and on a converging course, whilst the main body of the king's infantry was only six or so miles further behind.[37]

The next day things went horribly wrong for Essex's army. As it entered the open chalklands of the Lambourn Downs where the army should have picked up speed, it came under attack from the royalist horse supported, it seems, by a commanded party of 1,000 musketeers under Colonel George Lisle, though the fact that none of the accounts of the engagement mention its presence probably means it did not arrive in time.[38] For several hours on Aldbourne Chase the parliamentarians came to a complete halt, whilst the king's infantry continued to make very good progress towards Wantage, their intention being to block the enemy's path at Newbury on the London to Bath road twenty miles further on. This was the suggestion of Prince Rupert apparently in the teeth of opposition from Lord Forth,[39] who probably had concerns about the impact of forced marches on the fighting condition of his infantry regiments.[40] Essex's troops spent the night of 18 September in and around Hungerford in the Kennet valley, where they could join the Bath road for the last stage of their journey. They were now only ten miles short of Newbury, which the local parliamentarians had stuffed with provisions for man and horse. However, the next day's march would be once again across the open downs, and this would give the royalist cavalry the chance to delay their progress still further. Instead Parliament's lord general chose safety over speed.

On 19 September Essex ordered his men to cross to the south bank of the Kennet. This placed a major barrier between them and their pursuers, as there

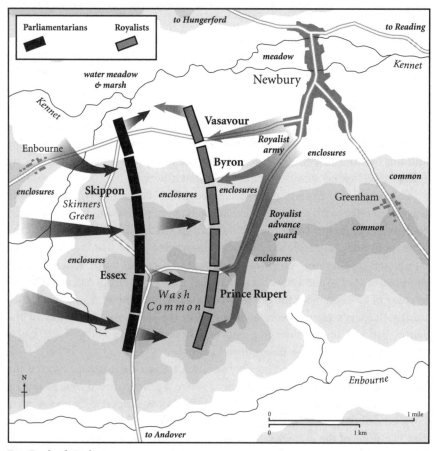

First Battle of Newbury

were no recognised fords between Hungerford and Newbury, but their progress eastwards was exceedingly slow as it was along narrow lanes through enclosed country. In the late afternoon the main body reached Enbourne, two miles short of the town, but the royalists had managed to get there first. From the low-lying ground beside the En brook, their troops of horse were visible on the escarpment to the right front, whilst quartermasters who had ventured into Newbury returned at speed with enemy cavalry at their heels. In the evening the king's infantry and the artillery train joined their horse and set up camp in and around the town.[41]

Essex had fallen into a trap, but there were several ways in which disaster could be avoided. He could fight his way into Newbury and then either join the Bath road by capturing the bridge over the Kennet or else carry on along the south bank of the river until he reached enclosed country near Aldermaston. Alternatively, he could reach Aldermaston by marching his army up the escarpment and across Wash Common and Greenham Common, thus bypassing Newbury to the south. Finally, he could remain where he was in the hope that Sir William Waller would come to his rescue or cause a diversion. All four strategies were risky, but in the end there was no choice. Storming Newbury Bridge might be possible given the size of his army, but first he had to get there. The enemy, however, had occupied a piece of open ground half a mile short of the town. The only access from the west was by a narrow lane, which meant it would be impossible to draw up a line of battle as any unit to emerge from the lane into the open would be pounced on before it could deploy. Remaining where he was was also out of the question as the army was desperately short of food. Essex's decision therefore was to try and distract the attention of the king and his generals by threatening to push troops down the road from Enbourne towards Newbury, whilst the rest of the army headed for Aldermaston over the downs as fast as it could. He hoped the feint would hold the attention of the royalists long enough for them not to be able to change front and launch a flank attack on his army as it made its way around the south side of Newbury.[42]

At first all went well. Although Prince Rupert had stationed a commanded party of horse and musketeers on Wash Common, they were apparently too far away to prevent Essex's advance guard climbing the escarpment soon after first light and establishing a strong presence behind a hedge that ran along the western edge of the common.[43] Some infantry units occupied Skinners Lane End at its north-west corner and an attempt by the commanded party to evict them failed, probably because the musketeers and horse had no answer to the disciplined pikes of Essex's own regiment, which was the lead formation. Rupert responded by ordering up more cavalry, whilst he hurried down into Newbury to ask Lord Forth for additional infantry. It seems that these were not immediately available, probably because of concern over the threat to Newbury from the direction of Enbourne, and when Rupert returned he wisely focused his attention on the enemy cavalry. These were beginning to form up 200 yards or so into the common to serve as a flank guard for the infantry regiments as they marched towards Aldermaston. The parliamentary horse put up a more impressive fight when they came under attack than they had done at Edgehill, but the royalists eventually pushed them back behind the hedge by sheer force of numbers after which they played no further part in the battle.[44] In the meantime some royalist infantry regiments had arrived on the common, and Rupert, taking advantage of a reordering of the enemy front line at Skinners Lane End, managed to push the enemy foot back behind the hedge in an engagement that was over by midday or very soon after.[45]

Two other engagements also came to an end at about the same time. A couple of London trained bands regiments found themselves, possibly by accident, in an exposed position on the far right of Essex's line beyond where the cavalry had tried to deploy. After enduring cannon fire for several hours and beating off a number of attacks by cavalry, they too appear to have sought shelter behind the hedge after coming under simultaneous attack from formations of horse and foot.[46]

Second, soon after dawn Sir John Byron's brigade of horse and his uncle Sir Nicholas Byron's brigade of foot received orders from Forth and the king to disrupt what appeared to be an attempt to establish an artillery platform on a hill overlooking the flat area directly to the west of Newbury, where the bulk of the king's army were preparing to foil any enemy attempt to advance from Enbourne towards the bridge over the Kennet. Against considerable opposition the two Byrons pushed the enemy back through several enclosures and captured the putative artillery platform.[47] However, the lord general appears not to have seen that if he sent more infantry brigades up the hill he stood a good chance of cutting Skinners Green Lane, the main route by which Essex's infantry regiments and heavy artillery were moving towards Wash Common. The light may have dawned on Sir John Byron in the final phase of his attack, but by that time it was too late. Essex had positioned a fresh infantry brigade behind the hedge bordering the lane, and the royalists, who had suffered very heavy casualties, were unable to hold onto the foothold they had gained. Stalemate then ensued, though Sir John's account suggests that the enemy made some attempts to push the royalists back down the hill later in the day.[48]

By early afternoon, therefore, Forth and Prince Rupert had pinned the enemy down all along the line. There were two possible ways forward. They could either try and force the enemy back down the escarpment to their start line, or else let them stew in their own juice whilst being ready to stifle any counterattack if they were foolish enough to try their luck on the common again. Unfortunately for the king's cause Rupert and Forth chose the former course of action, despite the fact that this meant attacking a hedge line defended by numerous artillery pieces and ever larger numbers of musketeers, as more and

more regiments crowded into the small area between the hedge and the escarpment. They ordered forward two of the infantry brigades that had stormed
Bristol, but these cowered in dead ground refusing to move because of the
strength of the enemy fire.[49] This totally untypical behaviour almost certainly
reflects the low courage threshold and inexperience of the new recruits. Rupert
then ordered his cavalry to attack the hedge and they obeyed,[50] suffering
appalling losses as a consequence but without making any headway.[51]

Very late in the afternoon, a witness on the parliamentary side noticed the
deployment of heavy artillery pieces on Wash Common.[52] Once these became
operational, they would cause great damage to Essex's infantry, which were now
more heavily massed than ever between the western boundary of Wash
Common and the escarpment. Every shot would hit a target, and Essex and his
officers must have been in dread of the carnage that would ensue on the
following day. Nevertheless they ordered their troops to remain where they
were rather than make a tactical withdrawal into the safety of the valley of the En
brook under cover of night, possibly because it would be impossible to drag
the artillery pieces back down the escarpment in the darkness. However,
when the parliamentarians awoke the following morning, they found that the
entire royalist army had fallen back into Newbury leaving wide open the way
to Aldermaston. Essex took no action until midday fearing an ambush on the
far side of the town, but the only action on the enemy's part was to fire the
occasional cannonball in the general direction of Wash Common.[53] In the afternoon he therefore led his army cautiously across the open ground towards
Aldermaston, drawing up in defensive formation from time to time just in case.
Prince Rupert eventually launched a cavalry attack on his rearguard as it passed
into the enclosures but the initiative got nowhere. Steady fire from musketeers
belonging to the London trained band regiments easily beat off the cavalry.

The reason most commonly stated for the decision of the royalist Council of
War to let the enemy go on their way was that the royalist army had almost
exhausted its stock of gunpowder, and that they could not be resupplied from
Oxford until midday on 22 September, but this is wrong. They still had seventy
barrels left.[54] It was the heavy losses in officers and men that weighed most
heavily on the minds of the council members. Essex's army on the other hand
was still very largely intact. It had also shown no sign of losing morale.
Moreover, some of the king's infantry had behaved in a cowardly fashion, whilst
the best of the rest had suffered heavy casualties and some of the crack cavalry
regiments had lost half or more of their strength.[55] Disengagement was the only
possible course of action in the circumstances.

Prince Rupert and Lord Forth were clearly to blame for the debacle at
Newbury, first for not occupying Wash Common in force on the night of
19 September and then for sending horse to attack enemy musketeers and
artillery pieces protected by hedges on the afternoon of the 20th. However, it

was Essex's finest hour. His army's escape owed much to his grim resolution in the face of adversity, and also to the earl not losing his head when the plan to bypass Newbury fell at the first hurdle. Both were qualities which had characterised his generalship in very different circumstances at Edgehill. Accounts of the battle include the usual formulaic phrases about his personal bravery and about how he inspired his men, but there is no doubt that he controlled the battle throughout. The Official Account describes him as giving directions to various units 'whenever there was occasion'. It also gives specific instances of his rotating front-line regiments as they became exhausted and ordering up reserves when the foothold his troops had gained on Wash Common came under determined enemy attack.[56] If Essex had not stood his ground, his army would have surrendered at Enbourne on the 22nd or the 23rd and Newbury would almost certainly have been the climactic victory for the king's generals.

CHAPTER 7

Odds Even

FIGHTING IN THE PROVINCES, AUGUST 1643–APRIL 1644

THE 1643 campaigning season for the armies that had fought at the First Battle of Newbury ended with the royalist reoccupation of Reading at the end of September, though brigades from both performed specific tasks from time to time, usually in support of provincial commanders whose war continued remorselessly throughout the winter. Only in England to the south of the Thames was there a break of four weeks or so from mid-January 1644 onwards when snow carpeted the land.[1] The inquest into the success or failure of the commanders-in-chief in carrying out their political masters' war aims therefore began earlier than 1642, as did planning for the 1644 campaigning season, but for the moment the strategic initiative still rested with the king. The earl of Essex had saved the parliamentary cause at Newbury but he had certainly not won the war.

Developments outside England added to the threats and also to the opportunities facing the strategists on both sides. In August 1643 the king's representatives had made a truce with the Irish Confederacy, the constitutional body set up by the rebels of 1641–2 to govern the part of the country they controlled. This enabled Charles to recall three-quarters of the English army. The regiments in the Dublin area were to be shipped to North Wales, whilst those operating around Cork were to disembark at Bristol, Bridgwater and other ports in the south-west. However, this bonus was offset by an alliance between the English Parliament and the Scottish Covenanters. The king was openly consorting with the hated Irish Catholics who had slaughtered Scottish settlers in Ulster in their thousands in 1641 and early 1642. The truce also imperilled the Scottish army in Ireland, which would now be facing the entire military might of the Catholic Confederacy. Moreover, the additional military advantage the truce would give to the king's cause in England raised the collapse of the parliamentary cause from a possibility to a probability. After victory there an attack on Scotland would surely follow as the king took revenge on his northern subjects, who had so humiliated him by consigning his model of State Protestantism and most of the monarchy's constitutional powers to the historical dustbin. The Solemn League and Covenant, by which the Scottish junta agreed to provide an army of 21,000 men for the war in England, followed soon after the truce in Ireland,[2] but it was chicken and egg not cause and effect. During the summer the two sets of negotiations had run in parallel with one another.

Lord Forth had achieved nothing of consequence in the 1643 campaign other than successfully managing the non-confrontation with the earl of Essex's army in May and early June. On two important occasions, at Reading in April and at Gloucester in September, he had failed. He was also guilty by association of squandering the king's horse in foolhardy attacks on enemy infantry during the First Battle of Newbury. However, Forth was a survivor. He had learned the old soldier's trick of avoiding responsibility when military operations did not go according to plan, and with over thirty years' experience he was a grandmaster at pulling the wool over his superior's eyes. His well-honed skills emerge from Clarendon's fascinating character sketch. He 'often pretended not to have heard what he did not then contradict, and thought fit afterwards to disclaim. He was a man of few words, and of great compliance and usually delivered that as his opinion which he foresaw would be grateful to the king.'

As early as the summer of 1643 strong rumours that Prince Rupert was soon to replace Lord Forth were circulating in the king's army,[3] but the prince had not achieved the spectacular victory he needed to achieve his ambition. He had done well when given his head, as in the storming of Lichfield and Bristol. He had also out-manoeuvred Essex in mid-September and pinned his army in the fields to the west of Newbury, but it had then escaped from the trap he had laid for it. Moreover, Rupert had enemies. He did not tolerate fools gladly and was quick to take offence. Those royalists whose friends and relatives had died at Bristol and Newbury bitterly resented the tactics he had employed. In addition, powerful interests at court, one led by the queen who could not stomach his dislike of Roman Catholics and the other associated with people like Clarendon and Sir John Culpeper who favoured a gentlemanly war and a negotiated peace, resented his influence over the king and did what they could to lessen it.[4] Finally, some of Rupert's own cavalry officers disliked him intensely, most particularly Henry, Lord Wilmot.[5]

However, Lord Forth and Prince Rupert were lucky. When the inquest into the summer campaign got back to first principles, the commander of the Army of the North, the earl of Newcastle, emerged as the obvious scapegoat for all that had happened rather than the generals and politicians who had been more intimately involved in the run of misconceived decisions culminating in the carnage at Newbury.[6] Through his flagrant disregard of a string of orders from the king to march south, Newcastle was guilty by default. He had left Charles with no alternative to setting siege to Gloucester, and all the ill consequences that had flowed from it were ultimately his fault. If he had joined the king instead of blockading Hull, his and the Oxford army could easily have overrun huge tracts of the Home Counties, the East Midlands and East Anglia, thus putting intolerable pressure on Parliament as food supplies for London dropped to a trickle.

But to what extent was Newcastle guilty of sabotaging what was possibly the best chance the king had of bringing the war to a successful conclusion? Historians have dismissed him as brave but unsoldierly and lacking in both aggression and strategic vision,[7] whilst contemporaries condemned him for putting personal and provincial interests before his first duty which was to obey the king. Their analysis of his motives ranged from fear of leaving an undefeated enemy in his rear and the impact that this would have on the morale of his army, to an all-consuming ambition to be the general who won the war for the king. However, courtiers' tittle-tattle[8] and the weasel words of politicians and generals defending their corners are no more than that. In the interests of equity the case for the defence deserves to be heard.

By late July 1643 the earl of Newcastle had accomplished two of his objectives. The queen, her munitions convoy and its escort had reached Oxford without a hitch, and he had defeated the Fairfaxes, overrun their base in the West Riding and bottled them up in the port of Hull. As a mark of the king's favour he was now marquis of Newcastle.[9] His next imperative, it seems, was to join the king at Oxford with the rest of the northern army. This had featured in Newcastle's orders from November 1642 onwards, most particularly in a letter from the king written in late May, but the plan had encountered overwhelming opposition from the leaders of the Yorkshire royalists once it changed from a remote possibility to the next probable military operation.[10] At a Council of War held at Pontefract on 4 June in the presence of the queen,[11] Newcastle acknowledged the promise he had made on first arriving in Yorkshire. He would not march south until the county was at peace.[12]

After his victory at Adwalton Moor on 30 June 1643, Newcastle probably thought he had satisfied all the concerns of the Yorkshire royalists. The Fairfaxes' army was no more, and by mid-July he seemed to be on his way south. After overseeing recruiting operations in Derbyshire he moved into Lincolnshire where he captured Gainsborough on 30 July and Lincoln by 4 August, forcing Eastern Association forces to retreat to Boston and into the Fenlands.[13] In front of him stretched a broad highway leading towards Oxford, free from enemy forces capable of stopping his progress, Essex and his army having left Great Brickhill for the London area a few days earlier. At this point the marquis received two communications, one from the Yorkshire gentry and the other from the king. The first announced that Parliament's northern army, presumed dead, had suddenly taken on new life. The Fairfaxes had overrun the East Riding and their cavalry were raiding as far as the outskirts of York. He should therefore pay regard to the promises he had made about safeguarding the security of Yorkshire.[14] This would have placed Newcastle in a quandary had the second letter contained a clear order to march to Oxford. Sadly, the king's letter does not survive, but it almost certainly contained nothing more than a request to know what the marquis's intentions were.[15] Not surprisingly, he took what in the circumstances was the honourable course of action, and Newcastle's life was ruled by honour. He informed the king that conditions in the north had deteriorated and that he was therefore duty-bound to return to Yorkshire.[16]

The king's response was to ask the queen, who knew Newcastle best, to suggest a compromise, namely that he should send some of his forces into East Anglia,[17] possibly to cooperate with the cavalry regiments which had gone south in June.[18] This would mean that he could also remain strong in Yorkshire, as well as calm any fears he might have about his army being absorbed into the king's. And there was a further honour to add to the marquisate. He was granted the right to confer knighthoods on his leading supporters.[19] Newcastle's reply, which was probably in the negative, does not survive,[20] but pressure on him probably eased as August came to a close. Once Essex's army left the safety of the London area, the king and his military advisers probably thought there was a good chance of bringing the war to an end without further help from the north. Not surprisingly, however, interest in the marquis's army revived after the First Battle of Newbury, but by then it was too late. An enthusiastic letter from Rupert about invading the Eastern Association, which no longer survives, elicited a very downbeat reply. Parliament and the Scots were now allies, a Scottish army would shortly be crossing the border, and the marquis had no resources to spare for campaigning in the south.[21]

For some weeks after his return to London in late September, the earl of Essex's star was in the ascendant, and he exploited his advantage to the full. A well-argued defence of his conduct between the capture of Reading and the surrender of Bristol appeared in print soon after the victory at Newbury. Needless to say, it was highly critical of Waller, and the earl demanded that he should be given operational control over Waller's new army. This induced Parliament to put pressure on Sir William to surrender his commission, which he did with little grace. Soon afterwards Essex's army won an almost bloodless victory by forcing the royalists to abandon Newport Pagnell near Bedford on 29 October, thus frustrating Prince Rupert's plans for invading East Anglia without the marquis of Newcastle's help. Rupert's response was to occupy Towcester, but this outpost was too close to Northampton and Newport for comfort and its garrison withdrew to Oxford without incident early in January 1644.[22]

During October and November 1643, Parliament made no quibbles about the lord general's requests for money to pay his army, but the halcyon days were soon over. First, the glory gained at Gloucester and Newbury quickly faded as comparisons were made between his relapse into inactivity and the energy displayed by the other army generals. Sir William Waller was running rings around the royalists in Hampshire and Sussex from mid-December onwards, whilst the Fairfaxes had forced the marquis of Newcastle to abandon the siege of Hull and then evicted his supporters from all their garrisons in Lincolnshire.

Moreover, the operations around Newport Pagnell did nothing to enhance Essex's personal reputation for sound generalship, as Philip Skippon, his major general of foot, was the commander on the spot.[23] As in the winter of 1642–3, Essex appeared to have gone into hibernation.

Second, John Pym died on 8 December. Pym's skills in managing Parliament had prevented the lord general being overwhelmed by the attacks made against him during June and July. Later, Pym seems to have encouraged Essex in his successful attempt to bring Sir William Waller to heel. However, within four days of Pym's death, the Committee of Safety, no longer Pym's poodle, began exerting a tighter control over military operations.[24] Before the end of the month it had forced the lord general much against his will to move his army from St Albans to the Windsor area where he could better assist Waller and put pressure on the new royalist garrison at Reading. His argument that this would leave the garrison at Newport Pagnell open to attack fell on deaf ears. The interchange of letters that accompany this spat are shot through with sarcasm and barely concealed acrimony. Bulstrode Whitelock was not exaggerating when he wrote of 'a little discontent between Essex and the Committee of Safety' and of the earl being 'not well pleased with some members and proceedings of the House of Commons'.[25]

Third, the unique position that Essex's army had enjoyed as Parliament's sword and buckler had gone for good. Twenty thousand or so Scots under the highly experienced professional soldier, Alexander Leslie, Earl of Leven, crossed into England in January, and a revitalised army of the Eastern Association was due shortly to exceed Essex's in size. In 1642 and 1643 his army was a heavy financial liability but indispensable for the achievement of Parliament's war aims. In 1644 it was as expensive but no longer indispensable.

With no aces left in his hand, Essex quickly lost two important political battles. A new 'war cabinet', the Committee of Both Kingdoms, took over the strategic and operational role of the Committee of Safety. Sitting on it were Scottish representatives, who at this stage in the war were no friends of the lord general, and who came from a military tradition that held its army generals on tight leading strings.[26] In addition, the committee's English members included many of Essex's opponents, including the odious Sir Henry Vane. Second, the lord general lost power over other army generals. The commander of the army of the Eastern Association, promoted to the rank of lieutenant general, was now his equal in the eyes of their political masters,[27] whilst Waller acquired a greater measure of independence,[28] though he was still subject to Essex's orders when the two armies were in the field together.[29] At the same time the lord general found it increasingly difficult to get Parliament to approve measures for paying and resourcing his army. Suggestions that it should be disbanded and its various units added to Parliament's other armies came to nothing, but lack of interest in the House of Commons, the Committee of Both Kingdoms and the city of

London resulted in his infantry not being ready to leave winter quarters until the middle of May.[30]

The army general in fashion in the early months of 1644 was not Sir William Waller but the new kid on the block, Edward Montague, Second Earl of Manchester, who had replaced Lord Grey of Wark as commander of the Eastern Association army the previous August. Manchester is usually seen as a kind of political and military innocent, a 'sweet, meek man', sound in matters of religion but not a warrior either by training or by inclination, in the last resort in favour of the war ending in a negotiated peace, not outright victory. This is a travesty. The earl may have been a novice in military matters,[31] but politically he had been in the thick of things in the lead-up to the outbreak of the Civil War.[32] Clarendon singled him out as one of the six most important men in the junta determined to reduce royal power and introduce godly reform in the winter of 1640–41.[33] In 1643 he was still one of the acknowledged leaders of the parliamentary party, being not only speaker of the House of Lords but also one of the slightly different group of six who had secretly contacted the queen in April concerning a new round of peace negotiations.[34]

Manchester showed his political skills immediately on taking up his commission in August 1643. In less than six weeks he had revived Lord Grey's corps with a strong dose of military resources. Also, within days of taking up his command, he had shown his determination to be his own man. He had successfully resisted Essex's order for his cavalry to take part in the expedition to Gloucester on the grounds that if they left the Eastern Association, the marquis of Newcastle's cavalry would quickly overrun the Fenlands. When the town of King's Lynn declared for the king, Manchester immediately set siege to it and when it fell in mid-September, he sent his infantry regiment by sea to Hull to strengthen Lord Fairfax's garrison. He then led the rest of his forces into Lincolnshire to help persuade the marquis of Newcastle to give up the siege. In the event Newcastle abandoned it of his own accord, having appreciated the enormity of the task and the danger that it would severely limit his options when the Scots invaded. However, cavalry regiments from the Eastern Association army helped Sir Thomas Fairfax and Lord Willoughby of Parham win a major cavalry engagement against the Lincolnshire and Newark royalists at Winceby on 11 October.[35] Manchester himself commanded the infantry, which arrived too late to take part in the engagement, but he wrote the 'evening of the battle' letter to the House of Lords describing the victory.[36] In two months he had achieved far more than Lord Grey of Wark in eight.

It was not only his achievements between August and October that made Manchester the darling of those MPs who were impatient with the earl of Essex. Manchester also had the enthusiastic support of a much smaller group for whom the principal purpose of the war was to prepare the way for root and branch religious reform, in that he shared with them the view that the best way of winning was for his to be a godly army. Officers were to be chosen in accordance with principles first enunciated by Lord Brooke at Warwick in February 1643.[37] They should be 'honest citizens . . . whose hearts go with their hands', men who fought 'for God, their religion, the laws of the land and the subjects' liberty and safety'.[38] In endeavouring to create an ideologically committed army, Manchester received immense assistance from his lieutenant general of cavalry, Oliver Cromwell, who had a similar mindset, and who had the political skills to further the cause of the general and his army in the House of Commons.[39] He had brought about the downfall of the traitor Sir John Hotham the younger. He had ensured that a demar-cation dispute between Manchester and Lord Willoughby of Parham over supreme command in Lincolnshire was decided in Manchester's favour. He had helped persuade Lord Fairfax to ship his cavalry from Hull, where they were dying through drinking brackish water, to fight in the campaign that reached such a happy conclu-sion at Winceby. However, Cromwell's tactics in two of the three battles in which he fought in 1643, Grantham and Winceby,[40] are not a clear pointer to the outstanding military career that lay ahead of him.[41]

The two major campaigns of the winter months began to all intents and purposes in November 1643. Sir William Waller, with a new army raised partly in London and partly in the four counties of the Southeast Association of which he was now major general,[42] found himself once more facing Sir Ralph, now Lord Hopton. Waller's orders, issued on or soon after 9 October, were to defend the Association should Hopton attack and then, if the opportunity arose, to set about reconquering the territory he had lost in the summer.[43] Ten days earlier Hopton had received his orders. As field marshal general of the western army he was to clear Dorset, Wiltshire and Hampshire of the enemy 'and so point forward as far as he could go towards London'. This meant putting together a new corps from what was left of Hertford's command, whilst Prince Maurice's part of the old western army continued with its operations against parliamentary-held towns in Devonshire.[44] In retrospect the king's mistake was not to give Maurice the more active role and instruct Hopton to return to the far south-west to complete the job he had begun the previous autumn.

At first all went very well for the royalists. On 7 November Waller set out from Farnham, his new army base, heading for Winchester, but with his army incomplete.[45] However, Hopton reached Winchester first, responding to the unexpected news that Sir William Ogle had seized the city in a coup. Waller then fell back, as he normally did when taken by surprise, and set siege to Basing House in north-east Hampshire, whose owner, the marquis of Winchester, had garrisoned it for the king. When Hopton, strengthened by forces from Oxford and Reading, marched to its relief, Waller returned to Farnham. A stand-off followed lasting for about a week, but Waller would not fight and Hopton fell back grudgingly on Winchester, his forces having consumed all the provisions for horse and man to be found in south-west Surrey.[46] This was Hopton's first mistake. Whilst he held the initiative, he ought to have called Sir William's bluff by bypassing Farnham, cutting his communications with the rest of the Association and with London, and thus eventually forcing him out of his bolt-hole. His next mistake was to go into winter quarters in Hampshire on the assumption that Waller would do the same. There was nowhere in the county large enough to accommodate Hopton's entire army and so he split it into several divisions, the principal brigades being quartered at Winchester, Alton and Petersfield in comfortable billets but too far apart to assist one another in an emergency.[47] This foolishness he compounded by occupying Arundel and stationing the Petersfield brigade there without first securing the pass over the South Downs at Midhurst, which blocked the route from Farnham into West Sussex.[48]

This was just the kind of game Waller enjoyed. From Farnham he could strike at two of Hopton's brigades in the knowledge that help was too far away. Also the wooded landscape interspersed with chalky upland favoured the kind of surprise tactics in which he excelled. First he surrounded the brigade at Alton after a night march. He attacked at dawn from the direction of Winchester, and had snuffed out the last pockets of resistance by midday. He then drove the brigade at Arundel out of the town into the castle where overcrowding and a dead ox in the well caused an outbreak of dysentery. Hopton received assistance from Oxford in the shape of Lord Wilmot and 1,000 cavalry and dragoons, but this was not to be a repeat of Roundway Down. Instead of advancing to meet the enemy, Waller drew up his army in a strong defensive position five miles short of Arundel, which Hopton dared not attack because the bulk of his infantry were either dead, prisoners of war or trapped behind the walls of Arundel Castle. When the town surrendered on 6 January 1644, the expectation on both sides was that Sir William would quickly set about reconquering the west, but he insisted on having time to establish a garrison at Arundel and to recruit his foot regiments. The blizzard that followed soon afterwards meant that he remained in West Sussex for the next few weeks, but the supplies he received from London and from Kent meant that when the weather improved in early March he was ready to take the offensive.[49]

The Committee of Both Kingdoms originally intended Sir William and his army to 'slip into the west', whilst Hopton dealt with a new threat to Basing House, but when Sir Richard Grenville, Waller's new cavalry commander, deserted to the king taking Parliament's plans with him, his instructions were merely to move on Winchester.[50] As for Hopton, his subordination to Prince Maurice was confirmed by the latter's promotion to lieutenant general of the south-east,[51] but Waller took the field before the prince and his army had left their winter quarters to the north of Plymouth. Hopton therefore received a minder in the shape of Lord Forth, who joined him on 13 March with 1,200 foot and 800 horse just in time to face the parliamentary army as it advanced.[52]

However, the royalists were still heavily outnumbered. Waller had about 10,000 men, Essex having been ordered to send Sir William Balfour, his lieutenant general, into Sussex with very substantial cavalry reinforcements. All Hopton and Forth had was about 6,500 men, at least half of whom were cavalry.[53]

The battle fought between Cheriton and West Meon on 29 March followed two days of manoeuvring for position on the chalk downs of east Hampshire. Neither set of generals was hankering after a battle. Waller and Balfour had strict orders from the Committee of Both Kingdoms only to look for a fight if the circumstances were such that victory was certain, 'you knowing we have no other reserve ready if you should receive a blow'.[54] Forth and Hopton were also circumspect, probably because of the small size of their army compared with that of the enemy. Their preference was probably to spin out time until Prince Maurice arrived. In the meantime they hoped to wrong-foot Sir William, forcing

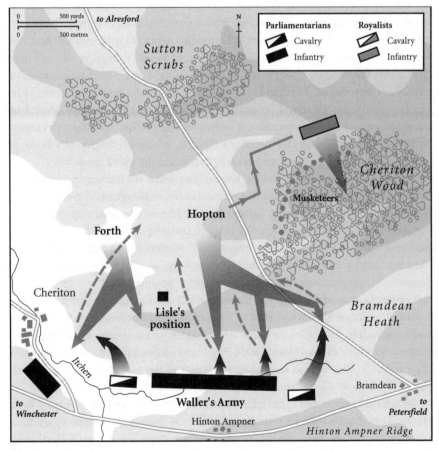

Cheriton

him to make a hurried and disorganised retreat, which their cavalry could with luck turn into a rout. Such tactics would also have the advantage of conserving their infantry until such a time as they were on more equal terms with the enemy.[55] However, more by accident than design, the armies boxed themselves into a corner from which they could not extricate themselves without a fight or a humiliating and possibly costly retreat.

After an encouraging start by the royalists, the battle became a complete shambles. During the night of 28–29 March, Waller and Balfour, who seem to have been in joint command, sent a body of infantry to occupy Cheriton Wood which threatened the flank of the enemy advance guard. They hoped that this would force the royalists to fall back, or if not, make it difficult for them to disrupt the parliamentary army's withdrawal towards Petersfield, a move that appears to have been decided at a Council of War the previous evening. The western army musketeers reacted promptly and captured the wood after a sharp fight, but Forth rejected Hopton's offer to chase the enemy so hard that their main body was thrown into disorder, thus creating rich pickings for the royalist cavalry. Forth was of the opinion that Waller was very likely to retreat of his own accord,[56] but then the other wing of the royalist army got into trouble. A major infantry attack was under way against the van of Waller's army, of which Forth denied all knowledge, though it was on so large a scale that he must have planned it in advance. The intention was to put more pressure on the enemy to retreat, but Waller's strength in depth began to tell and the royalist attack lost momentum and began to crumble. Forth then ordered his last infantry reserves to stabilise the situation and disaster followed. Whilst on their way a body of Waller's cavalry cut them off and captured or killed the lot of them.[57]

Forth then responded as Prince Rupert had done at Newbury by sending a large brigade of cavalry to attack the enemy centre, but Waller had drawn it up in a formidable defensive position behind a hedge line on the steep slope of Hinton Ampner Down. Not surprisingly, the brigade failed to penetrate the enemy position and suffered heavy losses as a result.[58] However, unlike Essex, Waller then used his cavalry to counter-attack, but they were no more successful than the royalists, Hopton having drawn up his infantry behind a similar hedge line on the opposite side of the valley.[59] Stalemate followed as the central part of the battlefield became filled with a milling mass of disordered horse as more and more were drawn into the melee. In the end, pushes by parliamentary infantry around both flanks of the cavalry battle forced Forth and Hopton to order a general withdrawal, but Waller had no immediate response as the monster melee had swallowed up almost all his reserves.[60] By the time he had brought forward his uncommitted cavalry and some artillery pieces to drive the king's forces from their fall-back position, an orderly retreat was under way, helped by the heavily wooded country only three miles to the north. The consequence was that Forth and Hopton saved their infantry and artillery train from suffering any further losses.[61]

Waller and Balfour's cavalry sweeps through Hampshire and its environs over the next few days achieved nothing more than the surrender of the little garrison at Christchurch manned by recently raised local forces, which, sandwiched between the garrisons of Southampton and Poole, could not have survived for long in any circumstances.[62] When Forth and Hopton met up with most of the rest of the king's forces in the south of England at Aldbourne Chase on 10 April, the parliamentary army, intended to reconquer the south-west of England, scuttled back once more to Farnham, much to the anger of Waller's political masters and the scorn of the citizens of London.[63] However, it was a strategic miscalculation by the Committee of Both Kingdoms and Parliament that enabled the royalists to deliver their bloodless and highly effective counter-stroke. They could have prevented it happening by putting pressure on the king's headquarters, but Essex's infantry were not yet ready to take the field whereas Manchester's army was looking west rather than south. Manchester and his political masters were worried that a new army that Prince Rupert was putting together in the Welsh Marches had evil intentions towards the Eastern Association.

In strategic terms Hopton's campaign had been a disaster and as a consequence the Oxford army absorbed his army after the Aldbourne Chase rendezvous. Winchester admittedly was an asset, as its strong royalist garrison dominated central Hampshire until the autumn of 1645, but the downside was that Hopton's carelessness was responsible for the loss of 1,700 precious infantry at Alton and Arundel. The chances of fighting anything other than a defensive campaign in the south in the spring of 1644 had therefore largely disappeared.[64] If Prince Maurice's forces had been nearing Oxford, the royalist generals might have regained the initiative, but his orders were first to capture the little fishing port of Lyme on the border between Devon and Dorset.[65] To make matters worse, unless Lyme fell exceedingly quickly, Lord Forth would find himself facing two enemy armies, Essex's and Waller's. This was a return to the situation of the spring of 1643, but made worse by the possibility that the earl of Manchester's army might also become involved.[66]

The second major royalist strategic initiative in the winter of 1643–4 was the creation of a new army in the Welsh Marches, which was to reconquer Lancashire and Cheshire, and then cross the Pennines to assist the marquis of Newcastle against the Scots.[67] The core was to be made up of regiments withdrawn from Ireland. Principally infantrymen, they were to combine with troops from Oxford, principally cavalry,[68] and with Lord Capel's forces,[69] to form a body of some 7,000 men. The commander was to be the king's lieutenant general in Ireland, the marquis of Ormond, with Sir John, now Lord Byron, as his deputy.[70] However, at the end of December Prince Rupert took Ormond's place, the king having decided that the marquis was better employed in Dublin heading up efforts to turn the truce into an alliance to be followed by the dispatch of an Irish Catholic army to England.[71] But it took the prince over a month to reach Shrewsbury, Capel's army base.[72] In the meantime Sir Thomas Fairfax had given Byron a bloody nose at the battle of Nantwich.

By the time the first contingent of the English army left Dublin on 10 November, a major difficulty had arisen. No longer was the king in complete control of North Wales. After defeating Lord Capel in a scrappy encounter near Wem in October, Parliament's two commanders in the area, Sir William Brereton and Sir Thomas Middleton, assisted by regiments from Lancashire, captured the bridge over the River Dee at Farndon, overran the Wrexham area and captured Hawarden Castle, which guarded the principal route between the North Wales ports and Chester where the new royalist army was to assemble.[73] However, Brereton and Middleton failed to push forward to the North Wales coast, with the result that the first three Irish regiments had an unopposed landing. The parliamentarians then got cold feet. The Lancashire contingent, worried that a foray by the marquis of Newcastle into north Derbyshire foreshadowed a move into their own county, decided to return home. Having lost some of his best infantry, Brereton fell back across the Dee, thus allowing the brigade from Ireland to march to Chester unopposed. There Byron joined it a few days later with the contingents from Oxford and Shrewsbury, which had marked time in Shropshire until the danger from Brereton and Middleton passed.[74]

Within days of arriving at Chester, Byron began his allotted task. Sir William Brereton informed Parliament of the downturn in his fortunes and begged for support, but instead of waiting for reinforcements to arrive he engaged Byron's army in battle at Middlewich on 26 December. Unsurprisingly, he lost the encounter but the enclosed landscape enabled his infantry to retreat to Nantwich, which, though not a walled town, had acquired a formidable set of earthworks in the eleven months since becoming Sir William's operational headquarters. His cavalry, however, joined their Lancashire friends on the far side of the Mersey.[75]

Byron, having cleared much of the rest of Cheshire of enemy troops, then set siege to Nantwich. Sir Thomas Fairfax, who was in charge of the rescue attempt, took his time. The earl of Essex sent him a temporary commission as commander-in-chief in the north-west within days of the news of the landing of the Irish regiments arriving in London, but he did not set out with his father's mounted troops, 1,200 horse and 800 dragoons, until 29 December.[76] On arriving in Lancashire he found local commanders none too keen to cooperate, but he nevertheless ordered a rendezvous on Knutsford Heath for 24 January. Here, according to John Hodgson, the appearance of the troops was so scruffy that 'the good man wept when he looked upon us'.[77] However, Nantwich could not hold out much longer, and the hotchpotch of an army hurried on south.

The royalists were expecting some attempt to break up the siege and had scouts watching all the major approaches to the town. Moreover, it would have been easy to delay Fairfax's progress through the south Cheshire countryside, a landscape of tiny fields interspersed with small patches of lowland heath. However, Lord Byron was late to react. As a result he and most of his cavalry found themselves on the wrong side of a river in flood and were unable to play any part in the battle that followed.[78] Fairfax's role in the events of 25 January was also a limited one. Up to the point of contact his continuous use of the word 'we' to describe decisions made suggests very strongly that a Council of War presided over the approach march.[79] After that he took charge of the left wing where the royalist resistance lasted the longest. It was junior officers elsewhere who issued the battle-winning commands. The sally from Nantwich which undermined the entire royalist position was the initiative of the garrison commander Colonel George Booth, whilst a flank attack delivered by a few companies of foot led by a Captain Holt apparently caused the collapse of the royalist infantry regiments on the right wing.[80]

Factors beyond Fairfax's control largely determined the scale of the victory. The royalist troops of horse, which took no part in the battle, were able to act as an effective defensive shield to protect such of their infantry as were able to retreat from the battlefield in good order.[81] In addition, the landscape made it problematic for Fairfax to carry out the type of cavalry pursuit which in early modern warfare normally inflicted the greatest loss on a defeated army. Finally, the battle did not begin until about 3.30 p.m. and the onset of darkness enabled many royalists to escape.[82]

Nevertheless Sir Thomas gained the credit for the victory, but by the time he left Cheshire a month later he was only just beginning to exploit the battle in terms of recovering lost territory, as the royalists remained strong in the wider region.[83] Three new regiments crossed the Irish Sea in early February, two of infantry and one of cavalry, whilst Prince Rupert's arrival at Shrewsbury on 19 February, followed soon afterwards by that of his regiment of foot, did much to revive royalist spirits. Quick to seize the initiative, he was in action against one of Fairfax's cavalry regiments near Market Drayton in Shropshire on 5 March and inflicted many casualties.[84]

Later in the month during a brief pause in the vigorous shake-up he was giving to military administration in the counties he now controlled,[85] the prince was able to add significantly to his military reputation by riding across the width of Midland England and winning a famous victory outside Newark. After Sir Thomas Fairfax and his cavalry and dragoons had left for Lancashire, the forces remaining in Lincolnshire belonging to the Eastern Association combined with the troops from Nottinghamshire and adjacent counties under Sir John Meldrum to set siege to the town.[86] Assembling a 'flying army' of cavalry supported by musketeers on horseback to provide firepower, Rupert rode rapidly eastwards picking up reinforcements from royalist garrisons on the way. The battle that followed three miles to the south of Newark on 21 March was a desperate, frenzied affair, and like the prince's assault on Bristol it came close to disaster. It was also very much an encounter battle in which the army arrived on the scene in dribs and drabs. Rupert should therefore have remained in the rear as much decision making was required, but he decided that leadership from the front was the only way of stopping an enemy which was in retreat and likely to escape from his clutches if he waited for the rest of his units to arrive.

The prince's boldness was almost his undoing, but fortunately support troops led by Captain Clement Martin of Rupert's own regiment, and by Colonel Charles Gerard, showed the skills and initiative necessary for rescuing him from the pickle he had got himself into. Together they then routed the enemy army, which broke up into its component parts as sectional interests came to the fore, with most of the cavalry making their escape and leaving the infantry stranded on an island in the River Trent with only two days' food supply. Surrender on terms soon followed, and Rupert took charge of 13 to 14 artillery pieces and 3,000 to 4,000 muskets.[87] Gerard received his reward, being appointed Rupert's deputy in south-west Wales where he replaced Lord Carbery whose pacification of Pembrokeshire had fallen apart when the parliamentary cause started to make a comeback after the First Battle of Newbury. For the rest of the year and again in the spring of 1645 Gerard waged a highly successful containing operation against coastal strongholds, which could not be stormed without spectacular casualties.[88] In addition, he built up a strong strategic reserve of 3,000 to 4,000 men, which the king could employ in the Thames valley, the Midlands or the Welsh borderland as required, though the distances involved meant that the force could not arrive quickly on the scene.[89]

Prince Rupert's conduct of the engagement outside Newark has been seen as possibly his greatest feat of generalship.[90] However, the results, though important, were limited. He had saved the most important garrison on the 'east coast' corridor between Oxford and York, and Newark was to remain vitally important, both strategically and operationally, until the very end of the war. Local commanders also reoccupied parts of Lincolnshire, including the county town, and floated before Rupert's eyes all sorts of interesting ideas for building on his success, whilst the marquis of Newcastle begged him to send the troops from Ireland to York,[91] but the defeat at Cheriton just eight days later meant that orders for the prince to leave the Trent valley arrived within days of the victory outside Newark,[92] and he was back in Shrewsbury by 4 April.[93] Without his army the local cavaliers were not strong enough to hold onto Lincoln and Gainsborough, and both were back in parliamentary hands by early June. To make matters worse the regiments of Lincolnshire horse under Major General George Porter, which had assisted Rupert, lingered too long in the Newark area and helped to bring about a major disaster at Selby three weeks later.[94]

CHAPTER 8

Great Expectations

SELBY AND OXFORD

IN THE autumn of 1643 the king charged his generals with restarting the strategic initiative which had stalled at Newbury in late September, but such gains as they did make were concentrated in October, November and early December. From mid-December onwards there was a run of setbacks on most fronts: Prince Maurice had failed to capture Plymouth; the garrison at Towcester near Northampton had to be withdrawn; Lord Hopton had lost half his infantry at Alton and Arundel; Lord Byron had suffered defeat at Nantwich and Lords Forth and Hopton at Cheriton. Moreover, the two clear successes, the relief of Newark and deterring Waller from invading the West Country after Cheriton, were defensive operations pure and simple. They enabled the king's forces to cling onto what they already held, not to occupy new territory.

The achievements of the army generals of Parliament and the Scottish Covenanters were also largely of a defensive nature, but the prospects for the allies in the spring campaign looked bright. In the first place, the five field armies of the earls of Essex, Manchester and Leven, Lord Fairfax and Sir William Waller totalled over 40,000 men, whereas the king only had 35,000 at most under the command of Lord Forth, the marquis of Newcastle, Prince Rupert and Prince Maurice. Second, although the king's problems in obtaining arms and ammunition had eased very considerably through the acquisition of ports in Somerset and Dorset and the development of manufacturing facilities at Bristol, his English opponents were even better supplied with the accoutrements of war.[1] Third, the imbalance in cavalry numbers between the two sides in the Thames valley and the northern theatres of war had disappeared to all intents and purposes. Although the king's generals continued to command large numbers of horse, the allies probably had more cavalry than the royalists at Marston Moor (July 1644) and certainly had at the Second Battle of Newbury (October 1644) and at Naseby (June 1645).[2]

The best performer amongst the king's generals had been Prince Rupert, his great victory outside Newark in March offsetting worries about his judgement stemming from the bloodbaths at Bristol and Newbury. Lord Hopton had been the worst. It can, of course, be argued that what happened in Hampshire and Sussex in the winter of 1643 was not his fault as he was under-resourced for the task the king had given him. This is a constant refrain in the narrative of the campaign he wrote for Lord Clarendon, but it does not excuse him from being less than careful with what he did have. The disasters at Alton and Arundel were due to poor generalship, not lack of resources. On the other hand, it was Lord Forth, not Hopton, who was responsible for the bad decisions taken on the battlefield at Cheriton, but Forth as usual managed to avoid the blame.[3]

Despite the setbacks he suffered at Hull and Winceby, the military operations that the earl of Newcastle oversaw in the winter months served the king's cause well, given the odds piled up against him. First, he extended his control over north and central Derbyshire, thus securing his rear areas in advance of the Scottish invasion. Then, just before the Scottish army crossed the border on 25 January, he divided his army. Whilst he and General King faced the Scots with some 6,000 men, Lord Bellasis, previously a brigade commander in the Oxford army, took charge at York with a force of some 4,000 men with orders to defend south and central Yorkshire against the Fairfaxes.[4] During February and March, Newcastle delayed the Scots' advance, though outnumbered by a factor of almost three to one, but a climactic battle was out of the question unless somehow or other Bellasis was able to secure south Yorkshire and come to his assistance. Newcastle's dispatches are full of pessimistic comments but, though doubtless an accurate reflection of his state of mind, they were also both a bid for the return of regiments he had sent south in 1643 and an effective defence against his critics if things went wrong.[5] However, despite loud muttering about his failure to order his army south in the late summer of 1643, there were no moves to replace him.

This was not so with Prince Maurice, even though his part of the royalist army of the west had done reasonably well by securing the surrender of three of the four large enemy garrisons in Devonshire, Exeter, Barnstaple and Dartmouth, during September and October.[6] However, at the siege of Dartmouth Maurice fell seriously ill and this caused a fatal loss of momentum. As a result the siege of Plymouth did not begin until several weeks later than intended, by which time the town was better placed to defend itself. Infantry reinforcements had arrived by sea under Colonel James Wardlaw, who also put the garrison on a better military footing and uncovered a plot to betray part of the town's defences to the royalists.[7] Maurice's sole achievement was to capture Fort Stamford, from which his heavy artillery pieces could fire at targets on the quayside, but attempts to penetrate the outer ring of the town's defences failed, and the army retired into winter quarters north of the town on Christmas day.[8]

Soon after Maurice's army emerged from winter quarters rumours began to circulate that it was to be incorporated into the king's army, as Hopton's had been after the battle of Cheriton,[9] but for the present he was to focus on capturing the port of Lyme on the border between Devon and Dorset, the only parliamentary garrison left in the south-west of England apart from Plymouth. If it continued in enemy hands, it might disrupt the king's plans for a new Association to be presided over by the young Prince of Wales. Its purpose was to enhance the royalist war effort by mobilising the resources of the four counties of the south-west in the same way as the earl of Manchester had mobilised those of East Anglia through the Eastern Association.[10] The siege was not the prince's initiative designed to enhance his military reputation[11] or to avoid getting too close to the black hole of the Oxford army and suffering the same fate as Lord Hopton.[12]

As for Parliament's generals, Essex was beset with worries about deteriorating relations with his political masters,[13] whereas Waller had lost ground because of his cautious conduct of the Cheriton campaign. Manchester kept a low profile, focusing his attention on recruiting and on building up administrative and finan-cial support for his army. His troops, however, experienced mixed fortunes. Some had taken part in the unfortunate siege of Newark, whilst others had spent a quiet winter garrisoning Newport Pagnell and picking off the odd weak royalist garrison in the vicinity.[14] The Fairfaxes, on the other hand, had done very well. Lord Fairfax earned respect for his defence of Hull, whilst Sir Thomas had to all intents and purposes won the battle of Winceby by a well-timed charge. He had also gained the credit for defeating Lord Byron's army at Nantwich even though his personal contribution towards victory had been slight, but prior to the battle he had welded a disparate and none too enthusi-astic set of regiments into an effective fighting force.

Finally, there was the earl of Leven. Other than blockading the town of Newcastle and pushing the marquis of Newcastle's army slowly but remorselessly southwards, the campaign he fought in Northumberland and Durham during February and March had been unspectacular. There were a number of stand-offs and in the end Newcastle's army were outmanoeuvred while Leven, experienced professional that he was, took every care that the royalists were not able to use their better-armed and better-horsed cavalry against him in open country.[15]

A major change in the relationship between Parliament's army generals and their political masters coincided with the start of the 1644 campaigning season. The new Committee of Both Kingdoms exerted a much greater control over the operational side of warfare than the Committee of Safety had ever done. It began cautiously but even so the language of some of its early letters to commanders in the field shows in no uncertain terms that it intended to be in the driving seat and that its orders were mandatory, not a matter for discussion. If a general failed to obey, he received a rebuke. If his alternative plan worked, the Committee might be generous in its praise as, for example, with the Fairfaxes in April 1644, or sour and mean-spirited as with the earl of Essex in June.[16] Sometimes if there was time for a debate, tightly argued letters passed back and forth often ending in a compromise, as in June 1644 when the allied generals' determination to have as many troops as possible besieging York conflicted with the Committee's concern about defending Manchester against Prince Rupert.

However, the slowness of communications between London and most of the theatres of war meant that a general could frustrate the will of the Committee in the full knowledge that by the time the rebuke arrived events would have moved on to such an extent that the original order was no longer relevant. In such circumstances all the Committee members could do was to bite their collective tongue and bide their time. They were not in the business of sacking a general in mid-campaign.

A similar tightening up in control can be seen on the king's side. First, the king became more confident in his military leadership as he gained greater experience of war.[17] Second, as pressure grew on the Oxford army, the need to ensure that the provincial commanders obeyed orders became all the more acute. What made for uncertainty was the shifting patterns of the war, with advantage swinging backwards and forwards much more rapidly than in 1643, and also the greater distances being covered by the field armies. There was no overall strategic plan other than keeping the show on the road and defending Oxford and its environs. This required a deftness of touch,[18] but the speed of response to a rapidly changing military situation was helped enormously by the fact that the king was often with the field army during April and May and continuously from early June until mid-November.

For much of 1644 a small committee oversaw the overall direction of the war and advised the king on strategy. Its regular members were the junior secretary of state, George, Lord Digby; the duke of Richmond; Lord Culpeper; Lord Forth; and the commanders of the horse and foot in the field army, Lord Wilmot and Sir Jacob Astley.[19] Directions then went to the generals in the field in letters written by the king or by Digby.[20] Rupert attended the committee in April and early May and again in late September, but his long absences did nothing to enhance the lord general's influence on decision making. Forth was no more than one member of a consultative group, and the only move he is known to have initiated earned him an angry rebuke from the king.[21] Culpeper's influence also seems to have diminished, probably because he had been foremost in pushing for the siege of Gloucester. As time passed, he found himself increasingly overshadowed by Digby, his younger civilian colleague whose glib tongue, courtly arts and unbounded optimism gave him a powerful influence over the king.[22] Richmond, as the king's cousin, was the senior nobleman in the realm, and also a close friend of Prince Rupert. There seems little doubt that he ensured that the prince's views were put to the king, and his letters helped calm Rupert's fears that his enemies at court and on the council were undermining his relationship with his uncle. Richmond also provided Rupert with a channel of communication with the king that was independent of Digby, though relations between the two were nowhere near as bad in 1644 as they were to become in the following year. Wilmot hated Rupert and favoured a negotiated peace on the grounds that the king could not win the war, but he made little headway as

Charles did not like him and resented his attempt to impose his will on the committee.[23] Astley also had little impact. A military technician rather than an operational or strategic planner, he kept his mouth shut for most of the time. Also, unlike Wilmot, he was not an intriguer by nature.

As Prince Rupert's victory outside Newark and Sir William Waller's at Cheriton had led nowhere, the 1644 campaigning season proper began in the north of England with the storming of Selby on 11 April. Once Sir Thomas Fairfax had helped Brereton's Cheshire forces to their feet, his political masters decided that the two parts of the northern army should combine to re-establish control over the towns of the West Riding where Colonel John Lambert had gained a precarious foothold in early March. Sir Thomas was then to march north with his cavalry to assist the earl of Leven against the marquis of Newcastle.[24] However, Lord Fairfax remained at Hull, whilst Sir Thomas did no more than move some horse and two regiments of foot across the Pennines whilst he concentrated on capturing Latham House, the last enemy garrison in Lancashire. Lambert successfully blocked an attempt by Lord Bellasis to force him out of Bradford and then drove the royalists back towards York,[25] but he could do no more because of lack of numbers.

Sir Thomas did not cross into Yorkshire until the beginning of April, but when he did he moved like lightning. Picking up Lambert's force at Leeds, he marched across the county to Ferrybridge, where he met his father and the troops from Hull.[26] However, instead of going to the assistance of the Scottish army in County Durham, they decided to try and make the most of an opportunity to inflict a devastating defeat on Lord Bellasis, who had ordered a general rendezvous of all his forces at Selby, twelve miles to the south of York, where the road to Newark crossed the River Ouse. The Committee of Both Kingdoms was not happy,[27] but any animosity towards the commanders in Yorkshire was overtaken by events.

The Fairfaxes attacked Selby on 11 April with a force of about 7,000 men, their own brigades and a substantial portion of Meldrum's army which Prince Rupert had routed less than three weeks earlier.[28] Bellasis had considerably fewer men. The parliamentarians assaulted the town from three directions but for several hours they could not achieve a breakthrough. Then Lord Fairfax's regiment of foot found a weak spot in the defences near the banks of the Ouse, where a Captain Wilson betrayed his trust, either through cowardice or knavery. The gap opened up enabled Sir Thomas to lead his cavalry behind the royalist defences and into the town. Bellasis charged them immediately with the small body of horse he still had with him, the rest having already made their escape over the Ouse bridge, but the younger Fairfax quickly took Bellasis and the rest prisoner. The royalists then surrendered – over 500 horse and 1,600 foot soldiers, not counting officers, according to Lord Fairfax.[29]

The marquis of Newcastle quite fortuitously was about to carry out a planned withdrawal across the Tees into Yorkshire, and he immediately led his army back towards York, where it arrived without incident on 19 April. Newcastle and his infantry regiments prepared to defend the city, but the cavalry, from that point onwards known as the Northern Horse, were to ride to Newark where they would be of much better use as part of a relief force. On the way south, however, he found time to write to the king complaining not about Bellasis's defence of Selby but about the shortcomings of George Porter and the earl of Loughborough, whose forces in the Trent valley had done nothing to prevent Meldrum marching to join the Fairfaxes.[30]

The Scots did not pursue Newcastle's forces closely, probably because this was a job for cavalry, and the type of horse General Leslie had at the time was not suitable for attacking an army retreating in good order.[31] It is, however, most surprising that the Fairfaxes did nothing to impede Newcastle's army as it approached York. If they had done so, the Scots would have had the chance to catch the royalists up and force them to fight, with very good prospects of landing a knockout blow. Possibly the casualties sustained at Selby had sapped their ardour, possibly they were low on ammunition or lacking intelligence of the movements of the enemy and of the Scots, but the failure of Lord Fairfax to exploit his victory prepared the way for the long and tedious siege of York and for the battle of Marston Moor, which almost destroyed his army. Clearly the follow-up to Selby did not come halfway towards fulfilling the Committee of both kingdoms' hopes (as expressed in a letter to Lord Fairfax written immediately afterwards) 'that not only the settlement of the north but of the whole kingdom may be speedily effected'.[32]

In the south it took another three weeks for full-scale campaigning to begin, but the orders that Essex and Waller received on 8 May were vague. They were to march against the enemy wherever they appeared in a body in the south and west of England.[33] However, it can be inferred from correspondence between the commanders of the two armies and the Committee that they had specific instructions to destroy the Oxford army in battle or, at the very least, to drive the king from his headquarters. If his generals left a garrison behind, they were to set siege to the city. Their chances of doing so were much greater than in the spring of 1643. Essex seemed enthusiastically committed to obeying the Committee's orders despite his long wait for resources, whilst Waller, though not shorn of the independence he had gained earlier in the year, accepted the role of subordinate with good grace as the two armies would be campaigning together.[34] Admittedly, shortage of ammunition no longer determined what the Oxford army could or could not do, but they outnumbered it by a factor of almost three to two. In addition, Essex had more than enough cavalry to fight a battle in open country.[35] There was also little prospect of Essex and Waller being disturbed in their work of smoking the king out of his headquarters. Prince Maurice was still besieging Lyme and was under orders to remain there, whereas the risk of Prince Rupert intervening in the Thames valley theatre of war in the immediate future was minimal. His first priority, agreed at a Council of War held at Wallingford on 26 April, was to put together a force in the Welsh borders to rescue the marquis of Newcastle and his infantry from York,[36] and Rupert had duly left Shrewsbury for the north on 15 May.[37] Moreover, should he return mission unaccomplished, he would have the Eastern Association army to contend with. A fortnight earlier the Committee of Both Kingdoms had ordered Manchester and his men to follow Rupert's army wherever it went.[38]

Those at the meeting at Wallingford had also decided how the war in the Thames valley was to be conducted in Rupert's absence. The main field army was too weak to face Essex and Waller, and on Rupert's recommendation the infantry were to be distributed amongst the principal garrisons – Oxford, Reading, Wallingford, Abingdon and Banbury. This would tie down one or both enemy generals, as Essex was unlikely to ignore current western European military doctrine that a general should not advance into hostile territory leaving large enemy garrisons in his rear. The king's cavalry, on the other hand, were to join Prince Maurice. This would give him a large enough army to fight Waller should Sir William advance into the West Country whilst Essex was keeping an eye on Oxford and its attendant garrisons.[39] However, no sooner had Rupert left than the king's military subcommittee reverted to an earlier plan on Forth's advice . There was insufficient infantry for all five garrisons to be strong enough to withstand a determined enemy attack, and so a measure of downsizing was necessary. When Essex and Waller set out from Beaconsfield and Farnham respectively on 15 May, the troops defending Reading abandoned the town and joined the field army, having slighted the fortifications constructed with much care during the winter.[40]

The king and his military advisers expected one enemy army to advance on Oxford along the north bank of the Thames and the other along the south bank. As all the bridges from Wallingford northwards were under royalist control, this would allow them to concentrate their entire strength against one or the other enemy army as occasion offered.[41] However, Essex quickly pricked this balloon by deciding that both armies should operate on the south bank. The king's military committee considered offering battle, but quickly decided that the enemy's strength made this far too dangerous. Their only option was to fall back as slowly as possible towards Oxford in the hope that the enemy would make a mistake which they could exploit. It was also decided in principle to abandon Abingdon, as it had no defence works of any significance on the south bank of the Thames. As the enemy neared Abingdon, the lord general, apparently on Wilmot's advice, withdrew the garrison without seeking the king's final approval. Charles was exceedingly angry when it proved impossible to reverse the order before the enemy occupied the town, but he decided to bide his time. This was not the moment to remove both his senior commanders.[42]

Whilst Waller's army secured Abingdon, Essex's army crossed the Thames by a ford and made its way around the east side of Oxford until, as in 1643, it encountered the king's infantry defending the crossings over the River Cherwell. For three days Sir Jacob Astley held the parliamentarians at bay, but then Waller, advancing westwards from Abingdon, captured New Bridge. This not only stopped the royalists retreating towards Bristol, it also allowed his forces to cross the Thames and attack the defensive line along the Cherwell from the rear. The king's army responded by seeking shelter behind the fortifications of Oxford, but this allowed Essex to occupy Woodstock, thus sealing off the best escape route into the Cotswolds.[43] Waller, however, did not complete the encirclement of Oxford. Instead of occupying Witney, he rested his army whilst pioneers set about strengthening the bridge so that it could carry the weight of his artillery train.[44]

Oxford was not a safe refuge for Charles and his army until such time as one or both of his nephews came to the rescue. Essex and Waller had sufficient troops to impose a complete blockade of the city, and its magazine only contained sufficient supplies to feed the king's troops for a fortnight. If the army remained where it was, the king and the Prince of Wales would be in enemy hands before the end of June and Parliament would have achieved its principal war aim. The only way of escaping such a fate was to adopt the only part of Rupert's plan that was still practicable. The slow-moving formations of pikes were to remain at Oxford, whilst the horse and most of the musketeers made for Worcester through the narrow gap between New Bridge and Woodstock.

The risks of the flying army being ambushed were enormous, but a deception might lessen the danger. The colours of the regiments of the king's army left on display outside the walls of Oxford and visible from Essex's forward positions gave the impression that the king and his commanders had every intention of remaining where they were. To reinforce the impression, a strong royalist force issued out of the south side of the city and threatened to retake Abingdon. In alarm Waller fell back towards Abingdon, leaving only a token force at New Bridge. This left a corridor some five miles wide through which the royalists could escape, but they would have to be quick. Essex's commanders at Woodstock were well placed to hinder their progress until such time as Waller arrived. On the night of 3–4 June, 3,000 to 4,000 cavalry and 2,500 to 3,000 musketeers probably riding piggyback, led by Forth, Astley and Wilmot, and accompanied by the king and the Prince of Wales, passed through the corridor without alerting the enemy. On the following night they quartered at Bourton-on-the-Water and by the next day they had reached Evesham, where the bridge over the Avon could be defended against multitudes. On the 6th they were at Worcester and by nightfall on the far side of the Severn with their flanks secure, as all the bridges and fords above Upton were in friendly hands.[45] There the flying army remained for the next ten days.[46]

Essex and Waller's armies set off in pursuit but they were slow off the mark, deceived, it seems, by the regimental colours still on display outside the walls of

Oxford. On the 5th Waller's army reached Burford and Essex's arrived at Chipping Norton, but by then the king's flying army was already in Worcestershire.[47] At this point the Committee of Both Kingdoms issued a new set of orders. Essex was immediately to send a party of cavalry and dragoons to relieve Lyme, and if the two generals decided that they were unable to engage the Oxford army in battle within six days, Waller's army was to advance into the West Country whilst Essex was to follow the king, drawing on local forces as and when necessary.[48] The lord general saw red. For the past fortnight leading an army group that at last was large and well equipped enough for its allotted task, he had achieved unprecedented success. The king had fled from Oxford and he and Waller had him on the run. Now the army group was to be split up at the whim of the Committee, and all the advantage gained would be thrown away. Goaded beyond endurance by inappropriate and ill-informed orders from on high, wounded by repeated blows to his pride, and humiliated by his image in the press which stopped just short of commenting on his impotence (a condition that had dogged both his marriages), Essex took the bull by the horns. To save his honour and his reputation he must win a spectacular military success similar to the relief of Gloucester, but this time it would be offensive rather than defensive in spirit, active rather than passive.

In order to retain the initiative, the lord general turned the Committee's orders on their head. Accepting the strategic necessity for relieving Lyme, he ridiculed the Committee's naivety in thinking that a brigade was all that was required given the strength of Prince Maurice's position. His own army would relieve Lyme and then go on to reconquer the West Country, whilst Waller's would combine with local forces to stop the flying army joining Prince Rupert or returning to Oxford. The latter was a task tailor-made for Sir William as his army had a higher proportion of mounted troops and a much smaller artillery train.[49] It could fly. His was too ponderous to do so, but it did have the infantry and artillery to fight its way through the enclosures that began five miles short of Lyme.

Clarendon claimed that Waller 'opposed this resolution all he could', urging that 'the west was assigned to him as his province', and that the consent of the Committee of Both Kingdoms was necessary before the armies could go their separate ways,[50] but he was mistaken. Waller accepted the military logic of the lord general's argument. His report to the Committee of the discussions at Chipping Norton where Essex's views had prevailed was a neutral one,[51] and even when Parliament and the Committee expressed great resentment at what Essex had done, Waller failed to add his pennyworth. Possibly he liked the idea of king chasing as it gave him a good chance of receiving all the credit for capturing Charles and bringing him back to Westminster as a prisoner.[52]

Essex was expecting a comeback and he prepared his ground well with a detailed report of the Council of War signed by his leading officers.[53] At first the instincts of his political masters were to give him a severe reprimand 'for disobeying the commands of the Houses and the Committee of Both

Kingdoms', whilst Sir Arthur Haselrig favoured dismissal.[54] However, the earl had many friends in the Upper House who delayed matters, thus allowing tempers to die down. As a result the formal rebuke from Parliament did not leave Westminster until three weeks had passed, and the tone was sulky rather than incandescent with rage. Having reviewed the evidence of the ways in which Essex had subverted the Committee's operational plans, and having read the correspondence that passed between the Committee and the earl, the two Houses declared that they were of the opinion 'that if the resolutions of the Houses and the directions of the Committee had been followed, the public affairs had been in a better condition' and that 'in some of your letters to the Committee and to the two Houses there are some expressions that might well have been forborne'. However, 'to make the best use of their affairs as they now stand they find themselves necessitated to new counsels and would have your lordship to take all advantages on the enemy and use your best endeavours for the reducing of the west'.[55]

The muted reaction also reflected the fact that the first phase of Essex's plan had worked well and was certainly not a strategic blunder of the first order.[56] Waller quickly increased the force under his command to some 12,000 men and took up a position at Stourbridge in north Worcestershire which made it impossible for the flying army to join Prince Rupert.[57] In the meantime, as Essex advanced through Wiltshire into Dorset, Prince Maurice abandoned the siege of Lyme and also Weymouth, the port through which much of the arms and ammunition obtained from continental suppliers had reached Oxford. The earl also looked set fair to bottle up Maurice's army in the far south-west of England and to capture the queen, who was at Exeter in transit for France and ill after childbirth. It was only when Waller allowed the flying army to escape from its bolthole on the far side of the River Severn that Essex's grand plan began to fall apart, as also did the understanding between Parliament's two army generals in the south.[58] However, the longer-term results of Essex's kicking over the traces need to be put into context. They are best seen as part and parcel of the much more extensive setback to Parliament's war aims that occurred in the second half of 1644, for which all its army generals were responsible.

CHAPTER 9

The Marston Moor Campaign

WHILST TWO of Parliament's generals were putting the king's military position in south central England under near intolerable pressure, Prince Rupert was trying to put together a force capable of rescuing the marquis of Newcastle and his infantry from York. The matter was not that pressing as the earl of Leven and Lord Fairfax could not cut the city off completely from the surrounding countryside and appeared to have ruled out the idea of storming it. Their focus was on drawing in the army of the Eastern Association. Only then would there be sufficient troops to make the blockade watertight and starve the marquis of Newcastle's forces into surrender.[1]

The earl of Manchester's army had begun the 1644 campaigning season facing south when it looked as if Lord Forth, reinforced by Prince Rupert's forces from the Welsh borderland and Prince Maurice's from Devonshire, would begin his spring offensive before the earl of Essex was ready to take the field. However, during the course of May, Manchester drew ever northwards, as it became more and more certain that Prince Rupert would be heading for York. By the middle of the month the earl's infantry were besieging Lincoln, whilst most of the cavalry had joined those of Lord Fairfax and the Scots in the Lower Trent valley ready to block Rupert's most direct route via Newark and the Great North Road. Once Lincoln had fallen, the earl of Manchester's infantry regiments made directly for York, where they arrived on 4 June.[2]

The allied leadership were right.[3] Rupert's first intention was to relieve York from a southerly direction via Newark or Sheffield, but his visit to Oxford in late April and early May to discuss strategy for the spring campaign caused too long a delay. Leaving Shrewsbury on 15 May with his own regiments of horse and foot, he met Lord Byron with the Anglo-Irish forces at Whitchurch two days later and was on his way to join the Northern Horse in the Peak District when he learned that local royalists had lost control of the vital crossing point over the River Ouse at Cawood, ten miles short of York.[4] Rupert therefore fell back on an alternative plan suggested during April but rejected because it would take too much time, namely overrunning Lancashire and then, having increased his forces by recruitment, advancing from Preston towards York via the Ribble valley. After crossing the Mersey at Stockport he sent the northern cavalry,

which had joined him in early June, into Cumbria in search of reinforcements.
He then captured Bolton and Liverpool by storm and looked set to consolidate
his control over Lancashire by attacking Manchester, but time was now pressing
and Rupert was not a free agent.

From the earliest discussions in mid-April as to how York was to be relieved,
the king had made it clear to Rupert that he must spend as little time as possible
in the north given the size of the force that Parliament's generals were likely to
deploy in the spring campaign in the south. Anxiety eased slightly during
Rupert's visit to Oxford, with Waller's army lying quietly at Farnham, Essex's
still in winter quarters and Manchester's busy in Lincolnshire. However, anxiety
returned during the fourth week of May as Essex's and Waller's armies menaced
the royalist headquarters. The escape of the king and his flying army did not help
matters. In fact it increased the anxiety, as part of the Oxford army was penned
in on the far bank of the River Severn and the rest was sixty miles away to the
east with one or two enemy armies in between.

The king's letter from Worcester dated 7 June ordered the prince to advance
on York immediately and fight a battle against the Scots.[5] A week later the
demand for a speedy resolution to the military crisis in the north culminated in
the infamous letter, sent by Charles from Bewdley near Kidderminster, which
Rupert allegedly carried with him until his dying day as an instant defence
against criticism of his rashness in fighting a force much larger than his own at
Marston Moor. On its own the letter can be read in several ways, but it was only
one of a succession of letters beginning in late May and ending on 15 June with
an almost identical refrain.[6] There is thus no doubt that Rupert was right and
Clarendon and his other contemporary critics were wrong about the root cause
of the disaster to the royalist armies in the north which was to occur on the
evening of 2 July 1644. It was not the overweening self-confidence of the young
prince that brusquely ignored wise advice from older and more experienced
soldiers. Rupert was under the strictest orders to fight a battle before returning
south, and this he proceeded to do.

Rupert's conduct of the march to York was masterly. He started out from
Preston on 20 June. Leaving garrisons at the principal passes should he decide
to return to Lancashire, he met up with the Northern Horse at Skipton on the
26th and reached Knaresborough less than twenty miles from the city on the
30th. Abandoning the siege, the allied generals drew up their horse and foot on
Marston Moor, an area of open lowland moor four miles to the west astride the
enemy's most likely line of advance. However, Rupert bypassed York and
entered the city from the north-east direction, having encountered no opposition whatsoever. On the afternoon of 1 July the allied forces heard the celebrations to their rear, but they could do nothing about it.[7] On the following day the
earl of Leven, who was in overall command, ordered the three armies to make
for the bridge over the River Wharfe at Tadcaster, six miles to the south. If they

held the river line, they could block the prince's progress should he decide to head for Newark or Sheffield. They would also be ideally placed for a rendezvous with forces from Lancashire, Cheshire and the North Midlands led by Sir John Meldrum, which were approaching rapidly from the south-west.[8] As a precaution given the prince's habit of attacking retreating armies, the earl of Leven kept a strong force of cavalry as a rearguard led by the three lieutenant generals, Oliver Cromwell, Sir Thomas Fairfax and David Leslie.

From their vantage point on Braham Hill between Tockwith and Long Marston villages, the only substantial feature in the landscape between York and Tadcaster, the lieutenant generals saw much to their surprise that the prince's army was drawing up on Marston Moor in battle formation. This suggested that Rupert's intention was not to carry out a conventional harassing operation using horse alone but to launch a general assault on the rearguard. General Leven therefore ordered the rest of his troops, some of whom were only a mile from the bridge at Tadcaster, to hurry back towards Braham Hill to save Cromwell and his associates from being overwhelmed. If they and their men were put to flight, Rupert's horsemen had quite a good chance of getting amongst the infantry regiments trapped on the wrong side of the Wharfe and capturing or slaughtering the lot of them. There was even the possibility that Rupert was preparing for a set-piece battle in open country, which was just what they wanted as their forces out numbered the enemy by three to two.[9]

What was truly in Rupert's mind? The various royalist sources do not tell exactly the same tale, but there is enough compatibility to suggest very strongly that the prince wanted the type of pursuit that his deployment suggested to Cromwell, Fairfax and Leslie. However, the marquis of Newcastle's regiments of foot did not appear at first light as promised. When it became clear by mid-morning that the enemy was returning to Braham Hill in force, Rupert faced the prospect of a general encounter but does not appear to have been too concerned. It was more likely to lead to the decisive result his uncle wanted than an assault on the enemy rearguard, which could only hope at best to inflict a modicum of damage. On the other hand it was also far more risky.

According to Sir Hugh Cholmley, the marquis of Newcastle dissuaded Rupert from attacking until the northern infantry arrived.[10] Rupert was also keen not to be drawn into an engagement prematurely. Otherwise he would not have allowed a formation occupying part of Braham Hill close to Tockwith village to retreat when it came under enemy pressure.[11] When Newcastle's infantry eventually did arrive in the mid-afternoon with General King at their head, they were fewer than expected and possibly in some disorder, having spent the morning plundering the enemy entrenchments around York.[12] The writer of Rupert's diary also claimed that they were all drunk. An allied artillery bombardment of the royalist line followed, the customary softening-up stage of a battle that preceded an all-out attack, but it stopped at about 6.00 p.m. to be succeeded

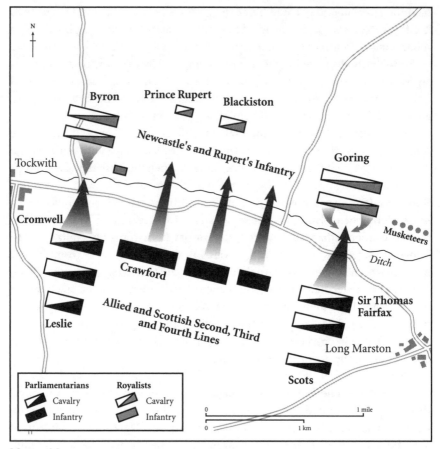

Marston Moor

by nothing more daunting than communal psalm singing. Not surprisingly, Rupert decided that he would not have to fight a battle on 2 July 1644 and allowed his troops to stand down. He sat on the ground to eat his evening meal whilst the marquis of Newcastle retired to his coach to smoke a pipe prior to settling down for the night.[13]

What was happening on Marston Moor could be seen from the top of Braham Hill.[14] The only inference the enemy generals could draw from it was that Rupert had not attacked whilst their forces were deploying because he did not think himself strong enough. They had seen Newcastle's infantry arriving during the afternoon, and must have assumed that, as the prince did not react aggressively to the bombardment, he was waiting for further reinforcements, which would arrive during the night, and that he would attack at dawn. The longer he remained inactive, given his reputation as an attacking general, the stronger this sentiment would have become, and with it apprehension as to what might follow, as they had doubts about the resilience of some of their own troops. The stops and starts of the past two days must have had a dispiriting effect and the malaise could only worsen by morning. They had left their provisions in the trenches around York and they had nothing to slake their thirst, having drunk the wells dry at Long Marston the previous night. Yet they could see the royalist troops on the moor below in confident mood lighting fires and preparing their food which had just arrived from York.[15] The obvious response to all of this was to attack before nightfall rather than wait for the following day, as there was a fair prospect of taking the enemy by surprise before thirst and the smell of cooking had the chance to eat any further into morale.

De Gomme's depiction of the deployment of the royalist armies shows Rupert's cavalry on the right wing under the command of Lord Byron and the bulk of the Northern Horse supported by East Midlands' garrison regiments on the left under George Goring. The first line of the infantry comprised the regiments of foot the prince had brought with him, with Newcastle's regiments of foot in the second and third line supported by a brigade of cavalry under Sir William Blackiston. The small reserve, entirely cavalry, consisted of the prince's and George Porter's lifeguards of horse and a small brigade of Lincolnshire horse under Sir William Widdrington.[16]

When Rupert asked General King what he thought of the way in which he had drawn up the royalist armies, King did not mince his words. The details provided by the two witnesses overlap rather than intermesh, but the gist of King's criticism was that the deployment drew on book learning, not practical experience, and that it was totally unfit for purpose.[17] The prince had managed to position his troops in such a way that the enemy held all the advantages. If he decided to attack, his troops would be advancing uphill against a much larger force, and there was no prospect of taking the enemy by surprise during daylight hours as the allied generals had a panoramic view from Braham Hill. To make matters worse the two armies were so close together that the prince could not easily disengage. Fighting could therefore start by accident. King could also have added that Rupert could not see what reserves Leven had hiding behind the hill. Moreover, the flat expanse of Marston Moor gave little advantage to the royalists should the allied armies attack. There was nothing in the landscape on which to anchor either of the flanks, and the boggy and waterlogged areas were too scattered to act as a hindrance. The only feature of any military significance was a ditch and a hedge marking the boundary between the open fields on the slope of the hill and the moor itself. These could adversely affect the enemy's ability to deploy in battle formation on the moor should they decide to attack, but neither the ditch nor the hedge formed a continuous barrier.[18]

However, Rupert did what he could. According to De Gomme's plan and one allied account of the battle, he placed infantry detachments where there was no hedge or ditch to hinder the enemy from crossing from the cultivated land onto the moor.[19] He also stationed small bodies of musketeers close to his cavalry regiments on both wings to provide supportive fire. The only other possible defensive measure was the stationing of Blackiston's cavalry brigade in the centre left slightly in advance of the third line of the infantry. In continental armies it was common practice to intersperse horse and foot in this way,[20] but as Rupert had insufficient infantry units at Marston Moor to form a complete third line, he may merely have placed Blackiston's men there to fill the gap.[21]

The final drawback for a general deploying his troops on Marston Moor was its surroundings, which made it difficult to carry out an orderly withdrawal should the battle go against him. To the rear and to the right of the royalist position were the rivers Ouse and Nidd. To the left, there was a narrow corridor of land leading in the direction of York and containing a number of small fields and crofts.[22] Normally an enclosed landscape benefited the defeated party as it made it easy for a rearguard to frustrate the pursuing cavalry. However, the enclosures did not form a continuous band across the width of the corridor and could easily be bypassed. They were therefore more likely to serve as traps than as safe havens for the infantry.

Leven's plan of attack was simple, and understandably so. First, if he tried something complicated with an army of almost 30,000 men, there was no reliable way of sending new orders to the unit or corps commanders if things started to go wrong. Second, the position on Braham Hill was a cramped one. Ideally, he would have liked a much longer frontage so that he could use his superior numbers to outflank the enemy. There was, of course, plenty of space on the moor itself, but expanding the length of the line of battle after crossing the ditch was out of the question. Rupert's front line, stuffed with formations of experienced musketeers from the army in Ireland, was very close to the edge of the cultivated land and ready to blow the vanguard away should it try something fancy. Finally, as explained above, there was a very good chance of taking the royalists by surprise whilst they were messing. In such circumstances, Leven decided that his best option was to attack at the same instant all along the line in overwhelming force.[23]

Simplicity was also the hallmark of the deployment. Leven drew up the cavalry in two lines, with the Eastern Association horse under Oliver Cromwell on the left wing close to Tockwith village and the Yorkshire and Lancashire regiments under Sir Thomas Fairfax on the right, nearest to Long Marston. A third line or reserve comprised three Scottish regiments per wing with David Leslie's men directly behind Oliver Cromwell's and Lord Eglinton's behind Sir Thomas's. There is some uncertainty as to how Leven deployed the infantry,[24] but they made up three full lines and a fourth half line of which the second and the fourth consisted entirely of Scottish regiments. The first line had two of the earl of Manchester's infantry brigades on the left. Also in the front line were two Scottish brigades and two of Lord Fairfax's. The third line comprised the remaining brigades belonging to Fairfax's and Manchester's armies and a number of Scottish regiments.[25]

Whether Leven issued any instructions as to how the battle was to be fought is not known. He did not write his own account and the narratives of the other army generals and their immediate subordinates provide no detail.[26] This is understandable. The magnitude of the victory was what their readers wanted to savour. Providing a nuanced narrative of great length was likely to cause confusion and controversy. It might also serve as a hostage to fortune by providing ammunition for critics, particularly as Leven's tactics went horribly wrong within a quarter of an hour of the start of the fighting. All that can be said with a fair degree of certainty is that the manoeuvre which was to decide the outcome of the battle was not part of the original battle plan.

One thing that is very clear is once he had deployed the allied armies Leven reverted to being general of the Covenanter army. He did not see himself as having any higher role to play in managing the battle. This is not necessarily a sign of narrow-mindedness or an inordinate regard for protocol. Once the battle was under way, it would be pot luck if any orders he sent to the other armies would reach them or reach them in time to be relevant. He must also have expected that his superiority in numbers would result in a quick victory. However, he was guilty of over-confidence. A prudent general with so large an army group should at the very least have retained a proper reserve of horse and foot under his direct command which he could commit to the fray as and when necessary. Instead his only action during the battle was to beseech the Scottish infantry not to take to their heels when they came under royalist cavalry attack. When this fell on deaf ears, he quickly followed them–to his eternal regret, according to that old gossip Sir James Turner.[27]

Of the other army generals, Manchester appears to have been with his regiment of foot in the third line, but when the third line collapsed he withdrew a mile or so from the fighting only to return in the closing stages of the battle with a hotchpotch formation of Scots he had persuaded to accompany him.[28] Nothing is known about Lord Fairfax's conduct other than that he fled from the battlefield and did not return. The fact that he did not receive a mention in the lengthy account of Marston Moor written by his political adviser, Thomas Stockdale, suggests very strongly that the part he played was too embarrassing to warrant even a bland generalisation.[29] However, he did perk up sufficiently on the following day to write to the mayor of Hull and Mr Farrar of Halifax telling them that all was well.[30]

There was little more than two hours of daylight left when the allied armies attacked.[31] Close to Tockwith village the Eastern Association horse moved without a hitch down the slope of Braham Hill into the open moorland. Lord Byron on the royalist right wing, seeing that his men were too busy eating to launch an immediate counter-attack, got together what troops he could and charged the enemy. His intention was almost certainly to create a breathing space for the rest of the royalist right wing to pick up their swords and pistols, mount their horses and get into close order. Cromwell quickly routed this scratch force,[32] but the rest of the royalist right wing assisted by the cavalry reserve led by Rupert himself halted Cromwell's charge and may indeed have begun to push the roundheads back.[33] After a melee probably lasting a quarter of an hour or so, the Scottish horse in the allied third line attacked or threatened to attack Rupert's regiments in their exposed flank, whereupon the entire royalist right wing fled from the battlefield.[34] Meanwhile the two brigades of Eastern Association infantry under Major General Lawrence Crawford, stationed immediately adjacent to their cavalry at the far left of the front line, had driven back the enemy foot facing them, probably by outflanking them and attacking from two directions. What had made this possible was the action of a royalist cavalry regiment, which had wheeled to the right to charge Cromwell's Ironsides in the flank, thus creating a gap in the enemy front line.[35]

Elsewhere, however, Rupert's plan worked. As the infantry brigades on the right of the allies' first line, primarily Lord Fairfax's men, broke through the royalist units facing them, Blackiston's brigade charged them. They broke in their turn, carrying with them some of the Scottish regiments in the second line, but the royalist cavalry did not have time to regroup before being charged and dispersed by the pikes of a regiment in the third line.[36] At about the same time or a little later, the commanded musketeers on the royalist left wing supporting Goring's Northern Horse poured devastating fire into Sir Thomas Fairfax's cavalry regiments as they tried to deploy on the moor. In almost total disarray it only needed a charge by the first line of royalist horse led by Goring in person to put them to flight.[37] The whole of the allied third line and the two regiments in the fourth then joined them, some after being ridden over by enemy horse, others without firing a shot.[38] At that stage in the battle almost half the allied army was on the run, the whole of Lord Fairfax's army, over half of the Scots, and Manchester's own regiment of foot.

In the final phase of this part of the battle the triumphant first line of the Northern Horse chased the enemy for miles across central Yorkshire, thus helping to spread the false news that Rupert had won the battle. Some troopers, however, remained to plunder the allied baggage train, but the second line of the Northern Horse under Sir Charles Lucas had learned the lesson of Edgehill and remained on the battlefield. However, they then committed another fundamental mistake by attacking the only Scottish infantry brigade in the first line that had not taken to its heels. It made sense to charge formations that looked shaky and ready to run away, but those which did not could easily see off mounted men who did not have the support of musketeers and/or artillery. Lord Lindsay and Lord Maitland's regiments duly withstood three charges, and then sent the royalist horse packing when more infantry came to their aid.[39]

Prince Rupert's first mistake had been to rule out an enemy attack taking place before night fell. His second was to ignore a basic rule of command and control. Having lost the fight on the right wing, he disappeared from the battlefield only to return to York at 11 o'clock at night when it was all over. The most likely explanation, given the prince's martial qualities and character, is that he was cut off from the rest of his army by enemy troops, and one parliamentary account, which describes him as hiding in a bean field to evade capture, may not be far from the truth.[40] However, Sir Thomas Fairfax, who was in exactly the same circumstances on the allied right wing, managed to make his way through the enemy to the other, victorious wing. If Rupert had done the same, he might have been able to put together a coherent defence against the enemy counterattack which was to decide the battle. This was the substance of Lord Byron's devastating criticism.[41] There had occurred 'such gross errors as I have not patience to describe'. Although the enemy had 10,000 more men in the field than the royalists, it was:

> our own wilfulness and rashness that overthrew us. Notwithstanding all the advantages we gave them, which were as great as ever were in any battle, the victory was so doubtful that, had the prince but stayed in the field to own it, the day had been ours the rout being much greater on their side than ours.[42]

Rupert had not been wrong in taking personal charge of the attempt to prop up the tottering right wing. In terms of military doctrine then current an army general would not be doing his job if he did not put himself at the head of a move to avert certain defeat. On the other hand he ought to have appointed somebody else to take over the running of the battle should he be killed or become incommunicado. This he had not done. The marquis of Newcastle had retired for the night after being reassured by Rupert that he would not be needed until morning.[43] Once he realised that a battle was under way, Newcastle bestirred himself, but his heroic actions as described by his wife were those of a captain of horse, not an army general.[44]

There was nobody else of sufficient seniority in a position to step into the breach. Of the seconds-in-command, Goring, like Rupert, having won his personal victory on the left wing, disappeared for the duration of the battle, whilst General King had his hands full with the infantry.[45] Sir John Urry, a general but lower down the hierarchy of command, apparently had the chance to attack the enemy in the final stage of the battle using some of Goring's cavalry, but he refused to do so on the grounds that they were no longer in close order and would therefore be ineffective.[46] Others, however, came to the conclusion that Urry had an ulterior motive, especially when he changed sides two months later,[47] and it cannot be denied that a body of 2,000 or so horse, however disorganised, charging into the fray from an unexpected direction in the gathering

gloom would have caused confusion, if nothing worse, amongst allied formations busy slaughtering royalist pikemen and musketeers. However, when all is
said and done, Byron's criticism sticks. Rupert's failure to make provision for his
replacement largely explains why the royalist armies were unable to make an
appropriate response to the remarkable recovery the enemy made from the
devastating blows delivered by Blackiston and Goring.

That such a recovery was possible on the allied side, despite the fact that all
three army generals had fled, was because some of their subordinates took
control of the battlefield, David Leslie and Lawrence Crawford certainly, Oliver
Cromwell probably, and Sir Thomas Fairfax possibly.[48] Instead of pursuing the
enemy right wing as it fled from the battlefield, or conducting a fighting retreat
towards the bridge over the Wharfe at Tadcaster (which would have enabled
them to link up with Meldrum's brigades), they devised a new battle plan, by
which the horse, foot and dragoons in the Tockwith part of Marston Moor were
to wheel to the right and mop up what was left of the enemy army.[49] Together
they dealt with the remaining royalist brigades one by one until by nightfall
there was not a single formation left standing. The principal royalist formation
still intact when the manoeuvre began, the core of the marquis of Newcastle's
infantry, the so-called Whitecoats, fought very hard. They refused to surrender
when they ran out of gunpowder and died where they stood.[50] This, together
with the fact that the full moon enabled the allied cavalry to pursue the enemy
to within a mile of York, explains the very high ratio of slain to those taken prisoner at Marston Moor in comparison with all the other major battles fought in
England and Scotland between 1642 and 1651.[51]

As for the royalist cavalry on the left wing, some, almost certainly what was
left of Sir Charles Lucas's men, fell victim to Cromwell's and Leslie's cavalry as
darkness fell.[52] The rest remained on the edge of the battlefield amongst the
wreckage of the enemy baggage train until midnight or later when they received
orders to return to York.[53] Several thousand strong, they formed the nucleus of
the force that Prince Rupert led back into Lancashire the following day, whilst
the marquis of Newcastle, General King and their closest associates left for the
Continent, claiming they could do no more for the royalist cause. Rupert's
suggestion that they should begin recruiting again in parts of west and south
Yorkshire, where there were still royalist garrisons, fell on deaf ears.[54] Rupert
himself probably thought that by keeping the royalist cause alive in the north, he
and the marquis of Newcastle would be able to relieve the pressure on his uncle
by limiting the allied generals' ability to send troops into the Thames valley
theatre of war. However, he need not have worried. Lack of vision and the
conflicting aims of the victorious allies meant that none of their troops arrived
in the south until mid-September.

The allied generals began well by resuming the siege of York, which surrendered a fortnight later, but then they informed the Committee of Both Kingdoms

that it would be best if the armies went their different ways, with the Scots focusing on the siege of Newcastle, Lord Fairfax on eliminating the remaining royalist garrisons in Yorkshire, and the earl of Manchester on keeping an eye on Prince Rupert. The only justification, and quite a weak one at that, was that the Army of the Covenant and Fairfax's army needed time to recover their composure and to recruit after what had come very close to being a pyrrhic victory. The Committee lamely gave its consent but what followed was an immediate loss of strategic momentum, which was not helped by what was happening in the south. By the beginning of August the king's generals were in the driving seat yet again.

CHAPTER 10

The Generals in Jeopardy

CROPREDY BRIDGE AND LOSTWITHIEL

IF THE prospect of the speedy surrender of the royalist western army at Devizes in early July 1643 formed the first high point of Sir William Waller's career as an army general, the assemblage of a vast host at Stourbridge twenty miles to the north of Worcester on 14 June 1644 was the second. His army, supplemented by that of the earl of Denbigh, drawn out of the Midlands' garrisons from Coventry in the east to Wem in the west, and by several regiments from Cheshire, was in an enviable position. With only 3,000 infantry made up entirely of musketeers, Charles had no chance of defeating him in battle, whereas if he tried to outflank him by crossing the Severn at Bridgnorth or Shrewsbury, Sir William would get there first because of the superior road network on the north side of the river. All Waller needed to do to force the flying army into the hill country of south Shropshire, and thus farther than ever from Oxford and the armies of Prince Rupert and Prince Maurice, was to cross to the west bank, an operation he earmarked for the 16th or the 17th,[1] but for once in his long career of wrong-footing the enemy, Sir William himself was to be wrong-footed.

Seeing that there was no chance of breaking through Waller's troop concentration, and knowing that remaining where they were was only feasible in the short term, the king's military committee had no option other than to try and return to Oxford. The flying army crossed the Severn at Worcester at noon on 16 June and marched rapidly via Evesham into the Cotswolds. Two days later it met the Oxford brigades at Witney.[2] Charles's enemies estimated that the Oxford army was now 8,000–12,000 strong, his friends that it comprised 6,000 foot and 4,000–5,000 horse or 5,500 foot and 4,000 horse.[3]

Waller was very slow to respond. Even though he knew that the king's musketeers had gone downriver by barge from Bewdley on 15 June, he underestimated the royalist generals, despite the earl of Essex having carried out a very similar manoeuvre not so far away at the start of the Newbury campaign. In a letter to the Committee of Both Kingdoms, Sir William claimed he had thought the voyage to Worcester was a feint, as his scouts reported that most of the enemy horse were still in the Bewdley area. As a result, when the flying army suddenly set out for the Cotswolds, his infantry were not ready to march. He could only follow with cavalry and dragoons, but by the time they reached Evesham they were beginning to flag. As the enemy still had a lead of twenty miles,[4] he gave up the chase; this implies that if he had driven his troops any harder they would have been in no condition to fight when they caught up with them.

However, Waller should at least have taken precautions. Given the size of his army he could easily have stationed a force of cavalry and dragoons at one of the passes on the road between Worcester and Evesham road to delay the progress of the flying army. This may well have been an effective deterrent, as the king's Council of War spent the evening of 15 June arguing over whether or not to risk leaving the comparative safety of the Severn valley and heading for the hills.[5] The final decision was the king's, but the march could not have gone as smoothly as it did without some excellent staff work. Sadly, neither Lord Digby in the letter he wrote to Prince Rupert describing the escape,[6] nor Sir Edward Walker in his narrative of the 1644 campaign, tells us who was responsible, but the failure to give credit to anybody hints that it was probably Lord Wilmot whose dismissal, long planned, was only a few weeks away.

Waller's letters to the Committee of Both Kingdoms reporting the king's escape contain little in the way of apology. After all, he had achieved his principal short-term objective of stopping the king joining Prince Rupert. Although he would welcome fresh advice or new instructions, for the moment he proposed to lead his troops into the south-west of England, which was where Parliament had intended him to operate. To that end he marched them from Evesham to the outskirts of Gloucester, which he reached on 20 June, but without his West Midlands and Cheshire auxiliaries. Their orders were to move north to close the ring around Prince Rupert.[7]

The Committee had second thoughts about the direction of Waller's march when the royalist army took up quarters in north Buckinghamshire rather than resting awhile at Oxford. This raised a number of alarming prospects. The enemy might be about to invade the Eastern Association, to march towards Prince Rupert by way of Newark, or to threaten London. Waller was therefore to place his army in such a position as to cut communications between the royalists and Oxford. At the same time the Committee made reassuring noises in letters it sent to the earl of Manchester and to the Committee of the Eastern Association. Colonel Richard Browne was assembling a large force to the north of London made up of trained band regiments from the capital and the Home Counties. Its orders were to join Waller.[8] There was no need for the earl of Manchester's army to quit the siege of York and march south to save the Association.

Promises about Browne Force may have been unduly optimistic, but on the other side of the fence all was confusion. The king's military advisers were bitterly divided. Wilmot spoke vehemently in favour of marching towards London, but the king was suspicious and refused to make any decision before he had heard from the Privy Council at Oxford. By the time their pessimistic report on the state of the city's defences arrived, the argument for waiting on events had become irrefutable. Waller was approaching fast.[9] Whatever the next operation was to be, its chances of success would be all the greater if he could be defeated first.

At the end of June the two armies were manoeuvring for position in the Upper Cherwell valley to the north of the royalist stronghold of Banbury. On 29 June Waller deployed his army in battle formation at Hanwell on the eastern slope of the Edgehill plateau, but the royalist high command refused to take the bait.[10] Instead the Oxford army set off northwards on the Northamptonshire side of the Cherwell heading for Daventry. Sir William shadowed it, taking a road that ran along the other side of the valley. The van and centre of the royalist army under the king and Lord Forth put on speed in the hope of surprising some troops of horse understood to be crossing its line of march. However, they did not bother to inform the rearguard, a body of 1,000 commanded foot under Colonel Anthony Thelwall supported by the cavalry brigades of the earl of Northampton and the earl of Cleveland. As a result, a gap opened up between the rearguard and the rest of the army, and Waller seized the chance of cutting it off and destroying it in one of those sudden attacks for which he was renowned.

Sir William sent two parties across the Cherwell, one at Great Bourton to attack the rearguard and prevent it returning to Banbury, and the other a mile to the north at Cropredy to stop the main body coming to its rescue.[11] However, according to Lieutenant Colonel Birch, Sir William chose the wrong troops for the job. Instead of employing his own rearguard, made up of his best musketeers supported by horse, he gave the first task to cavalry alone, which did not have the requisite firepower. Lieutenant General John Middleton had the more difficult task of fighting off the royalist centre. Under his command were the rest of the cavalry supported by a mixed bag of weak infantry regiments and most of the artillery pieces. In reserve were the Tower Hamlets regiment which should have been in the van.[12] The rest of Waller's army remained on the far side of the Cherwell, but their chance of intervening quickly in the event of a setback was negligible because of the narrowness of the bridge at Cropredy.[13]

Waller also completely misjudged the speed with which the royalists would react. Thelwall, assisted by Northampton's brigade, brushed off the attack on the rearguard. Nevertheless, the parliamentary horse managed to fall back in good order across the Cherwell and Northampton's men did not pursue them. Middleton's attack initially made better progress but in the end it was brought to a halt by a charge from Cleveland's brigade. Middleton's cavalry reserves then intervened, only to be blown away by horse from the main body of the royalist army. In their headlong dash for safety, they did not give a thought to their support troops. As a result the royalists captured or killed several hundred foot and took eight artillery pieces. Waller's General of Artillery James Wemyss also fell into their hands.[14] When brought before the king, he had the cheek to claim that 'his heart had always been with His Majesty'. It did not help him. He spent the rest of the war as a prisoner in Ludlow Castle.

The Tower Hamlets regiment prevented further disaster. Taking up a position covering the approach to Cropredy bridge, it put up a strong barrage of covering fire, which stopped the royalists in their tracks and permitted what was left of the support group to reach safety. Sir William then ordered his badly shaken assault force to fall back on the rest of his infantry drawn up on Bourton Hill. For twenty-four hours the two sides watched each other. Waller did not try and re-cross the Cherwell whilst the strength of his position deterred the king's commanders from going into attack mode. At nightfall on 30 June the royalists marched back towards Banbury.[15] Soon afterwards they set off westwards worried by the approach of Colonel Browne whose 3,000 foot would make Waller's army too large to face in a set-piece battle. The king and his advisers were also waiting for news of Prince Rupert's confrontation with the allied armies before deciding what to do next. Until then the Avon valley was a good place to rest their troops. If Waller gave chase they could easily avoid an encounter by crossing the Severn as they had done a month earlier.[16]

It took three days for news of the latest move of the king's army to reach Waller. In the meantime he took precautions to prevent it resuming its northwards march by moving his army to Towcester where it rendezvoused with Browne's brigade on 2 July. Realising by then that the Oxford army was heading back towards the Severn valley, Waller focused on sweeping the countryside clean of horses so that he could mount his musketeers. This would take some days to accomplish, but his men would benefit from the rest and recuperation.[17]

Cropredy Bridge was no more than a spoiling operation which failed to develop into a full-scale battle, but for Waller the results were to be dire. After chasing the king all over the Midlands in the summer heat he was worried about how much longer he could keep his troops motivated,[18] and the campaign duly ground to a halt with the arrival of Browne's brigade. This, the London trained bands regiments decided, was their relief. Several hundred men deserted their colours immediately, and within two days most of the remainder left for home in a column of march providing, they claimed, a fitting escort for the bodies of two of their officers who had died of disease.[19] The rest only put off their departure on the brigade commander's promise that their tour of duty would last no longer than three weeks. Browne's regiments were also 'in no good temper, some of his Essex men threatening already to quit and the Hertfordshire men expressing their impatient suffering during a night or two's ill quartering'. Soon afterwards they mutinied, probably on hearing that they were to join the chase, and when Browne remonstrated with them they struck him in the face. In Sir William's view the whole lot of them were 'only fit for a gallows here and a Hell hereafter'.[20]

In a letter written on 2 July to the Committee of Both Kingdoms, Waller was adamant:

> an army composed of these men will never go through with your service, and till you have an army merely your own, that you may command, it is in a manner impossible to do anything of importance.[21]

Generations of writers have seen this remark as the first hint of a new type of army, the New Model, which would enable a new commander-in-chief, Sir Thomas Fairfax, to win the First Civil War.[22] By implication it was also evidence of Waller's foresight and his incisive military thinking, a mark of good general-ship. However, his words were not prophetic. They were not even relevant to the issue of remodelling the militia. Waller had not proposed an army far larger than any yet put into the field, officered by men approved by Parliament, regu-larly paid and totally committed to winning the war. Instead he was expressing his exasperation at the behaviour of the London trained bands, which were a loose cannon because they were under the command of the City Militia Committee, not Parliament and the Committee of Both Kingdoms. Waller's remark was no more than that, but it was heartfelt nevertheless, based on bitter experience of being let down at critical moments, as at Basing House in November 1643, in April 1644 after the battle of Cheriton,[23] and again in July. Other problems were to give rise to the idea of a New Model, namely the shrinkage in size of all the field armies and the inability of the first- and second-generation generals to win an outright victory.

After the losses at Cropredy Bridge and the disintegration of the City brigade, Waller's infantry strength was now only half that of the enemy. He could there-fore no longer follow the Oxford army confident that he could defeat it in battle if the opportunity arose. Moreover, Browne's men had let him down even more emphatically than the London trained bands. They had their own priorities. Now the king's army was no longer a threat to the Eastern Association or to the capital, they made for Greenland House near Henley-on-Thames, which threat-ened the barge traffic in foodstuffs between Reading and the capital. From mid-July onwards troops of cavalry were also beginning to disobey orders or to abscond, and others were recalled by their county committees. Waller therefore headed for Abingdon, his only conquest in the campaign, where he quartered his remaining infantry.[24] He pointedly ignored several orders to march into the west, but did not receive a reprimand for his actions.[25] Presumably when he attended the Committee of Both Kingdoms in person on 27 July he was able to convince it that his army would be annihilated if it followed the Oxford army too closely,[26] but to keep its good will he promised to send his horse and dragoons westwards in due course to help secure those parts of Dorset and Somerset conquered by the earl of Essex. With the lord general's army now in Devonshire, the two counties were potentially at risk from the royalist garrisons at Bath, Bristol and Bridgwater.

Sir William's last letter to the Committee before leaving for what was to be a long stay in London ended with his oft-repeated refrain. If it chose to employ him again as army general, 'I desire I may have a commission only subordinate to both Houses and the Committee of Both Kingdoms'.[27] But he was not the only general to resent being under the command of other generals. The boot was on the other foot when Richard Browne reminded the Committee that he was not at Waller's beck and call. He had a commission as major general of three counties from the earl of Essex and therefore was not subject to orders from anybody other than the lord general, the Committee and Parliament.[28]

The Oxford army remained in the Vale of Evesham for over a week before Prince Rupert's dispatch arrived, announcing that he had suffered a defeat (at Marston Moor), but the key message was almost certainly an optimistic one.[29] He had saved much of his own army; two of the three enemy armies were in disarray, having been routed in the first hour of the battle; York was still holding out; and he had returned to Lancashire to recruit after which he would march once more to its relief. This was important intelligence for the king and his military committee as it confirmed their view that nothing was to be gained by marching north. At the same time Waller's problems since Cropredy Bridge, of which they were well aware, convinced them that his army was incapable of setting siege to Oxford and could therefore be ignored. The best strategy was therefore to march into the south-west of England and fight the earl of Essex, hopefully in tandem with Prince Maurice. It also helped quieten the king's worries about the queen.[30] If Exeter surrendered and she fell into enemy hands, Charles would have to sue for peace to save her life, as Parliament had declared her guilty of high treason for bringing arms and ammunition into England.[31] The Oxford army therefore set out for Exeter on 11 July. Marching via Bath and Ilchester, it reached the Devonshire border less than two weeks later.[32]

The earl of Essex in the meantime had done very little. After relieving Lyme he had rested his army for a few days at Chard instead of pursuing Prince Maurice or setting siege to Exeter. He had then marched it to Tiverton, fifteen miles to the north of the city, where it remained for a further fortnight.[33] However, two easy parliamentary successes followed. When the prince withdrew the garrison from Barnstaple to strengthen his army, the townspeople declared for Parliament, whilst the small garrison in Taunton Castle surrendered a week earlier at the approach of a body of troops from Chard.[34]

Prince Maurice took advantage of the earl's inactivity to escort the queen from Exeter to the borders of Cornwall, where he remained until he was certain she had set sail for France. He then returned eastwards, his army strengthened by Cornish troops from the blockade of Plymouth, but he had no intention of engaging Essex in battle. Instead his destination was Exeter, whose defences were immeasurably stronger than they had been in the earl of Stamford's time.[35] Maurice does not seem to have been aware that his uncle and the main field army were on a converging course,[36] but Essex knew that it had recently arrived at Bath. Whilst at Tiverton, the earl's Council of War discussed whether to continue with the conquest of Devonshire or to return east in order to confront Lord Forth. It decided on the former course of action, satisfied that Waller could deal with, or at least distract, the Oxford army without their army needing to become involved.[37]

Essex had received no more than a slap on the wrist for turning the strategical orders of the Committee of Both Kingdoms upside down. Having had their say, his political masters seem to have decided to let him get on with the job of reconquering the south-west. Whilst he informed the Committee of his operational decisions and the reasons for them, they focused on supplying him with money to pay his troops and purchase necessities such as ammunition.[38] However, Parliament ignored Essex's request to encourage leading members of the gentry, who had fled to London in 1643, to return to the West Country and begin putting in place the administrative apparatus needed to supply his troops with provisions and to nurture newly raised regiments.[39] Even if the two Houses had listened, it is doubtful that a new structure could have been put together before the Oxford army arrived, but the consequences soon became apparent. Essex's troops seized meat on the hoof and other foodstuffs for man and beast, thus alienating the Devonians.[40] Lack of resources also affected recruiting. Colonel Robert Bennett regretfully disbanded the troops he had raised in the Barnstaple area because of lack of money to pay them.[41]

On 19 July the parliamentary army left Tiverton and headed towards the Tamar valley. Essex's objective was to raise the morale of the Plymouth garrison. It had been under blockade for over a year and was demoralised by lack of pay for its officers and men and shortage of fodder for its cavalry horses.[42] Hopes of defeating Prince Maurice in battle or driving him and his forces into the furthest reaches of Cornwall must also have entered Essex's mind, but they were quickly overtaken by events. Maurice's army had set out for Exeter from Okehampton a few days earlier, and the two armies were on a collision course. However, the prince had the better intelligence, and by neatly sidestepping the oncoming enemy he managed to put the River Exe between himself and them, a sensible precaution should Essex change his mind and decide to come after him. The lord general, however, continued remorselessly towards Plymouth and the royalist army of the west reached safety virtually without loss.[43] Not long afterwards Maurice learned that salvation was at hand. The Oxford army had arrived at Honiton only thirteen miles away.

The parliamentary army stopped at Tavistock close to the Tamar valley, made contact with the garrison of Plymouth and drove the blockading force commanded by Sir Richard Grenville back into Cornwall. The king's military advisers expected Essex to return eastward and set siege to Dartmouth, but he continued his westward course.[44] Lord Robartes, one of the leading Cornish landowners, who also happened to be a major general in Essex's army, had convinced the Council of War that there was extensive support for Parliament in the county.[45] He may also have suggested that the flow of arms and ammunition from the Continent on which the royalist war effort depended could be severely disrupted or brought to a halt by seizing the king's revenue from tin mining, as this was how the trade was being financed.[46]

After withdrawing horse and foot from the Plymouth garrison, Essex's army marched to Bodmin, the county town, whose market was allegedly a place to obtain provisions in prodigious quantities. On the way there it drove Grenville's men out of the ports of Saltash and Fowey. The rumour was that they had fled as far west as Pendennis and St Michael's Mount, but they stopped at Truro where a letter from the king encouraged Sir Richard to raise the county against the invaders, as he and Prince Maurice were on Essex's tail and determined to destroy the enemy. This was true. Leaving Exeter on 27 July, the Oxford army and the army of the west were at Launceston by 1 August and at Liskeard two days later.

The earl of Essex knew little about the movements of the enemy other than that they were approaching fast. His letters to the Committee of Both Kingdoms written on 30 July and 4 August were full of gloom. The abundance of victuals promised by those who had pushed hardest for the invasion of Cornwall had not materialised; three armies were advancing towards him from the east and another from the west; and where were the friendly forces that he understood Parliament had ordered to pursue the king? However, he and his men would do their utmost 'though we perish in the attempt', but they put their trust 'in God's blessing, the courage of our officers and soldiers, and our faithfulness to the cause'.[47]

To improve his chances Essex fell back from Bodmin to Lostwithiel, a town close to the south coast of the county and situated on the Fowey river, a creek navigable to ships of a reasonable size. He could thus keep contact with the earl of Warwick's fleet, which had just dropped anchor off Plymouth. As for land-based assistance, the best Parliament and the Committee could do in the short run was order Waller's cavalry and dragoons to impede royalist operations by disrupting food convoys heading for Cornwall.[48]

Not surprisingly, the London journals were soon warning their readers that Essex was caught in a trap and in need of divine assistance,[49] but the situation in which he found himself was desperate rather than hopeless. First, he could not be forced to fight a battle against his will. The valley of the River Fowey, with its small fields, narrow lanes, steep slopes and numerous creeks, favoured an army determined to remain on the defensive. As at Newbury, he ought to be able to inflict very heavy casualties on the enemy at minimum cost if they were foolish enough to attack him.[50] Second, the close proximity of Warwick's fleet meant that he should be able to receive supplies of ammunition, food and fodder by sea.[51] The royalist commanders, on the other hand, dependent for provisions on a countryside already picked clean by his troops, would see their strength wither away as hunger began to bite. Third, should the Lostwithiel position become untenable for any reason, there was a good chance that he could save most, if not all, of his army. He controlled the ports of Fowey and Parr on St Austell bay through which he could evacuate his infantry. As for his horse, the fifteen-mile perimeter of the defended area[52] was too long for the royalists to be strong everywhere. They should therefore find it possible to make a breakout with a fair prospect of reaching Plymouth before the enemy caught them up.

For a time Essex's prospects of avoiding a military disaster improved. Charles has traditionally been portrayed as managing the complex military operations described as the battle of Lostwithiel with considerable ability and commendable enterprise,[53] but the origin of this narrative lies in Clarendon's account, which is heavily reliant on *Historical Discourses*, the propaganda effort written by Sir Edward Walker and corrected by the king, which portrayed Charles as wise sovereign, compassionate ruler and competent military commander all rolled into one.[54] However, although the king may have competently managed the last day or so of the four-week operation, the rest was a bit of a shambles.

First, a serious attempt to evict the enemy from Lostwithiel and its environs ought to have started in early August. Instead, it did not begin until almost the end of the month, by which time shortage of food and absenteeism were having a significant effect on the numbers of troops that the king's generals had available for action. However, the only military move of the first fortnight was a very positive one, the occupation of the whole of the east bank of the Fowey river. This meant that Fowey was no longer of any military value to Essex, but it did not prevent essential supplies reaching the parliamentary army via Parr and two small coves between there and Fowey.[55]

The reasons for the delay were purely political. The king and his advisers hoped that the treatment Essex and his army had received from their political masters from the spring of 1643 onwards would cause them to respond favourably to the idea of the two armies making a joint approach to Parliament in favour of a negotiated peace which, if rejected, would be followed by a joint advance on London. However, honeyed words from the king conveyed to Essex by Essex's favourite nephew Lord Beauchamp met with a stony response. He would have none of it,[56] knowing full well that his enemies at Westminster would pounce on the slightest sign that he had exceeded the powers granted to him by his commission and begin a new round of demands for his dismissal.[57]

The rest from active campaigning also gave the king the chance to remove Wilmot from his command. He was arrested on 8 August, and immediately replaced as lieutenant general by George Goring who had just arrived from the north trailing clouds of glory after his personal triumph at Marston Moor.[58] Prince Rupert feared that Goring would rubbish his conduct of the battle in order to replace him as the king's chief military adviser. The letter to his friend, the duke of Richmond in which he opened his heart does not survive, but Richmond wrote back to reassure him, and soon afterwards Lord Digby informed him that the king would commission him as lord general as soon as a way could be found of removing the earl of Forth without reflecting on his honour.[59] However, Forth was probably already on gardening leave. Although he got close enough to the fighting to be wounded at the Second Battle of Newbury, it was Prince Maurice and Goring who played the active role in the various engagements fought by the Oxford army from early August onwards.

With politics out of the way, military operations could begin, but the king's generals had lost three weeks of the campaigning season.[60] The softening-up process began on 21 August. Over the next few days the royalist artillery pieces bombarded the parliamentary enclave but to little effect. Pressure on Essex's defensive perimeter began on 26–27 August with the capture of Parr but, although the royalist forces evicted the enemy from some tactically important pieces of high ground around Lostwithiel, Essex's army maintained its grip on the town itself and the corridor of land that led down the west side of the river to Fowey and to the coves beyond where small boats could still unload military supplies on the beaches.[61] On 31 August the royalists launched a series of massive attacks on the Lostwithiel to Fowey road. After two days of fighting, the morale of some of Essex's infantry regiments collapsed, the road was cut, and with it went the last, faint hope of evacuation by sea. However, on the night of the 30th Sir William Balfour managed to lead almost the whole of Essex's cavalry to safety by storming through a gap between Prince Maurice's and the king's armies. The darkness and the misty conditions made the task of interception difficult, but the king and his military advisers knew that a breakout was only hours away when a deserter spilled the beans just as it was beginning to get dark. The royalist commanders therefore had time to set up an ambush on the cavalry's intended route to Liskeard, but all they did was quarter fifty musketeers in a house nearby,[62] and these men let the enemy pass without firing a shot. Joseph Jane was surely right to accuse Charles's generals of 'sloth and improvidence'.[63]

The only other senior officers to escape from what was now truly a trap were the lord general and a couple of his senior commanders, Lord Robartes and Sir John Merrick. They set sail for Plymouth in a fishing boat on 2 September, leaving Major General Philip Skippon in charge. Skippon summoned a Council of War and suggested that the infantry should also attempt a breakout, but it was bravado speaking. The chances of success without cavalry support were zero and the officers were right to reject the idea. The only alternative was negotiation and within twenty-four hours the deed was done. The foot were to march to Southampton under armed escort without having to give their word that they would never fight against the king again. However, they left all their weapons and military supplies in royalist hands apart from officers' hand arms. The king also gratefully took possession of Essex's train of artillery.[64] The king's magnanimity was not just a public relations exercise or an attempt to persuade the rank and file to change sides. Behind it lay a major practical consideration. By early September the supply situation had become critical.[65] He could scarcely feed his own troops, and on political and humanitarian grounds he could not keep 6,000–7,000 men captive and allow them to die of starvation.

On the day that Skippon surrendered, the lord general wrote to Parliament describing all that had happened to him and his army since their arrival in Cornwall. Essex was full of righteous indignation against those who had watched his army fall into a trap and then failed to do anything to help him escape. He was happy to attend an inquiry at which he would reveal all: 'how our poor army was neglected . . . shall be known to the world . . . this business shall not sleep if it be in my power'. The most telling sections, however, were those in which he praised the endurance, the courage and the loyalty of his troops, and reminded his political masters that, as their orders were for him to reconquer the south-west, a big enough military rumpus should have been created in south-central England to deter the Oxford army from pursuing him.[66] The underlying messages are clear. The first comment mocked Sir William Waller's inability to inspire his troops, the second attempted to shift the blame for the surrender onto others who had let him down either deliberately or through operational incompetence.

But had Essex and his army been left swinging in the wind by their political masters in revenge for his past deeds? Denzil Holles stated as much and Bulstrode Whitelock dropped hints, but the evidence is circumstantial, and Waller's allegation in his memoirs that he was used by others to get at Essex could apply as easily to the early summer of 1643 as to the late summer of 1644. In addition, it is difficult to see Essex's opponents daring to go so far as to sacrifice his army to further their political ends or as retribution for his highhanded behaviour earlier in the year.[67] Moreover, the reaction of Parliament to the surrender at Lostwithiel would have been very different if either had been the case. When Essex arrived in south Hampshire to meet his infantry he was greeted with a message from the speakers of both Houses of Parliament. Instead of denouncing the way in which he had led the expedition into the south-west from beginning to end or from Tiverton onwards, they absolved him from blame. They also agreed to rearm and reclothe his men as quickly as possible and to supply him with a new train of artillery so that he could take the field again before the end of the campaigning season.[68]

In addition, the behaviour of Parliament and the Committee of Both Kingdoms in July and August 1644 does not suggest evil intent towards the lord general. They did what they could to support Essex's army whilst it was in Devon and Cornwall, sending him money to pay his troops, and also military supplies such as ammunition, though there were delays caused by matters over which they had no control. Adverse winds, for example, prevented the earl of Warwick's ships passing freely backwards and forwards between Plymouth and Fowey and Parr for much of August.[69] It was also not the Committee's fault that the intelligence they sent Essex after he left Tiverton concerning the movements of the Oxford army was woefully out of date.[70] But what the men at Westminster did not do was keep Essex fully informed about the progress of the war elsewhere, which should then have had a powerful influence on his decision-making. The Committee of Both Kingdoms, for example, did not write to him about Cropredy Bridge or the difficulties Waller and Browne were experiencing in keeping their forces together. However, it did tell Essex that the strength of Waller's army had fallen to fewer than 4,000 men in a letter dated 16 July, and this almost certainly reached him before he invaded Cornwall.[71] This should have been a strong enough warning to be wary. With so few men under his command Sir William was most unlikely to be able to deter the Oxford army from marching westwards.

However, the most remarkable aspect of the whole affair was the loyalty that Essex's officers and men showed towards their general. The expectation on both sides was that the infantry would desert in droves during the gruelling march to Southampton, but a hard core of 3,000 or so reached south Hampshire.[72] Moreover, when Essex's enemies were looking for damning evidence about his handling of operations in Devon and Cornwall, most particularly how he reacted to the king's peace feelers, only Colonel John Weare was willing to oblige, but the poor performance of Weare's troops told against him, as did the evidence that he had deserted, albeit temporarily, to the enemy.[73] Thus the care the lord general had shown towards his men, and the frequent letters he had written to his political masters on their behalf throughout his lord generalship, gained their due reward. His enemies at Westminster had probably hoped to bring him down over the Cornish business, but they could pin nothing on him.[74] Instead their sights shifted to the earl of Manchester.

CHAPTER 11

The March to Newbury

SAVING THE SOUTH

THE MAELSTROM that engulfed the earl of Manchester in the autumn and winter of 1644 far surpassed earlier attacks on the earl of Essex. The occasion was the remarkable decline in the military effectiveness of the army of the Eastern Association. At Marston Moor on 2 July it had turned near certain defeat into total victory, but it proved utterly incapable of winning the war in the south. The stock explanation is that Manchester lost the will to fight, but this is questionable at the very least and may be totally erroneous. The circumstances surrounding the malaise that affected the army are complicated and Manchester's role in it can be read in various ways.

On taking up his command in August 1643, Manchester had put his muscle behind the moral crusade for a godly army first articulated by Lord Brooke.[1] Godly officers were common elsewhere in Parliament's armies, but by the start of the spring campaign Manchester's army had become widely recognised as possessing ideological commitment in its purest form. Yet that very purity was soon to become a weakness, as Independent officers, who wanted some form of toleration for a wide swath of Protestant religious opinion after the war had ended, clashed with Presbyterians, who wanted complete uniformity in religious doctrine and practice enforced by the state. It mirrored in a more acute form the divisions in Parliament over the post-war settlement of religion, and it can be argued that, as with lack of resources on the king's side, this was the factor which would have ensured that the longer the war lasted the less likely were Parliament's generals to win it outright. However, although religious differences fuelled intrigues to remove one officer and to promote another between Marston Moor and the surrender of Essex's army at Lostwithiel, with serious fighting in the offing the two factions, the Independents led by Lieutenant General Oliver Cromwell and the Presbyterians by Major General Lawrence Crawford, agreed to bury their differences,[2] and in the campaign that followed there is not a single clear instance of opportunities being lost because of tensions and rivalries within the officer corps.

Another possible reason for the declining military effectiveness of the army of the Eastern Association was an inequitable distribution of resources. Manchester may have seen this as a way of bringing the factions into line, but the only suggestion that he favoured one part of his army at the expense of another is in letters written by Cromwell, Henry Ireton, Manchester's commissary general, and John Crewe, a member of the Committee of Both Kingdoms.[3] They all date from an eleven-day period in early September, and Cromwell's letter, typically, can be read in a number of different ways.[4] A more persuasive argument is that the effectiveness of the army as a whole declined in the second half of 1644 because the Eastern Association no longer had sufficient resources to go around. Diminishing returns, most especially in military manpower, was something to be expected over time, but Parliament placed extra burdens on the Association during its army's absence in the north. Most particularly, it was funding a second army charged with defending London and the Home Counties, Browne Force, and it also took over some responsibility for garrisoning Abingdon from late July onwards. As a result when Manchester's army arrived back in the Association in September there were few recruits left.[5]

Turning now to the sea change in Manchester's attitude towards the war, the most charitable explanation is that he encountered the bloody side of warfare at close quarters for the first time on the battlefield of Marston Moor and suffered traumatic shock which influenced his behaviour for the rest of the campaign.[6] However, the evidence is weak: the Scot Robert Baillie's description of the earl as a 'mild, meek man', and what Simeon Ashe, the earl's chaplain, had to say about his own reaction to the bloodshed in a pamphlet written in Manchester's defence months later.[7]

The most widely held explanation of Manchester's behaviour is political rather than psychological, namely that for him the victory at Marston Moor had been too decisive. The earl had always favoured a peace treaty between the royalists and the parliamentarians, and had fought strenuously during the first two years of the war to prevent the king winning an outright victory.[8] Marston Moor, however, tipped the balance too far in the opposite direction. The greatest danger now was that Parliament would win outright, and he therefore decided to do something about restoring the equilibrium. For the rest of the year, using a variety of excuses and stratagems, he tried to avoid coming into contact with the enemy and held his troops back when fighting became inevitable.[9] Behind closed doors his enemies had no hesitation in describing such behaviour as treasonable,[10] but evidence of a deliberate campaign on Manchester's part to avoid a climactic victory is very largely circumstantial or else just plain wrong.[11]

Alternatively, the earl was the victim of a most successful spin campaign intended to protect Oliver Cromwell's military reputation by concealing his poor record in the second half of 1644. From the morning after Marston Moor, when he failed to harry the remnant of Prince Rupert's army as it retreated across the Pennines into Lancashire to the end of the Newbury campaign four and a half months later, Cromwell and his cavalry had done nothing of significance, and this was not because he was following the earl of Manchester's orders to be easy on the enemy. In such circumstances the best response for the Cromwellians in the army was to opt for attack as the best form of defence and fix the blame on somebody else, namely their commanding officer, who had lost their confidence.[12] Previously, Cromwell and his friends had got all they had wanted from their army general. Now such unequivocal support could no longer be relied upon, but not only was Manchester trying to be even-handed in dealing with factional strife within his army, he was also no longer 'one of us', having put his name to a letter to the Committee of Both Kingdoms, written immediately after the capture of York, which put pressure on Parliament to institute State Presbyterianism in England.[13] In the autumn, the countess of Manchester tried to dissuade Cromwell from attacking her husband openly by avowing that 'her lord did exceedingly honour and respect him'. Oliver's reply was 'I wish I could see it'.[14]

In Cromwell the earl of Manchester faced a formidable adversary. Earlier in the war he had brought about the downfall of Sir John Hotham junior and the resignation of Lord Willoughby of Parham,[15] and early on in the autumn campaign one of Cromwell's civilian allies tried to warn Manchester of the danger he faced in getting on the wrong side of Oliver.[16] In addition to his fellow Independents in the Eastern Association army, he had powerful allies and associates in both Houses and in the Committee of Both Kingdoms, who saw the future political advantage of advancing the military career of somebody who was not only totally dedicated to winning the war outright but sound on matters of religion. For the same reasons Oliver had the enthusiastic support of some of the editors of the London journals and their fellow workers in the mid-seventeenth-century media, Independent ministers in the city and the provinces. But this time Cromwell's adversary was not a loose cannon teetering on the edge of changing sides, or a backwoods peer whose angry response to attack received few backers, but an important politician in his own right, who had experienced every aspect of generalship apart from managing a battle.[17] He had also stood shoulder to shoulder with the earl of Leven and Lord Fairfax in arguing the toss with the Committee of Both Kingdoms prior to the battle of Marston Moor about sending forces to strengthen the parliamentary garrison at Manchester, and then in insisting on a strategic plan for the north of England after the surrender of York.[18] Not surprisingly, such a track record gave the earl the confidence to fight his corner.

To sum up, Manchester may have been naive to suppose that an army officered by men displaying a wide and diverse range of religious enthusiasms would remain united when a good chance of final victory replaced the grim prospect of defeat, but he was not a gentle soul unfitted for the highest command once the chips were down, nor an effete nobleman as portrayed by Robert Morley in the film *Cromwell*. These popular images of Manchester are to be found in a less extreme form in biographies of Cromwell and in general and specific studies of the war, but they are false. They owe their origins primarily to lies and half-truths put about by Oliver and his supporters in the winter of 1644.[19] Underneath an urbane and debonair exterior Manchester hid a back-bone of steel. He was as assertive in the face of criticism as the earl of Essex, more skilled in appealing to the uncommitted, and often better informed. Instead of collapsing under a barrage of abuse from Cromwell and his supporters, he stood up for himself.[20] His very effective counter-attack in the House of Lords ensured that the row between Cromwell and himself ended in stalemate, not in his downfall or disappearance from public life.[21]

An alternative explanation of Cromwell's behaviour in the autumn campaign may be discovered by turning the accusation he flung at his army commander on its head: 'there is good reason to conceive that this backwardness and neglect in his lordship to take advantage against the enemy was out of a design or desire not to prosecute the war to a final victory'.[22] Complete victory in the autumn of 1644 would not have furthered the war aims of the Independents. They were on the back foot in the debate in the national synod which was advising Parliament on the new Reformation of religion, and the Scots, whose army had regained much of the reputation lost at Marston Moor by storming Newcastle, were egging on the English Presbyterians. The surest way of achieving the Independents' war aims was for final victory to be won at a later date by an army no longer commanded by the first and second generation generals. Cromwell may therefore have deliberately set out to ensure that the autumn campaign was inconclusive by doing just enough to avoid defeat.

However, in Cromwell's case as in Manchester's, the evidence for this expla-nation of his inactivity is largely either circumstantial or tainted by prejudice. There are factors other than political expediency that could account for his uncharacteristic behaviour. First, he may have been ill. He suffered from peri-odic bouts of ill health, physical and mental, from the mid-1630s onwards, but there is no mention of one coinciding with the autumn campaign. Second, he may have had worries about the morale of his cavalry, which had been under-mined by lack of pay and the disputes between Crawford's faction and his own. He therefore dared not use them in battle for fear they would turn tail, thus destroying both his and their reputation as God's chosen instrument. A third possibility is that Cromwell and his allies believed that Manchester had now served his purpose, and that Oliver's hour had come. By bringing about the earl's downfall they could shoehorn Cromwell into the highest level of command, initially as his successor in the Eastern Association army,[23] and then as commander-in-chief once the earl of Essex had retired or been dismissed.

The sorry tale of the decline of the army of the Eastern Association as told by Cromwell and his supporters runs as follows. For six weeks after the capture of York on 16 July, Manchester did nothing of any military significance. With some reluctance he sent detachments to capture minor royalist garrisons in Derbyshire and South Yorkshire, but ignored suggestions from his officers and from the Lincolnshire and Nottinghamshire county committees that he should set siege to the strategically important town of Newark, safe haven for a small army of royalists, even though the army was at Lincoln, only sixteen miles away. However, this section of the case against the earl is a pack of lies. His forces captured Sheffield Castle, Welbeck House and Wingfield Manor in good order, and the correspondence between Manchester and the Committee of Both Kingdoms in London shows no signs of reluctance to move on his part or rebukes for inactivity on theirs.[24] Manchester's brief, as in the spring, was to shadow Prince Rupert, who was actively recruiting in Lancashire and Cheshire, and might at any moment break loose and march south or back across the Pennines.[25] It was therefore essential that the earl should keep his army intact and not weaken it by storming enemy garrisons. As for the siege of Newark, it was the earl who suggested it to the Committee of Both Kingdoms, tentatively on 22 July, and then more forcibly on 12 August, supported by the Lincolnshire and Nottinghamshire county committees. The Committee, however, firmly turned the suggestion down. Newark could wait for the moment. Manchester's priority was to keep an eye on Prince Rupert.[26]

Cromwell's accusation that his general refused to obey the Committee's instructions to put pressure on Rupert in mid-August by advancing on Chester, which was now his headquarters, is a half-truth rather than an outright lie. Manchester certainly pointed out the impracticality of such an operation in his reply to the Committee's command, but he backed up his argument with a detailed pessimistic military appraisal of the operation compiled by his chief officers.[27] Nevertheless, towards the end of the month the earl of Manchester did send a large body of horse towards Chester, and they were to be followed shortly by the rest of the army. However, he abandoned the operation after learning that Rupert and his forces were on the march through the Welsh borderland, destination unknown.[28]

As soon as the Committee learned that Rupert had left Chester, the earl was reminded of his orders to follow the prince wherever he went. The letter left London on 28 August and by 3 September the Eastern Association army was marching south from Lincoln. It was to head for either Woodstock or Abingdon depending on the direction of the prince's march. If Rupert was heading for Bristol and the West Country, Abingdon was best. If he was heading for the royalist garrison at Banbury, which was being besieged by local forces, Woodstock was preferable.[29] It was not until the army reached Huntington, where the earl of Manchester hoped to pick up supplies from the Eastern Association, that news broke of the surrender of Essex's army at Lostwithiel.[30] Parliament's immediate fear was that the royalist armies in Cornwall would march eastwards at full speed, with very little to stop them overrunning the whole of England south of the Thames and threatening London. The Eastern

Association army was therefore to march at once towards Dorchester in Dorset where it was to rendezvous with Sir William Balfour's cavalry and whatever forces Sir William Waller could muster.[31] To this instruction Manchester gave his enthusiastic and unconditional agreement,[32] but within days the Dorset operation was on the back burner not, as Cromwell put it, because Manchester opposed it, but because by then it had become apparent that the king's generals were going to take their time. Instead of heading for the capital at full speed, they were having a stab at capturing Plymouth.[33] Moreover, there were other considerations nearer to home. Rupert had gone to Bristol rather than Banbury, but his troops were still on the far side of the Severn in Herefordshire and Shropshire poised to go who knows where. There was therefore good reason for Manchester not to make too much haste until the strategic picture clarified. Some of Cromwell's cavalry regiments, however, were to go to Banbury in case Rupert's first objective was to relieve the besieged garrison.

In the second week in September the earl of Manchester travelled to London where he attended the House of Lords on the 13th and the 16th. He also took part in discussions concerning strategy at the Committee of Both Kingdoms on the 12th, the 14th and the 19th. In the meantime his army moved on to St Albans where it arrived on 11 September, having covered 120 miles in eight days, including a four-day stop at Huntingdon.[34] There it remained until the earl returned on 22 September.[35] Throughout that time enemy intentions remained unclear. The only decision the Committee felt able to make was that the royalist forces returning from Cornwall should be kept as far to the west as possible so that they could not disturb the siege of Banbury, or those of Basing House and Donnington Castle. If they capitulated, the area from which the Oxford garrison drew its sustenance would be severely restricted, making it impossible for the king's commanders to quarter a large army in the Thames valley during the winter.[36] In addition, it would be very difficult if not impossible for Prince Maurice and Lord Forth to rendezvous with Prince Rupert if they could be brought to a halt in Devonshire or west Somerset.

It was not until the earl was on his way back to St Albans that the situation clarified. The Committee had received good intelligence that the king was withdrawing his siege artillery from its positions around Plymouth, and also that part of his army was on the march. Parliament therefore ordered Manchester and Sir William Waller for a second time to join forces with Essex's cavalry and block the royalists' advance.[37] This time, however, the earl had doubts about the wisdom of so speedy a response, and had said as much at the Committee of Both Kingdoms a few days earlier.[38] On a head count alone the force that would assemble at Shaftesbury in Dorset, Waller's preferred rendezvous, was not large enough to make victory likely, let alone assured, and if it were to be defeated, the king could march on London and dictate his own peace terms. On the most optimistic reckoning it would comprise 5,000 foot and probably 6,000 horse, similar in size to the combined strength of the armies led by Lord Forth and Prince Maurice.[39] However, probably between a quarter and a fifth of the horse were dragoons, which would be of little use in battle on the chalk downs of southern England. They were not trained to fight on horseback as cavalry, and they could not operate as an infantry unit in open country as they had no pikes. Finally, the figures included Waller's 1,500 infantry, but these were scattered in ones and twos amongst the south coast garrisons from Plymouth to Poole, and it can be inferred from the earl's letters that he doubted whether they could be reassembled in time.[40] Although Manchester did not spell it out, he strongly implied that it would be best to wait for infantry reinforcements, Essex's regiments re-forming in south Hampshire and a large brigade of trained bands which the London Militia Committee had promised to supply. Only then should Parliament's generals contemplate fighting what could well be the climactic battle of the civil war.

During the period from 21 September to 5 October, Cromwell's charge that Manchester deliberately procrastinated is correct, but the reason was military rather political in nature. Manchester's army took a week to march the forty miles from St Albans to Reading, and another week passed before he sent cavalry and dragoons to join Waller, who by then had fallen back from Shaftesbury into central Wiltshire. Newbury was as far west as he would send his infantry. It lay in a hollow in the chalk downs and was therefore open to cavalry attack, but it was only three miles from the safety of enclosed country.[41]

As the days passed, communications between the Committee and the earl became shorter and sharper, but there was an ebb and flow in the level of assertiveness in the commands issued by Parliament and the Committee, and this suggests that there was some support for Manchester's argument for caution. In early October, however, his political masters backed down. Essex's infantry were to join Waller and Manchester as soon as they possibly could;[42] London was to assemble an infantry brigade that included its best trained band regiments;[43] and the three army generals were to agree on the best place for a grand rendezvous.[44] There is, however, no doubt that Manchester's arguing the toss had angered a larger element at Westminster than the House of Commons radicals. They must also have had serious worries about whether he would obey orders when the king's forces were within striking distance and pre-battle manoeuvring began in earnest.

A further concern with command and control was whether the senior commanders as a group would be able to sink their differences given their past record. In early September when it seemed that only Manchester, Waller, Balfour and Cromwell would have to work together, their political masters were content with written promises that they would subordinate their personal feelings to the common good. However, this had not prevented bickering.[45] In addition, Waller's faith in the earl of Manchester deteriorated as the westward march of the Eastern Association army failed to materialise. Moreover, Essex, more cantankerous than ever, would now be involved. The refurbishment of his infantry was almost complete, and he was building up a head of steam over essential military supplies that had failed to arrive and were holding things up. He could also not resist having a dig at Waller, who in his opinion was not doing enough to delay the royalist armies. Waller should have used his mounted troops to raid their quarters, instead of just falling back as they advanced and making sure that the distance between him and them was great enough to ensure that a fight did not break out by accident.[46] Finally, Essex implied that, as senior general, he expected to take charge of the campaign. With egos inflamed by grievances ancient and modern, it all looked like a recipe for disaster if the three army generals faced the enemy together without some overall political supervision.

On 14 October, therefore, on the instructions of the two Houses of Parliament, the Committee of Both Kingdoms set up a mechanism for ensuring that their senior commanders worked together in harmony and obeyed the orders of their political masters. All significant military decisions were to be taken by a steering committee drawn exclusively from members of the Committee – Essex himself, Manchester, Waller, Cromwell, Lord Robartes, Sir Arthur Haselrig and two civilians sent down from London, John Crewe and the Scot Archibald Johnston. Six days later the various components of the army group came together at Basingstoke.[47] The earl of Manchester had achieved his aim. Parliament's generals would be facing the enemy with a balanced force of 10,000–11,000 foot and 7,000–8,000 horse,[48] more than enough to win the decisive battle of the English Civil War before winter set in.

CHAPTER 12

The Second and Third Battles
of Newbury

PARLIAMENT AND the Committee of Both Kingdoms had the time to put their
house in order because for most of September the king's Council of War was
busy with matters of military administration, re-establishing control over the
four counties of the south-west, raising supplies and recruits for the two armies,
and making provisions for the blockade of Plymouth, Lyme and Taunton.[1]
Discussions concerning the strategy for the rest of the campaign came next
when Prince Rupert met his uncle and brother at Sherborne on 30 September.
He promised to assemble a force of some 6,000 men made up of his and the
marquis of Newcastle's cavalry, a corps of infantry that Charles Gerard had
raised in South Wales, and what infantry the garrison of Bristol could spare. It
was to meet the victors of Lostwithiel at Marlborough at the beginning of
November and together they would invade East Anglia, relieving Banbury on
the way.[2] However, within a day or so of Rupert's return to Bristol the king
received intelligence that Banbury, Donnington Castle and Basing House were
in imminent danger of surrendering. The first priority must therefore be to ride
to their rescue before it was too late.[3] By pushing due east towards Basing Lord
Forth and Prince Maurice would have some chance of inflicting damage on
Waller's cavalry and dragoons. There was also the possibility of borrowing
400 musketeers from Winchester to replace those left behind in garrison at
Sherborne.[4]

Waller's forces were indeed almost caught by surprise by royalist cavalry at
Andover on 18 October as they fell back towards Basingstoke, but Prince
Maurice's infantry failed to arrive on time. The next day the king's armies
reached Whitchurch in the chalk downs just to the north of Winchester, but on
the 20th as they were preparing for the short march to Basing House scouts
discovered the burgeoning enemy army group blocking their way. For the
present relieving Basing was out of the question, but Donnington Castle near
Newbury was another matter. Executing a ninety-degree turn to the north, they
headed for a triangle of land between Newbury and Donnington where the
Rivers Kennet and Lambourn joined, which they could hold against all odds for
at least a week – or so they assured Prince Rupert. If he had not joined them by
then, they would return to Oxford via Wallingford. This should not be difficult.

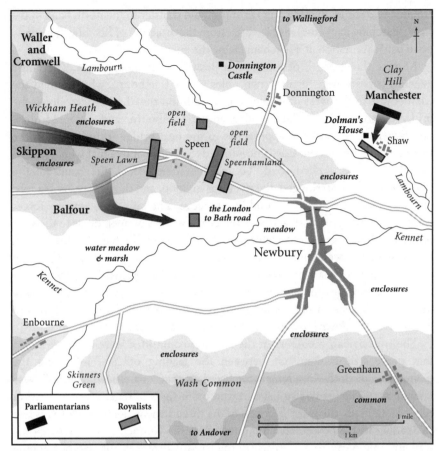

Second Battle of Newbury

By then the enemy concentration ought to have broken up through shortage of provisions. So confident were the committee advising the king of the strength of the Newbury position that they sent one of the strongest and most experienced brigades of horse under James Compton, Third Earl of Northampton, to Oxford with orders to take what forces the garrison could spare and to relieve Banbury. The garrison had been driven back into the castle which, pummelled by heavy artillery, was falling to pieces about their ears.[5]

Essex, Manchester and Waller had expected to fight a battle on 21 September.[6] The enemy's march to Newbury therefore caught them by surprise and they were unable to harry them as they withdrew. The only consolation, and a small one at that, was a cavalry raid on enemy quarters at Aldermaston under the cover of darkness, which took fifty royalists prisoner. When mounted patrols arrived at Newbury, they found that the king's forces were defending the far end of the bridge over the Kennet. Storming it was out of the question, and so the steering committee decided that the army group should transfer to the north bank of the river. Marching back towards Newbury from the direction of Reading, they drew up in battle formation at Thatcham facing the enemy.[7]

At once the strength of the royalist position became apparent. The king's generals had strongly fortified two miles of the Lambourn, which joined the Kennet just to the west of Thatcham. In addition they had broken down the bridge that carried the Bath road over the Lambourn, and occupied Shaw House, which covered the approaches to the next bridge to the north in the same way as Donnington Castle dominated the bridge above that which carried the Newbury to Oxford road. To make matters worse, the banks of the Lambourn were waterlogged, the river was in flood, and the nearest usable ford was at Boxford, two miles beyond Donnington. The bulk of the enemy forces were in support spread out across several square miles of open fields to the west of the Lambourn known to history as Speenhamland, the name of the largest. To the west of Speenhamland was the village of Church Speen, a good place of retreat. Situated on a steep spur of land, it gave easy access to open country beyond, yet was surrounded on almost all sides by small closes where a body of infantry could make a stand, thus giving time for the rest of the king's forces to escape over the downs towards Hungerford or Lambourn.[8]

The two civilian members of the steering committee were highly gratified that peace had broken out between the leading officers, informing the Committee of Both Kingdoms after five days that 'our officers continue very unanimous'. They may also have heaved more sighs of relief when the earl of Essex, potentially the most fractious of the three army generals, took to his bed at Reading with a bowel infection,[9] and when the Council of War agreed on a way not only of making a breach in the royalist defences but also of trapping them in the angle between the two rivers. The plan was to attack them simultaneously from two directions. The Eastern Association infantry under Manchester and Crawford supported by 1,500–1,800 horse from all three armies was to threaten the bridge at Shaw with the aim of pinning down the royalist reserves, whilst the remaining three-quarters of the army under Waller's overall command would march all the way around the enemy position and attack it in overwhelming strength from the west.[10] However, the decision having been taken, Essex's officers asserted their claim to be in the van.[11] If the altercation and subsequent rearrangement of the right pincer caused Waller's force to camp for the night well short of the place intended, thus making the following day's march longer, it almost certainly saved the royalists' bacon.[12]

Waller Force set out from Clay Hill, three-quarters of a mile to the east of the Lambourn, at about midday on 26 October. It marched in a wide arc to the north of the royalist position so as to avoid artillery fire from Donnington Castle, bivouacking at Chieveley (close to the current service station on the M4 motorway). Crossing the Lambourn at Boxford in the morning, it deployed on

Wickham Heath two miles to the west of Church Speen at about two o'clock in the afternoon. Essex's cavalry and Manchester's regiment of horse under Sir William Balfour drew up on the right close to the escarpment separating the Speen spur from the Kennet valley. Essex's large regiment under Philip Skippon was in the centre, and Cromwell and Waller's regiments of horse on the left between Skippon's men and the Lambourn. Behind the lord general's regiment were five London trained bands and the other regiments of foot belonging to Essex's army.[13]

From the start the king's generals understood the purpose of the outflanking movement and ordered a barricade to be constructed covering the western approaches to Church Speen. Defending it were Prince Maurice's infantry strengthened by the Duke of York's regiment from the Oxford army and assisted by a small brigade of western horse. The position had no natural defences, but the enemy approach would be hindered by a narrow belt of enclosures at Stonecross and Wood Speen between Wickham Heath and Speen fields. This slowed down and probably disordered the enemy formations as they advanced, but its significance can be exaggerated.[14] The width of the belt of enclosures at Wood Speen was no more than 300 metres.[15]

The plan of attack on Church Speen was well conceived, but when it began there were only two hours of daylight left and it took Essex's foot regiment about an hour to capture the barricade. Although the royalists lost about one hundred men and at least eight artillery pieces, their retreat through Speen seems to have been an orderly one, and they found no difficulty in establishing a new defensive line along the hedge separating the closes around the village from the open fields to the east. Given the fading light, Waller decided not to launch an attack on Speenhamland itself until morning.[16] However, the capture of the barricade allowed Balfour's cavalry to use a lane leading down the escarpment into the Kennet valley to threaten Newbury bridge, one of the enemy armies' two possible escape routes. As light was fading, a vanguard of some 500 horse supported by a small body of musketeers made considerable progress, pushing a brigade of enemy cavalry back almost as far as the bridge. However, the last royalist reserves on that wing charged Balfour's men in the flank and they retreated sharply, leaving numerous musketeers to be cut down by the enemy troops of horse.[17] By then it must have been almost dark, and Balfour ignored the temptation to order a second push even though reinforcements had made their way down the escarpment and drawn up behind him in the narrow field between it and the water meadows beside the Kennet.

The centre and the right wing of Waller's force had thus made very commendable progress given the time of day at which the attack began. Elsewhere there had been no progress at all. Manchester's attack on the defences of Shaw bridge went in much later than intended. The signal to attack was the firing of a cannon to indicate that Waller Force was in place. The cannon was duly fired at about

3.00 p.m., but Manchester ignored it and also the sound of musket fire that accompanied the assault on the barricade. In the event the attack did not begin until dusk, but the opposition was formidable, some of the best infantry in the king's army drawn up behind hedges and in trenches in what had been the moat of Shaw House.[18] To make matters worse two of Manchester's infantry formations fired on one another in the gathering gloom, and the assaults got nowhere. As the attackers fell back to their starting point, the handful of royalist horse on the east bank of the Lambourn chased them and captured at least one field piece.[19]

Manchester's opponents on his own side were adamant that the debacle at Shaw was first-class evidence of procrastination designed to achieve his political aims,[20] but when all is said and done, Manchester commanded less than a third of the army group and his role in the battle plan was a subsidiary one. The attack on the line of the Lambourn was not intended to do anything more than draw in enemy reserves, which it may have succeeded in doing much earlier in the day.[21] The reason for the failure of the overall plan must therefore lie elsewhere. One factor was the lateness of the attack on Speen combined with the resistance put up by Prince Maurice's infantry. The other was the lack of success of Cromwell's and Waller's regiments of horse on the left wing at Church Speen. The landscape to the north of the village in the Lambourn valley was much more suitable for a conventional cavalry encounter than that over which Balfour's men fought. In addition, the cavalry regiments deployed there ought to have been in a position to launch an attack at the same time as the infantry assault on the barricade went in, not, as in Balfour's case, after it had achieved its objective. But whatever role Waller had planned for his and the Eastern Association regiments of horse, it went off like a damp squib. The silence in the parliamentary sources about what happened on the left wing is deafening, though punctuated by tiny squeaks of self-justification, but royalist sources, although ignorant of the enemy's intentions, are full enough to construct a narrative of what happened.

The parliamentary vanguard pushed through the enclosures at Wood Speen and was crossing a deep ditch when Lord Goring's lifeguard and the earl of Cleveland's brigade of horse attacked it and put it to flight. This is not surprising as troops of horse were particularly vulnerable in such circumstances. However, the main body should have prevented the royalists building on their success by charging them as they tried to exploit their advantage. This did not happen. Cleveland's brigade redeployed without hindrance on the far side of the ditch, and then wheeled to the left towards the infantry engagement. In doing so, it presented its flank to the rest of the parliamentary horse on the left wing, giving them a golden opportunity to attack and turn a small setback into a major success, but they did not move. John Middleton, Waller's lieutenant general, tried to persuade the Eastern Association horse to counter-attack but few obeyed and the royalists quickly routed them.[22] Cleveland then charged Waller's infantry reserves three times. After this the remnant of his brigade, now in total disorder having lost their commander and a number of officers, drifted back to their start line.[23] At this point the general officers on the parliamentary left wing should have implemented a new tactical plan to exploit the royalist setback, the most obvious being to cross the ditch in force and either capture Donnington bridge or move towards the centre of the royalist position on Speenhamland where the reserves were situated. However, Waller had probably been swept from the battlefield with his fleeing cavalry after the fight at the ditch,[24] whilst Cromwell, his deputy, apparently did nothing.

One possible reason for caution was that Oliver did not know what was lurking on the other side of the ditch. All that Waller Force had seen so far of the enemy horse was Cleveland's brigade and some western army cavalry chased from the approaches to Church Speen soon after 3.00 p.m. They would have known that Northampton's brigade was elsewhere, but Forth and Maurice could still have had 3,000 or so horse drawn up in a defensive position supported by the fire of at least one and possibly two brigades of infantry and the train of artillery. However, Cromwell should have ordered a reconnaissance. The contrast with the boldness of the extempore battle plan devised in not dissimilar circumstances during the battle of Marston Moor makes his behaviour all the more remarkable (unless, of course, he had a hidden agenda).[25]

Nevertheless, the steering committee was happy with what the generals had achieved. They had pushed the enemy into a much smaller perimeter than they had held at 3.00 p.m. and they were ripe for the picking. When day dawned Balfour could push forward at full strength to capture Newbury Bridge, whilst the left-wing horse with infantry support could block the other exit from Speenhamland over Donnington bridge. Surrounded and with no hope of escape or rescue, the enemy would quickly surrender. The generals would thus have annihilated two royalist armies (leaving only Rupert in the field with a force under a fifth the size of theirs) but the biggest prize would be the king and the Prince of Wales. During the night, however, the chance of a climactic victory vanished through undue caution, crass negligence, or something worse.

Some four hours after darkness fell, the king's forces began their retreat from Shaw and Speenhamland towards Wallingford.[26] However, their chances of escape were very slim.[27] If not scattered in an engagement in the Lambourn valley once the enemy realised what was happening, they were likely to be brought to a halt by parliamentary cavalry on the chalk downs above Donnington until such time as the parliamentary infantry arrived and blew them away. To make matters worse, they could not conceal what they were doing from the enemy. Sir Edward Walker wrote subsequently that the enemy 'could not but have heard our retreat',[28] and he was right. Skippon's men lining the hedge that separated the closes around Church Speen from Speenhamland quickly realised that the royalists from Shaw were marching past their position and raised the alarm. They apparently begged the Eastern Association troops of horse to do something, but their pleas were ignored.[29]

By 9.00 p.m. news of the enemy retreat had reached the steering committee quartered for the night at Church Speen and they agreed to launch an attack, but then reversed their decision, almost certainly on Cromwell's advice.[30] Possibly they had concerns that night fighting would lead to units falling foul of one another or so disorder the cavalry that they were incapable of fighting the following day. However, they were happy to discuss using such a tactic a fortnight later on the same ground in somewhat similar circumstances.[31] Possibly they thought the royalists were merely crossing the Lambourn to regroup on Donnington Common under the protection of the guns of Donnington Castle,[32] but Sir Simon D'Ewes's précis of Waller's account of the battle read to the House of Commons on 29 October shows that the steering committee knew the royalists were retreating not to, but past, Donnington Castle.[33]

But even if the steering committee considered that a night attack in force with the moon shining in the sky was too risky, there was an alternative. Waller could have sent scouts onto the downs in the evening. He would then have discovered the direction of the royalists' line of march and could have taken steps to get a large body of horse and dragoons to the environs of Wallingford before dawn, with a fair chance of beating up the enemy rearguard at the very least before they crossed the Thames. But Sir William did not even go for the easy option, although movements of troops by night were common during the civil war,[34] and also surprise cavalry attacks.[35] Moreover, retracing their steps over Boxford ford onto the downs was simplicity itself compared with the night march he had conducted prior to the engagement at Alton. The upshot was that when dawn broke, Waller had no idea where the enemy were.[36]

The royalist moonlight flit was an outstanding success. Having left their artillery trains behind in Donnington Castle because they would slow down progress, the two armies reached the bridge over the Thames at Wallingford still in military formation at dawn or soon after. Later that day they took up quarters under the protective wing of the Oxford garrison.[37] The credit should go to Prince Maurice, as Lord Forth was still at Donnington Castle, having sustained a wound during the battle, whilst the king and the Prince of Wales were riding like the wind in search of Prince Rupert, as Charles had no confidence that his armies would reach safety.

For Waller and Cromwell, the cavalry commanders who had achieved nothing on the battlefield or in its immediate aftermath, the imperative was to prevent the royalist forces making their grand rendezvous with Prince Rupert. They argued strongly in favour of the entire army group taking a wide right hook into the Cotswolds via Abingdon and probably Lechlade so as to block the route from Worcester or Upton where he was most likely to have crossed the River Severn, but the earl of Manchester and a majority of the steering committee disagreed.[38]

The royalist rendezvous duly took place at Burford on 2 November,[39] but the decision was a sensible one in the circumstances. The parliamentary infantry and artillery trains could only make slow progress across the heavy clay lands of the Thames valley, and if the troops of horse arrived well before the foot, they might be badly mauled. It made much more sense to wait for the royalists to return to collect their cannon and then do battle with them. The Committee of Both Kingdoms, desperate for a decisive engagement, approved the decision.[40]

Whilst Manchester and Waller waited for the royalists to reappear, they resumed the siege of Donnington Castle, but they did not have to wait for long. The governor, alarmed at the number of mouths he had to feed and at the prospect of the castle being stormed, sent a panicky letter to Secretary of State Sir Edward Nicholas at Oxford begging for help.[41] On 6 November the armies that had fought at Speen and Shaw, Rupert's force, and a sizeable contingent from the Oxford garrison, assembled on an open space to the north of the city and set out for the bridge at Wallingford.[42] Their brief was not only to recover the artillery but also to relieve Basing House, which was still under siege.

In the fortnight between the Second Battle of Newbury and the next encounter important changes took place in both army groups at the highest level of command. Prince Rupert finally replaced the earl of Forth as lord general of the king's army.[43] On Parliament's side, the two civilian members of the Committee of Both Kingdoms returned to Westminster and the steering committee's jurisdiction came to an end.[44] Manchester, Waller and Balfour (in Essex's absence the most senior officer in the lord general's army), advised by a Council of War, took over collective responsibility for operations until the end of the campaigning season.[45]

On 8 November, Parliament's generals knew that the king's forces had reached Wallingford and were therefore highly likely to cross the Thames and head for Donnington.[46] Crawford and Skippon had visited a site at Compton where the armies could be drawn up in open country to block their advance,[47] but as scouts were not watching Wallingford bridge the first news that the enemy were in Berkshire did not arrive at Newbury until late in the afternoon. The intention was to fight a battle the following day,[48] but there seems to have been no sense of urgency. The enemy were able to reach Donnington Castle without incident and by midday they had drawn up in classic battle formation on Speenhamland, facing east.[49] Skippon had already deployed the infantry behind the hedge dividing Speenhamland from Shaw fields, which also covered the approach to Newbury bridge. Troops on the other bank of the Kennet could therefore cross the river in safety and take up their position in the line of battle for an engagement. However, most of the cavalry, which had orders to rendezvous on Wash Common at first light, did not reach the north bank of the Kennet in force until late in the afternoon, by which time it was almost dark.[50]

The excuse was that some regiments were in billets at some distance from Newbury, but royalist sources show that the enemy cavalry spent most of the day in a large body moving backwards and forwards to no apparent purpose on the slopes of the downs to the south of the river. As a result the only fighting that took place on the 9th was some light skirmishing.[51]

Overnight the royalist forces withdrew from the Lambourn valley and took up a position on the downs at Winterbourne covering the road to Wantage.[52] By that time the parliamentary forces had drawn up in battle array on Speenhamland. Their commanders then carried out a reconnaissance and followed it up with a Council of War. The royalists appeared to be offering battle yet again. All that the army group had to do was to march towards them. Sir Arthur Haselrig opened the discussion with an eloquent plea for caution. The war could be lost at a single blow. The royalists were stronger than they had been two weeks earlier and their morale was high. Parliament's forces, however, were in a bedraggled state, ravaged by weeks of campaigning in atrocious weather, the cavalry horses in particular being in very poor condition.

The discussion that followed was variously described at a later date by those present, but there is little doubt that some generals did have some concerns about morale. Others thought the royalists were trying to entice them into abandoning the line of the Kennet so they could sneak around behind them and relieve Basing House. There was also some support for giving battle. Manchester's own contribution to the discussion was to make light of Cromwell's argument that if they delayed Parliament would find itself facing a French invasion in the spring brokered by the queen. In the end the earl's summing up reflected majority, possibly by then unanimous, opinion that this was not the moment to fight a battle in open country. The armies were therefore to remain at Newbury.[53] Unfortunately for his reputation he repeated the gist of Haselrig's words. Later some of his colleagues twisted them into a denunciation of any and every effort to bring the war to a satisfactory end by fighting.

Parliament and the Committee of Both Kingdoms reacted angrily:

> We have received your letters concerning the relief of Donnington Castle by the enemy, and are very sorry that they met not with that opposition that was expected from an army which God hath blessed lately with so happy a victory against them.[54]

Haselrig travelled to Westminster to explain the generals' reasoning, but the House of Commons was unreceptive.[55] At this point the common front of the military men towards their political masters collapsed. To save their own reputations they began briefing against one another. The weeklies duly reported that such and such a general had spoken in favour of fighting, which they had all probably done at some point or other between 8 and 10 November, but there is little

doubt that most of them had also put counter-arguments and that all had eventually gone along with the party line.[56] Meanwhile the military situation in the
Newbury area was deteriorating. The armies shrank in size when rumours circulated that they were about to go into winter quarters, and when resources to keep
them in the field such as pay and foodstuffs failed to materialise. On about the
20th, Newbury was abandoned as indefensible. This exposed the forces besieging
Basing House to annihilation as the royalist armies were still in the field, and they
withdrew to a safe distance a day later. A party of Oxford garrison horse then
relieved the garrison on the 22nd without encountering any opposition, whereupon the royalist armies ended the campaign and entered winter quarters in
villages and towns to the west and north of Oxford and in the Cotswolds.[57]

As the campaigning came to a close, the confrontation between Parliament's
generals in the south and their political masters grew more and more serious. On
the day the royalists relieved Basing House the Committee of Both Kingdoms
instituted its own inquiry into what had happened in the Newbury campaign and
on 23 November Waller and Cromwell received the command to give the House
of Commons an account of the generals' performance since the rendezvous at
Basingstoke five weeks earlier.[58] This widening of the scope of the investigation
from the events of 8–10 November to the whole of the Newbury campaign is
interesting, and was possibly in anticipation of an attack in the Lords by the earl
of Essex on the House of Commons' two favourite generals. He had recovered
from his illness, and his friends saw his star in the ascendant once more.[59] He
could not be blamed for what had happened at the Second or Third Battles of
Newbury, and his regiments, commanded by Skippon and Balfour, had
performed significantly better than their peers. He had also begun to gather new
evidence against his enemies[60] to add to that which he already claimed to possess
relating to the Cornish campaign.[61]

Waller and Cromwell addressed the Commons on 25 November and both
used the occasion to turn king's evidence (as it were) by placing the blame for
all the disappointments and failures exclusively on the shoulders of the earl of
Manchester. However, on the day Cromwell expanded their remit still further
and, beginning his narrative of events with the capture of York, he condemned
the earl for throwing away the chance of bringing the war to an end in 1644 on
three occasions – in Dorset in late September, at Newbury in October and at
Newbury again in November.[62] Waller may also have used the occasion to
attack the earl of Essex. Thus began the process by which the first two generations of Parliament's army commanders were to disappear from the scene.
Those members of the Commons exasperated by the generals' failure to bring
the war to a conclusion in 1644 probably expected a quick resolution with an
abject apology from the two earls, followed by their resignation and the appointment of new commanders. Despite his blustering, Essex did not have a leg to
stand on after what had happened at Lostwithiel; Manchester could not stand

against the mass of evidence that Cromwell, Waller and the Committee of Both
Kingdoms would bring against him; and Waller had probably had enough of
playing the commander-in-chief's understudy and would happily resign his
commission. But Cromwell had gone too far. The accusations he made against
Manchester amounted to a charge of high treason, and Manchester answered
like with like. He brought into the public arena intemperate statements that his
lieutenant general had made against all and sundry in the allied coalition. From
these it could be inferred that Oliver wished to see the peerage abolished, and
with it the House of Lords, and that he would fight the Scots to prevent a perse-
cuting Presbyterian Church being imposed on England as part of any peace
settlement.[63] Moreover, Essex was intriguing with the Covenanters to bring
Cromwell to trial for deliberately trying to drive a wedge between the allies.[64] To
make the charged atmosphere even worse, Manchester and Cromwell fought
out their verbal duel at a time when men accused of high treason in 1643, Sir
John Hotham senior and junior and Sir Alexander Carew, were being tried and
executed.[65] It was plain to see that either could follow the same path if his opponent's charges stuck, and that if one or the other suffered the death penalty the
parliamentary coalition would fly apart. At best this would prolong the war, at
worst lead to a civil war within a civil war which the king could exploit to regain
most, if not all, of what he had lost in England and Scotland since 1637.

CHAPTER 13

The Reckoning

A NEW GENERAL AND A NEW ARMY

THE OUTSTANDING military development of the winter of 1644 was the creation of the New Model Army, nationally financed, larger than any previous army, commanded by a new general with a hand-picked officer corps, and strategically and operationally under the control of the Committee of Both Kingdoms. This was a new venture. The appointment of the steering committee did not pave the way for it,[1] and it had nothing whatsoever to do with Sir William Waller's cry of despair after Cropredy Bridge.[2] This is not to deny that problems of command, recruitment and maintenance and how to solve them were a general concern in the summer and autumn of 1644.[3] However, root and branch reform would be a contentious issue for the parliamentary coalition and it made sense to defer it. It was only practicable during the close season, and the military men could well have achieved outright victory before winter set in.

The point at which dodging the issue became unavoidable was on 14 November when the House of Commons rejected Sir Arthur Haselrig's explanation for the royalist relief of Donnington Castle and the non-battle of Newbury.[4] If Parliament was to win the war, both the incompetence of the generals and the poor state of the armies had to be addressed, and for the next two months or so they ran on parallel lines with sometimes one taking the lead and sometimes the other. The House of Commons set the ball rolling on the 19th. The Committee of Both Kingdoms was 'to consider the state and condition of all the forces under the command of Parliament and to put them into such a posture as may make them useful and advantageous to the kingdom'.[5] There was no direct mention of the generals, but it is surely no coincidence that on the 22nd the House of Commons began its inquiry into who was responsible for turning a first-class opportunity of winning the war in the south into a major humiliation.

The Committee of Both Kingdoms held meetings about reform of the militia on 4, 10 and 13 December. In the meantime the composition of the officer corps, and with it the future of the army generals, came under the spotlight. On 9 December the committee of the House of Commons charged with examining Cromwell's and Waller's charges against the earl of Manchester recommended that members of both Houses who held commissions in the armed forces should surrender them, a proposal that would remove Essex and Manchester at one stroke, but also Lord Fairfax,[6] Sir William Waller and Oliver Cromwell.

In the debate Cromwell firmly tied the purge of the officer corps to the creation of the new army:

> It is now a time to speak or forever hold the tongue. The important occasion now is no less than to save a nation out of a bleeding, nay a dying condition . . . without a more speedy, vigorous and effectual prosecution of the war . . . we shall make the kingdom weary of us and hate the name of Parliament . . . I do conceive if the army be not put into another method and the war more vigorously pursued, the people can bear the war no longer and will enforce you to a dishonourable peace.

He went on to speak forcibly against an inquiry into errors made by the army commanders as 'they can rarely be avoided in military affairs'. He himself had been 'guilty of oversights'. Instead Parliament should focus on the remedy. The purge of the officer corps would ensure that nobody could accuse its members of prolonging the fighting to feather their own nests, and he did not doubt that any and every officer who also sat in Parliament as a commoner or a peer would be willing to give up his position in the army for the unity of the cause.[7]

In the House of Commons debate on 17 December to discuss the ordinance embodying the 'self-denying principle', Bulstrode Whitelock referred to 'the great work of the new modelling of your armies'.[8] A single army was the agreed solution and on the 24th the Commons asked the Committee for a speedy response to questions concerning the number of regiments of horse and foot required, their size and the names of their colonels. Further discussion took place in the Committee on the 27th, and on the 31st it agreed that the new army establishment should be 16,000 foot, 8,000 horse and 1,500 dragoons, and that the infantry regiments should be 1,200 strong. After a sub-committee had reported on how the army was to be financed, and the horse and foot had been reduced by 2,000 men each and the dragoons by 500, the full proposal went to the House of Commons on 9 January.[9]

It was clear for all to see that the New Model Army would not only replace but also absorb the troops who had fought in the Newbury campaign. There would be no funds left to pay the old armies once the new one was in place, and it would be quite impracticable to recruit over 21,000 men and give them a sound military training before the royalist forces took the field in March or April. In the meantime the inquiry into what had happened in the Newbury campaign was grinding to a halt due to a procedural deadlock between the Lords and the Commons.[10] But the row between Cromwell and Manchester was a long time a-dying. The earl was very keen to clear his name, whilst his opponents gave the inquiry an encouraging kick whenever the momentum for military reform appeared to be slackening.

The House of Commons had accepted the Self-Denying Ordinance on 19 December, having two days earlier decided by a narrow majority that its provisions covered everybody, including the earl of Essex. The Lords sat on the ordinance for over a fortnight but then rejected it outright on 13 January 1645. They took exception to the sidelining of so many experienced officers and the effect this would have on the fighting capacity of the armed forces. They also objected to the fact that members of the House of Commons could continue in military service merely by resigning their seats, whilst peers could not do so as their membership of the House of Lords was for life.[11]

The Lower House chose for the moment to focus on remodelling the militia rather than challenging the Lords on the principle of self-denial, but the way in which they proceeded showed that it still lay at the heart of the reform programme. On 21 January the MPs voted by a sizeable majority that Sir Thomas Fairfax should be commander-in-chief 'of all forces to be raised by the new established army according to the new model', with Philip Skippon as his major general. Skippon had shown his martial spirit in the Lostwithiel and Newbury campaigns, whilst Sir Thomas had displayed a real capacity for military leadership at the level of army general, most notably in the Nantwich campaign.[12] He had also spent the entire war in the north of England and thus avoided becoming involved in the quarrels between the commanders in the south. Oliver Cromwell, who had fought with him at Winceby and Marston Moor, would have spoken of his bravery and boldness, his commitment to winning the war and his simple, unostentatious piety.[13]

The draft ordinance for the New Model Army also named the colonels of horse and foot, drawn from all three of the earlier armies, but it left the post of commander of the horse vacant.[14] The rumour was that John Middleton, Waller's lieutenant general, was the likeliest candidate, probably because his name came first after Fairfax in the list of cavalry colonels.[15] However, if this was indeed the intention, it came to nothing as Middleton resigned in April 1645 together with the other Scottish colonels, probably because their political masters disapproved of the number of Independent officers selected for the New Model.[16]

Sir Thomas was to have complete authority over all forces in England and Wales other than his father's Army of the North and the Scottish army,[17] and army pay was to be financed by a tax on the English counties and towns south of the Trent that were firmly under Parliament's control.[18] However, the wording of the clause that described Fairfax's authority in strategic and operational matters made it very clear that he was the servant, not the master. He was to 'rule, govern, command, dispose and employ the said army . . . in all defences, offences, invasions, executions . . . [but] be subject to such orders and directions as he hath or shall receive from both Houses of Parliament or from the Committee of Both Kingdoms'.[19] However, this had an interesting corollary. The former army generals, though no longer field commanders, remained on the Committee and would potentially have greater influence over strategy and operations after laying down their commissions than they had had before. Moreover, when the revised Self-Denying Ordinance became law on 3 April, they would have the chance to be there every time the Committee met if they so desired.[20]

There was no such remodelling of the royalist armies in the winter of 1644.[21] All the changes that took place were at the highest level of command. Prince Rupert had already replaced Lord Forth. Prince Maurice then took over Rupert's command in Wales and the Welsh Marches, whilst George Goring took charge of what was left of the western army. But that was all. Unlike Hopton's army after Cheriton, the formations that joined the Oxford army between August and November 1644 kept their separate identities. This was partly a matter of quartering,[22] but there is little doubt that the army of the west and Charles Gerard's corps went their separate ways in December and April respectively because of fear of mutiny. The Northern Horse, commanded by Sir Marmaduke Langdale after George Goring's promotion, were less restive because they knew that their passionate desire to return to the north had Prince Rupert's complete backing. Their self-esteem was also high thanks to an operation they carried out with total success during March. After a long trek from Banbury into west Yorkshire, they broke up the siege of Pontefract Castle, defeated part of Lord Fairfax's army commanded by Colonel John Lambert, and returned safely to royalist-controlled south Shropshire, all in the space of just over a fortnight.[23]

From November onwards both sides were intent on avoiding military operations for several months. For Parliament a time of reduced activity was essential to enable the various components of the new army to come together and bed down. The task of the king's generals was to recruit their field armies, which had shrunk alarmingly during the autumn campaign. However, for both sides strategic necessity made for exceptions in the case of Taunton and Chester. Parliament saw its continuing control of Taunton as essential for scuppering the king's plans to raise troops and revenue from the four counties of south-west England.[24] To that end Charles had set up an Association managed by a committee of the Privy Council under the nominal presidency of the Prince of Wales, which was to meet at Bristol. Chester, on the other hand, was vital to the king's hopes of persuading the Irish Confederates to send troops to England to support the royalist war effort. In due course the siege of Taunton was to tie down well over 10,000 soldiers from both sides, whilst Parliament's attempts to capture Chester and the king's to retain it were to last a whole year and occupy the attention of at least 7,000 troops.

Before leaving Somerset in early October 1644, the king's advisers had made arrangements for Taunton to be besieged by local forces under the command of the governor of Bridgwater, Edmund Wyndham.[25] On 6 November, well before the Newbury campaign was over, Parliament ordered Sir William Waller to combine the infantry he had left behind in the Dorset garrisons with regiments of horse from the army group surplus to requirements to create a relief expedition, which was to be led by his major general of foot, the Scottish professional James Holbourne.[26] This Waller did, and as Holbourne Force approached, the Somerset royalists fell back, allowing it to reach Taunton without incident on 14 December, but instead of immediately returning the way it had come, it settled down in West Somerset.[27] Holbourne believed that Sir William was to follow at the head of the rest of his army. Together they could then strengthen Parliament's hold over the neck of the south-west peninsula, which was at its narrowest between Taunton and Lyme, and ruin once and for all the king's plans for a royalist equivalent of the Eastern Association.[28]

The Taunton area provided none too comfortable a billet for Holbourne Force, with Exmoor and the Blackdown Hills to the west and the south, the sea to the north, and to the east a string of enemy garrisons guarding the crossing points over the rivers Parrett and Yeo between Bridgwater and Ilminster. As time passed, the situation worsened. First, the enemy received reinforcements from east Somerset under Lord Hopton, who took charge of operations against Taunton.[29] Second, some of Holbourne's cavalry left without permission. Arriving in south Wiltshire, they tried to establish a garrison at Salisbury, but George Goring quickly evicted them.[30] In late December, having replaced Prince Maurice as lieutenant general in command of the four counties of south-east England, Goring led the army of the west into Hampshire strengthened by some cavalry brigades from the Oxford army. His objective was to capture Portsmouth by guile.[31] However, it came to nothing, as did an attempt to storm Christchurch, and he fell back into Wiltshire. However, his raids on parliamentary regiments in billets along the Surrey/Hampshire border caused some alarm and enhanced his reputation as an energetic commander, though in reality they inflicted little damage.

Quartered in the villages around Salisbury, Goring's cavalry had unrestricted command over the chalk downs and were well placed to turn east Dorset into a no-go area should Holbourne try and return without an escort. To make matters worse, Sir William Waller kept putting off his departure. His regiments were under strength and either refused to accept his overall command (in the case of Essex's cavalry) or else demanded the pay they were owed before moving out of winter quarters (as with his own and Manchester's). Lack of military equipment was also a problem. On 2 February he wrote to the Committee of Both Kingdoms as follows: 'The officers this day re-presented some particulars wherein their regiments were defective, 600 pikes, 1,000 swords, 1,000 bandoliers, 2,000 knapsacks and 2,000 pairs of stockings'.[32] Holbourne therefore had no option. The enemy had pinned him in west Somerset and there he would remain until he could be rescued. By early March his men were chronically short of provisions, but help was at last on the way.

The winter of 1644–5 is a particularly difficult time to get into the mind of the king and his military advisers. Their strategic aims in England were simple and straightforward – to establish the new Association in the south-west, to retain control of Wales and the Welsh borderland, and to draw once more on the resources of the north of England which had great potential as a recruiting ground – but the interface between aspiration and delivery is largely hidden from history. Sir Edward Walker did not take up his pen until the field army was flexing its muscles for the spring campaign, and the flow of suggestions, intelligence and orders between the king at Oxford and the generals in the provinces is a fitful one. Rupert was in the Welsh borderland for over two months in the late winter and early spring, but precious few letters exist between uncle and nephew compared with periods in 1643 and 1644 when the two were apart, and as in 1644 the king's correspondence with Prince Maurice no longer survives.

Fortunately, the orders issued to commanders in the south-west of England still exist or can be inferred from the records of the Prince of Wales's Council, which took up residence in Bristol at the beginning of March. These are very revealing. Lack of a clear and consistent chain of command, overlapping jurisdictions and conflicts of personality were the key elements. The consequence was a succession of missed opportunities and what can only be described as military fiascos. The temptation is to follow Lord Clarendon and blame everything on the personalities, ambitions and sheer incompetence of the generals, most particularly George Goring. More at fault, however, was the Council, which had an excessively elevated view of its own authority and a determination that the mediocre and politically unambitious Lord Hopton should be army general in the west, but the root cause was the king himself. He failed to knock heads together at the start and the subsequent trumpet calls from on high gave a series of uncertain notes. These inflamed the struggle for power at the provincial level and ensured that the western army did not play its full part in the decisive Naseby campaign of May–June 1645.[33]

The first debacle occurred in mid-February. The Dorset royalists under Sir Lewis Dyve operating out of Sherborne captured Weymouth without apparently seeking permission from the king or informing other commanders in the region. However, they were not strong enough to overrun the adjacent town of Melcombe on the other side of the River Frome. Dyve then asked Goring for help. He apparently sent some musketeers on horseback, and later visited Weymouth in person, but before he returned with the rest of his army the enemy had mounted a successful counter-attack using an unguarded bridge over the Frome. Two days later Goring launched a night attack in the hope of recovering the town, but the enemy using cannon loaded with case shot inflicted heavy losses on the assault parties and caused them to retreat. Goring then abandoned the operation and marched northwards into Somerset.[34] There he received orders from the king, issued on 4 March, to take charge of the operations against

Holbourne Force and Waller's relief expedition which was on its way at last. He was to use his own troops, those he found in Somerset, and two infantry brigades marching up from Devon and Cornwall under Sir John Berkeley and Sir Richard Grenville respectively.[35] This placed Goring under the jurisdiction of the Prince of Wales's Council, which proceeded to give him detailed operational instructions. Goring had no option for the moment but to obey, because Prince Maurice's commission as lieutenant general of the south-west was in abeyance, but he was as determined to obtain a free hand over military operations as the Council was to stop him, and this poisoned relations between them for as long as Goring was commanding an army in the west.[36]

By the time Goring heard from the king, Waller, with Cromwell as his second in command, was heading for Bristol rather than Taunton with a force of about 3,000 horse and dragoons drawn from his own and the earl of Manchester's armies.[37] On the way he destroyed James Long's regiment of horse in typical fashion in north Wiltshire by decoying it into a carefully prepared ambush.[38] His hope was that Parliament's supporters would betray Bristol and with it the Prince of Wales and his council, but after he had quartered for ten days or so at Marshfield in south Gloucestershire waiting on events, the principal plotters arrived with news that the enemy had discovered their plans. Waller's disappointment is very apparent from a letter he wrote to the speaker of the House of Commons on 25 March,[39] but he still had his principal task to complete and a cunning plan was already well under way for setting Major General Holbourne free. Waller's cavalry and dragoons rode back across Wiltshire from the northwest corner to the south-east, arriving at Ringwood just over the Hampshire border on the 27th, as if in preparation for an advance along the sea coast as far as Axminster and then into Somerset over the Blackdown Hills.[40] Goring had prior knowledge of the move and took the bait, advancing with all his forces as far east as Sharston, close to Stonehenge, but Waller's retreat was a deception. Cromwell and his brigade had left the Bristol area some days before Waller. Thought by Goring to be even further to the east, they were already making their way rapidly in the opposite direction. Hugging the coast, they duly arrived at Axminster where Holbourne joined them with between 1,500 and 2,000 infantry, cavalry and dragoons. On 30 March or thereabouts they met Waller and the rest of the relief force at Cerne Abbas to the north of Weymouth, and then took up quarters in villages around Shaftesbury where the counties of Dorset, Somerset and Wiltshire joined. This was uncomfortably close to Goring's army,[41] and he made up for his disappointment as he had done two months earlier by picking off individual regiments of Waller's brigade whilst they slept.[42] Goaded into action, Waller, Cromwell and Holbourne advanced towards him looking for a battle. They reached Bruton where the chalk downs meet the flat lands of central Somerset. Goring reacted by retreating to Wells, but they hesitated and then fell back towards Salisbury. They were too short of good-quality infantry to risk venturing into the enclosed country which lay between the two armies.[43]

Goring, however, was in fighting mood. On 7 April he put a plan to the Prince's Council for advancing on Salisbury. At first the Council made encouraging noises, but then changed its tune when Sir Richard Grenville reported that his Cornish infantry refused to move any further east than Taunton until it had been captured. Grenville also claimed that he could take it by storm provided that he had the use of Goring's and Berkeley's infantry as well as his own. The Council agreed and ordered Goring to send the western army regiments of foot to Taunton, the capture of which became Grenville's responsibility. However, the general and his cavalry were to remain where they were to frustrate any attempt by Waller to intervene. Goring was upset and protested in no uncertain terms, but even if he had had his way, he would not have caught Waller and Cromwell.[44] On 17 April the Committee of Both Kingdoms brought their operation to a close. Waller then resigned his commission as major general of the west, well within the forty days' grace allowed by the Self-Denying Ordinance to commanders who were also members of Parliament.[45] Reflecting on his last campaign in his memoirs, he described it as 'hopeless employment', not a bad description as he had not managed to inflict any significant damage on the enemy, but at least he had rescued Holbourne and run rings around the king's newest army general.[46]

George Goring, the elder son of the earl of Norwich, came from a family of courtiers and royal officials, which probably explains his expertise in the arts of flattery and intrigue and also his extravagant ways. Having married the daughter of the wealthy earl of Clare in the mid-1620s, he quickly spent her dowry and piled up a mountain of debts. He was in such straits by 1633 that a prolonged stay on the Continent was the only solution, and Lord Clare came up with the money to purchase a colonelcy in the Dutch army. Goring fought with great bravery on the Continent for the next four years, but returned to England with a leg wound, the pain from which was to return from time to time. The effect this had on his powers of command is uncertain, but it may account for his notorious dependency on alcohol.

Goring's tale-telling about intrigues to use military force to put pressure on Parliament in the year before the outbreak of the Civil War was greatly to the advantage of the future parliamentary leadership, and they therefore had no objection to his remaining governor of Portsmouth, an office conferred on him by the king in 1639. However, when civil war became a real possibility in the summer of 1642 he agreed to turn the garrison and its huge arsenal of military supplies over to the king's supporters.[47] Unfortunately, news that parliamentary troops were on their way to reinforce the garrison impelled him to reveal his true colours much earlier than he had intended. Three weeks later he surrendered on terms as there was no prospect of relief. He then left for the Continent. There he renewed his acquaintance with the queen, and won great favour with her and the king by helping to organise her expedition to England. His reward was to be appointed General of Horse in the marquis of Newcastle's army.

Goring's career in the royalist northern command was brief but spectacular. He soundly defeated Sir Thomas Fairfax in an action on Seacroft Moor near Leeds in March 1643, but two months later the Fairfaxes captured him at Wakefield along with several thousand men and a magazine of military supplies. Too ill to take charge of the defence and with ill-starred subordinates, he nevertheless fought like a lion once the parliamentary attack began and only failed to beat it off by a whisker. However, he landed on his feet, finishing up as a prisoner at the Lion Inn in Holbourne, where he could indulge his love of the bottle. When the House of Commons heard of this, they quickly moved him to the Tower.[48]

After almost a year's captivity Goring gained his release in exchange for a Scottish earl, and was at Newark on the way north to resume his command when he learned of the disaster at Selby from some three thousand of his own cavalry who had just arrived there from the north. He provided good quarters for them in the Trent valley and then commanded them most successfully in Prince Rupert's northern expedition.[49] It was not, however, the king's intention that Goring should remain in the north. He wanted him as Wilmot's replacement in the Oxford army, but agreed that Rupert could keep him until after he had fought the Scots.[50] Once what was left of the royalist armies reached Lancashire after Marston Moor, Rupert released him. He then took charge of Wilmot's cavalry in Cornwall on 7 August, leading them with some distinction for the rest of the 1644 campaign.[51]

Although Goring's reputation as a cavalry commander in the winter of 1644 rivalled that of Prince Rupert,[52] evidence that he was suitable for promotion to army general was equivocal. He had shown tactical skills of a high order at Seacroft Moor in March 1643 and considerable promise in the first stages of the battle of Marston Moor and the Second Battle of Newbury. He had won over Wilmot's officers, a ticklish task, and he also seems to have found it easy to work with other commanders provided they did not threaten his position.[53] However, the disappointing campaign in Hampshire and the loss of Weymouth suggests that, as a general, Goring was somewhat unlucky,[54] but generals make their own luck and his misfortunes stemmed largely from a failure to take much interest in obtaining accurate intelligence about the movements of the enemy. Again and again in 1645 he was taken by surprise, though often he had enough presence of mind to avoid complete disaster. Clarendon's comment on a military commander whom he loathed and despised for once seems apposite. Goring was characterised by 'natural invigilance'.[55]

On balance, despite his boasting and the supportive noises made by other royalists with whom he corresponded, Goring could take little credit for his first campaign in the west, especially when it became clear that Holbourne had left a garrison at Taunton sufficiently strong in infantry to defend the town but unencumbered by masses of cavalry and dragoons (whose horses ate up supplies at a prodigious rate). Moreover, the commander was Robert Blake, the future Commonwealth admiral, who had successfully defended Lyme against Prince Maurice the previous year.[56] However, Goring had not lost territory in the early months of 1645, which could not be said of Prince Maurice.

Maurice left Oxford for Worcester on 14 January to take up his new command.[57] His task was to raise infantry for the field army. In the counties of North Wales impressing men by force was to be the principal means, but the king hoped he could persuade the loyalist and neutral landowners in the counties of the West Midlands to raise volunteers through a new Association modelled on the one in the West Country that was to be nurtured by the Prince of Wales's Council. Maurice was pessimistic. The concessions the king had made in advance to gain support would vastly increase the powers of the civilian administrators, some of whom were 'cunning', and this would hasten the 'destruction of military power and discipline'.[58] Nevertheless for the rest of January, he was busy laying the foundations of the Association in Worcestershire and south Shropshire, but on 3 February or thereabouts he must have received orders from the king to put together an ad hoc army for a special mission.[59] A grave emergency had arisen in the far north of his command. Chester was about to surrender to Sir William Brereton.[60]

Brereton began his preparations to capture Chester in December 1644 by establishing a fort at Christleton, two miles down the present-day A41 road towards Whitchurch, blocking the easiest route for a relief force to approach the city. When Lord Byron, still major general for North Wales and the Borders, tried to storm it on 19 January, Brereton found out in advance, set up an ambush and captured or killed many of his officers and men.[61] A week later Brereton tried to rush the city's defences under cover of darkness. The defenders saw off the attack before scaling ladders could be put in place,[62] but soon afterwards he sent troops across Farndon bridge into Wales, thus completing the encirclement of Chester and making a blockade practicable for the first time. With little food in its magazine and its population swollen by refugees, the city could not hold out for long and Byron was in despair.[63]

Maurice, however, was being asked to perform a miracle. Although he could scrape together a relief force from the Shropshire and Worcestershire garrisons, some locally raised horse, and the remnants of the Anglo-Irish regiments quartered in and around Shrewsbury for the winter, Brereton had twice as many troops drawn from several counties.[64] A direct advance via Whitchurch was out of the question, Sir William having drawn up his forces in open country just to the south of that town ready to fight a conventional battle. Marching through the lowlands of Maelor and east Denbighshire with the Welsh hills to his left would be safer, as much of the countryside was enclosed, but Brereton could quickly get his troops to the far side of the Dee via Farndon bridge and hit him in his open flank. Maurice therefore took a much more circuitous route through the hills where there was a string of royalist strongpoints beginning at Chirk Castle, and this apparently deterred the cautious Brereton from attacking him. On 21 February Maurice reached Chester by way of Ruthin and Hawarden, whereupon Sir William abandoned the siege.[65] This was as fine an achievement as selling a dummy to Essex's army near Tiverton in July, but the prince's triumph was short-lived. Two days later the Shropshire parliamentarians, assisted by some infantry provided by Brereton, surprised Shrewsbury under cover of darkness, and quickly captured the town and the castle. The myth is that somebody opened one of the town gates and let the enemy in, but the real reason was that the expedition to Chester had run the garrison down to an unacceptably low level.[66]

Prince Rupert took the news badly, as he had improved Shrewsbury's fortifications and built up a large magazine there during his generalship, but the king charged him with recovering what he could from the collapse of royal power in the Welsh borderland and the prince left Oxford in a hurry.[67] By the beginning of March, according to intelligence sent to Sir William Brereton by Edward Massey, the governor of Gloucester, he was busy rousing the field army infantry from their billets in the Cotswolds. General Charles Gerard's infantry brigade was also on the move from its winter quarters in Monmouthshire.[68] On 8 March Rupert was at Ludlow with the bulk of his forces, but in low spirits. He had lost few troops at Shrewsbury but the enemy had captured 2,000 weapons, 100 barrels of gunpowder and vast quantities of food and fodder.[69] To make matters worse, Wales was on the verge of revolt; his train of artillery had not arrived; some of his officers had questioned his orders; and he could not see how he could rescue Prince Maurice unless the king also took the field.[70] Soon afterwards Sir Marmaduke Langdale and his brigades arrived after their success at Pontefract. This must have helped raise his spirits as later letters to his friend Will Legge, the governor of Oxford, are more cheerful, but he was also winning successes against the odds.[71] When Rupert made a move towards Chester, Sir William, not wishing to suffer a repeat of what had happened outside Newark twelve months earlier, withdrew into central Cheshire to await the arrival of Scottish reinforcements. As a result the two princes were able to rendezvous between Whitchurch and Wrexham without incident on 17 March.[72]

The Committee of Both Kingdoms and all London with it were full of anxiety. What would the princes do next? Were they about to move into Lancashire to relieve Lathom House and raise recruits, as Rupert had done in 1644? Would they try to retake Shrewsbury? Neither seems likely in retrospect. If they went any further north, they risked being trapped as the Scottish army was just the other side of the Pennines.[73] Shrewsbury, moreover, was a tough nut to crack. It could not be starved into surrender before the arrival of Brereton with Scottish reinforcements, and an effective breach could not be made in its walls without Rupert's artillery pieces, which were still at Oxford.[74]

Having relieved Beeston Castle, one of Chester's out-garrisons, Rupert and Maurice set off in a south-easterly direction as if heading for Worcester. However, when they reached Newport, they heard that the plundering and extortions of royalist troops in Herefordshire had provoked a serious uprising and that the rebels were threatening to attack the county town. They therefore crossed the Severn at Bewdley. Arriving at Hereford on 29 March,[75] they quickly dealt with those insurgents who had not already made themselves scarce on hearing of their approach. The princes then resumed their recruiting operations, their only military operation being a successful surprise attack on some of the Gloucester garrison cavalry at Ledbury on 22 April.[76] By then they had probably raised 1,000 men for the Oxford army and were ready to take the field, having presumably trained them in the use of pike and musket. However, they undermined their own efforts by allowing Gerard's corps to return to south-west Wales where the local parliamentarians with some outside help had overrun much of Pembrokeshire and parts of Cardigan and Carmarthen.[77] Brereton in the meantime had resumed his siege of Chester, having failed to persuade his Scottish reinforcements under David Leslie that they should combine forces and follow the princes into the marcher counties.[78]

The royalist generals had performed reasonably well given the resources at their disposal, but the king made a serious mistake at the start of the campaign by ordering Maurice to do too much with too few troops at too short notice.[79] Given that most of the king's veteran infantry were in winter quarters only two days' march from Worcester, it is amazing that they did not receive orders to join him for the expedition to Chester, and if Maurice had had another 2,000 or so infantry, it is possible that Shrewsbury might not have been drained of reliable troops. But it was Maurice as provincial commander rather than Rupert as lord general who carried the can. Although still responsible for North Wales and the border counties, Maurice never again held a field command. Overshadowed by his more outgoing and intelligent elder brother, he was written off by Clarendon as boorish and quarrelsome and too keen on the company of his social inferiors. However, he had been a steady and occasionally inspired commander of such of his uncle's armies that had come his way.

One final military operation took place in advance of the spring campaign. On 20 April the Committee of Both Kingdoms ordered Oliver Cromwell to use the cavalry and dragoons he had commanded in the West Country to prevent the king and the royalist artillery train leaving Oxford to join Rupert and Maurice. Cromwell duly rounded up all the draught horses he could find, but also did all he could to terrorise the enemy in the Thames and Cherwell valleys. He routed the earl of Northampton's cavalry brigade at Islip on the 24th. Three days later at Bampton-in-the-Bush he destroyed part of George Lisle's infantry brigade, the defenders of Shaw House in the Second Battle of Newbury, having earlier browbeaten the garrison of Bletchingdon House into surrender. Next he set siege to Faringdon, but the garrison commander realised that Oliver had no chance of storming the defences with cavalry and dragoons and treated his request to surrender with scorn.[80] In early May, Goring rode to the rescue, and Cromwell withdrew towards Reading and Newbury, thus allowing the king to join his nephews in the Cotswolds with the artillery train. Nevertheless Oliver had shown good evidence that he possessed the ability to run a successful operation on his own. In the short run he had also gained the initiative for his commander-in-chief. The king had expected to begin operations in mid-April. Instead it was Sir Thomas Fairfax who was first to take the field.[81]

CHAPTER 14

Fairfax, Rupert and the Battle of Naseby

S IR THOMAS Fairfax's command emerged from the chrysalis on 30 April 1645. His first orders were to lead the infantry and some of the cavalry on another relief expedition to Taunton, whilst the remainder were to continue helping Cromwell harass the king's forces in the Oxford area.[1] Halfway to Taunton new instructions arrived from Westminster. A battle was imminent somewhere to the south of Oxford. Rupert, Maurice and the king had rendezvoused in the Cotswolds and were likely to try and crush Cromwell Force in what might well be the Fourth Battle of Newbury. However, four regiments of New Model foot and one of horse, strengthened by local forces formerly part of Sir William Waller's army, were to continue towards Taunton under the command of Colonel Ralph Weldon.[2]

When it became apparent that the king was not looking for a battle in Berkshire but hurriedly marching north in the direction of Chester, Cromwell Force, strengthened by New Model infantry and troops from Abingdon under Major General Richard Browne, received instructions to follow him. Oliver was to rendezvous with the Scottish army, which had orders to march south once the enemy field army became active. Together they would be strong enough to fight Prince Rupert or at least to regain the initiative. Fairfax, on the other hand, was to hold himself in readiness to follow in the tracks of Weldon Force should it find difficulty in breaking through to Taunton.[3]

News of the relief of Taunton reached London on 14 May. Parliament then decided, on the recommendation of the Committee of Both Kingdoms, that the New Model Army should set siege to Oxford. The king would be diverted from his objective, whatever it was, by the need to save his headquarters. In addition, according to Lord Savile, who had recently spent some time in Oxford, a show of force should be sufficient to persuade discontented royalist officers to betray the city. Cromwell and Browne were therefore to return to the Thames valley with their infantry to assist Fairfax, whilst their cavalry and dragoons under Bartholomew Vermuyden, the senior colonel of horse, continued northwards in search of the Scots.[4]

The Oxford army, having convinced Sir William Brereton that it would be politic to abandon the siege of Chester, marched from north Shropshire into the

East Midlands heading for Newark, the jumping-off point for an invasion of the north of England, victory over the Scots and a vigorous recruiting drive, which ought to see the marquis of Newcastle's surviving infantry return to the colours. Instead the royalists took Leicester by storm in the hope of causing the New Model Army to abandon its operations against Oxford. Parliament duly obliged in the belief that the king's next move would be the long-promised invasion of the Eastern Association. Fairfax was to up sticks once more and deploy the New Model Army in the Upper Ouse valley guarding one of the principal gateways into the Fenlands. Vermuyden was to join him, and also Cromwell whom Parliament had sent into the Eastern Association almost a week earlier to organise resistance at the regional level.[5]

Instead, however, the royalist army marched south rather than east, taking up a position near Daventry on 4 June, even though its commanders knew before arriving there that the siege of Oxford was over. Nevertheless to Parliament and the Committee of Both Kingdoms the move to Daventry made sense. It gave the royalist high command a plethora of options. They could return to Oxford, advance into the Cotswolds and so into the south-west, march north towards Yorkshire, withdraw into the safety of the middle Severn valley, or attack the New Model Army in north Buckinghamshire. Alternatively, they could be waiting for reinforcements from the West Country and/or South Wales, as the latest intelligence suggested that Goring and Gerard were already well on their way.[6] To close down some of these options, Fairfax's orders were to advance on Daventry at full speed as soon as Vermuyden's regiments joined him.[7]

Amongst all this operational uncertainty Taunton continued to cause concern. The intention was for the relief force to strengthen parliamentary control over west Somerset by establishing a garrison at Ilminster,[8] or else to attempt a breakout,[9] but the military situation soon deteriorated. By late May, Weldon Force was in the same condition as Holbourne's earlier in the year, penned in by superior enemy forces and running short of supplies. Edward Massey, the governor of Gloucester, who had won a string of victories over local royalist forces in 1644 and early 1645 and was not a MP, took Waller's place as major general of the west on 24 May. His orders were to assemble yet another relief expedition from the south-coast garrisons, his Gloucestershire command, and those cavalry regiments formerly in Essex's and Waller's armies that had failed to make the cut for the New Model Army.[10] Massey, however, made slow progress, beset like his predecessor by lack of resources and demarcation disputes.[11]

In May and early June, Fairfax and the commanders of the various ad hoc groupings of New Model and non-New Model units were reacting to events as seen from Westminster rather than causing them to happen. The reason was that Parliament and the Committee of Both Kingdoms were pulling the strings, as the New Model ordinance had empowered them to do. The commanders in the field, often against their better judgement, had to dance to their tune, and they resented it. Fairfax disliked having to set siege to Oxford. Once it was over, he moaned to his father about spending 'time unprofitably before a town whilst the king hath time to strengthen himself'.[12] A similar sentiment is implicit in Cromwell's letter to Captain Stone reluctantly informing him that he had to leave the Midlands to take part in the siege.[13] In early June the shackles appeared to be about to tighten still further but on the 9th, seemingly against the odds, Fairfax gained operational freedom.[14]

The reason for this apparent volte-face was that Sir Thomas had completed his apprenticeship as army commander. When appointed commander-in-chief he was the only native Englishman who had led an army to victory but did not fall foul of the provisions of the Self-Denying Ordinance. However, Fairfax's experience as army general was limited, and Parliament and the Committee of Both Kingdoms must have had doubts about entrusting him with absolute command over what was now their only large army. This probably explains their initial decision to saddle him with a steering committee. However, pulling the strings on the Committee of Both Kingdoms were men like Essex and Manchester who may have felt, based on their experience of campaigning in 1644, that operational control from the centre was also on trial.

Fairfax began well by assembling the new expedition to Taunton so promptly. Then he had instantly obeyed the Committee's order to return eastwards despite the temptation to complete the mission. Moreover, the cunning he had shown in hoodwinking the enemy into believing his entire army was retreating earned its reward when the royalists scattered at Weldon Force's unexpected arrival, thinking it was the whole of the New Model Army. Finally, he had shown that he was capable of prudence as well as boldness. By taking a more circuitous return route through Hampshire and Berkshire, Fairfax ensured that the Oxford army had no chance of intercepting him. However, he was about to run into choppy waters.

Forced to sit down outside Oxford between 22 May and 2 June, Sir Thomas could do nothing to assist Massey in preparing his expedition. Nevertheless there were unfriendly comments in the London journals. For the same reason he could do nothing to curb the movements of the Oxford army across the Midlands culminating in the storming of Leicester. He got some of the blame, but it was unjustified. The Committee bore a measure of indirect responsibility by putting their trust in Lord Savile's gossip, but the real culprits were the earl of Leven and his political masters in Edinburgh. The Committee had intended the Scottish army to defend the North Midlands assisted by the forces under Vermuyden's command,[15] but Leven had a bigger priority. When in mid-May the royalist field army appeared to be making a beeline for Chester, his concern was that the king would send reinforcements up the west-coast route to Scotland to help the marquis of Montrose, whose victories in the Highlands and the Highland fringe were causing serious alarm to the Covenanter leadership. He therefore led the forces under his direct command, which had quartered for the winter in North Yorkshire, in the opposite direction. They finished up at Appleby in the Eden valley where they could keep in close touch with the rest of the Scottish army, which was laying siege to Carlisle. As a result the only troops the alliance had in the North Midlands in late May 1645 to confront Rupert's army were Vermuyden's regiments and a scattering of local garrison troops, which were neither battle-hardened nor battle-worthy.[16]

The abandonment of the siege of Oxford brought Fairfax no relief. In fact, the criticisms grew in intensity when, rather than marching quickly northwards to supervise arrangements for the defence of the Eastern Association, he tried to capture one of Oxford's out-garrisons as a sort of consolation prize. The Committee rapped him over the knuckles. He was told 'not to amuse yourself before Boarstall House' but to take immediate action to join up with other forces already gathering in the Buckingham area.[17] The committee at Cambridge, with administrative responsibility for the Eastern Association, went further, blaming him for languishing for three further days in the Oxford area instead of setting out immediately for East Anglia,[18] and Cromwell also stirred the pot. Writing to civilian colleagues in Suffolk on the same day, he passed on the news that 'the army at Oxford was not yesterday advanced, though it was ordered to do so'.[19] There was even talk in London of the earl of Essex being reappointed, presumably over Sir Thomas's head to avoid embarrassment.[20]

Discontent with army command came to a head on 4 June when the rulers of London, incensed at the storming of Leicester, the worst disaster to be suffered by a garrison town since the fall of Bristol almost two years earlier, presented a forthright petition to the Commons. Its principal demand was for the steering committee to be resurrected with representatives of the Committee of Both Kingdoms accompanying the army and having the power of veto over military decisions.[21] The clear implication was that Sir Thomas did not have the experience for supreme command, as unlike in 1644 there was no friction between the army commander and his senior officers which might impact disastrously on military decision-making.

The House of Commons responded positively, ordering the Committee of Both Kingdoms to nominate a new steering committee.[22] However, when the Committee debated the matter on 9 June, it informed the Commons that it could not nominate one which fairly represented Lords, Commons and Scots. This does not make sense. There were nineteen members present drawn from all three constituencies and from both the Independent and the Presbyterian factions in Parliament. Moreover, if there had been intense disagreement about the composition of the steering committee, it could not have conducted the vast amount of business it did on that day. In addition, if one faction had been strongly in favour of reinstating the steering committee, it would surely have raised the matter in one or other House. Instead the House of Commons accepted the Committee's decision, whilst the House of Lords passed no comment.

Almost certainly the membership issue was an excuse as the Committee had already resolved to give discretion to Sir Thomas and his officers, not to weigh him down with new chains. This it had said in so many words in a letter sent to Fairfax on the day the Londoners handed in their petition. He was 'to attend the motions of the king's army in such way, as being on the place, you may judge to be the best'.[23] His record over the past six weeks had been much more than satisfactory, and with a confrontation with the king's army in the offing, the army general advised by the Council of War was best placed to manage the run-up to the battle and the battle itself.[24]

The second demand of the London petition, that the Eastern Association should be strengthened by giving Oliver Cromwell power 'to raise and command the Association until some other course be taken to tend to the safety of the Association', was of no significance. It was not the first step towards his being appointed lieutenant general of horse in the New Model Army,[25] as the Committee had placed Oliver in overall charge of the forces of the Eastern Association during the previous week.[26] It took a completely different petition to raise Cromwell to the command of the New Model horse. This began with a proposal put by Fairfax to his Council of War on 8 June. As Cromwell's brigade was about to join forces with the New Model Army,[27] it made very good military sense to put his great abilities and experience to the best possible use 'in a time of so great an action'.[28]

The single point the New Model Army petition made, that there was no person with sufficient experience to command the horse in the approaching battle, was argument enough for the House of Commons. Middleton had resigned, Vermuyden had applied for leave to return to the Netherlands for personal reasons,[29] and Fairfax, despite his great experience in that role, could not lead the cavalry and perform effectively as army general. The petition may, of course, have been the culmination of a long-drawn-out intrigue to secure the post of lieutenant general of horse for Cromwell,[30] but I doubt it. The emergency was a real one and it arose from the particular military circumstances of the second week of June 1645. Moreover, the army officers were not asking for much. Cromwell's commission as lieutenant general, extended for another forty days from 12 May in accordance with the provisions of the Self-Denying Ordinance,[31] had another twelve days to run, and it should therefore be in force when the two armies squared up to one another. If so, he would be second in rank to Fairfax, and it would be contrary to military logic for him not to command the cavalry. In my opinion the petition was merely the New Model Army Council of War protecting itself against the chance that the battle might not take place until after Oliver's commission had expired.

In May 1645 Prince Rupert, like Fairfax, was under restraint, though of a less prescriptive nature. Though he was now lord general, the days were long gone when he dominated the Council of War. Charles had greater confidence both in his own abilities as commander-in-chief[32] and in his own competence to choose between several options.[33] Moreover, he had come to enjoy campaigning, and also to keeping his thumb on the pulse of military operations, which would be impossible if he remained at Oxford.[34] These developments potentially restricted the prince's independence as army commander, but at the start he retained considerable influence over his uncle and may have preferred to have him where he could see him.[35] He may also have been instrumental in removing some potential rivals from the king's presence. Nothing further was heard, for instance, of the king's proposal that Lord Forth should remain with the field army. Instead, late in the day, he joined the Prince of Wales's Council at Bristol.[36] Another rival, Lord Culpeper, was also a member of the Prince's Council, but not so easily sidelined. He continued to write to the king offering military advice,[37] as did the Prince's Council as a whole[38] and Sir Edward Nicholas, the mouthpiece of the privy councillors who remained at Oxford.[39] Thus, the king's power to pick and choose was probably greater than it had been in 1644 and he had no hesitation in using it. Writing to the queen just as the campaign was getting under way, he stated that the army was heading north, but that he might change his mind: 'if Fairfax be engaged far westwards, [he would] engage him there'.[40]

   Opposition to Rupert's northern strategy came to a head at a Council of War held on 8 May after the principal units of the Oxford army led by Rupert, Goring and King Charles himself had rendezvoused at Stow-on-the-Wold. Apparently only Rupert and the officers of the Northern Horse spoke in favour. A powerful body of opinion wanted to attack the New Model Army. However, the king decided on a compromise by which Goring returned to the West Country with the cavalry and dragoons he had brought with him.[41] Clarendon follows Walker in seeing this splitting of the field army as a fundamental strategic error,[42] but there is plentiful evidence that the king, Prince Rupert and Charles's other military advisers saw Goring as being only on temporary leave of absence, as did Goring himself.[43] On 19 May when the royal army was at Newport in Shropshire closing in on Chester and intelligence indicated that Fairfax and Cromwell were in pursuit, his orders were to leave the west and march as rapidly as possible to a rendezvous with the rest of the Oxford army in Leicestershire.[44] A week later when Oxford came under pressure from the New Model Army he was to march into the Thames valley, but if the enemy proved too strong he was to wait in the Newbury area until the rest of the army joined him.[45] In the event he never did return, but the reasons had little or nothing to do with the generals. Although Clarendon claims that Rupert did not want Goring anywhere near the king because of his silvery tongue, there is no other evidence that this was the case.[46]

   The extent to which Rupert was happy with the wanderings of the field army across the English Midlands after it left Stow-on-the-Wold must be a matter of speculation.[47] The northern scheme was still his obsession, and until 25 May everything was going his way. The attack on Leicester looks like a setback, but he did not take offence. He had planned and supervised the successful storming of the town, and it was a feather in his cap that it had gone so well. There is, however, a strong hint in both Walker's *Historical Discourses* and Rupert's diary that he opposed the decision to march south from Leicester to 'persuade' the Committee of Both Kingdoms to abandon the siege of Oxford.[48]

It is difficult not to see Rupert as chafing at the bit during the week spent at Daventry, but he did win some political skirmishes, successfully beating off an attempt by Sir Edward Nicholas to browbeat him into giving up the northern scheme, and thwarting a proposal of Lord Digby's that the king should return to Oxford rather than remain with the army.[49] The decision to set off northwards on 12 June, however, was probably not the prince's doing but a kneejerk reaction to news that Pontefract Castle, the only potential army base still in royalist hands in the north, would not be able to hold out for more than ten days.[50] Even so the king continued to keep his options open. For the moment, the army would go no further north than Belvoir Castle, the nearest of Newark's out-garrisons to Daventry.[51]

The jockeying for position that took place in the days immediately preceding the battle of Naseby gave Fairfax and Rupert the chance to show their mettle. Fairfax, whose army had quartered in the villages between Newport Pagnell and Olney from 6 June onwards, knew exactly where the Oxford army was,[52] but his approach march was an oddly circuitous one for a commander desperately keen to fight the enemy at the earliest opportunity. However, there were good reasons for it. Fairfax was expecting reinforcements, and they duly arrived, first some Northamptonshire cavalry, then Cromwell with 600 men from the Eastern Association, and finally Colonel Edward Rossiter's Lincolnshire regiment of horse.[53] Second, having petitioned Parliament for Cromwell to command the cavalry, it was not worth the risk of accidentally running into the enemy and having to fight a battle before he arrived.[54]

Setting out on 10 June, Sir Thomas marched off in the opposite direction, camping for the night at Stony Stratford on Watling Street. The decision to use a good road rather than heading across country to Northampton and so to Daventry was an understandable one given the size of his train, but instead of marching up Watling Street as far as Weedon, only five miles to the east of Daventry, the New Model Army left the road at Towcester and made off towards Northampton, thus adding an extra ten miles to the journey. It then camped for the night of the 11th/12th at Wootton, just short of the town.[55] On the following afternoon cavalry patrols clashed at Floore, a village somewhat nearer to Daventry than Northampton, but all the New Model Army did that day was march to Kislingbury, which was almost as close to the west side of Northampton as Wootton was to the south.

By the time Cromwell and his Eastern Association cavalry arrived early on 13 June, the Oxford army was on the move, but for quite a number of hours Fairfax was under the impression that it was heading towards Warwick and the Severn valley. As a result the New Model Army marched only seven miles that day, camping for the night in villages around Guilsborough on what is now the Northampton to Leicester road. That evening Sir Thomas learned from royalist cavalrymen captured in an alehouse at Naseby that the enemy army was at Market Harborough in the Welland valley, only eight miles from Guilsborough. Before first light the New Model Army was on its way, the king's forces turned to face it, and the two armies duly deployed at about 10 o'clock in the morning on either side of a small valley where Naseby and Sibbertoft parishes joined.[56] It was open-field country, but the site was a constricted one with a steep escarpment to the east and to the west a thick hedgerow separating Naseby's open fields from the small enclosures of what had once been the home manor of Sulby Abbey.

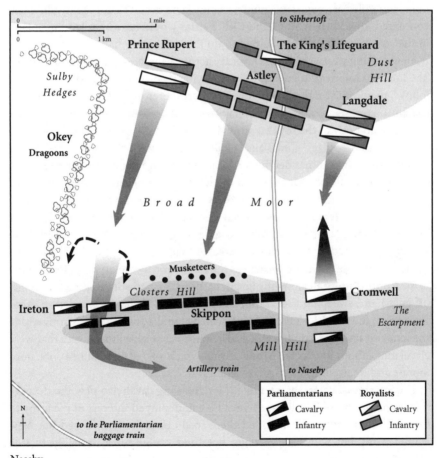

Naseby

What was happening on the other side of the hill is easy to understand at a generalised level, but some important detail is unclear. The intelligence that Rupert received throughout the Northamptonshire stage of the campaign was poor.[57] As a result the clash of patrols at Floore came as a complete surprise. The next day's march of some fifteen miles across country was a great success, but why did the king decide to confront the enemy on 14 June rather than continue north towards Belvoir? Lord Digby claimed that it was Rupert who persuaded his uncle to fight without consulting the Council of War. This may have been the case, even though *Historical Discourses* claimed that the prince did not want to fight, as the two statements are not contradictory.[58] The royalist high command was unaware that the New Model Army was so close until several hours after sunset, and complete disengagement the following morning would have been well nigh impossible. The River Welland, unlike the Thames and the Kennet, was too close to its source to have choke points where a party of infantry or dragoons could hold off the enemy for hours, and beyond the Welland lay miles and miles of open-field country. There is no doubt that if the royalists had continued towards Belvoir on the 14th, Fairfax would have handled the pursuit in the same way as he had planned to do the day before had the Oxford army been marching westward from Daventry across a similar agricultural landscape: 'the horse to interrupt their rear', thus delaying its progress, and 'the infantry to follow', to administer the killer blow.[59] Rupert therefore had no choice. He had to fight.

The main body of the royalist army deployed in two lines on Dust Hill facing towards Naseby village a mile and a half to the south, with the infantry in the centre, probably commanded by Sir Jacob Astley, and the cavalry on the wings, the right under Prince Maurice and the left under Sir Marmaduke Langdale.[60] There was also a strong reserve line of two infantry regiments, Prince Rupert's and the king's lifeguard. Sandwiched between them were the king and the queen's lifeguards of horse, fighting as a single body.[61] Rupert must have strongly suspected that his army was weaker than the New Model Army in both horse and foot. In such circumstances the best tactic was to attack in force at the earliest opportunity all along the line of battle in the hope of catching the enemy off-guard and sweeping them from the battlefield.[62] What he needed to avoid was prolonged hand-to-hand fighting, which would advantage the stronger side the longer it lasted. A sudden attack also made sense given the stories that were circulating about the New Model Army's lack of battle-readiness, its poor morale and quarrelling amongst its senior officers.

Rupert almost certainly intended the right-wing cavalry to play the decisive role, as he put himself at its head once he had deployed the rest of the army to his satisfaction. What he intended them to do once he had routed the New Model Army left wing is uncertain, but their orders were probably to ride around the back of the New Model infantry and attack the enemy right wing in the rear whilst they were locked in combat with Langdale's brigades,[63] a tactic used by the Duc d'Enghien in his victory over a larger Spanish army at Rocroi less than two years earlier.[64] With the whole of the New Model Army cavalry off the field, Rupert could then deal at leisure with the New Model Army infantry.

Skippon deployed the New Model infantry in a reasonably orthodox manner on Closters Hill despite the constricted nature of the site. He placed five regiments in the front line. In consequence the regiment on the extreme right, Sir Thomas Fairfax's, overlapped the royalist infantry formation. It could thus wheel to the left in textbook fashion and attack the enemy in the flank, a tactic that had probably helped the Eastern Association regiments win the infantry battle at Marston Moor. The second line comprised three strong regiments with a substantial gap between Colonel Edward Harley's on the left and Colonel Robert Hammond's and Thomas Rainsborough's on the right. This would allow sufficient room for the weaker regiments in the centre of the first line to fall back behind them and redeploy if driven back by the enemy, whilst their pursuers would find it difficult to push forward because of the intensive musketry fire from the second line.[65]

Cromwell, to whom Fairfax delegated the deployment of the horse, ordered Colonel John Okey's regiment of dragoons to line Sulby hedges so that they could fire into the flank of the royalist right-wing cavalry as they charged.[66] The New Model Army left wing commanded by Henry Ireton he drew up in two lines, the classic attacking formation for open country, as there was space to do so between the west edge of Closters Hill and the hedges. Because of the length of the infantry line Cromwell could not do the same on the right, where he stationed himself at the start of the battle. He therefore drew his squadrons up in three lines, with the third line forming a true reserve which he could use as and when required.

Fairfax's first intervention according to Lord Orrery was to order the first line of the infantry to fall back from the forward-facing slope of Closters Hill to the summit,[67] thus forcing the royalist infantry brigades to attack uphill. This could cause their tight formations to unravel before contact,[68] but it left insufficient space for the regiments in the second line to deploy on the hill itself. They therefore formed up in the narrow valley behind. His second intervention was not to begin the battle with a textbook-type cannonade. Possibly after the experience of Marston Moor he saw it as a complete waste of time, but the more likely explanation is that it was not his decision to make. Rupert dispensed with a cannonade to increase his chances of catching the New Model Army by surprise, and his attack went in before the New Model heavy artillery was in position.[69]

The traditional tale of the battle of Naseby is that the royalist right-wing cavalry defeated the New Model horse facing them, but then instead of turning to attack the rest of the enemy army they chased their defeated opponents all over the landscape just as they had done at Edgehill two and a half years earlier. However, if traced back through the literature, the source for this damning indictment turns out, not surprisingly, to be Lord Clarendon, whose word can never be trusted when writing about the king's commanders whom he disliked. In fact, the king's cavalry had learned not to behave in this manner by the time of Roundway Down, and at Naseby much of the right wing stopped and may have tried to carry out the manoeuvre suggested above.[70] However, blocking the best route for hitting the enemy right wing in the rear were the 3,000 or so New Model pikemen and musketeers in the second line of Skippon's infantry formation, and not unnaturally the royalist cavalry turned away. In the next valley short of Naseby village and to the rear of the main body of the enemy army they found the New Model artillery train. This was a less serious obstacle and so they attacked it causing some casualties, but they could not shift the artillerymen and fell back disconsolately towards their starting point.[71]

The failure of the royalist right wing to make any headway against the rest of the enemy army after routing the cavalry facing it may have owed something to the way in which Fairfax had drawn up his infantry and his artillery train. However, the sudden collapse of the rest of the royalist army half an hour into the battle owed much to Prince Rupert, who had conspicuously failed to combine the conflicting roles of leading from the front and managing the reserves. After putting himself at the head of the right-wing cavalry, he left his uncle instructions as to how to manage the reserve line in his absence. This arrangement, though risky, could have worked, but it was utterly dependent on the melee being over very quickly so that the prince could return before his instructions became overtaken by events or the king decided to disregard them. However, the melee was a prolonged affair lasting for twenty minutes or so.[72] When at last the enemy fled and the royalist horse moved off to carry out the next stage of the battle plan, Rupert rode back towards Dust Hill only to find the battle to all intents and purposes lost. The instructions he had left the king for managing the reserve line had unravelled in a spectacular manner.

Sir Marmaduke Langdale's first line on the royalist left wing had duly charged the enemy as instructed a split second after Prince Rupert, and Cromwell ordered his first line to ride forward to meet them. Initially, there was a very stiff fight in which squadrons in the New Model front line suffered heavy casualties, but it was not long before second-line formations came to their support and Langdale's men fell back under pressure of numbers.[73] At this point part or all of Langdale's second line appears to have made off without engaging the enemy.[74] As the royalist left wing collapsed, the king led forward the lifeguards, his aim being to charge Langdale's pursuers in the flank before they could attack the royalist infantry in the rear. However, this involved a ninety-degree wheel to the left that would bring them within range of the musketeers of Sir Thomas Fairfax's regiment of foot, which up to that point had played no part in the battle. It was therefore ready to deliver a full barrage of 900 or so musket balls into their ranks as they passed.[75]

This alone probably explains what happened next. A Scottish nobleman riding beside the king shouted that Charles was going to his death. Seizing the king's bridle he forced his horse to stop, whereupon the charge juddered to a halt. The next order was a ninety-degree wheel to the right and the lifeguard fell into confusion. This is scarcely surprising because if the troopers had obeyed it they would have either collided with the rear of their own infantry or else run head-on into the massed pikes and muskets of Fairfax's regiment. Totally confused, they turned tail and rode off towards Sulby Hedges in a disorderly mob where they were soundly peppered by Okey's dragoons.[76]

The royalist infantry in the meantime had been fighting their own battle largely undisturbed by what was happening on their flanks.[77] Initially, the first and presumably the second line of king's foot made good progress against the New Model first line, inflicting very heavy casualties on one regiment and probably driving back two or three more.[78] However, the New Model second line stabilised the situation and may have begun making headway against the royalists.[79] At this point the two regiments of foot in Rupert's reserve line should have moved forward in support, but a comment in one enemy report of the battle and strong archaeological evidence suggest that they remained exactly where they were. With the prince fighting on the right wing and the king leading the lifeguards in an attempt to restore the situation on the left, there was nobody to give them the order to advance.[80]

Whilst all this was going on, Cromwell used his cavalry reserves to complete the royalist defeat. Giving his first- and second-line troopers instructions not to chase Langdale's horse off the battlefield but to keep an eye on them as they fell back over the crest of Dust Hill, he ordered the rest of his squadrons to wipe out the two regiments of foot in the king's reserve line.[81] This they did, probably with some help from Okey's dragoons. As a result the main body of royalist infantry still fighting on the slopes of Closters Hill found themselves hemmed in on all sides. With no prospect of rescue, they promptly surrendered. A modern myth that some units made a fighting retreat from the battlefield to Wadborough Hill, two miles to the rear, where they fought it out until overwhelmed, is totally wrong.[82] Another more established myth – that the troopers who had defeated Langdale's men completed the encirclement of the royalist infantry – is also wrong. It was fresh troops who did the deed.[83]

In the meantime Rupert and the king were trying to put their cavalry in order somewhere near Sibbertoft village, but before the redeployment was complete Fairfax had drawn up his infantry and cavalry regiments in line of battle and they were clearly visible advancing on the royalist position. The king apparently tried to get an attack going, but prolonged resistance was impossible without infantry firepower. The charge spluttered out well before making contact, whereupon the royalist horse took to their heels. Chased by Cromwell's troopers, they did not stop until they reached Leicester.[84]

Of the two tactical decisions that appear to have swung the battle, one, the deployment of the dragoons along Sulby Hedges, was certainly Oliver Cromwell's idea, and the other, the use of the cavalry reserves to surround the royalist infantry, probably so.[85] But what was Fairfax's role in the battle? For most of the time he was in the central part of the battlefield encouraging his troops as they came under pressure and displaying his customary bravery under fire.[86] Whitelock, however, records one incident that puts his understanding of what an army general should or should not do on the battlefield in a very different light. Whitelock's informant, Captain Charles D'Oyley, who commanded Fairfax's lifeguard of horse, described an attack on the last enemy infantry brigade still fighting, which had already beaten off two charges by D'Oyley's troop. Sir Thomas rode up and ordered D'Oyley to attack it again from the front whilst he attacked it from the rear with a commanded body of horse. The tactic succeeded and the two officers met in the middle where Fairfax killed the ensign carrying the infantry colonel's colours,[87] but it was extremely foolhardy for the commander-in-chief to risk his life in such a manner when his army had clearly won the battle.[88]

CHAPTER 15

Fairfax and Goring

WHAT HAD happened on the battlefield at Naseby vindicated the decision of the Committee of Both Kingdoms to give Fairfax his operational independence but after persuading Leicester to surrender he was reluctant to take responsibility for the next decision, which was a strategic one, without the complete backing of his political masters. After their defeat the king, Prince Rupert and their cavalry, still several thousand strong, had made their way across the Midlands to Hereford where they met General Charles Gerard's corps and immediately set about raising new infantry regiments for the Oxford army colonels, most of whom had escaped from the battlefield on horseback.[1] Should the New Model Army follow the king or should it head for the south-west of England to do battle with Goring? The Committee of Both Kingdoms wanted to leave the choice to Fairfax, using almost the same words as it had done on 4 June.[2] He was as keen to deal with Goring as they were, but Fairfax also wanted the approval of Parliament,[3] because if he advanced into the south-west there was the risk that Rupert would threaten London or invade the Eastern Association. It was not until 28 June when Fairfax reached Marlborough that he received Parliament's permission to go after Goring.[4] There was now no longer any chance of the survivors of Naseby making a breakout. The Scottish army, which had set out from the far north of England before Naseby and was now at Nottingham, was heading towards Worcester. Once there it would be quite capable of deterring the king's forces from trying to venture into the English Midlands.[5]

The royalist game plan was to augment the size of Goring's army to such an extent that the New Model Army could be brought to battle a second time and defeated. Gerard's infantry and the newly raised Welsh regiments were to be shipped across the Bristol Channel, whilst the cavalry rode into the west via Worcester, the Cotswolds and the Wiltshire Downs. In the meantime the king would establish his headquarters at Bristol for the comeback campaign. Goring's role was to create sufficient time for all this to happen.[6] He failed, of course, but for many his part in the downfall of the royalist cause began six weeks earlier, that is, well before Naseby.

The charge is that after returning to Somerset in mid-May, Goring received several orders to rejoin the field army but chose to ignore them. As a result

Rupert had insufficient cavalry at Naseby to exploit his success on the right wing and/or to smother Cromwell's breakthrough on the left.[7] Goring was therefore responsible for the royalists losing the First Civil War. The point is worth making, but superior numbers have never been a guarantee of victory. Nobody can prove that Rupert would have saved the day had Goring and his cavalry been with him on Dust Hill, but more importantly the premise underpinning the accusation is false. The charge of disobedience is at best misconceived and at worst just plain wrong.

Any examination of Goring's personal contribution towards the disaster in Northamptonshire must begin with his standing with the king and his peers in late June and early July. Every piece of evidence from the royalist side points to his being in the highest favour, not the scapegoat for what had happened at Naseby. In addition, his letters to Prince Rupert and Lord Digby show that he regarded them as allies, if not friends, working towards a common goal. He had indeed received two orders to rejoin the Oxford army during the course of May, but his political masters, the Prince of Wales's Council, had stopped him leaving until the king had had time to look at their case for him staying where he was.[8] The enemy forces at Taunton and in the Dorset garrisons were now so strong that if he left the West Country Colonel Ralph Weldon would quickly overrun Somerset and Devon or else would follow him, bringing almost as many troops for the New Model Army as Goring would be adding to Prince Rupert's. By the first week in June there is no doubt whatsoever that the Prince's Council had convinced the king. Goring was to continue blockading Taunton.[9] The fact that the Oxford army spent over a week at Daventry had nothing to do with him. He was therefore in no way to blame either directly or indirectly for what happened at Naseby.

But what had been going on in Somerset in late May and early June? Goring had arrived two days too late to prevent Weldon relieving Taunton. That was also not his fault. He knew the New Model Army was on the march and his horse and dragoons had ridden south from Stow as fast as they could.[10] Goring naturally assumed that the royalist commanders in Somerset would be able to hold on until he arrived as they should be following the advice he had given them before his departure, which was in strict accordance with military doctrine of the day. This was to establish a cavalry screen at some distance from the siege to monitor any forward movement by the enemy, thus giving the siege commander plenty of time to organise his response.[11] However, Goring's words fell on deaf ears. The Prince's Council had approved the decision of the man in charge to concentrate his forces in western Somerset and to rely on intelligence provided by the Dorset royalists, who told him that Fairfax's whole army had reached Blandford and then retreated.[12] When he then heard to his amazement a few days later that enemy forces were at Chard, he panicked and his troops fled for their lives, their assumption being that the entire New Model Army was in the offing when in fact the besiegers probably had more troops than Weldon.[13]

When Goring arrived in west Somerset on 14 May, he ordered a general rendezvous at Kingsmoor near Ilchester, which according to John Digby produced an army of some 11,000 men divided pretty equally between horse and foot. Their task was to prevent the relief party making a breakout and rejoining Fairfax. On the 17th Weldon set out to do just this. The bulk of his force had reached Martock in the enclosed country fifteen miles to the east of Taunton when Goring struck.[14] This was his first mistake. He should have waited until the enemy reached the open country beyond. There he could have used his huge superiority in cavalry to delay their progress and then bring up infantry support to break up their formations with massed musket fire.

Weldon reacted quickly to the danger. He immediately fell back behind the line of the River Parrett just to the west of Martock and prepared to defend the crossing points. His intention was probably to conduct an orderly retreat to Taunton rather than to sidestep via Crewkerne to Axminster and the safety of the south coast garrisons, but the intelligence Goring received suggested that the enemy plan was indeed to follow Holbourne's route to the Channel coast. He therefore sent off 1,000 horse under Sir William Courtney towards Crewkerne with the rest to follow, the intention being to prevent Weldon reaching the broken country to the south of the town. He then ordered an infantry assault on the bridge over the Parrett at South Petherton, probably with the intention of trapping Weldon's force in a pincer movement. On taking charge of the vanguard he discovered that the enemy were heading for Taunton, not Crewkerne, and chased after them, leaving the infantry and the rest of the cavalry to follow in his wake. However, the latter continued towards Crewkerne and ran into Sir William Courtney's brigade rather than Weldon Force. Unfortunately, it took them two or three hours of fighting in which several troopers were killed before they discovered the truth of the matter. Goring in the meantime was over the hill and far away, sparring with the enemy rearguard and totally unaware of what was happening behind him.[15]

The affair at Petherton bridge on 19 May was another of Goring's fiascos (though he preferred to use the term 'fantastical accident'), but on this occasion the reason was not bad luck but his own inexperience in handling large bodies of men taking part in a complex operation. The upshot was that Weldon Force got back to Taunton with scarcely a scratch.[16] However, for the royalists the Petherton bridge incident was an opportunity lost rather than a disaster. Lord Culpeper's assessment is probably the fairest: Goring 'has sufficiently scared the rebels but not destroyed them',[17] and the strategic outcome was a reasonably positive one. Weldon's failure to achieve a breakout ensured that Fairfax's field army went into battle at Naseby minus one regiment of cavalry and with its infantry a third smaller than it could have been.

The military situation in west Somerset for the next seven weeks was a rerun of December to March. Goring could not lay close siege to Taunton or capture it by assault as it was defended by a force of 4,000–5,000 men. All he could do was institute a blockade and hope to force the garrison to surrender through starvation, a task he estimated would take him until the end of August.[18] Weldon's corps, on the other hand, was not strong enough to make its escape without help. All it could do was wait patiently for yet another relief expedition to break through the royalist cordon.

By 27 June at the latest Goring knew the results of the battle of Naseby, and also that Major General Edward Massey was trying to assemble a relief force.[19] He had two operational plans. If Massey was all he had to face, he would try and defeat him in battle as he closed in on Taunton. If he faced both Massey and Fairfax, he would withdraw into Devonshire and take up a strong defensive position in the enclosed country just over the county boundary. On 30 June, having received no orders from the king or Prince Rupert, and determined not to be surprised into an incautious move if the enemy crept up on him unawares, he informed the Prince's Council that he had abandoned the blockade of Taunton and ordered a rendezvous at Chard, thus blocking the route habitually taken by enemy relief forces. However, if overpressed by numbers, he would fall back into Devonshire.[20]

Within a day of writing to the Prince's Council, Goring received a new set of orders from the king, which required a completely different operational plan. His task was now to retain control of the West Country until the rest of the king's forces joined him and Charles himself moved his headquarters to Bristol, from where he could manage the war more effectively.[21] By then, however, he had probably received the unwelcome news that he would be facing both enemy armies.[22] The task of setting up a defensive perimeter covering the Somerset ports, the biggest of which was Bridgwater, and then holding it against a much larger force for a period of three to four weeks, seems in retrospect formidable if not well nigh impossible.[23] To make matters worse, Goring only had four days at most between receiving his orders and the enemy armies' arriving on his doorstep.[24] Fairfax and Massey, having met up at Blandford on 2 July, had reached Beaminster and the Chard area respectively by the 4th.[25] Goring's only advantages were the landscape of small fields, rivers and marshes that lay to the north of Chard, which by now he knew very well, and the certainty that the enemy would find very few provisions for men or horses. The harvest would not be in until September and the villages along the Somerset/Dorset border had already been picked clean by royalist troops.

Goring decided to use a defensive line following the rivers Parrett and Yeo to hold back the enemy until reinforcements from across the Bristol Channel made him strong enough to take the fight to them. Strengthening the line were four garrisons established during the siege of Taunton or earlier, defending the principal crossing points, Bridgwater in the north followed by Burrow, Langport and Ilchester. He could do nothing to prevent Weldon's regiments rejoining the

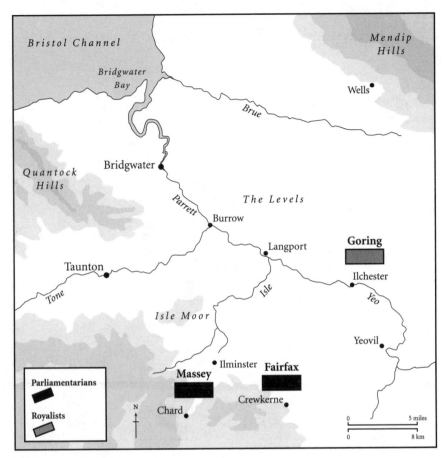

The Langport Campaign

New Model Army, which they did on 5 or 6 July,[26] but his was to be an active defence. For the next three days he kept the parliamentarians on their toes, inspiring one London journal to describe him as 'dancing from one side of the river to the other'.[27] However, numbers counted in the end, with Fairfax managing to force the river line at Yeovil. Goring successfully evacuated Ilchester, and fell back on Langport, the next garrison to the north. In addition, he ordered Major General George Porter with several brigades of cavalry to take up a position at Isle Moor on the west side of the Parrett. The purpose appears to have been a defensive one, namely to deter the garrison of Taunton from threatening Bridgwater or Burrow, but Fairfax thought it was a sign that Goring was about to try and capture Taunton by a surprise attack, its garrison having been greatly weakened by Weldon's departure. He therefore ordered Massey's army to see the royalists off and sent him four regiments of horse and dragoons and a commanded party of musketeers as reinforcements. Fairfax in his turn

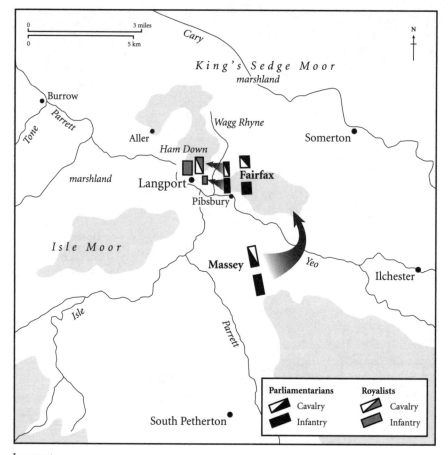

Langport

continued to advance along the east bank of the Parrett towards Langport. By the evening of 9 July his foremost units were at Long Sutton, three miles short of the town.

Porter, by all accounts the best company but the worst general officer in the king's employ, had given his men the day off. They spent it drinking and swimming in the River Isle. He had not posted any scouts and the first sign of Massey's approach was when enemy horsemen appeared on the horizon. What followed was a turkey shoot. Three of Goring's brigades fell apart, and even though he himself rode over from Langport to stop the rot, the incident at Isle Moor adversely affected the morale of the rest of his cavalry.[28]

At this point it is possible to determine what was going on in Goring's mind with a fair degree of certainty.[29] With Massey at Isle Moor threatening communications with Bridgwater on the west bank of the Parrett, Goring kept his army on the east bank, deploying it for the moment in a very confined space on Ham

Down just north of Langport. Although protected on one flank by the Parrett, it could easily be outflanked on the other, and was therefore not the place to remain for any length of time, as he was still outnumbered by two to one despite having recently received some infantry regiments from across the Bristol Channel. On the morning of 10 July his intention was to carry out an orderly retreat to Burrow, which was more easily defensible than Langport, having the extensive marshes of the Somerset levels protecting the flank that did not rest on the river.

The only serious threat to a prolonged standoff at Burrow would be a direct enemy attack in force on Bridgwater, but first Goring had to get to Burrow. Much the safest route was along the east bank of the Parrett, as Massey dominated the west. However, the country over which the army would have to pass presented certain difficulties. The Somerset levels were technically speaking open land with no hedges or walls, but as well as being marshy they were crisscrossed by drainage ditches with steep sides that were largely impassable to horses.[30] Control of the road to Burrow was therefore of vital importance, and there was only one pass, at Aller two miles beyond Langport. However, at some time in the night Goring must have received intelligence that Fairfax was in the process of withdrawing Massey's army and its reinforcements back across the Parrett. He therefore ordered Richard Bulstrode, his adjutant, to make preparations for the infantry and the artillery train and carriages to cross to the west bank and proceed to Burrow by that route, escorted by a brigade of cavalry under the command of Lord Wentworth.[31]

What followed provides a further example of Goring's inadequacy as an army commander. The staff work involved in crossing to the west bank was well done. By early morning on 10 July the artillery train was at Langport bridge, and the bulk of the infantry regiments with their cavalry escort were close behind in the town and its outskirts, ready to follow. Behind them on Ham Down was the rest of the cavalry.[32] However, the arrangements for protecting the rear of the army were far too casual. The approach to Langport from the direction of Long Sutton had few natural advantages for the defence. All that stood between the royalist army, drawn up in line of march, and the parliamentary forces on Long Sutton Down, was the valley of the Wagg Rhyne. The Rhyne itself was a small brook carrying little water, whilst the slope between it and Ham Down was a gentle one, though crisscrossed by a number of hedge lines. Over it passed a lane which crossed the brook by a ford and led in the direction of Somerton. To defend this apology for a pass, Goring assigned two field pieces and a couple of regiments of foot recently arrived from South Wales, who had had little experience of fighting, though their conduct suggests that they had received some training.[33] It was not normal practice to use greenish troops to cover the rear of an army with the enemy in hot pursuit. Commanders usually gave that sort of job to their best infantry and dragoons, as Lords Forth and Hopton had done at

Cheriton.[34] Their only reserve was a single cavalry formation, probably no more than 300 strong, drawn up on the down beyond.[35] What Goring should have done, given the lack of experience of the rearguard he had posted along the Wagg Rhyne, was position a much stronger brigade in close support to harass the enemy infantry as they passed through the last hedge line and emerged onto the open down.

Fairfax, concerned that he would have to retreat through lack of supplies if he did not immediately engage with the enemy, ordered an early morning attack on the pass without waiting for Massey to arrive. His heavy artillery plastered the enemy position, quickly knocking out their field pieces. For the assault stage he appointed a commanded party of a thousand or so musketeers and a forlorn hope of six troops of cavalry to exploit their success. The commanded musketeers briskly went about their work of clearing the enemy infantry from the hedges, whilst the heavy artillery, having accomplished their first task, raised their sights and caused alarm and despondency amongst Goring's already shaken cavalry which were sitting targets, as it were, on Ham Down.

When the first of the musketeers reached the hedge line bordering the down and began firing on the royalist cavalry beyond, Cromwell sent in half the cavalry, a squadron some 250 strong commanded by Major Christopher Bethell.[36] Only two abreast, they charged over the ford, up the lane and straight into the enemy support troops who, taken by surprise, began to give way. Goring himself led a counter-charge against the front and the flank of the enemy formation and for a time made headway against them, but he then allowed them to fall back and regroup. Having been joined by the rest of the forlorn hope, Bethell's troops charged again. The royalist formation then broke, the rest of the royalist cavalry set off after them, and the confrontation stage of the battle was over. However, there was enough time for Goring's artillery and infantry to cross Langport bridge including, amazingly, the two regiments that had tried to defend the pass. There was no pursuit. Royalist pioneers had destroyed the drawbridge and also set fire to the town. As a result Cromwell was left fuming on the wrong side of the river, whilst Massey, who should have been on the west bank ready to counter such a move, was out of the picture altogether. Led by Major General Joseph Wagstaffe, Goring's infantry and artillery train arrived safely at Bridgwater the following morning.[37]

Fairfax's caution was clearly responsible for the escape of the royalist infantry. First, given the numbers of troops at his disposal, he had no real excuse for not maintaining a strong presence on the west bank of the Parrett as a precaution against the enemy crossing Langport bridge.[38] Second, once the engagement at the lane head was over, he behaved exactly as he had done at Naseby. The pursuit of the royalists did not begin until the regiments on Sutton Down had taken up their correct places on the edge of Ham Down in battle array.[39] Possibly he held back because he could not see whether or not there was a

The true and liuely Pourtraicture
of Robert Earle of Essex his Excellence
Generall of the Army etc.

Guil.ᵐ Dobson pinxit

Guil.ᵐ ffaithorne sculp

London printed and Are to be sold by P. Stent at y.ᵉ white horse in guilt spurstreet without Newgate

1 The Earl of Essex

2 The King's Commanders

3 Prince Rupert

4 George Goring

5 The Earl of Clarendon

6 George, Lord Digby

The Effigies of the most Excellent & truly valliant Sr Thomas Fairfax Capr: tin Generall of the Armies raised for the preservation of Religion, defence of King Parliamt. & Kinadome London Printed and sold by Peter Stent.

7 Sir Thomas Fairfax

8 Oliver Cromwell

royalist line of battle waiting for him on the far side of Ham Down, but he could at least have allowed the two squadrons to continue their probing attack and then supported them with the other cavalry regiments as they arrived on the down. If he had done this instead of waiting, he would have stood a very good chance of capturing Langport bridge intact and preventing the enemy infantry making its escape, even if the troops of cavalry that made up his forlorn hope sustained heavier casualties in the process.

However, the fate of the royalist cavalry was a different matter altogether. They fled in disorder into the levels where the drainage ditches created bottle-necks and cul-de-sacs in which many troopers were slaughtered or taken pris-oner. Others, seeking to cross the drainage channels and dikes, dismounted and were hunted down in ones and twos like infantry. As a result Goring lost 1,500 horse, including many officers, but only a third that number of infantry, a most unusual occurrence in an early modern battle when the defeated army was as strong in horse as it was in foot.[40] Goring managed to escape, but the report he wrote three day later for Lord Digby describing the measures he had taken since the battle to preserve his forces was a gloomy one.[41] It was made even worse on 23 July when Fairfax stormed Bridgwater and captured a cornucopia of military supplies and 1,000 royalist foot soldiers.[42]

After Langport Sir Thomas Fairfax continued his conquest of England south of the Thames, showing much competence but little flair. After capturing Bridgwater, his first thought seems to have been to pursue Goring, but there were other considerations. Royalist garrisons situated on or close to the major roads from Donnington Castle and Basing House in the east to Sherborne and Devizes in the west threatened his supply routes, and the fate of Essex's army in Cornwall the previous year was a warning against relying on what could be brought in by sea.[43] Second, MPs for the southern counties pressed for the capture of all remaining enemy garrisons so as to make internal trade secure and thus hasten economic recovery. MPs with constituents living in London, the Home Counties and East Anglia had a different concern. If the king returned to Oxford with several thousand cavalry when the New Model Army was busy else-where, they could well plunder and devastate everywhere within a sixty-mile radius.[44] The advice of the Council of War that the New Model Army should deal with the back areas first may have prevented an all-out row. It also produced a string of successes. Between 30 July and 10 September, Fairfax and his regi-ments captured Sherborne, Bath and Bristol, whilst Massey's army remained in the Taunton area keeping an eye on Goring.

Now was the opportunity for Sir Thomas to invade the royalist far south-west, but there was still concern about south-central England reverting to lawlessness should he do so, and Cromwell duly set out in September with three regiments of foot to capture Devizes, Winchester and Basing House.[45] Anxiety returned two months later when the king returned to his capital for the winter, even though he left his few remaining forces in the Welsh Marches. By then Fairfax was in deepest Devonshire, but nonetheless the Committee of Both Kingdoms ordered him to send several regiments back east to help pen the royalists into their ring of garrisons around Oxford.[46]

Goring, on the other hand, was inactive from the time he retreated into north Devon after Langport until he left for France in mid-November, the only sign of his former liveliness being a successful attack on outposts of the New Model Army in the Blackdown hills on the night of 13 October as Fairfax at last crossed from Somerset into Devon.[47] He could still theoretically assemble an army of some size, and ought to have been able to deal with Massey's army if it tried to block his passage eastwards to disrupt Fairfax's siege operations. However, should he try and do so his communications with the far south-west would be threatened by the line of parliamentary garrisons across the neck of the south-western peninsula which Fairfax had completed with the capture of Bridgwater and Sherborne.[48] It was also highly unlikely that Fairfax would allow him free rein to destroy Massey, let alone risk him rejoining what was left of the king's field army without doing something about it.

However, there were other reasons for the passivity of the royalist western command. According to one account, Goring had lost interest in fighting.[49] This may have been because he saw the military situation as hopeless. Alternatively, he may have thought it best to keep as quiet as possible so as not to attract the attention of the New Model Army and its political masters. In time the king's forces might turn back the tide elsewhere in England and rescue him and his men, as Prince Maurice had been rescued in 1644.[50] Another factor was that Goring was in pain for much of the time and worn down by ongoing rows with the Prince's Council. Finally, when he did bestir himself, he had difficulties in getting together a serviceable field army. Cavalry he had in plenty, but on reaching safety in the Barnstaple area the infantry that escaped from Langport quickly dwindled to fewer than 2,000 men, most of the Cornish soldiers having returned home without leave.[51] As a result, when ordered to relieve Bristol, Goring was reliant on local administrators to impress men to fill up the ranks. This, of course, took time and the city surrendered well before he was ready to march.[52]

Prince Rupert faced different problems. His military reputation had suffered a devastating blow at Naseby, but he threw himself into implementing the new strategy. From late June onwards he was in the West Country discussing opera-tional matters with Goring and the Prince of Wales's Council, and then at Bristol strengthening its defences in preparation for his uncle's arrival,[53] but as a result he could play little part in the decision-making process, which became increas-ingly dominated by Lord Digby whose optimism buoyed up the king's spirits but clouded his judgement.[54] The effects were soon apparent. First, and not surprisingly after the defeat at Langport and the loss of Bridgwater, Digby informed Rupert that Charles would not be travelling to Bristol, but that it might be best for Rupert to remain there rather than return to South Wales.[55] The next decision was for the king and most of the 4,000 or so men he still had with him to join forces with the marquis of Montrose who was still winning victories in Scotland.[56] This was not to Rupert's liking and he did not mince his words in letters to his friends.[57] By early August the king and his advisers did not even seek his advice about future operations, though it did not help matters that the prince was openly expressing his opinion that the royalists could no longer win the war, and that the king should reopen negotiations with Parliament whilst he still had some troops under his command.[58]

The loss of Bristol on 11 September after a siege of only just over a fortnight was the final blow to the prince's reputation. His uncle dismissed him from all his military commands, but the lowest point in their relationship did not occur until the following month when there was an open row at Newark between Rupert's supporters and the king.[59] During the winter Charles and his nephew were reconciled, but the prince did little more than lead cavalry raids from Oxford and devise impracticable schemes for capturing Abingdon.[60] Sir Jacob, now Lord Astley, his replacement as lord general, fought a hopeless campaign in the Welsh borderland in December and January, trying to ensure that Chester and its dependent ports in North Wales remained in royalist hands, as the king's only hope of mounting a campaign in England in 1646 was if he received military assistance from the Irish Confederacy.[61] When the city surrendered in early February, Astley tried to join the king at Oxford, but local forces were sufficient to trap and destroy his tiny army at Stow-on-the-Wold on 21 March.[62]

Fairfax's conduct of the winter campaign in Devon and Cornwall, which began on 13 October 1645, was businesslike but devoid of decisive thrusts against the enemy. His defenders blame lack of supplies and the decline in the size of his army due to disease, desertion and the redeployment of New Model Army units elsewhere,[63] but it took him four months to force the surrender of the royalist army in the west and another two to capture the major garrisons, even though his army still outnumbered the enemy by a considerable margin.[64] He must also have been fully aware of the enemy's weaknesses. Encounters between the two armies at brigade level as at Bovey Tracey on 9 January 1646, for example, showed how far the king's cavalry had deteriorated as a fighting force.[65] Fairfax also knew from informants about the deep divisions between the Prince's Council and the leading officers in the army, which had not ceased with Goring's departure for France.[66]

Instead of trying to bring the enemy to battle before winter set in, Fairfax embarked on another series of sieges, though to be fair to Sir Thomas he conducted them with considerable skill. If there was a chance of capturing a town by an assault that would not be too expensive in casualties, he did so, as at Tiverton in November and at Dartmouth in January. Exeter he isolated from the surrounding countryside until the New Model Army was ready to deal with it. This was all that was necessary to protect his overland lines of communications and to prevent the garrison cavalry bringing in provisions.[67]

Instead, it was the royalists who went on the offensive. On Goring's departure the Prince of Wales's Council at last got its own way and appointed Lord Hopton as army general in the west. In early February 1646 he gathered a force of some 5,000 horse and foot and moved forward from the Tamar valley, his aim being to break the blockade of Exeter and liberate at least one of Goring's infantry brigades trapped there by the New Model Army's advance.[68] Fairfax advanced to meet Hopton, and the last battle in the west took place at Torrington on the night of 16–17 February. It began as an encounter between patrols, which developed into a full-scale engagement as darkness fell and the New Model infantry and dragoons sensed that the enemy infantry were not in a frame of mind to put up much resistance. As anticipated, most of the royalists fled when put under pressure, but the explosion of their magazine stored in Torrington church enabled Hopton to engineer his army's escape. He then fell back into Cornwall followed at a distance by the New Model Army.[69]

There was little in the way of fighting as the campaign drew to a close. Sir Thomas, keen to avoid unnecessary casualties, promised excellent terms to those who surrendered. Unsurprisingly, the royalist infantry melted away, whilst Goring's cavalry officers put increasing pressure on Hopton to capitulate. Resistance in the field ended in a negotiated surrender at Truro on 14 March.[70] Of the remaining royalist garrisons, Barnstaple and Exeter gave up the fight in April, whilst Pendennis Castle, where Hopton had sent his few remaining infantry, held out for a further five months.[71] However, the Prince of Wales and his Council had escaped long before via the Scilly Isles and Jersey to France.[72] This was clearly the fault of the navy, not of the New Model Army, but Fairfax clearly foresaw the consequences. The prince would be 'a [figure] head for malignants to draw to and grounds for other states' to intervene in England's internal affairs.[73]

CHAPTER 16

Warfare in Scotland and Ireland
1642–1648

T HERE WAS warfare in Ireland throughout the period covered by the English
Civil Wars and beyond, and in Scotland from 1644 onwards, but it was
significantly different from the fighting in England. In the first place it was
bloodier, partly because of traditional ways of doing things, partly because
combatants and non-combatants frequently owed their allegiance to different
religions rather than to different varieties of Protestantism. On the other hand,
campaigning in Ireland in particular tended to be less intense (though no less
painful for the civilian population), grinding to a halt at times because some
essential military supplies, such as muskets and gunpowder, could not be
imported in sufficient quantities as and when required.[1] Finally, in Ireland especially, coalitions fought coalitions,[2] and they were unstable, breaking up and re-
forming as the political and military situations evolved. This gave the army
generals another string to their bow. It made sense for generals to try and tempt
one coalition member to defect, but they always had to be wary of upsetting
their political masters by becoming too friendly with the enemy.[3]

Other circumstances affected for better or worse the freedom of generals to
campaign as they wished. The Scottish Covenanter government and the Irish
Confederacy tended to keep their army commanders on a tighter rein than did
either the English Parliament or the king, with members of the Scottish government accompanying their armies in the field and overruling their generals' decisions even on the battlefield.[4] On the other hand the commanders of English
armies in Scotland and Ireland, and also Irish loyalist commanders fighting the
Confederates in Ireland, were free from such encumbrances and also from operational control from Westminster because of the distances involved. However,
army generals fighting outside England in England's interests were still
dependent on their political masters for most of the military resources they
needed to fight a successful campaign, and they almost invariably found themselves lower down the pecking order than generals fighting closer to home.
Indeed the ebb and flow of fighting in Ireland between 1642 and 1648 is like a
mirror image of fighting in England and Scotland, with the Protestant alliance
making gains when the tempo of fighting in the larger island eased, and losing
ground when it picked up again.[5] However, the Confederate coalition was never

able to achieve sufficient single-mindedness or to generate sufficient momentum to rid the whole of Ireland of its enemies, whilst the latter were unable
to re-establish their hegemony until Oliver Cromwell came on the scene
in 1649.[6]

In theory, a general could have emerged in Ireland with the necessary mix of
military and diplomatic skills to win the war on a comparative shoestring, but
none did. However, by the same measure no general was sufficiently incompetent to bring about the downfall of the cause for which he fought. The
Confederate generals did not rise much above the level of mediocrity, even
Owen Roe O'Neill of the Ulster army. His distinguished lineage, and the natural
desire of later generations of Irish patriots to find a heroic figure for the wars of
the 1640s, have effectively concealed a truly mediocre record of only one victory
in eight years of fighting.[7] The Confederates' principal opponents, Robert
Monro the Scot, the fall-guy in O'Neill's only victory, at Benburb in 1646, and
the king's loyalist general, the marquis of Ormond, were of a similar low calibre.
The two brightest stars in the firmament were Michael Jones, who took over in
Leister in 1647 when Ormond made his peace with the English Parliament, and
Murrough O'Brien, Lord Inchiquin, who commanded the loyalist forces
in Munster. During the lull between the two English civil wars they won victories at Dungans Hill and Knocknannus respectively, but Jones's subsequent
rampage through central Ireland quickly lost momentum when the money ran
out, whereas Inchiquin's enthusiasm for the parliamentary cause waned as he
grew fearful of what the New Model Army and its political backers had in store
for King Charles I.[8]

However, as the topic of this book is to investigate the importance of generalship in bringing wars to a successful conclusion, there is no advantage in
spending any more time on the fighting in Ireland until the final round, which
began in 1649, as no general came within a country mile of achieving his political masters' war aims. Warfare in Scotland, however, cannot be ignored. Any
study of generalship in the wars fought in the British Isles in the mid seventeenth
century would be bizarre if it ignored James Graham, earl and later marquis of
Montrose, whose spectacular run of victories between September 1644 and
August 1645 have captured the imagination of writers from his own time
onwards.[9] In the last thirty years his image has become tarnished, but the
damage inflicted may be superficial rather than fundamental and thoroughly
deserves being put under the microscope.[10]

When the Covenanter government sent an army to assist Parliament in
January 1644, the king decided to open up a second front in Scotland. The
prime candidate as commander-in-chief was James Graham. Montrose had
almost certainly spent some time studying the art of war in the military academy
of the French King Louis XIII at Angers in the early 1630s.[11] He had also shown
some flair in Scotland in the late 1630s in browbeating actual and potential

Scotland, 1644–1651

opponents of the Covenanter cause. He was fully behind the early stage of the
Scottish revolution in which the principal aim of the king's antagonists was to
free the Scottish Presbyterian Church from being subverted by what they saw as
an English crypto-Papist crusade. However, he had broken with the Covenanter
leadership by 1641 when the conflict with the king shifted from defence of the
Scottish Church and its doctrine to an attack on Charles's executive power.
Montrose's motives were apparently a complicated mix. Thwarted ambition sat
side by side with genuine concern that a new constitution in which the king was
a mere puppet and the great landowners held the levers of power would end in
tears. How could families that had been at one another's throats for generations
be expected to provide stable government in the future?

Excluded from political life in the autumn of 1641 for his alleged involvement
in a plot to kidnap and murder three key members of the Covenanter leadership,
Montrose spent the next eighteen months in internal exile on his estates.
Rejecting the chance of high command in the Scottish army that was to invade
England on Parliament's behalf, he travelled to Oxford in August 1643. There he
claimed that the king's agent in Scotland, the duke of Hamilton, who had promised to ensure that Scotland remained neutral, was too incompetent to put the
case against the English alliance and probably in cahoots with the Covenanter
leadership. However, Montrose's lobbying came to nothing as Charles was
bewitched by Hamilton's bullish reports from the north and wary of Montrose's
alternative strategy, namely, to promote an uprising in Scotland which would
ensure the Covenanters were too busy at home to send an army into England.[12]

The king called on Montrose's services as soon as the Scots invaded, but the
prospects of opening up a second front were unpromising. The Covenanter
government enjoyed widespread support amongst all classes, who accepted the
argument that the human and material cost of intervening in English affairs was
a necessary price to pay for the security of the Presbyterian Church and freedom
from arbitrary royal government.[13] If Charles defeated Parliament, there was
little doubt that his next step would be to overthrow all that the Covenanters
had achieved.[14] Montrose therefore had a poor set of cards to play, but his hand
was weakened still further by the fact that he could not call on the support of a
legion of loyal tenants, as the Graham family's landed estates were small
compared with those of the great Scottish noblemen who backed the
Covenanter government.[15] Moreover, the heads of the two great landed families
who might have put their muscle behind the king's cause north of the border,
James Hamilton, First Duke of Hamilton, and George Gordon, Second Marquis
of Huntly, had their personal reasons for keeping their distance.

Hamilton's response to the failure of his attempt to keep Scotland neutral in
the English Civil War was to travel to Oxford accompanied by his brother, the
earl of Lanark, later the second duke. Hamilton was promptly clapped up in
prison on a charge of high treason, and for this he blamed Montrose's

badmouthing. However, the behaviour of his brother effectively undermined Hamilton's protestations of innocence. After escaping from Oxford disguised as a footman, Lanark returned to Scotland and entered the inner circle of the Covenanter government.[16]

Huntly also had personal grievances against James Graham. In 1639, when still a member of the Covenanter inner circle, Graham had undermined Huntly's efforts to raise north-east Scotland for the king and then dishonourably delivered him into the hands of his enemies. Moreover, in 1644, Huntly had a commission from the king as commander-in-chief of the loyalist forces in that part of the country, which he maintained took precedence over Montrose's.[17] Nevertheless cavalry commanded by his sons, James Gordon, Viscount Aboyne, and Lords George and Nathaniel Gordon, were to play a major part in four of Montrose's victories. The Hamilton interest not surprisingly backed the Covenanter government from beginning to end.

Montrose's first attempt to raise an army on the king's behalf ended in humiliation. The intention was for him to recruit in the Borders, whilst the Gordons did the same in their home territories. In addition, a force from Ireland provided by the Confederate government was to land in the western Highlands in April and mobilise the friendly clans. On 15 April 1644 Montrose duly left Carlisle and occupied Dumfries, the nearest Scottish town of any significant size. However, the bulk of Montrose's infantry, drawn from the Cumberland militia, left within two days of his crossing the border, and none of the noblemen of southern Scotland showed the slightest interest in declaring for the king. Finally, news arrived that a Covenanter army ten times as large as his own force was marching on Dumfries. With nothing heard from Ireland or, more surprisingly, from north-east Scotland, where Huntly had had men under arms since 16 March, Montrose and his little band of loyalists headed back across the border.[18] His only consolation was to be promoted to marquis in the Scottish peerage, presumably a reward for his unheeded warnings about the Hamiltons.

During the spring whilst the allied armies were besieging York, Montrose and the few hundred men he still had with him helped Sir Robert Clavering to attack the Scottish army's lines of communications in Northumberland. Prince Rupert ordered Carnaby south a week or so before the relief of York, but his brigade did not arrive until 4 July, two days after the battle of Marston Moor. It was not the best time for Montrose to ask for favours. Not only did Rupert brush aside his request for 500 horse to assist in another invasion of Scotland, he also ordered the Northumberland brigade to join what was left of his own army.[19]

Montrose, however, went solo a few days later. Returning to Carlisle he set out for Scotland in mid-August with only two companions. The prospects looked grim. Military assistance from the Gordons was now highly unlikely. What happened in the spring had exacerbated the poor relations between Huntly and Montrose. After Montrose's withdrawal from Dumfries, Covenanter troops had quickly suppressed the uprising in north-east Scotland and the marquis was now a fugitive in the Cairngorms with a price on his head. Not surprisingly, Huntly now felt twice betrayed by the Graham upstart. Montrose's only hope therefore was the Irish brigade, but all he had to go on were rumours that it had left Waterford for the Scottish west coast some weeks earlier.[20] Difficulties in finding suitable shipping, and the reluctance of both the king's man in Ireland, the marquis of Ormond, and the Confederate government to provide military supplies explains why the Irishes (as the Scots called them) missed the April deadline by three months.[21]

Montrose made for his family estates, and then immediately went into hiding, but not for long. A chance encounter with a messenger from the western Highlands brought news that a force of between 1,500 and 2,000 Irishes had landed somewhere to the north of Oban in July. However, the Highland clans had remained neutral at best, waiting for some evidence that the Irish brigade had sufficient muscle to be worth supporting. By late August the Irishes' options, limited from the start, had narrowed still further. They could not remain where they were as they had exhausted all the supplies the area could offer, and a force of Covenanters larger than their own was gathering at the west end of the Great Glen. In desperation they marched south into Atholl where there was a glimmer of hope they would receive a sympathetic reception given the area's traditional hostility towards the Campbell clan, whose head, the marquis of Argyll, was the leading Covenanter nobleman.[22] To prevent any misunderstandings between the starving Irish and the men of Atholl, Montrose made for Blair Atholl where he arrived just in time to prevent bloodshed. The following day he raised the royal standard, and the Scots and the Irish acknowledged his authority to command them through his commission as the king's lieutenant general in Scotland, which he had taken good care to bring with him.[23]

In the spring using troops belonging to the Irish Confederacy to help spark off an uprising in Scotland made good military sense, as what the Confederates were offering were not untried volunteers but regular infantry regiments, many of whose officers and men had considerable experience of war. The Irishes could therefore act as a nucleus around which thousands of Scottish royalists, some with military experience but many with none, could coalesce to form an effective field army. The Scots would also outnumber the Irishes and could thus restrain them by force should they show any inclination to plunder the civilian population. However, by August the other pieces were no longer on the board. The Border lords, who had not stirred in April, had no reason for altering their stance four months later, whereas the royalists of north-east Scotland, having been severely punished for the spring uprising,[24] would be very wary of taking up arms again. Montrose therefore faced the prospect of leading a force made up very largely of Irishes.

For Lowland Protestant Scots, however fervent their royalism, this was tanta-mount to supping with the Devil. First, some of the officers and rank and file of the

Irish brigade were guilty of slaughtering Scottish settlers in Ulster in 1642 at the start of the troubles in Ireland. Second, the Irish brigade and some of the Highland clans who were likely to follow them into Montrose's army were fervent Roman Catholics. Third, as Montrose did not have a loyal hinterland in the north-east or the south to supply his troops with food and pay, they were likely to systematically plunder town and countryside alike wherever they went. Finally, the commander of the Irish corps was not the moderate and slippery aristocrat Lord Antrim who had brokered the original agreement, but Alasdair MacColla, a man with a ferocious and bloodstained reputation, who had led raiding parties in the Western Isles since 1638 and campaigned against the Scottish settlers in Ulster in 1642.

For Montrose, the political damage done by associating with the Irishes was not their only drawback. Although MacColla willingly served under the marquis as major general of foot, he is better thought of as an ally rather than as a subordinate officer because he had war aims of his own. His prime ambition was to recover lands in south-west Scotland seized from his father by the Campbell family with royal connivance some twenty years earlier. Although not in direct conflict with Montrose's war aims, this did mean that on occasion he had no compunction about upping sticks and taking most of the Irishes with him.[25]

Whereas for centuries afterwards Montrose enjoyed the reputation of a military genius,[26] his current image is that of a highly ambitious self-publicist with major flaws in his generalship who became blinded by his own egoism, as victory followed victory in circumstances that should have ended in defeat.[27] The principal characteristic of his campaigning at its prime was gross carelessness, particularly with regard to keeping a track of the movements of the enemy.[28] From the eventual consequences of such pigheadedness he managed to escape, but not so many of his most loyal followers who paid for it with their lives at Philiphaugh on 13 September 1645 or in the judicial murders that followed.[29] Another charge against him is that, though brave, he had little conception of how an army general should behave himself on the battlefield. Once a battle had begun, he let it run its course or else, to be less charitable, lost control of proceedings. He owed his victories to the fighting qualities of the Irishes under MacColla's inspired and inspirational leadership, of which he was the fortunate (and ungrateful) beneficiary.[30]

This shocking indictment of one of history's heroes is difficult to evaluate because of the nature of the source material. Montrose's dispatches to the king describing his successes are self-regarding and overly optimistic in the conclusions he drew from them, but the context is very important. He was bidding for resources against other royalist commanders and, unlike Prince Rupert or Lord Goring, he had only one shot at getting his voice heard.[31] The few accounts of Montrose's campaigns written by contemporaries go into much greater detail, but they have the disadvantage of being positioned,[32] or written many years after the event, or both.[33] What is lacking, of course, is the two-way flow of correspondence between the English army generals and their political masters, the weekly journals written from a range of political perspectives and contemporary or near contemporary battle plans. It is such material that often makes it possible to identify the lies and half-truths that so frequently distort the memoirs and biographies written by contemporaries. However, the locations of Montrose's battles are well known and few have been victims of new build, so the impact of the landscape on the shape of the fighting is not difficult to ascertain.[34]

Montrose's victories began at Tippermuir, just to the west of Perth, on 1 September 1644. Six more followed in quick succession: Aberdeen (13 September), Fyvie (28 October), Inverlochy (2 February 1645), Auldearn (8 May), Alford (2 July) and Kilsyth (15 August). However, this triumphant roll call is not quite what it seems. Apart from the first two, which were set-piece battles, and the last when the two sides were pretty evenly balanced and looking for a climactic victory, Montrose fought them on the run, often in unexpected and desperate circumstances when he was outnumbered and the odds were very firmly against a royalist victory. This was not so much because he had a blind spot about intelligence as because he did not have sufficient cavalry both to patrol widely and to ensure that he had a large enough body of horse always to hand in the event of an unexpected encounter. How then did he win his victories?

In a rosy glow of nostalgia for the so-called Celtic way of fighting, much is made of the Highland Charge of men on foot wielding bladed weapons who could overwhelm formations of musketeers by their sheer speed.[35] However, there is no question whatsoever that in three of Montrose's four major victories – Auldearn, Alford and Kilsyth – it was cavalry charging sword in hand in the manner of Prince Rupert's squadrons at Edgehill or Naseby that played the decisive role.[36] Admittedly, Montrose was less heavily outnumbered in horse than he was in foot, as the Covenanter generals were ill-provided with cavalry.[37] Moreover, those cavalry they did have were armed primarily with lances.[38] These were excellent for pursuing a defeated enemy trying to get away on foot, but not of great value on the battlefield other than if they were facing enemy lancers (which they were not) or in the reserve line as at Marston Moor when they could charge into the flank of the enemy horse whilst it was engaged in a melee. It was not until after Kilsyth that Montrose faced a large body of cavalry, sent from England under the command of Lieutenant General David Leslie,[39] who duly brought Montrose's victories to an end at Philiphaugh on 13 September (though not in a classic cavalry encounter).[40] However, it is going too far to attribute Montrose's success solely to the way in which he used his cavalry.[41]

The second factor that helps to explain Montrose's string of successes was the way in which he behaved in battle. It is true that he had to fight before he was ready on a number of occasions, but once the battle had begun he displayed an inspired sense of what to do with the forces he still had to hand. Very frequently he sent them with precision to that part of the battlefield where their presence was sufficient to rout the enemy already in hand-to-hand combat with his vanguard. At Auldearn and Kilsyth, for example, it was his cavalry reserves that secured the victory in this way. At Alford it was his infantry reserve that broke the deadlock in the cavalry melee.[42] The enemy generals on the other hand could make no such response, having opted for an inflexible battle plan or chosen to fight before assembling all their available forces. Even allowing for some exaggeration on the part of the royalist chroniclers, Montrose's presence of mind, his intuitive reactions and his sheer understanding of the role of an army general on the mid-seventeenth-century battlefield shine through their narratives. On these grounds alone his personal contribution to the victories of the royalist army he commanded should not be underplayed or rubbished. As for Alasdair MacColla's contribution to victory, he was never in overall charge of any battle nor at Montrose's right hand when he made a battle-winning decision. Instead he did his job, fighting bravely and with great distinction as major general of the infantry.[43] He may indeed have invented the highly effective Highland Charge,[44] but it is equally possible that the success of the Irish brigade owed more to his subordinate officers, some of whom had far greater experience of campaigning than did MacColla.[45]

However, what really counted was not the Highland Charge per se but the variety of battlefield tactics that Montrose's infantry were capable of executing, most particularly the Irish brigade. He certainly made good use of the Charge at Tippermuir, Aberdeen, Inverlochy and Kilsyth, but it was not appropriate in every circumstance, as MacColla was to find to his cost at Knocknannus in Ireland in 1647.[46] The important thing is that the Irish brigade was capable of so much more, largely because it was not one of the intensively drilled formations of massed automata to which seventeenth-century army generals educated in the ideas of Prince Maurice of Nassau aspired. At Aberdeen the infantry opened its ranks to let in a troop of Covenanter cavalry and then closed ranks behind them and slaughtered the lot.[47] At Auldearn they fought desperately, making excellent use of the defensive potential of the small village into which they had managed to retreat until Montrose managed to come to their rescue with the rest of the army.[48] At Alford they terminated a cavalry melee by crawling under the bellies of the enemy horses and attacking them with swords.[49] At Fyvie they used the cover of woodland to deliver skirmishing, as opposed to barrage fire, which discomforted the enemy cavalry advancing towards them across open ground.[50] At Inverlochy, on the other hand, they showed themselves perfectly capable of producing a conventional musketry barrage at point-blank range and then of attacking the enemy infantry at the trot rather than the gallop.[51] They also played their part in combined operations on at least two occasions when Montrose used a small body of infantry in combination with an even smaller body of cavalry to foil an enemy attack on his flank.[52]

Overall, then, it was the synergy of horse and foot that lay at the heart of Montrose's success on the battlefield. But when all is said and done, it was

188

THE WARRIOR GENERALS

Covenanter grand strategy which allowed his campaigning to blossom in the way that it did. What in 1644 had been an irritant was by the spring of 1645 a major concern and in the late summer a deadly challenge for the Covenanter cause. This apparent blindness to the potential seriousness of Montrose's activities stemmed from the Covenanter leadership's conviction that the Scottish revolution would only be really secure if the English adopted Scottish Presbyterianism. In the winter of 1644 the chances of achieving this essential war aim were less than they had been a year before, because of the growing strength of Independency in the House of Commons and also in the army of the Eastern Association which was bound to be a powerful influence in the New Model Army. It was therefore vital for the Scottish army to play the key role in crushing the royalist cause in England in 1645, and to that end it had to be as strong as possible.

In hindsight the most sensible response to Montrose would have been to withdraw most of the Scottish regiments from England at the end of the 1644 campaigning season and use them to destroy his little army before the New Model Army took the field. This could have been done without loss of face. The capture of Newcastle in late October had won back most of the reputation the Scottish army had lost at Marston Moor, but all the Covenanter leadership did was replace the not unwilling marquis of Argyll with professionals, the turncoat Sir John Urry and William Baillie, lieutenant general of infantry in the army in England, who happened to be visiting Edinburgh on private business.[53] Between them they ought to have possessed the skills necessary to finish Montrose off, but neither was up to the task.

Turning to Montrose, it is difficult to identify circumstances in which, by behaving differently, he could have done any more to make his conquests permanent or to help the king's cause in England. Greater persistence in April 1644 is unlikely to have achieved success, as the spearhead of his later campaign, MacColla's brigade, was still in Ireland; and establishing a working relationship with Huntly, already very problematic, was not likely to have been improved by Montrose arriving in north-east Scotland with fewer than 200 cavalry. Turning to the campaign that began in the late summer, what Montrose needed was a home area under his secure control if he was to have a chance of replacing the Covenanters with a royalist government, and he allegedly threw his only chance away after his second victory by allowing the Irishes and their Highland allies to sack Aberdeen, the provincial capital of the only part of lowland Scotland to have shown any sympathy for the king's cause. The sack, then, was a highly significant own goal, and a powerful sign of his lack of political understanding.[54] However, Montrose had no chance of holding the city at that point in time. The marquis of Argyll was approaching rapidly from the south with a far larger force than his own, and the last thing Montrose wanted at that stage in the campaign was to be trapped in a city under siege. He had fewer than 2,000 men under his command, Aberdeen was weakly fortified, and there was no prospect of relief. However, there was an alternative. He could simply have marched away, as he had done in the case of Perth after his first victory at Tippermuir in September 1644, in the hope of returning at a later date when circumstances might have changed for the better.

After his victory at Kilsyth ten months later the lack of such a home area was to be a crucial weakness in re-establishing royal authority in Scotland, and this, rather than blind belief in his own destiny, probably explains Montrose's foray into the Borders with a skeleton force which led to the humiliation at Philiphaugh on 13 September. However, the size of that force was the evidence of another weakness, the fragility of the coalition he had led to victory. With the Covenanter government scattered to the four corners of the realm, the army of 5,000 men that had won at Kilsyth quickly fell apart. There was no longer a powerful enough incentive to bind them together, and it would have taken the wisdom of Solomon on Montrose's part to convince his partners not to leave him and go their separate ways in pursuit of their own war aims. MacColla had helped his general conquer Scotland for the king. Now was the time to pay greater attention to family concerns, and he and many of the Irishes left for Argyll to stake their claim to the lost lands. The Gordons and their supporters were similarly intent on re-establishing their control over the north-east, lost after the suppression of their uprising in the spring of 1644. Both parties were also probably disappointed by the meagre fruits of victory. Montrose refused MacColla the sack of Glasgow, and instead of appointing James Gordon, Viscount Aboyne, as his lieutenant general of cavalry he chose the earl of Crawford, who had fought in the war in England as a none too successful brigadier.[55] As for the Scottish clansmen, they headed for home, keen to put their booty in safe custody and to help their families bring in the harvest.[56]

To make matters worse, there was no prospect of outside help for Montrose in his hour of victory. The Confederates had sent Alasdair MacColla to cause trouble in Scotland so as to induce the Covenanter government to remove its army from Ulster, but although some troops had returned home, the rest showed every intention of clinging onto their strongholds of Carrickfergus and Belfast. There was some talk of sending more men to Scotland in the autumn of 1645, but by then it was too late. As for assistance from England, Charles I was as deaf to Montrose's pleas for cavalry in 1645 as Prince Rupert had been in 1644. It was not until some weeks after Langport when his cause in England was in ruins that Charles showed any enthusiasm for the Scottish option, but when a small body of horse did cross the border in October, Montrose was back in the Highlands and on the run with fewer men in arms than he had had a year earlier.[57]

It was Montrose's desperate attempt to establish a secure home area by conjuring up the spirit of popular royalism based on the fickle promises of the great Border landowners that led to his downfall at Philiphaugh on

13 September. Caught totally by surprise at dawn by David Leslie at the head of 4,000 or so horse,[58] his newly raised levies took to their heels and his small body of Irishes were quickly overwhelmed. A charge by Montrose's cavalry, so effective in the past in turning near disaster into victory, failed because they were too few,[59] and although the marquis escaped and continued in the field until ordered to give up by the king in May 1646, Philiphaugh had broken the spell and Leslie felt confident enough to return to England within two months of his victory.[60] Despite Montrose's expertise as an army general, the qualities of his troops, and the mistakes and shortcomings of his enemies, his fate was very similar to that of other commanders of bandit armies throughout human history who were capable of winning battles but not of winning a war. His campaign of 1644–5 was therefore no more than a short-lived but stupendous spectacle, a nova which briefly outshone all other stars in the firmament but which finished up as a red dwarf.

CHAPTER 17

The Second English Civil War

THE FIRST English Civil War had ended to all intents and purposes in the spring of 1646. Both the royalist armies had surrendered; the few remaining major garrisons could not hold out for long as there was no prospect of relief; and by the end of May the governors were under instruction from the king to negotiate the best terms they could with their besiegers. But there was still a war to win in Ireland, and the obvious way for the two Houses of Parliament to bring it to a successful conclusion was to ship the New Model Army there. However, using the New Model Army to conquer Ireland was seemingly a taboo subject, the elephant in the room. Instead Parliament tried a different tack, namely piecemeal reinforcement of the loyalist forces already in Ireland so as to create an army large enough to defeat the Confederates. This was to be under the command of a new lord lieutenant, Lord Lisle.

Redeployment was to be the key. Reaching a crescendo between 28 July and 6 August, the House of Commons passed a large number of orders for the disbandment of non-New Model units, both field regiments and garrisons, the largest being Major General Massey's army of the west. In most cases it required those in charge of the process to drum up volunteers interested in furthering their military careers on the other side of the Irish Sea.[1] The measures passed without division, but in the middle of the proceedings there was a proposal that four regiments of foot and two regiments of horse from the New Model Army should also be sent to Ireland. This provoked a heated debate in the Commons stretching over two days in which Oliver Cromwell played a leading role in opposing the measure. In the end a single vote decided that the New Model Army should remain intact and at home, and that was the end of the matter for the time being.

The principal argument against running down the size the New Model Army was not that the 1645 ordinance authorised it only to defend 'the laws and liberties of the kingdom'[2] (in other words, England), but that it needed to be as strong as possible in case the Covenanter government decided to use its army to intervene in English politics.[3] After the forces led by Lords Hopton and Astley had left the scene, King Charles, recognising that there was no possible mileage in prolonging the war but a good chance of using peace negotiations to drive wedges between the partners in the enemy coalition, had surrendered to Lieutenant General David Leslie who was supervising the forces besieging Newark. Immediately afterwards the garrison surrendered on the king's instructions and the Scots rushed him off to their army base at Newcastle so as to forestall any attempt by the New Model Army to mount a 'rescue operation'.[4] The fear at Westminster was that Charles would agree to accept Presbyterianism as the state religion for all three of his kingdoms, whereupon the Scottish army would march south to impose the now joint war aim of king and Covenanters on the English.[5] At first sight this seems a convincing argument. However, the New Model Army shorn of six regiments would still have outnumbered the Scottish army by a factor of almost two to one.[6] It is therefore difficult to escape the conclusion that this early on Cromwell and the Independents in the Commons saw splitting the New Model Army as removing the most powerful card from their hand,[7] though not necessarily at this stage the ace of trumps, and that they deliberately played on anti-Scottish sentiment in the Commons to ensure that it did not happen.

In January 1647 the Scottish army left the scene. Once it became apparent to the Covenanter government that Charles would not convert to Presbyterianism, and that he was spinning out peace negotiations in order to perplex and divide his enemies, their overriding concern became achieving agreement with the English Parliament over how much money was owing to them. Once their back pay arrived at Newcastle the Scots handed the king over to a New Model Army escort. Still a prisoner, he took up residence at Holdenby House in Northamptonshire, and negotiations with Parliament continued.[8] On arriving home, the Scots army disbanded apart from five small infantry regiments and a single cavalry regiment retained for home defence purposes.[9]

The events of early 1647 meant that Cromwell's justification for keeping the entire New Model Army in England no longer had any relevance. He also lost the backing of those MPs who had supported him in July solely because of their anxieties about the Scots.[10] To make matters worse, building up an army large enough to reconquer Ireland from the disbanded provincial forces had failed. A new expeditionary force had therefore to be created and the way in which Parliament went about creating it finally broke the coalition that had won the First Civil War.

The Independents' opponents came up with a scheme to kill three birds with one stone, namely to reconquer Ireland, weaken the influence of Cromwell and his supporters in the New Model Army and create a peace dividend for the English taxpayer by significantly reducing military expenditure. It led to an army coup, which in its turn divided the Scottish leadership and helped ignite a second civil war, which for the English royalists would only have been a pipe dream without Scottish military assistance. In addition, the growing resentment of English taxpayers at the escalating expense and the deteriorating conduct of the New Model Army provided the king with a new set of supporters. For them Charles's real appeal was that he represented a happier past when taxes were low and disorder rarely to be encountered, a time when the country was free from soldiers and from religious turmoil, and the threat that they both posed to the hegemony of the landed classes and the urban elites. What galvanised these neo-royalists into action, be it taking up arms at one extreme or mere grumbling at the other, was not devotion to the king but despair and disgust at what they saw as the breakdown of traditional values and power structures.

The first decision that emerged from the House of Commons on 18 February 1647 was to keep a force of 6,400 cavalry and dragoons in England. In the unlikely event of an army having to take the field, garrisons would supply suffi-cient infantry. Nothing was said for the moment about the size of the expedition to be sent to Ireland, but the clear implication was that any New Model infantry not selected would be disbanded. In addition, the commissions of Cromwell and some of his leading supporters would lapse, as the Self-Denying Ordinance was to be strictly enforced.[11] Finally, there was no guarantee that officers and soldiers who had no place in the new military establishment would have their arrears paid in full or be immune from prosecution for criminal acts committed whilst they had been in arms. Instead, they were to trust in Parliament's honour and integrity.

The New Model officers and rank and file reacted badly to the proposals. It was further evidence of the ungrateful, even vindictive behaviour of the two Houses of Parliament since the previous spring when the New Model Army had finally destroyed the English royalists' capacity to wage war. Neither House had done anything to stem a barrage of criticism from outside Parliament. This focused on the unnecessary cost of keeping so many men under arms, and on security issues in the widest sense from the spread of unorthodox religious opin-ions and practices, such as soldiers presuming to preach the word of God, to violence of soldiers against civilians, to the practice of recruiting former royalist soldiers to fill up the ranks.[12] Moreover, speakers in both Houses had repeatedly aired such complaints, with the most outlandish accusations being given an earnest and lengthy hearing.

The extent to which the army's reaction was spontaneous or planned in advance can only be a matter of conjecture. However, the general view is that Parliament would have succeeded in partially disbanding the New Model Army had due regard for the soldiers' concerns been apparent from the start, and had Parliament treated the first petitions from the army with calm consideration rather than yet more abuse.[13] Nevertheless, the furious language of the so-called Declaration of Dislike passed by the Commons on 30 March 1647, which turned what appeared to be an honest exchange of views into a confrontation, is perfectly understandable. Some of the army's demands were a direct assault on Parliament's sovereignty, fundamental to which was the subordination of the military to the civilian power, with Parliament having absolute authority over the armed services. A clause in the soldiers' petition, which asked that those who had volunteered for the New Model Army or its predecessors should be able to refuse to serve in Ireland, may have been just about acceptable; but the officers' demand that they should know what regiments were to be sent to Ireland and who was to command them was beyond the pale, as they were in effect claiming the right of veto over military appointments, which the New Model Army ordinance had vested in the two Houses, not in the commander-in-chief.[14]

The various stages of the army coup, beginning in early June with the seizure of the king at Holdenby House, Northamptonshire, and his transfer to army headquarters, and ending with the suppression of a mutiny of the radical rank and file in mid-December by Cromwell and Fairfax, lie outside the parameters of a book on generalship and the wars of the 1640s. However, one highly significant effect was that the leading army officers, the so-called grandees, acquired a share of sovereignty, which included conducting head-to-head negotiations with the king over such matters as religious toleration and the future constitution. They also ensured that those men who they regarded as enemies were to be excluded from taking their seats in Parliament. Even though the number involved was small compared with what was to happen later, the army had established an important principle.

However, there was a reconciliation in the early months of 1648. The radicals had demanded sweeping changes in the nature of Parliament and its procedures. Their expulsion from the army after the suppression of the mutiny won the grandees more friends in both Houses of Parliament than they had had at the time of the coup. The reduction in size of the New Model Army from 27,000 to 24,000 men proposed by the army leadership and the disbandment of more non-New Model Army regiments enabled expenditure, and therefore taxation, to be cut, to the great satisfaction of others.[15] Finally, as rumblings of thunder could be heard in the distance, the New Model Army Council of War made abundantly clear its commitment to one for all and all for one in a new civil war. In a letter read in the House of Lords on 17 January 1648, the officers rejoiced at 'the carrying on of this great common cause wherein both Houses of Parliament stand engaged'.[16] What was taking place was probably a true coming together of the old coalition minus the Scots, not a mere papering over of the cracks, as very few members of the Lords or the Commons who had supported Parliament between 1642 and 1646 fought for the king in 1648.[17] However, it is not surprising that the war aims were of a consensual nature, namely to preserve what Parliament had won in the First Civil War.

The way in which the revived coalition conducted the war at the strategic and operational levels also looked like a return to the certainties of the past. Parliament continued to give orders to the high command concerning strategy, and the Committee at Derby House, a reconstituted Committee of Both Kingdoms (though now with responsibility for only England and Ireland), acted as the principal means of communication between the two from early January 1648 onwards,[18] though army commanders still wrote occasionally to the two Houses. Thus, during the war the New Model Army would be firmly under political control, though the Committee was even more dominated by the Independents than the original had been. However, one of the most assiduous attenders throughout was the earl of Manchester, despite being very busy as speaker of the House of Lords,[19] and for much of the time he was the only member present with recent and direct experience of land warfare.[20] It would be wrong, however, to argue strongly from this that Manchester had a major hand in determining strategy, but it seems unlikely, given his other responsibility, that he would have bothered to attend the Committee so often if his advice fell on deaf ears or if there were others present to represent his opinions.[21]

If the war aims of Parliament were non-controversial and lacking in detail, those of the neo-royalists were so variegated as to verge on the contradictory. For the Scots the preservation of their Church was of fundamental importance and this was to be achieved by a Presbyterian settlement of religion in Charles I's other two kingdoms. But this was hardly likely to win friends amongst those many former royalists in England and Wales whose reason for fighting for the king in the first war was that he had taken up arms in defence of the Anglican Church as established by Queen Elizabeth. The pronouncements of the king's English supporters, on the other hand, were unfocused. In some places the emphasis was on happenings since 1645 in the hope of winning over former supporters of Parliament. Elsewhere the proclamations merely repeated the king's justifications for going to war in 1642.[22]

The way in which the triumph of such a multiplicity of interests was to be achieved was equally imprecise. By taking refuge on the Isle of Wight, the king had merely swopped one prison for another, as he quickly found himself once more under house arrest and largely cut off from contact with the outside world. The understanding was that the Scottish invasion would coincide with uprisings in many parts of England, but there could be no central direction with the king a prisoner and nobody in overall command of the armed forces. However, the strength of the king's cause in the Second Civil War lay in its geographical spread rather than its organisation. Between 27 April and 27 May, fears were expressed in Parliament of possible uprisings throughout East Anglia and the Home Counties, at Bristol, in Leicestershire and Yorkshire, at Coventry, on the Isle of Wight, in the counties along the Welsh border and in London.[23] If the Committee at Derby House's response had been to send troops to all these potential trouble spots, the New Model Army would have been spread very thinly indeed, but fortunately there were fewer serious uprisings than had been anticipated, and they and the Scottish invasion did not coincide. Parliament's reaction was also judicious. Quite early on in the emergency it decided to send Sir Thomas Fairfax with a large force to the Scottish border to deter the Scots from invading,[24] though the ostensible objective was to recapture Carlisle and Berwick. These well-fortified towns had been seized in March and April respectively by English troops under Sir Marmaduke Langdale, which the Scottish authorities had allowed to assemble on their side of the border prior to the attack.[25] The rest of the New Model Army took up quarters largely in those parts of the country where rumours of unrest turned into outright military resistance, but Fairfax's determination, somewhat against the wishes of Parliament, to keep a strong brigade in the south-west throughout the summer and autumn turned out to be an unnecessary precaution.[26]

The first incident in the Second Civil War was the seizure of Pembroke Castle by disgruntled former officers and soldiers of Parliament in late February 1648. Parliament responded by ordering Fairfax to send a large enough force to south-west Wales to put down the uprising, and he duly dispatched four regiments under the command of Colonel Thomas Horton. Once the seriousness of the uprising became apparent, he sent a second brigade to South Wales under the command of Lieutenant General Cromwell.[27] Horton defeated the rebels at St Fagans near Cardiff on 8 May, but the survivors fell back on their base and defied the New Model Army until the arrival of a siege train early in July changed their minds and they begged for terms.[28] Cromwell was therefore hundreds of miles away when Kent erupted in late May, and responsibility for repressing that rebellion fell entirely on Fairfax's shoulders. Defending London was of far greater immediate importance than facing down the Scots, and John Lambert, commander of a motley collection of Lancashire, Yorkshire and New Model regiments operating out of Newcastle, assumed responsibility for the defence of the Borders on the understanding that Cromwell would replace him once he had put down the unrest in Wales.[29]

The campaign that Fairfax fought in Kent and Essex in the spring and summer of 1648 was his last, but not his greatest, triumph. Advancing rapidly from Clapham Common where he had met his three infantry and four cavalry regiments, all from the New Model Army, the lord general showed his customary skill in engaging with the enemy. The royalists had decided to defend the line of the River Medway and placed detachments guarding the crossings at Rochester, Aylesford and Maidstone. Fairfax's line of march took advantage of stretches of woodland to conceal his approach. Crossing the river by an unguarded bridge between Rochester and Aylesford on 1 June, he approached the main enemy concentration at Maidstone from an unexpected direction and, despite the pouring rain, he ordered an infantry assault on the town at nightfall. All went well initially, but this was not to be a repeat of Torrington. Sir George Lisle, who commanded at Shaw House during the Second Battle of Newbury, had put up barricades covering the approaches to the town, turned houses and shops into strongpoints, and placed his eight cannon where they had a good field of fire along the streets. The New Model vanguard not surprisingly came to a halt on entering the built-up area where they found themselves facing case shot and intensive barrages delivered by musketeers firing from behind cover.

Fairfax responded in typical fashion. Despite suffering from gout, he took personal charge of the fighting and displayed the courage under fire for which he was renowned. Nevertheless it took almost six hours to clear the town of enemy in what Fairfax described as 'a very fierce and hard dispute'.[30] There was no pursuit, despite the fact that the New Model Army lost only some thirty or so officers and men. The lord general allowed fugitives from the town and else-where to march unhindered across the front of the New Model Army as far as Deptford, where they were able to cross the Thames almost unmolested using what boats they could find. On the day following the battle Fairfax could have used his regiments of horse to delay them, thus giving his infantry time to catch up and destroy them either en route or at the waterside. His preparatory work had certainly been sensible, as he had already deployed most of his mounted troops in a position to the south of Maidstone to prevent the enemy receiving reinforcements from Rochester. However, in the lame words of Sir Thomas's own report, 'Our men [were] not able to make so speedy a march after them as was necessary'.[31] He thus displayed in a more extreme form the blind spot in his generalship that had been apparent at Langport, and to a lesser extent at Nantwich and Torrington, the inability to make the most of an impressive victory by following it up with an effective pursuit.[32]

On the afternoon after the battle Fairfax collected his army together, sent some of it to capture enemy-held ports on the sea coast of Kent and with the rest followed the enemy into Essex, eventually forcing them to take refuge in the town of Colchester, but his vanguard failed to rush the gates quickly enough. A reception party drove them back and they suffered heavy casualties as a result.[33] There then followed a protracted siege which sorely tried Sir Thomas's patience. It did not end until 27 August, by which time the war was to all intents and purposes over, Oliver Cromwell having destroyed the Scottish army and its English allies in a week-long campaign in Lancashire earlier in the month.[34] At the surrender of Colchester there was an ominous pointer to the future. Fairfax summarily executed Sir George Lisle and Sir Charles Lucas, the king's commander in Essex, for breaking their parole.[35]

Cromwell's first campaign as general in command of a marching army began once Pembroke Castle had surrendered on 11 July.[36] He immediately set out for the north, as his presence there was now essential. A large Scottish army had crossed the border commanded by the same duke of Hamilton who had failed to keep Scotland out of the First English Civil War. With little military experi-ence, Hamilton owed his position to his exalted social status. Like his prede-cessor in the north of England, the marquis of Newcastle, he was utterly dependent on the advice of others.

Internal unrest in Scotland had delayed the long-expected attack, and the prin-cipal uprisings in the southern kingdom had collapsed or were on the verge of collapse when Hamilton's host crossed the border. Invading England on behalf of Charles I was not popular, as the guarantees the duke and his supporters, the Engagers, had obtained from the king with regard to Presbyterianism becoming the state religion throughout the British Isles were limited and partial. Many leading figures, such as the marquis of Argyll and the lord general in Scotland, the old earl of Leven, had refused to accept them as sufficient cause for fighting on the king's behalf and obstructed the duke at every turn.[37] Nevertheless Fairfax's brigade was still outside Colchester, and other brigades of the New Model Army were on home security duties in the south-west and around London, and Cromwell had few regiments at his disposal.[38] The forces already in the north of England would therefore be of vital importance, and Lambert was under the strictest instructions to avoid getting into a fight before Cromwell arrived.[39]

Major General John Lambert was the outstanding figure amongst the fourth generation of Parliament's generals, those who came to prominence during the Second Civil War, but his earlier military career had been far from promising. At Marston Moor on 2 July 1644 when leading the second line of cavalry on the right wing of the allied army, he had failed to exploit the advantage gained by Sir Thomas Fairfax on the far right, and left the field early with the rest of the Yorkshire and Scottish horse on that wing. In the following spring Sir Marmaduke Langdale had given him a bloody nose at the relief of Pontefract Castle, probably because Lambert failed to use his infantry to best advantage. However, Lambert had been a close political associate of the Fairfax family throughout the First Civil War, and used this to ingratiate himself with Oliver Cromwell, who gave him great responsibility in the wars of 1648–51. Lambert was not renowned for his religious enthusiasm, which makes Cromwell's patronage seem rather odd, but where Oliver saw leadership potential he exploited it. This was even more striking in the case of George Monck, confined to the Tower of London for three years after being taken prisoner on the royalist side at the battle of Nantwich on 30 January 1644. Less flamboyant and less blatantly ambitious than Lambert, but a sound administrator and a profound military thinker, he had been permitted by Parliament to command the English forces in Ulster, probably through the influence of Lord Lisle to whom he gave the military treatise he had written during his captivity.[40] After a sticky patch in 1649, he became the third member of Oliver Cromwell's team in the war against the Scots in 1650–51.[41]

In the spring and early summer of 1648 Lambert had done very well indeed, first driving the northern royalists back to the gates of Carlisle, and then when the Scots invaded delaying their progress without getting into serious trouble. After nearly getting caught at Appleby he withdrew to Barnard Castle on the borders of County Durham and Yorkshire, putting almost thirty miles of difficult country between his men and Hamilton's army. Should the duke try to deal with him before heading south, his plan was to withdraw to Newcastle, the principal parliamentary garrison in the north, and bide his time. However, the enemy decided to ignore him, and Lambert Force had almost a fortnight's rest before the arrival of cavalry from Cromwell's brigade gave it the protection necessary for traversing the open-field country of the Vale of York. Moving south parallel to the enemy line of advance but fifty or so miles to the east, it rendezvoused with Oliver and his infantry regiments at Wetherby on 12 August.[42] The short campaign that followed was masterly. In less than two weeks Cromwell destroyed an army twice the size of his own by a mixture of single-mindedness, good fortune and an intuitive grasp of the tactics needed for annihilating the enemy, as opposed to merely defeating him,[43] but he could not have achieved what he did had not Hamilton made a succession of basic military errors.

The day after the rendezvous the parliamentary army set off in the direction of Preston, the lowest crossing point of the River Ribble. Cromwell understood that the duke had fixed upon it as his own place of rendezvous with Sir Marmaduke Langdale's corps, which he had detached to guard his army's flank against being attacked from the Yorkshire side of the Pennines. Another corps commanded by Major General George Monro, consisting of regiments recently arrived from Ulster, was quite a number of miles behind the main army, apparently waiting for military supplies from Scotland before joining the duke.[44] At a Council of War held two evenings before the battle took place Cromwell and his officers decided to head straight for Preston at full speed so as to force Hamilton to fight before his whole army came together. What made this attractive was that Langdale's corps was making for Preston by the same road and could be harassed as it fell back towards the Scottish army.[45] However, although Cromwell was probably aware of Monro's whereabouts,[46] he did not know that the odds in his favour had increased still further. Hamilton was without most of his cavalry. They had pushed on to Wigan, fifteen miles further south, under his instructions, apparently in search of food and fodder.[47]

The Scottish commanders at Preston were allegedly unaware of Cromwell's movements,[48] but they knew that an enemy force was following Langdale, as he had told them so. They also knew that enemy patrols had recently attacked cavalry units in their quarters to the north of the Ribble.[49] However, the duke and his advisers chose to believe that the main body of Cromwell's army was to the south of the river, and that the body following Langdale was no more than a diversionary force. In retrospect this seems an amazingly wrongheaded appraisal of what was going on in the enemy general's mind. When they met, Lambert would have told Oliver that the Scottish army was much larger than their combined forces.[50] In such circumstances he would surely not have decided to advance towards Preston along both banks of the river. Crossing places were few, thus making it extremely difficult, if not impossible, for one part of the army to go to the aid of the other if it got into difficulties.

The battle that followed was nothing like a conventional one fought in open country. This was partly because of the nature of the landscape, which did not provide a large enough arena, and partly because of Scottish misapprehensions about the direction of the enemy approach. Instead, almost all the fighting took place at two locations several miles apart and on a very narrow front with only parts of the armies heavily engaged. The first engagement was between Cromwell's army and Sir Marmaduke Langdale's troops. After being hustled some ten miles down the road from Clitheroe during the morning by Oliver's vanguard, Langdale turned to face the enemy at Ribbleton Moor's End just short of Preston, where the landscape favoured the defence. The approach to the position from the east was across a piece of muddy open ground, which posed all sorts of problems for the parliamentary cavalry. The road then disappeared into enclosures. This meant infantry fighting would be at close quarters with the progress of the troops of horse slowed to the speed at which the infantry could clear the enemy from the hedgerows. Langdale, on the other hand, though outnumbered by perhaps two to one, could use the enclosures to hold off the enemy until such time as the Scots

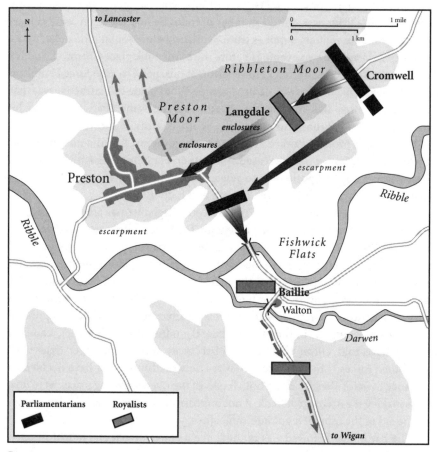

Preston

sent him reinforcements or he received orders to fall back on the main body of the army. Unsurprisingly, having chosen his position, his next action was to cry for help. However, the duke and his advisers decided that Langdale was strong enough to fend off what they still saw as a diversionary attack whilst they prepared to face the main body of Cromwell's army on the south bank of the Ribble. The Scottish infantry brigades were therefore to cross the river and deploy just beyond the bridge as they arrived in Preston from the north.[51]

Cromwell drew up his men in a reasonably conventional manner, with five regiments of infantry in the first line and two in the reserve. The bulk of the cavalry he deployed on the wings, but he kept two of the best New Model regiments of horse in the centre with another behind them in reserve. Their instructions were similar to Major Bethell's at Langport, to charge up the lane once the royalist infantry showed signs of retreating so as to turn a retreat in good order into headlong flight.[52] However, at Ribbleton Moor's End the defending force was stronger and probably more committed than that which Goring drew up along the Wagg Rhyne, whilst Cromwell, unlike Fairfax, had no cannon with which to soften up the enemy. He had wanted to reach Preston in double quick time and had therefore left his artillery train behind at Wetherby.

In some desperation Cromwell ordered his cavalry regiments in the centre to charge up the lane into the midst of the enemy position before it was properly cleared, but some Scottish lancers saw them off, the only reinforcements Hamilton sent to Langdale that are known to have arrived.[53] Cromwell then set off for the right wing with the intention of bringing into play two infantry regiments that had not yet made contact with the enemy, but before he had the chance to reposition them, a development at the opposite end of the line brought the first engagement to an abrupt end. According to Lieutenant John Hodgson, this was all his doing. Hodgson pointed out to Lambert, who was in temporary charge of the battle, that the greatest danger was now to the left wing. Lambert ordered Hodgson to instruct the Lancashire regiments in the reserve line to take up a position guarding that flank, but the effect was almost certainly far greater than either had anticipated. A tactic intended to counter a massive attack from the Scots (who had yet to make their presence felt on the battlefield) became a forward thrust into a vacuum, as the reserves encountered no enemy troops whatsoever. As a result the Lancashire regiments, supported by one New Model regiment, marched rapidly past Langdale's position using a lane that serendipitously joined the main road south between Preston town and the bridge over the Ribble, and at a time when the whole of the Scottish infantry had crossed the river. Once there they set up a defensive position which not only blocked Langdale's intended line of retreat,[54] but also cut the duke of Hamilton off from the rest of his army.[55]

Once Langdale and his men realised they had been outflanked they fled, and having no other option sought sanctuary in the streets of Preston with Cromwell's cavalry at their heels. There an almighty jam developed as they ran into the duke and some Scottish horse entering the town at right angles and vainly trying to reach the bridge. After a brief attempt to hold onto the town the royalists scattered. Oliver's troopers hunted the English infantry down in Preston itself and in the fields beyond. However, sufficient Scottish horse escaped for Cromwell to think it worthwhile sending two cavalry regiments after them as they headed for Lancaster.[56]

The second engagement began as soon as Cromwell's infantry had deployed along the escarpment that separated Preston town from the bridge over the Ribble. They found the bridge defended by up to two brigades of Scottish infantry but without artillery support.[57] The parliamentary commanders were also without cannon but their musketeers lined the hedges that ran along the escarpment, and they were close enough to the bridge to pour devastating fire into the ranks of its defenders. Later they used the same technique to drive off an attempt by the Scots to reinforce the defenders and to cover the massed charge of pikes that eventually took the bridge by storm, one of the few occasions in the wars in Britain between 1642 and 1651 when this time-honoured tactic was employed. Such was the momentum of the charge that the infantry, and the handful of cavalry that were in close support, were also able to rush the bridge over the Darwen five hundred yards further on, whilst the rest of the Scottish infantry looked on disconsolately from Wardle Hill, a mile to the south, as darkness fell.

The duke of Hamilton played as little part in the second engagement as he had done in the first. Ejected from Preston, he and a small band of followers had difficulty crossing the Ribble. Eventually they managed to ford the river and arrived on Wardle Hill just in time to chew over the second disaster of the day.[58] Cromwell's role in the engagement at Preston bridge is much less certain. He was not in the habit of writing much about his personal role in any battle for fear that God would punish him for the sin of pride,[59] and there is no parliamentary account that sheds any light on what his terseness may or may not conceal.[60] The infantry attack on the bridge, however, is most unlikely to have been planned in advance, as Cromwell did not know that the bulk of the enemy army was crossing the river whilst he was fighting Langdale, and therefore that the lane that passed to the south of Langdale's position might be used to separate one part of the enemy army from the other.[61] Of the various components of the battle plan, only one rests on firm documentary evidence. Ralph Assheton, the commander of the Lancashire brigade, masterminded the pike charge that cleared the bridge over the Ribble.[62] The softening-up operation and the overall scheme of attack may have been the work of the officers of the reserve regiments who were on the spot, or that of Cromwell, or Lambert, or of both Cromwell and Lambert.

Overnight the Scottish high command continued its run of unforced errors. The cavalry returned from Wigan following orders sent during the course of the engagement at Ribbleton Moor's End, but they arrived back in the Ribble valley far too late to be of any assistance and ran straight into Cromwell's cavalry. They were therefore in no good state when they eventually managed to rejoin the rest of their army. Hamilton and his advisers in the meantime had decided to march south, their only hope being to join the forces being raised in north-west Wales by Lord Byron, but these were 150 miles away. In the interest of speed they abandoned their ammunition wagons and the rest of their train, but this ensured that the Scottish musketeers would cease to be of any military value as soon as they had used up the powder they carried on their persons. Chased through Wigan towards Warrington and the crossing over the Mersey, the Scottish army made a stand at a pass at Winwick, two miles short of the town, where the infantry held up the New Model Army for some hours.[63] As Cromwell pointed out in his report, the enemy could have crossed the river unimpeded whilst the engagement was taking place,[64] as parliamentary troops had yet to reach the Cheshire bank, but for the infantry further progress to the south and west was dependent on the firepower of the musketeers, and after Winwick there was no gunpowder left. A Council of War therefore decided that the infantry should surrender but that the cavalry should try to escape. The infantry officers duly made terms with Cromwell at Warrington on 20 August, but it did the cavalry no good. With the crossings over the Dee guarded by Cheshire forces, they tried to make their way to Pontefract, the nearest fortress held for the king. Harried by Cromwell's cavalry and by local forces, they came to a halt through exhaustion all over the North Midlands, Hamilton with many of his officers being captured at Uttoxeter in Staffordshire on the 25th.[65]

But that was not quite the end of the campaign. What followed next shows another facet of Cromwell's capacity for high command, and one for which he had had copious training – political generalship. Part of the Scottish army had escaped his clutches: the infantry regiments blockading Lancaster Castle, Monro's brigade and the cavalry that had arrived at Preston too late to cross the bridge. The troops of horse that Cromwell had sent after them were too few to cut off their retreat, and under Monro's command they quickly recrossed the border. Avoiding Edinburgh, which the anti-Engagers had fortified, Monro occupied Stirling Castle, probably the strongest defensive position in Lowland Scotland capable of accommodating an army.[66]

Cromwell headed northwards after giving his troops some time for rest and recuperation. His orders from Parliament were to recapture Carlisle and Berwick, but he saw it as his first priority not to allow the two Scottish factions time to sink their differences in the face of a foreign invasion. Arriving before Berwick, he opened up negotiations with the Anti-Engagers, but in order not to alienate Scottish opinion he only occupied sufficient Scottish soil to complete the blockade of the town.[67] By the treaty of Stirling the Engagers allowed their opponents to conduct the negotiations, and by late September a rough agreement was in place between the Anti-Engagers representing the entire Scottish nation and Cromwell. The final details came together during his visit to Edinburgh in October. There he wooed the enemy with honeyed words about Protestant solidarity in the face of the Devil's brood of Engagers and royalists, but he also ratcheted up the terms, the most important being that Engagers were to be excluded from positions of power including the army, with Monro Force being shipped back to Ireland. As a corollary, New Model horse and dragoons were to remain in Scotland under John Lambert's command until the Anti-Engagers had raised a home defence force from their own supporters.[68] Keen to see the back of what looked like an army of occupation, they had it in place within a month and Lambert and his men duly returned to England.

CHAPTER 18

The British Wars 1649–1652

IRELAND

OLIVER CROMWELL returned to England in mid-October 1648, and spent the next six weeks supervising the sieges of Pontefract and Scarborough, the last garrisons holding out in the north for the king. This distanced him from the early stages of the second army coup, first the demand from the army that King Charles should be brought to trial to answer for the crimes he had committed against the people of England (who were the true sovereign), and then the forcible expulsion by the army of about one hundred members of the House of Commons to ensure that its will prevailed.[1] There is, however, no doubt that Cromwell approved in general terms of the actions the army was taking,[2] and after some hesitation on first arriving back in London he eventually put all his substantial political and indeed physical muscle behind the king's trial and execution.[3] Fairfax went some way along that road. He did not attend the trial but did nothing to stop the execution.[4] His behaviour is understandable in terms of his remit as army commander. He was not the king's general; the king had broken his parole and could not expect pardon; responsibility for the deaths of many rested on his shoulders.

Cromwell and his associates also axed the House of Lords, the institution of monarchy and the Committee at Derby House. From the end of February 1649 the House of Commons working through a Council of State, the new executive committee, was sole sovereign, governing the country on behalf of the people of England and Wales. However, this was no more than a fig leaf. It was the New Model Army represented by its leading officers that was the true sovereign, as membership of both bodies was ultimately in its gift. This was, of course, an affront to the other western European powers, and much mumbling went on about invading England and removing its new republic by force, but with France and Spain at war the prospect of continental intervention in English affairs was most unlikely for the time being.

In the spring of 1649 the most immediate danger to the Commonwealth was from Ireland, where James Butler, Marquis of Ormond, had returned some months earlier. Using a religious and constitutional template provided by the queen and the Prince of Wales, by mid- to late January he had brought almost all the conflicting interests, both Protestant and Catholic, into a coalition to promote the Stuart cause ranging from Confederates at one extreme through

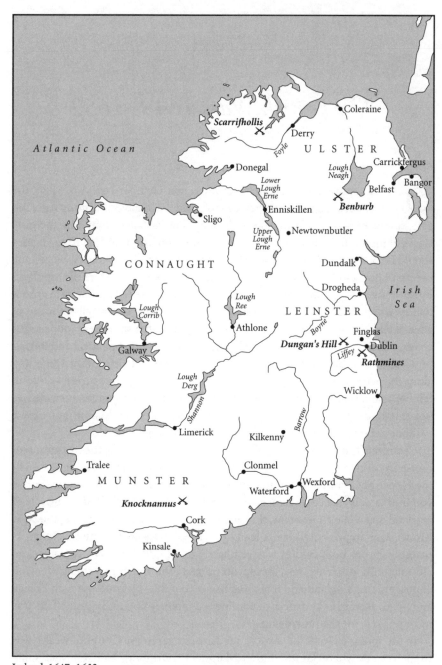

Ireland, 1647–1652

loyalists of both faiths to Ulster Presbyterians and the few remaining Scottish troops at the other. Ormond also had the support of a considerable number of royalist refugees from England, many of whom were former soldiers. The only leading dissenters were, at one extreme, ultra-Catholics, including members of the hierarchy and General Owen Roe O'Neill and the Ulster army for whom the concessions to Irish Catholicism and to Irish liberties did not go far enough, and at the other extreme loyalist commanders who preferred for a variety of reasons to remain in the Commonwealth's employ: Michael Jones at Dublin, George Monck at Dundalk and Sir Charles Coote at Derry.[5]

This was a completely different situation to that which had prevailed at the end of the First Civil War. The House of Commons and the Council of State had to take immediate action, as the royalists intended to use Ireland as the launching pad for an invasion of England. Moreover, an Irish invasion was practicable for the first time and not simply because the enemy had few security fears at home as they controlled so much of the country. For the first time the commanders in Ireland would have a fleet with sufficient capacity to bring over a large army. Ships belonging to the English navy had turned royalist in April 1648. Bottled up in the port of Helvoetsluys in the Netherlands by the parliamentary navy, they escaped at the time of the second army coup and, commanded by Prince Rupert, they duly arrived at Kinsale in late January 1649.[6]

Parliament appointed Oliver Cromwell as lord lieutenant of Ireland and commander of an expeditionary force charged with making a pre-emptive strike. It was to be drawn from the New Model Army, which should have made matters easy, but it did not set sail for another five months. This was partly because of Cromwell's determination that his expedition should be satisfactorily resourced, and partly because of discontent in the army against serving in Ireland, which led to mutinies in nine regiments, mainly horse, with rumblings in several others.[7] Leadership was assumed by radical elements, which were able to take advantage of long-standing grievances such as arrears of pay and the fear that once the troops got to Ireland they would sicken and die through neglect and the unhealthy climate as English armies there had done in the past. General Fairfax, who had kept very quiet during the time of the king's trial and execution and pleaded illness as a reason for not leading the Irish expedition, took on a new lease of life. The radicals represented a threat to army unity and to the social order, and he vigorously put down the mutinies with Cromwell's assistance. The number of summary executions that followed was small, but the general did disband one entire regiment and several troops and companies belonging to other regiments. This was probably what many of the rank-and-file supporters of the mutiny had wanted, but they lost out on the other half of their desires. They never saw their pay arrears.[8]

The expeditionary force, some 12,000 strong, duly landed at the port of Dublin in three waves between 15 and 25 August, only for Cromwell to discover

that the army he was expecting to face had fallen apart.[9] The marquis of Ormond
had begun campaigning in March, but for the first four months he focused his
attention on Ulster, the main centre of opposition. He not only drove O'Neill
out of the centre and east of the province but also secured the capitulation of
most of the English forces there. Colonel Monck's entire brigade deserted
despite profuse promises that they would remain loyal. When Monck returned
to England he faced a sticky interview with Cromwell and a grilling in the House
of Commons because of the terms of a truce he had made with O'Neill earlier in
the year, but in the end he escaped with nothing more than a reprimand.[10]

Ormond appeared to have frittered away his time on minor operations,[11] but
there were grave problems in attacking Dublin with its garrison of several thousand men commanded by the victor of Dungan's Hill, Michael Jones. However,
by mid-July with an army variously estimated as being between 11,000 and
21,000 strong, the marquis did at last close in on the Irish capital.[12] The
rendezvous was at Finglas ten miles to the north-west, but capturing Dublin
would not be an easy option. Michael Jones had received reinforcements during
the summer, and this ruled out storming the city. On the other hand, the royalists did not have the means of starving the city into surrender as the English fleet
had regained control of the sea, having stationed enough ships off Kinsale to
keep Prince Rupert in port.[13] Finally, Ormond knew that Cromwell's arrival was
imminent.

After considerable discussion the royalist Council of War agreed to leave
Lord Dillon with 3,000 men at Finglas to prevent the Dublin garrison foraging
on the north side of the River Liffey, whilst the rest of the army moved to
Rathmines on the south side with the object of making it as difficult as possible
for Cromwell to land his troops. This seems the most sensible course of action
in the circumstances, but a second decision was more questionable.[14] There
were rumours of mutinies in Munster associated with the landing of English
troops there, and Ormond sent Lord Inchiquin, his most uniformly successful
commander, to investigate and he took with him two of the marquis's best regiments of horse.[15]

To put his plan into execution Ormond sent Major General Purcell on 1
August with 1,500 foot, some pioneers and a small cavalry escort to build a gun
platform at Baggotsrath in artillery range of the deepwater quay where Cromwell's
troops would have to disembark. He himself remained at Rathmines, a mile or so
to the west, and quartered his regiments in the surrounding villages and hamlets.
However, he failed to consider what Michael Jones might do in response.

Over the past year Jones's letters to London had become increasingly
gloomy. Garrison after garrison had gone over to the enemy. He had received
reinforcements from England but not the wherewithal to feed and pay them. He
was now penned into a very small space with a force of perhaps as many as 8,000
men. If Cromwell was unable to land at Dublin, he would be on his own for

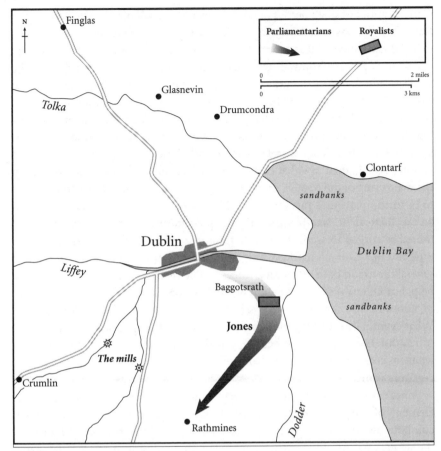

Parliamentarians   Royalists

Rathmines

several more weeks, the only other ports in Commonwealth hands being in the far north-west of the island. In the meantime his forces would be desperately short of bread, as the enemy had cut off the water which drove the machinery that powered Dublin's flour mills. He was also fearful of traitors in the ranks who would work on the discontent to such an extent that he would have to sue for terms. The position of the gun platform was the last straw. In addition to allowing the royalists to bombard the deepwater quay, their cannon would also dominate the only piece of open ground where he could graze his cavalry horses.[16] It was therefore essential to remove the royalists from Baggotsrath before they could fortify it, and the only answer was a sally in force.

Early on the morning of the following day, 2 August, Michael Jones left the city at the head of some 5,000 men.[17] What followed was a massive indictment of Ormond's generalship. The marquis had a well-deserved reputation as a military administrator. He was also an able negotiator and coalition builder, and had won a number of small battles in the first year and a half of the 'rebellion', but at Rathmines he was in sole charge of a large army for the first time and he totally misread the military situation.[18] Probably unaware of the pickle Jones was in, and knowing that Cromwell was expected any day, he did not expect to be attacked and therefore did little to provide the builders of the gun platform with close support, and when he heard musket fire from that direction he was very slow to react. Having been up all night on military business, he had retired to his tent for a sleep and probably refused to be disturbed. After putting up a fierce fight, Purcell Force lost control of Baggotsrath. Jones, having beaten off a feeble counter-attack, then saw that he had an unprecedented opportunity to beat up the major part of the royalist army. The forces to the south of the Liffey seemed to be in complete disarray. Ormond had not even devised a rudimentary line of battle. Instead he was feeding in units piecemeal. The parliamentary forces therefore surged forward through Rathmines, eliminating enemy units one by one, and in a running battle lasting into the afternoon Jones captured or killed several thousand of the Coalition forces.[19] The marquis sent to Lord Dillon for help, but Dillon wisely declined. If he crossed the Liffey, his men were likely to be consumed in the same way.[20] However, he may have helped stop the rot. What eventually brought Jones's men to a halt was the approach of a large body of royalist horse. It did not engage, but they were too exhausted to follow it when it crossed to the north bank of the Liffey from where it had almost certainly come.[21]

Jones's victory had been an opportunistic one. It owed everything to the element of surprise and to numerical superiority at the point of contact, compounded by Ormond's lack of foresight and sluggish reaction.[22] However, the scrappy nature of the engagement meant that militarily it was less damaging to the enemy than Dungan's Hill had been. Many royalists therefore escaped in the confusion. Also, Dillon's forces remained in the field, and there was a strong possibility that O'Neill would join the coalition in the autumn with an army of 5,000 men. Ormond's letters written immediately after the battle were therefore quite optimistic.[23]

Left in peace for a few days whilst Cromwell's army recovered from its sea voyage, Ormond had time to consider the options. After consulting his Council of War he decided to strengthen the garrison at Drogheda, thirty miles to the north of Dublin, with 2,000 infantry, half Catholic and half Protestant. Its purpose was to serve as bait for the enemy forces but one that it would be difficult for them to swallow. Ormond envisaged them being involved in a lengthy siege, which would give him time to assemble a large enough army to engage them in battle. He also hoped that 'Colonel Hunger and Major Sickness' would improve the odds in his favour by cutting a swathe through their ranks. Ormond therefore withdrew to a safe distance to wait on events,[24] and for the hoped-for arrival of Owen O'Neill and the army of Ulster.

By the end of August, Cromwell was ready for action. Together with Jones's troops, he commanded an army of 20,000 or so men, which was both well paid and extremely well resourced. It was also free from interference from Parliament or the Committee of State, but not merely because of the distances involved. The army officers had insisted from the start that Oliver should enjoy complete political autonomy in Ireland, including the right to negotiate with the enemy on behalf of Parliament and the Council of State.[25] This privilege he was to use to very great effect. Even before leaving England, Oliver won over Roger Boyles, Lord Broghill, the future earl of Orrery. The Boyles, a settler family with Puritan sympathies, jostled with Lord Inchiquin for political dominance in Munster. Broghill would therefore be a useful ally in winning over the Munster Protestants of English descent who presently sided with Ormond.[26] However, Cromwell's time as commander-in-chief in Ireland is the most controversial phase of his military career. His skills as a general were in command and control on the battlefield, but he signally failed to engage the Coalition forces in battle. Instead he conducted one siege after another whilst lacking not only the experience but also the patience required for that type of warfare. As a result he tried to cut corners and in the process all around were soaked in blood, the enemy, his own troops and innocent civilians.[27]

Cromwell began by storming Drogheda and Wexford on 10 September and 11 October 1649 and slaughtering thousands, but he failed to capture Dungannon and Waterford before the weather closed in for the winter in early December. In the spring of 1650, he determined to capture Kilkenny, the former Confederate capital, in double-quick time. Storming the city was costly and unsuccessful, but it so terrorised the townspeople that they easily browbeat the garrison commander into capitulating on 27 March, which encouraged Oliver to do the same at Clonmel six weeks later with disastrous consequences. Three thousand officers and men died or were wounded in two attacks on the breach his artillery had made in the town walls, by far the worst setback in the New Model Army's entire history. To make matters worse, Clonmel surrendered on terms the following day but not the garrison, which had marched away under cover of night. Cromwell's men then put the seal on their disgrace by slaughtering hundreds of stragglers who had failed to keep pace with the retreating soldiers.[28]

After a succession of orders to return to England, Cromwell finally left on 23 May 1650, but without finishing the task set him and war dragged on for a further two years. The campaign he fought in Ireland therefore represented a major discontinuity in the spectacular run of successes, which began at Marston Moor in July 1644 and was to end at Worcester seven years later. However, this narrative is misleading in a number of respects. Cromwell's achievements in Ireland were manifold, and the alleged shortcomings of his generalship as displayed there need modifying in several important respects.

There is no doubt whatsoever that Cromwell broke the back of Ormond's coalition and paved the way for the end game which others had to play for him for reasons beyond his control. Moreover, the fact that he did not have to fight a battle is all due credit to Michael Jones, but no reflection on his abilities as a general. It takes two to tango, and the most Ormond could put in the field after Rathmines and Drogheda was a force less than half the size of Cromwell's and Jones's forces combined. As a result, all he could do was shadow the Commonwealth army at a safe distance hoping that it would disintegrate as the weather deteriorated and its supplies ran out.[29] However, unlike many earlier English expeditions to Ireland that had begun well, the victors did not run out of steam, and this was due to the energy displayed by Cromwell and his subordinates, and the continuous flow of resources he had ensured they would have at their beck and call.[30] The results were impressive. In early August 1649 the Commonwealth controlled no more than a handful of garrisons around the coast. By the end of May 1650 its forces had overrun most of Leinster and almost the whole of Munster, whilst in Ulster Sir Charles Coote aided by New Model regiments had recovered more than he had lost the previous summer.[31] A month later Coote put the final stamp on his own achievements by destroying what had been Owen O'Neill's army at the battle of Scarrifhollis after which he summarily executed its commander, the bishop of Clogher. However, O'Neill's reputation was not damaged as a result. He had died in November of the previous year leading his army south to join Ormond, and the bishop had ignored the advice of the professional soldiers in his entourage.[32]

Cromwell's military successes also ran in tandem with major political victories over Ormond. The marquis's misfortunes, first his defeat at Rathmines, then the loss of the rest of his infantry at Drogheda, and finally his failure to do anything to assist Wexford, caused Catholic members of the coalition to lose confidence in him, a sentiment approved of by many of their priests who had never been happy with the Ormond peace. His authority also suffered from the increasing tendency of the Protestant side of the coalition to disintegrate. In Munster soldiers and landowners made their peace with the Commonwealth in droves during the autumn and winter of 1649, won over by Broghill's blandishments, the New Model Army's successes at Drogheda and Wexford, and Cromwell's propaganda campaign focusing on Protestant solidarity.[33] In Ulster also the Presbyterian settlers, who had joined the Ormond peace and fought against Coote and Monck, saw the light and changed sides. However, Cromwell was not interested in bargaining with Catholic officers, politicians or priests. His well-publicised belief in religious toleration did not extend to the celebration of the Mass. In his view, Roman Catholicism was a debased and corrupt type of Christianity whose practice led to eternal damnation. However, his hostility was religious rather than racial. The benighted native Irish were lost sheep who had been led astray by their clergy. He encouraged them to surrender in the hope that they would see the error of their ways and become good Protestants.[34]

Finally, Cromwell's so-called barbarous and costly siege tactics need to be seen in context. Despite Ormond's horrified reaction,[35] what had happened at Drogheda and Wexford was not untypical of warfare in western and central Europe in the mid seventeenth century or indeed in Scotland. It was the gentlemanly manner of fighting in England that was the exception. What is remarkable is that Cromwell expressed 'remorse and regret' after Drogheda where a very large percentage of the dead were soldiers, whilst remaining silent in the case of Wexford where a much higher proportion were civilians.[36] Damage to public relations or concern about his future reputation caused by the slaughter of non-combatants does not therefore seem to have been a worry. However, there was one significant difference between the two. Wexford had a garrison that was very largely Catholic, whereas Drogheda's was half Protestant. It is therefore possible that Cromwell's remorse and regret was part of his propaganda campaign for winning over former loyalists in the rest of Ireland. It was not a general apology for losing control of his men. Those killed at Drogheda who had washed 'their hands in so much innocent blood'[37] were Protestants who had done so fighting the forces of Parliament in England and then in Ireland, not in massacring Protestants in Ulster in 1642. If so, the message may have got through: Cromwell did not want to kill fellow Protestants even if they had innocent blood on their hands. This may therefore be another reason why so many Protestants made their peace with the Commonwealth by the time Cromwell left Ireland.

Turning to later episodes in the campaign, the failure to capture Dungannon and Waterford in the late autumn is not worthy of comment one way or the other: the weather and the time of the year, not Cromwell's ability or lack of ability, were the causes.[38] As for Kilkenny and Clonmel, he does seem to have expected the enemy to surrender after token resistance at his army's approach. There was, however, nothing tactically wrong with the attack on Clonmel other than that Cromwell did not call it off once he became aware of the losses his assault troops were sustaining through enemy counter-measures.[39] In addition, the casualties reputedly sustained at Clonmel, up to 3,000 New Model Army soldiers killed and wounded in the two assaults, are much exaggerated. Five hundred to 1,000 is more likely.[40] Storming a city was almost invariably costly, unless some other factor intervened, as for example at Wexford where the garrison did not put up much of a fight because they thought surrender negotiations had come to a successful conclusion. Perhaps Cromwell's error was impatience,[41] but caused by priorities rather than pride. He was in a hurry because of what was happening elsewhere in the British Isles, not because he was mustard keen to protect his reputation as an army commander, as such a sentiment was evidence of the sin of pride, which would leave him wide open to heavenly chastisement.[42] Indeed, he quit Ireland leaving his successor Henry Ireton, the lord deputy, with the best possible chance of bringing the war to a swift conclusion.

It was Ireton's fault, not his, that this did not happen. Unlike Cromwell, Ireton lacked the political skills to exploit the divisions between his opponents.

Although supplies of men and materials from England continued to flow into Ireland despite the outbreak of war with the Scots, siege remorselessly followed siege with the besieged resisting to the last, possibly because of the summary execution of senior figures who surrendered and the slaughter of almost the whole of the Ulster army following the battle of Scarrifhollis on 21 June 1650. The capture of Limerick took up almost the whole of the 1651 campaigning season, and the last major garrison, Galway, was still resisting in April 1652 after a nine months' siege. Even so, the war could have dragged on even longer had there not been a concession on the part of the English. Irish Catholic soldiers who surrendered on terms could go abroad and fight in the armies of France and Spain.[43] Politics thus provided the key where terror kept the door to peace bolted and barred. But what a peace! Ireland lost 15 to 20 per cent of its population in the wars and the famine that followed,[44] the Church was driven underground and guerrilla warfare continued. Moreover, the Protestant ascendancy was more firmly in the saddle than ever before as the estates of Catholics deemed to be traitors fell directly or indirectly into the hands of army officers and civilian speculators.

CHAPTER 19

The British Wars 1650–1651

SCOTLAND AND ENGLAND

THE SUCCESSION of messages Cromwell received begging him to return to England was an indication of worsening relations between the Commonwealth government and Scotland. Robbed of its king by the New Model Army and the purged House of Commons, the Scottish government had duly proclaimed the Prince of Wales as King Charles II. Initially, the House of Commons and the Council of State did no more than issue a formal protest reminding the marquis of Argyll and his colleagues of their shared experience of the treachery of the House of Stuart. A declaration of war would have been a gross over reaction. In the early months of 1649 young Charles was a long way from actually sitting on the Scottish throne, let alone invading England at the head of a Scottish army.

The Anti-Engagers believed that the disasters of 1648 were divine punishment for straying from the path of righteousness along which the Scottish people had travelled since the first agitation against the policies of King Charles I eleven years before. The only way to secure the future of the Scottish revolution now that England was under Independent control was for government policy and practice to conform to the tenets of Presbyterianism in every respect. This did not rule out entering into negotiations with the new king, but there could be no concessions. God's continued favour depended upon it. The Anti-Engagers' representatives therefore made it clear to Charles from the start that he must become the creature of the Covenant by accepting Presbyterianism not just as the only permitted religion in all three of his kingdoms but also in his own household. There were to be no exceptions, however exalted that person's status. In addition, he would not recover the political powers his father had surrendered. There was less chance of going astray if a godly collective exercised them rather than a single person. Charles II's role as monarch would therefore be a ceremonial one. In addition former royalists, both English and Scottish, and former Engagers must play no part in civilian or military affairs. Finally, he must disassociate himself completely from his supporters in Ireland. Catholics and Protestants who were not Presbyterians were clearly God's enemies. To make common cause with them against the English republic was to lay the godly open to the fate that had befallen the Engagers in 1648.[1]

In August 1649 when Cromwell left England, young Charles had no intention of agreeing to so humiliating a set of conditions, and negotiations with the Covenanters were not a priority so long as he had hopes of success in Ireland. However, the defeat at Rathmines and the unravelling of the Ormond coalition meant that the Scottish option was the only one left for regaining his father's thrones, however distasteful the medicine he would have to swallow.[2] By the spring of 1650 agreement was close, and Scotland replaced Ireland as the principal threat to the security of the Commonwealth regime. There young Charles would have the backing not of a coalition of opposites brought together by Ormond's glib diplomacy and fear of the English Republic but of a single-minded body of Protestants who, if not the entire nation, were most unlikely to have their mission to bend the other two British kingdoms to their will opposed or undermined by those they excluded from power, be they Engagers or royalists. Moreover, in command of the Covenanter army was the country's most successful general, David Leslie, the victor of Philiphaugh, and in the eyes of the Scots, of Marston Moor also. Leslie had had no truck with the Engagers in 1648, but since the end of the First English Civil War he had kept his military muscles in tone. He had expelled Alasdair MacColla and his family from the Highlands and the Isles in 1646–7 and he had also conducted successful operations against royalists in various parts of Scotland in 1649–50.[3]

Immediately after Cromwell's return, the English Council of State decided on a pre-emptive strike using regiments stationed in England. The original intention was for Fairfax and Cromwell to be in harness once more, but Fairfax would only agree to be the commander-in-chief if the Scots invaded England. He still saw himself as bound by the oath he had sworn in 1643 to stand by the Solemn League and Covenant, and his conscience told him that the Scots would not invade.[4] Parliament accepted his resignation with regret and immediately appointed Oliver Cromwell as its second lord general.[5]

The English army crossed the border in late July 1650. At Cromwell's disposal were about 12,000 foot and 4,000 horse commanded respectively by George Monck and John Lambert. The route chosen for the invasion was the Great North Road, which hugged the North Sea coast and led straight to Edinburgh, only fifty miles from the border. Logistical preparations were as sound as they had been for the Irish expedition a year earlier, with most of the heavy equipment going by sea to Newcastle, which was to serve as the campaign headquarters,[6] whilst other supplies could be delivered to the army through any one of the string of ports that lay along the route, the principal ones being Berwick and Dunbar.

The Covenanters were ready for him. Volunteers had flocked to the colours, giving Leslie an army that was considerably larger than Cromwell's. The commitment to godliness, however, persisted, with royalists and Engagers, many of them experienced officers, being discharged just as the campaign was about to start. This is one reason cited for what happened, particularly by such habitual groaners as Sir Edward Walker,[7] but the purged army was much more than an ideologically uniform rabble. Many of the officers and quite a number of the rank and file had fought in the wars in England and Scotland between 1644 and 1647. In addition, Leslie had a sound operational plan. He had systematically stripped the landscape of southern Scotland of anything that would be of assistance to the enemy army, and constructed a fortified line protecting the Edinburgh area and the port of Leith behind which he placed his army.[8]

What the Covenanter government and its general had in mind was a Fabian campaign. Cromwell dared not attack the lines of Edinburgh head on because of the casualties the New Model Army would incur, and Leslie had no intention of leaving it voluntarily unless to harass a demoralised enemy as it fell back towards the border. The odds against Leslie being forced to move because his troops were starving were very long, as the English fleet could not hope to intercept more than a small percentage of the food and other supplies crossing the Firth of Forth from the Kingdom of Fife, given the length of the shoreline to be patrolled and the narrowness of the Firth.[9] It would also be very difficult for Cromwell to force Leslie to shift his ground by turning his flank. One rested on the sea, the other on the short stretch of the River Forth between the mountains and the estuary. At its centre stood Stirling Castle, constructed on one of the best defensive sites in Scotland, and commanding what for an army was the only practicable crossing.[10]

Cromwell set up his forward base at Musselburgh, seven miles short of the Scottish capital, on 22 July. However, his attempts over the next five weeks to tempt or browbeat Leslie failed completely. The losses sustained in probing attacks had been small but the unseasonable weather took a much bigger toll,[11] and on 31 August Cromwell ordered his forces to retreat to Dunbar. Leslie followed at a discrete distance in case it was all a trick, and took care to quarter his army in an impregnable position on Doon Hill overlooking the town. He also sent a mounted force to the pass at Cocksburnpath some miles to the south, thus cutting road communications between Dunbar and Berwick. So far the Fabian strategy had worked like a dream, but Leslie had yet to strike the killer blow. Even so, the odds favoured the Scots. It might be possible for the English cavalry to stage a breakout, as Balfour's had done at Lostwithiel, but Cromwell's only chance of saving the rest of his army was to evacuate it by sea. Although his troops could board ship straight from the quayside, the process was likely to be a messy one. The Scots had every chance of cutting up his rearguard, or even inflicting severe damage on his main body should discipline break down during embarkation.[12]

On 2 September the Scots saw the sick and wounded being shipped out of Dunbar and assumed that the rest of the army would soon follow. This was too good a chance to be missed and, according to some contemporary accounts, the

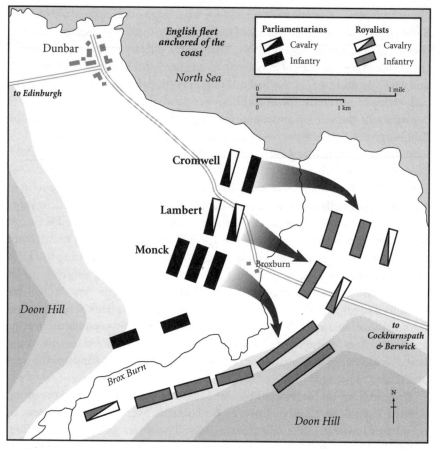

Dunbar

representatives of the Covenanter government, egged on by their ministers, forced Leslie to quit Doon Hill against his will so as to make it easier to massacre the English.[13] The redeployment began in the middle part of the day,[14] and by nightfall the Scots had set up camp along the far bank of the Brox Burn, which wound its way around the east and south sides of Dunbar at a distance of about a mile. Cromwell immediately saw this as a sign of God's providence, evidence of which had been missing for the past six weeks. There was now a good chance of fighting a battle in circumstances that did not unduly favour the enemy, and he and his two deputies spent the afternoon preparing a battle plan. They explained it to the Council of War in the evening and gained the officers' approval.[15] The attack would be launched two hours before dawn on the following day.

In the battle that followed Cromwell's tactics foreshadowed the oblique order of attack for which Frederick the Great was to become so famous a century later. The first assault led by his two protégés, Lambert and Monck, was

against the centre of the Scottish line. Its purpose was to hold the enemy's attention, and against heavy opposition they managed to establish a precarious
bridgehead where the road to England crossed the Brox Burn. At the same time
Cromwell's heavy artillery blazed away against Scottish positions to the north of
the road, raising expectations that the Scottish left wing would be next to come
under attack.[16] In the meantime, the New Model Army reserves had crossed the
burn close to where it met the sea. Under Cromwell's personal guidance they
then deployed themselves in such a way as to outflank and even overlap the right
wing of the Scottish army. Thanks to the darkness, and possibly a sea mist, they
did all of this without being seen.

At about 8 a.m. the reserves launched a massive attack on the flank and rear
of the enemy right wing. It too met with considerable opposition at first, particularly from the Scottish infantry,[17] but Leslie was unable to send reinforcements
because the centre already had its hands full, whilst the left wing could not move,
squeezed between Doon Hill, the Brox Burn and the fighting in the centre.[18] To
make matters worse, as the right wing started to disintegrate the fugitives tried
to make their escape through the main body of the Scottish army, thus
disrupting any attempt by uncommitted units to make a stand which would have
delayed the pursuit and enabled more Scots to escape.[19] Oliver had greeted the
rising sun with the words 'Now let God arise and his enemies should be scattered', and his prophecy was fulfilled in spectacular fashion.[20] Although most of
Leslie's cavalry managed to outpace their pursuers, he lost almost the entire
Scottish infantry who were either killed or captured on the spot or cut down in
a pursuit lasting the rest of the day.[21]

In his declaration after the battle David Leslie tried to convince his listeners
that he should not bear full responsibility for what had happened at Dunbar.[22]
This may be true of the decision to quit Doon Hill,[23] but he was directly responsible for two elementary errors in the way the Scottish army had deployed on the
afternoon of 2 September. First, he failed to ensure that the flat coastal plain to
the east of the Brox Burn, the most likely place for the English cavalry to attempt
a breakout, was as full of Scottish troops as possible. What makes this even more
surprising is the claim that he himself was preparing to attack across the burn the
next day at the same spot so as to force the English back into the streets of
Dunbar, thus making an orderly disembarkation that much more difficult.[24] The
other error was his failure to extend his line of battle as far as the sea cliffs. Had
he done so, Cromwell could not have outflanked him and delivered the devastating attack that decided the battle. Why Leslie did not do so is perplexing. It
was certainly not through shortage of men. He could easily have filled the space
between the Great North Road and the sea with brigades of foot supported by
cavalry. All I can suggest is that keeping a large force of infantry on the left wing
close to the built-up area enabled him to launch an assault on the town as soon
as Cromwell started evacuating his army.

Another reason for the Scottish defeat mentioned soon after the battle was its army's laid-back attitude. Many officers and men had fallen under their ministers' spell. They believed that a cosy relationship now existed between the Army of the Covenant and God, as shown by the ease with which it had captured the dreaded Montrose and his force of German and Danish mercenaries, which had landed in the north of the country earlier in the year. Officers allegedly found comfortable billets for themselves at a distance from their men, whilst the commander of the Scottish infantry, John Holbourne, apparently ordered his musketeers to keep only two lengths of matches alight per company, thus making it almost impossible for the musketeers to react quickly to a surprise attack.[25] However, there is no evidence that a casual attitude towards gathering intelligence or a refusal to listen to reports that conflicted with the high command's preconceived notions were of any significance whatsoever in the Scottish defeat.[26]

Dunbar was by no means a climactic battle despite the huge Scottish losses and the surrender of the Scottish capital (but not Edinburgh Castle) a few days later. It was not just that Leslie's cavalry, unlike their compatriots in 1648, could find refuge in friendly territory once the immediate pursuit was over. Cromwell still had Stirling Castle to contend with, and unsurprisingly Leslie chose it as the rallying point for what was left of his army. However, in tactical terms Dunbar was more clearly Cromwell's victory than Preston had been. Lambert and Monck were heavily involved at the planning stage but in the execution their job was to pin the enemy down. It was Oliver who had delivered the killer blow.[27] Lambert, however, was clearly responsible for the second success of the 1650 campaign, routing a small army raised in south-west Scotland in an encounter battle at Hamilton on 30 November.[28] Yet the victory was not of strategic importance, as the men of Ayr and Galloway were not on their way to join Leslie at Stirling. Indeed the Covenanters of the south-west were unhappy at letting the king return to Scotland, saw Dunbar as the consequence, and were edging towards a position of neutrality encouraged by Cromwell's serpent tongue. Their inquest into God's providence was wrongly conceived. Cromwell gained the victory because the New Model Army was right in His eyes, not because He wished to punish the Scots for dallying with the second Charles Stuart. Such talk probably did little if anything to weaken the south-westerners' resolve, but it certainly weakened that of Sir William Dundas, who surrendered Edinburgh Castle in December even though he still had plenty of gunpowder and victuals left.[29]

The final phase of Cromwell's conquest of Scotland did not begin for another six months. Bad weather forced the New Model Army into winter quarters south of the River Forth in December, but when better conditions returned, it had no chance of winning a quick final victory, partly because Oliver was seriously ill at various times between February and May 1651,[30] and partly because of the operational problems the high command faced in forcing the Scots to fight.

From late September 1650 onwards he gave Leslie several inducements to leave the safety of Stirling, but Leslie refused to play ball,[31] and the defences along the River Forth were far too strong to be attacked head-on without incurring huge casualties. However, all was not well on the north bank. The Scots were short of supplies. They were also quarrelling amongst themselves about the best way forward, and this may explain their lacklustre reaction when the English did strike.[32]

In letters written in June and July 1651, Cromwell described himself as being in an operational impasse. If the Scots were able to maintain their position at Stirling until the end of the customary campaigning season, the English army would wither away through disease and desertion during the months that followed, whilst the Scottish soldiers, used to a harsher climate, would fare much better. By the spring of 1652 the military balance between the two sides would have tipped firmly in the Scots' favour and defeat would probably follow.[33] However, Oliver was being a little economical with the truth. He had begun planning an amphibious landing on the north shore of the Firth of Forth in the autumn of 1650 as soon as it became clear that Leslie intended to play a second Fabian game at Stirling. In December the English government placed orders at Newcastle for the construction of large numbers of flat-bottomed boats suitable for transporting cavalry horses and heavy artillery, but nothing could be done until they were ready.[34]

The 'landing craft' duly arrived in the Firth of Forth in June but they remained at their moorings for a month. The New Model Army was busy else-where. One reading of its peregrinations during late June and July is that they represent a desperate attempt to avoid the risks associated with an amphibious operation. One final attempt was therefore made to tempt Leslie from his lair, first by advancing to within two miles of Stirling, and then by a march westwards seemingly with the intention of attacking Glasgow. Only when Leslie failed to react did Cromwell reluctantly give the command for an assault on the north shore of the Firth. Another view is that the purpose of the marching backwards and forwards was to distract Leslie's attention from what was happening on the south shore.[35] If so, why was Leslie taken in? The Scottish general would certainly have known from spies that the English now had vessels suitable for mounting a seaborne assault on the coast of Fife, but lack of a vantage point on the low-lying north shore may have made it impossible for him to see how many troops Cromwell had assembled for the assault. Alternatively, he may have worried about moving troops into Fife in large numbers in case the landing craft were merely a feint to distract him from the main attack further to the west.

On 17 July the flat-bottomed boats landed a party of a thousand or so troops under Colonel Overton's command at North Queensferry. Taken by surprise, the Scots' high command hesitated. This gave the English time to expand their bridgehead, and within a few days several thousand more horse and foot had crossed the Firth, with John Lambert taking charge of operations.[36] Still concerned that the New Model Army would deliver its main attack on the lines of Stirling as Cromwell was still hovering nearby, Leslie only sent a small body of men to drive the enemy from Fife. This was to prove his undoing. Lambert drew up his army at Inverkeithing, three miles to the north of North Queensferry, with his infantry in the centre and his cavalry on the wings. However, he placed the bulk of his horse on the right wing as the ground in front of the other wing was unsuitable for a cavalry charge. The Scots' position was on high ground and he naturally expected them to attack, but for some hours nothing happened. As time passed Lambert became increasingly convinced that the enemy commander was waiting for reinforcements. He then received a message from Cromwell. He had given up the attempt to lure Leslie from the lines of Stirling and was heading for the embarkation point. Although encouraging news in one respect, the distances involved meant that Leslie was highly likely to arrive at Inverkeithing first. Lambert therefore went into attack mode. The English cavalry on the right wing duly charged the enemy horse and almost immediately afterwards the two infantry bodies locked horns. The melee was a prolonged affair and the Scots seemed to be gaining the upper hand until Lambert's dragoons moved forward from the reserves and began directing heavy fire into the rear of the enemy formation. At this point the Scottish cavalry took to their heels. Many of their infantry followed but two veteran regiments held their ground, presumably in an attempt to cover the retreat. However, their self-sacrifice was to no avail. The retreat became a rout and the Scots sustained very heavy casualties.[37]

Although the fighting had only been on the scale of Montrose's battles, Inverkeithing was more decisive than Dunbar as Lambert had forced the lines of Stirling and completely undermined Leslie's operational plan.[38] Most of the rest of the English army then crossed the Forth by boat, an operation that took over a week, but instead of advancing on Stirling Castle they marched due north towards Perth, thus at one and the same time blocking the Scottish army's line of retreat towards Aberdeen and the eastern Highlands and cutting it off from the Kingdom of Fife, its principal source of food and fodder.[39]

After Inverkeithing the Scottish high command had to make a decisive response, but it was in disarray. Leslie apparently wanted to stay put, but by then the old Covenanter leadership, with which he had worked so closely over the years, had lost control. The defeats of the godly at Dunbar and Hamilton had undermined their credibility. It took some time for their grip on strategy to crumble, but by July the royalists and a number of former Engagers with young Charles at their head were firmly in the driving seat. His plan was to invade England with the aim of raising a huge army from men who had fought for his father in the First and Second Civil Wars and from disgruntled former supporters of Parliament. However, in so far as the old royalists were concerned, it did not have much hope of success. Many had supported the king in the First

Civil War to preserve Anglicanism against critics who were primarily Presbyterian. Yet they were being asked to join a Presbyterian army led by a Presbyterian king and consisting primarily of Scotsmen whose treachery had so hampered Charles I's war effort. As for the English Presbyterians, they chose to keep their heads down, and even the king's supporters among the Scottish nobility blanched at the task in hand. The English option was a gamble, but nobody could think of anything better, and Leslie's army duly set out from Stirling for the English border on 31 July.[40]

It is possible that by advancing on Perth rather than Stirling, Cromwell intentionally left the door into England ajar,[41] and that this was his masterstroke for ending a war that had lasted much longer than anticipated. There is little doubt that he saw a move in a southerly direction as one option available to the enemy, but the letters he wrote prior to the event suggest that he considered it unlikely. Moreover, if the enemy did make a run for it, they would not get far. Troops gathering in southern Scotland under the command of Major General Thomas Harrison should be strong enough to delay them until his army arrived.[42] Instead Cromwell saw the most likely result of his advance on Perth would be Leslie's army rushing north to free up its lines of communication, thus giving him a very good chance of destroying it in a conventional battle in the valley of the River Tay. Only when the invasion of England was clearly under way did Cromwell suggest that he had expected it all along.[43] Then he was very profuse with advice as to how to counteract it, but the Council of State was already busy ordering the county militia regiments to assemble at various points to delay the Scots' progress towards London.

Cromwell shortened his regiments' march south by ferrying them back across the Firth of Forth, but the king's army, at least 10,000 Scots and about 2,000 English exiles, was several days' march ahead. By the time he reached Newcastle on 12 August they were in central Lancashire.[44] He sent Lambert and Harrison ahead with most of the regiments of horse to hold them at the crossing of the Mersey, but the royalists brushed them aside. The Council of State suspected lack of will on the part of the two commanders, particularly when they did nothing to slow down the enemy's march across the English Midlands.[45] However, to be fair to Lambert and Harrison they were probably under orders from Cromwell to shadow the enemy rather than get involved in a major engagement. In battle their regiments would be the core of the New Model cavalry, and if they suffered some mishap prior to the event or got overtired, the outcome could well be catastrophic. As it happened, the threat to London was not an immediate one. Charles's army was heading for the Severn valley, probably in the hope of picking up recruits. Only then would a march on the capital be practicable. Shrewsbury refused to admit the Scottish king, but Worcester, which the local militia was not strong enough to defend, would provide an equally suitable temporary headquarters.[46]

Cromwell's army continued on its way south through Ripon, Macclesfield and Leicester, rendezvousing with Harrison and Lambert at Warwick on 25 August. It then moved forward to Evesham in the Avon valley, thus taking up a position astride the road from Worcester to London. There it paused for a week, which is hardly surprising as it had marched over 300 miles in nineteen days. The rest also allowed time for some of the militia regiments to arrive,[47] and for Cromwell and his officers to put together a plan of attack. A direct advance on Worcester from Evesham was not the best way of achieving closure, as the Scots could withdraw into the hill country of the Welsh borderland, breaking the bridge over the Severn down behind them. The most important priority was therefore to get substantial numbers of troops to the far bank of the river to cut off their retreat, but the nearest bridges were at Upton ten miles below the city and at Bewdley fifteen miles in the opposite direction.

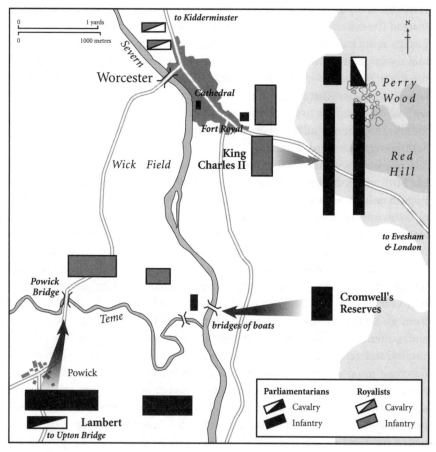

Worcester

The battle that followed on 3 September took place over much of the same ground as the first engagement of the First Civil War almost exactly nine years earlier, and Cromwell adopted the outline of Essex's tactical plan of 1642. He would attack Worcester from two directions, with the vanguard crossing the Severn at Upton and proceeding up the west bank of the river whilst the rest of the army approached the city from the east. This time, however, the army general would be in command of the vanguard.[48] There was one other tactical innovation. Essex had been unable to reinforce his vanguard when it got into difficulties at Powick bridge. Cromwell assumed that the enemy would defend the line of the Teme at Powick as in 1642, and to ensure that his vanguard could be reinforced he arranged for bridges of boats to be constructed on the morning of the battle, one across the Teme and the other across the Severn. To lessen the bridges' susceptibility to attack, he ordered the western end of the Severn bridge and the northern end of the Teme bridge to be no more than a pistol shot apart so that a single body of musketeers could defend them both and be reinforced by one or both parts of the army if it came under attack.[49] Nevertheless the battle plan did contain an element of risk. It left the troops on the east bank potentially open to attack from almost the whole of the royalist army, as Leslie could rely on holding the line of the Teme for some time with nothing stronger than an infantry brigade. However, although the brunt of the royalist attack did indeed fall on the militia regiments which made up much of the first line of battle on the east bank, Cromwell had stuffed the second line with New Model foot, and he had also placed regiments of New Model horse in close support.[50]

Who was in actual command on the royalist side is a matter of doubt. It should have been David Leslie, but he appears not to have issued or been ordered to issue any orders once the battle was under way. He was criticised subsequently for holding back the Scottish cavalry when they could have supported the royalist attack on the militia regiments, but the charge did not stick as he was ennobled at the Restoration without doing anything in the intervening nine years that might have served to rebuild a shattered reputation.[51] But whatever the circumstances, the pre-battle preparations were sound, repairs having been made to the city walls and to Fort Royal, which protected the eastern approaches to the city. In addition, a brigade of foot stationed at Upton had orders to block any attempt by the enemy to cross to the west bank of the Severn.

Cromwell's first move was to secure the crossing point at Upton. On 27 August Lambert's scouts discovered that although the drawbridge was no longer in place it was possible to reach the far side using a plank laid across the hole in the roadway. Under the cover of darkness a small body of musketeers tiptoed across and set up a defensive position in the town church which was adjacent to the bridge. This came under heavy enemy attack, but Lambert was able to get more troops across the river using a ford.[52] The royalists then fell back to Powick and prepared to defend the line of the Teme.

By midday on 3 September, the anniversary of Dunbar, the bridges of boats were complete, whereupon Cromwell launched his attack on Powick Bridge, whilst the enemy focused their attention on trying to eliminate the bridgehead at the conjunction of the Severn and the Teme. The fight at the Teme was certainly not a walkover. The Scots fought back, forcing Cromwell to draw in some reserves from the east bank of the Severn, which he encouraged in their attack by urging them on from the rear as he had done with the reserves at Dunbar. However, after about two hours of fighting the enemy broke and fell back towards the western suburbs of Worcester with the New Model soldiers in pursuit. At this point the king ordered an infantry attack to be launched against the rest of the enemy army drawn up on Red Hill facing the eastern side of the city. Initially, it seems to have made good headway against the militia regiments, but Cromwell responded quickly. He led reserve units to their support using the bridge of boats over the Severn, hitting the royalists in the flank and forcing them back into the city.

The final stage of the battle took the form of bloody hand-to-hand fighting in the streets of Worcester and its suburbs, as the royalist infantry tried to create time for the cavalry to escape, taking the king with them.[53] A cavalry screen of sorts protected the king for the first fifteen miles of his flight northwards, but from then onwards he was under civilian protection, as he dodged enemy horse patrols and search parties until he managed to escape to France from Sussex six weeks later. As for the rest of his army, Cromwell and the Council of State had organised the pursuit well in advance, assisted as in 1648 by local militias and stray troops of New Model horse. These focused very successfully on the principal choke points along the routes that the Scots would have to use in order to reach Scotland.[54] It was Preston all over again, but with the much greater distances involved even fewer got home. By the end about 10,000 Scots and English were prisoners and about 2,000 were dead, compared with about 100 fatalities in the New Model Army and the militia regiments.

The last of Cromwell's major victories as army commander had been in many ways the easiest. For the first time his forces outnumbered the enemy, but he was campaigning in an awkward military landscape and the enemy, though demoralised, were also desperate. However, as at Dunbar it is impossible to fault his leadership. In Scotland, too, formal fighting was pretty well at an end. George Monck, whom Cromwell had left in charge with 5,000–6,000 men, secured the surrender of Stirling Castle through negotiation, captured members of the Scottish government whom he found hiding in the little town of Alyth on the edge of the Highlands, and cowed Lowland Scotland into submission by storming and sacking Dundee. All three events took place before the battle of Worcester. Monck's expeditious handling of the fag end of the Scottish campaign laid the foundation for a most impressive career in which his earlier shortcomings were very largely forgotten. It also confirmed Cromwell's willingness to reward outstanding ability where he saw it, regardless of the officer's background.[55] From 1651 until the Restoration of King Charles in 1660, England and Scotland were a single country with the gains of the Scottish revolution largely dissipated. Religious toleration for Protestants and an English army of occupation were major blows to Scottish pride. On the other hand toleration did little to weaken Presbyterianism in the long run, as the English sects were far less of a threat than resurgent quasi-Anglicanism would have been had Charles I won the wars for the three kingdoms.

Although there was still some tidying up in Ireland and guerrilla warfare remained a problem in both Scotland and Ireland for some time to come, the generals' tale finishes to all intents and purposes at Worcester. By their victories Fairfax had won the First English Civil War, Cromwell and Fairfax the Second, and Cromwell the Anglo-Scottish War, and a succession of generals had ground down the Irish. However, the landscape of command was very different to what it had been in 1642. No longer was the commander-in-chief merely the state's servant. He and his officers enjoyed a share of sovereignty and, when push came to shove, theirs was the ultimate power in the land. The mailed fist had only emerged occasionally from the velvet glove between 1647 and 1651. The velvet fell to the floor two years later. Oliver Cromwell as head of the army expelled the remaining members of the House of Commons and disbanded the Council of State. He and his fellow officers then set about trying to construct the type of constitution that must have been in embryonic form in Cromwell's mind from the start. If God's will was to prevail, those who were right with God ought to be in control of all the levers of political power.

CHAPTER 20

Generals

THE AUDIT

THERE ARE, of course, problems in separating out the impact of the army generals from the background noise of special pleading and extraneous detail to be found in contemporary sources, the gaps in the coverage of events, and the misapprehensions and misreadings of texts to be found in works written since. Such problems are also compounded by the impossibility of explaining what would have happened, as opposed to what could have happened, if the army generals had taken different decisions. However, an audit of their performances can shed light on three very important facets of the relationship between generalship and the outcome of the British Wars: the occasions on which they made a material contribution to how they progressed and how they ended; the tactics they employed to achieve their sovereigns' war aims; and the strengths and weaknesses of individual generals, which obviously had a significant impact on their ability to achieve success in the tasks they were set.

In the first place, army generals clearly did have a significant influence on the progress and outcome of wars. They could and did win and lose wars in a single afternoon, frequently with the assistance for good or ill of the enemy generals. What happened on the battlefield at Preston in 1648 and Worcester in 1651, and in the days that followed, brought two of the four wars to a speedy end. The destruction of the king's veteran infantry at Naseby followed by the rapid exploitation of that victory, made Parliament's victory in the First Civil War a near certainty. However, the royalist cause should have been mortally wounded eight months earlier at Newbury if Sir William Waller had attacked the position at Church Speen two hours earlier or if Cromwell's cavalry had done its job on the left wing. Only in Ireland can it be argued with conviction that victory was very largely determined by resources. The English and their allies failed to conquer the island between 1642 and 1648 because of the fitful supplies of men and materials crossing the Irish Sea. There was no decisive battle in 1649–50, but the sheer volume of resources transported to Ireland eventually smothered the enemy by their sheer bulk. On the other hand, it can also be argued that the Irish war lasted three years longer than it might have done had Michael Jones's foray in force against Baggotsrath not turned by accident into a battle, which he did not have the military strength to exploit. If the encounter had taken place in

October or November instead of August, with Ormond's and O'Neill's forces on one side and Cromwell's and Jones's on the other, there is every possibility that the winning side would have achieved a victory as climactic as at Naseby.

As in most wars, the general's tale was not a uniform one of triumph and/or disaster, but for most of the time one of frustration and disappointment, of opportunities missed, of coping with political masters who expected the earth but failed to provide the resources needed, and who interfered with the running of campaigns and sometimes of battles. There were numerous occasions when generals at the time or subsequently expressed unhappiness with the strategies they had been ordered to implement, and they reacted by failing to carry them out as ordered. However, when such events are thoroughly investigated, the more notorious ones turn out to be nothing of the sort. Frequently cited examples of the ways in which army generals subverted the king's strategy – the marquis of Newcastle in August 1643, Prince Maurice in May 1644 and George Goring in May–June 1645 – are the fabrications of historians led astray by Lord Clarendon's vendetta against some of the king's commanders. Similarly, the decisions of the earls of Essex and Manchester to tamper with Parliament's strategy in June and September–October 1644 respectively did more good than harm overall and cannot be shown to have prolonged the First English Civil War. Essex's mistake was to go a step too far by invading Cornwall, Manchester's to offend too many important politicians and soldiers. In fact the most baleful examples of the generals in the field affecting the progress of the wars were the decision of Lords Leven, Manchester and Fairfax to go their separate ways after capturing York, the earl of Essex's conduct of the run-up to the battle of Edgehill, and Sir William Waller's failure to obey Essex's operational commands whilst campaigning in the Severn valley in April and May 1643.

In the campaigns of 1648–51 the synergy between commanders and their political masters was much greater on the parliamentary/Commonwealth side partly because the generals were on a looser rein. As for the enemy, General Leslie may have had his judgement overruled by his political masters on occasion, but it was not a major factor in the defeat of the Scots in the war of 1650–51. Claims that they forced him to change his battle plan on the eve of Dunbar are not that convincing, and the allegation that he underperformed in the Worcester campaign because he disapproved of the whole idea seems improbable on the available evidence. Similarly, the marquis of Ormond's decision not to attack Dublin in the spring of 1649 was not because he was incapable of identifying what should or should not be a priority, but rather because it made sound military sense. Blockading the capital at a time when he needed to keep part of his army in Ulster watching the forces commanded by O'Neill, Monck and Coote was an open invitation to Michael Jones to use interior lines to pick off his units one by one.

Most army generals displayed many of the martial qualities that writers have identified as essential for success for well over 2,000 years: gaining the trust of officers and men by acts of personal bravery and by providing for their physical needs; paying due regard to intelligence; reading the landscape and seeing its potential; resilience and fortitude in the face of setbacks; choosing able subordinates; seizing the right moment for inflicting the maximum damage on the enemy; and so forth. However, the methods they used to achieve success were very much determined by the times in which they lived. In the mid seventeenth century, doctrine was not as prescriptive as it was to become when writers of military treatises became thoroughly wedded to the idea that warfare was science. On the other hand, there were no contemporary developments in military hardware capable of transforming the ways in which army generals fought battles.

Artillery pieces were either too heavy to move about the battlefield or had too small a bore to inflict much damage on the enemy. The bayonet had yet to be invented, so infantry units were made up of two types of soldier, one manhandling a fifteen-foot pike, and this placed limits on mobility, however well trained in foot drill the unit was. The matchlock musket with its very low rate of fire remained the norm because it was both cheap and durable; and the problem of supplying men fighting on horseback with projectile weapons of sufficient power to overcome infantry would not be solved even partially until field artillery became more mobile. Such circumstances restricted the scope for tactical innovation. Similarly, lack of visibility on the seventeenth-century battlefield once the muskets and artillery pieces opened fire with their black-powder gunpowder, combined with the absence of modern means of communication, meant that it was extremely difficult for a general to control a battle once it got under way. Nevertheless, successful generals displayed a flexibility of mind that enabled them to tweak conventional tactics to suit their purposes, to deploy their armies in such a way as to make best use of the landscape over which they were fighting and to produce imaginative solutions to problems on the battlefield as they arose.

The first supposed tactical innovation was nothing of the sort. The parliamentarians did not win because Prince Rupert taught them the cavalry charge, which they then transformed by instilling such discipline into their troopers that they could regroup after a charge and then charge again. The difference between Essex's use of cavalry at Edgehill and Cromwell's at Marston Moor was a matter of numbers, not doctrine. Essex gave his cavalry a defensive role at Edgehill because Prince Rupert's men outnumbered them. In such circumstances it made sense to wait for the enemy to charge in the belief that massed musketeers to their front and on their flanks would so ravage their ranks that the attack would grind to a halt. Any idea that Essex was somehow adverse to the charge must be wrong because of the way in which Balfour Force and his own lifeguard performed later in the battle. The way in which they charged, regrouped and then charged again also suggests that those units at least had already attained a high level of discipline. Regrouping and then carrying out a second charge, however, was an

extremely difficult manoeuvre for large masses of cavalry to perform. It happened
in what must have been exceptional circumstances at Marston Moor,[1] but was
not repeated at Naseby despite frequent claims to the contrary or indeed at any
later battle fought by the New Model Army. Moreover, there is no evidence that
it was ideological motivation and/or discipline as opposed to superior numbers
that enabled Cromwell's Ironsides to outperform Rupert's cavalry from 1644
onwards. Thus, whatever his other talents, Oliver Cromwell did nothing unique
in a tactical sense with the Eastern Association cavalry which enabled it to win the
First Civil War for Parliament.

The second development was reasonably innovative: the use of infantry
formations to support cavalry and vice versa. Such combined tactics can be seen
in action on a small scale in the attack by Essex on the earl of Lindsey's two regiments at Edgehill. Army generals used similar methods to dislodge determined
enemy units in almost every major battle thereafter, but not on a large scale until
Dunbar when both the assault across the Brox Burn led by John Lambert and
George Monck, and Cromwell's flank attack, used combined arms tactics.
Equally novel, though less common, was the practice in battles fought in
enclosed landscapes in particular for commanded parties of musketeers to be
drawn from several regiments and moved about the battlefield independent of
their pikemen.

The third innovation was different in type in that it was an emerging doctrine
at the battlefield rather than the unit level. Making effective use of the reserve line
was something that distinguished the parliamentary army generals from the
royalists and the Scots army generals. It was not until Marston Moor that a
royalist army general created a substantial reserve line, and then it was not strong
enough to perform all the tasks required of it, most particularly on the all-impor-
tant right wing. The cavalry reserves, however, had done very well in the centre,
and Rupert used a similar battle formation at the Third Battle of Newbury. At
Naseby there was an even stronger reserve line, but it was totally ineffective
because Rupert failed to solve the dilemma of how to lead from the front and
commit his reserves when the climactic moment of the battle arrived. What
distinguished Rupert's imaginative failures from Parliament's successes was
command and control. At Edgehill and at the First Battle of Newbury, Essex's
management of the reserve infantry steadied the battle line and probably saved
his army from disaster. At Marston Moor the infantry reserves fled, but the third
line of the cavalry on the left wing under David Leslie's command played a not
inconsiderable part in the victory. The Second Battle of Newbury marks a step
backward. Waller's reserves for the attack on the royalist position at Church
Speen, though very numerous, played no part in the battle because they had no
overall commander. Philip Skippon led the infantry vanguard, Sir William
Balfour the cavalry on the right wing and Cromwell the cavalry on the left. Waller,
who should have been in overall charge, became involved in a cavalry melee at the

very start of the battle, was probably swept from the battlefield as a result, and exerted no overall control until after the capture of Church Speen by which time it was too dark to exploit Skippon's success.

It was very different at Naseby. A sea change had taken place in command and control in that two of the three generals were in charge of the support troops. Skippon led up the second line of infantry, checked the enemy advance through his first line and then started pushing them back. Cromwell on the right wing then launched the battle-winning move using the reserve cavalry once his first line had opened up a corridor through which they could charge. Without any doubt it was the New Model reserves that decided the battle.

Good practice continued at Preston, where Lambert sent in the infantry reserves when Cromwell was absent elsewhere, and they seized the northern approaches to the bridge over the Ribble, the jugular vein connecting the two parts of the duke of Hamilton's army. However, the most clear-cut example of the use of the reserves to win a battle was at Dunbar, where the attack instituted by Cromwell on the exposed flank of the Scottish right wing caused the rout of the entire enemy army. At Worcester, too, the lord general managed the reserves with aplomb, first giving support to the vanguard under pressure at the bridge of boats at Powick, and then moving troops to the east bank of the Severn to counter the only serious royalist counter-attack of the day.

Other developments at the tactical level also deserve mention, though they are problematic or of lesser overall significance. The hypothesis that the ratio of musketeers to pikemen increased over time so as to give the infantry greater firepower is an unproven one.[2] The so-called Highland Charge, with which Montrose allegedly won his victories, was a valuable innovation, but it was the flexibility in infantry tactics of MacColla's brigade that really counted on the battlefield, and cavalry used in the manner of Prince Rupert. An amphibious assault was of enormous significance in turning the flank of the Scottish army position at Stirling in 1651, but rarely did opportunities occur for using such a tactic. Finally, as the armies became better trained, night attacks became a practicable proposition. Fairfax used that tactic at Torrington and at Maidstone, and Cromwell would have done so at Dunbar had Lambert been ready in time, but they had one major disadvantage. Pursuit of a defeated enemy was far more difficult than in the full light of day.

Finally, what does an audit of the individual generals reveal? Prince Rupert's career as army general as opposed to General of Horse was disappointing, as he lost both the major battles in which he was in overall command. The writer of his 'diary' blamed others for what happened, but his battle plans for Marston Moor and Naseby were too clever by half, and he failed to develop a means of leading from the front and managing the reserve line.

The other army generals bar one who fought in the wars in the British Isles between 1642 and 1651 lacked at least one important attribute. Sir Thomas

Fairfax did not know how to manage the immediate aftermath of a battle, Sir William Waller how to fight one. The earl of Essex, on the other hand, despite his lacklustre record, had two outstanding virtues, fortitude and unflappability, which stood him in very good stead when staring disaster in the face at Edgehill and the First Battle of Newbury.

As for the king's second lord general, the earl of Forth, there is not one scintilla of evidence that the successful if quixotic campaigns of the king's main field army from October 1642 to October 1644 owed anything to his advice, wise or otherwise, or that the disasters of June and July 1645 would not have occurred if he had still been in post. He was also probably responsible for the defeat at Cheriton. The earl, later marquis, of Montrose, on the other hand, was a consummate performer on the battlefield, though often in adverse circumstances for which he himself was to some extent to blame. Recent research would have us think well of Lord Fairfax for the Fabian campaign he fought in the north between October 1642 and April 1644.[3] However, his performance on the battlefield left a lot to be desired, and nothing whatsoever can be said in favour of the duke of Hamilton, the marquis of Ormond or the earl of Manchester in that respect.

The most successful army general by far when it came to achieving his sovereign's war aims was Oliver Cromwell. Seemingly able to pull out of the army generals' bag of tricks whatever was needed in the circumstances, he won all three of his major battles expeditiously and achieved great success in all the campaigns he led personally including that in Ireland, but from 1649 he had the inestimable advantage of having the sovereign under his thumb and military resources were therefore adequate or more than adequate for his needs. He also had the knack of choosing able subordinates, though Lambert was not Cromwell's *éminence grise* from the Preston campaign onwards but merely an able lieutenant. Generals fighting wars on the Continent in the mid to late seventeenth century often commanded larger armies, but in the context of the type of wars in which he fought, Cromwell was nothing short of outstanding.

Notes

Abbreviations

BL	British Library
Bodleian	The Bodleian Library, Oxford
CRO	County Record Office
CSP	Calendar of State Papers
HMC	Historical Manuscripts Commission
NAS	National Archives, Scotland
ODNB	*Oxford Dictionary of National Biography*

Chapter 1: The Generals

1. British Library, 1103, d. 77 (5). Byron's relation of the battle is printed in full in P. Young, 'The Royalist Army at the Battle of Roundway Down', *Journal of the Society for Army Historical Research* XXXI (1953), pp. 130–1. The western army cavalry, which had escaped from Devizes in a madcap ride over the downs during the early hours of 11 July, were too shattered by the experience to make up a fourth brigade, but some volunteers from Prince Maurice's regiment fought as a squadron in Wilmot's brigade: see P. Young, ed., 'The Vindication of Richard Atkyns Esquire', *Military Memoirs of the English Civil War* (London, 1967), pp. 62–3.

2. Hopton claimed that he had argued vehemently in favour of leaving the town, but failed to persuade the Council of War: see Ralph, Lord Hopton, 'Bellum Civile', C. Chadwyck-Healey, ed., *Somerset Record Society* 18 (1902), but as elsewhere in his memoirs he was probably trying to defend himself against criticism by putting his own conduct in the best possible light.

3. Young, 'Roundway Down', p. 131. Dragoons in the mid seventeenth century were mounted musketeers, who normally fought on foot as irregular infantry.

4. HMC, Portland MSS III, p. 113.

5. J. Adair, *Roundhead General: The Campaigns of Sir William Waller* (Stroud, 1997), p. 93. For the letter he refers to, see Bodleian, Tanner MSS 62, ff. 164–5.

6. Edward Hyde, Lord Clarendon, *The History of the Rebellion and Civil Wars in England*, ed. W. Macray, (Oxford, 1888), book V, paragraph 447n. For a more detailed appraisal of Clarendon's bias against Rupert and George Goring, see below, pp. 39, 146, 149, 163–4.

7. HMC, Portland MSS III, p. 113.

8. Ibid. Waller thought on similar lines about the defeat at Roundway Down, as is very apparent from what he wrote in his spiritual autobiography. His overweening pride and self-esteem are apparent in the words he used in a letter to Parliament penned two days before the battle, describing the military prospects: '. . . we have such experience of God that we doubt not to give you a good account of Sir Ralph Hopton': see Bodleian, Tanner MSS 62, ff. 128, 164–5; Wadham College Library, MSS Collection, A18.14.

9. Only in the Lostwithiel campaign did Charles assume the role of army general, though typically his reasons were political rather than military. Moreover, his actual involvement in operations against the earl of Essex may have been exaggerated for propaganda purposes by Sir Edward Walker, his secretary at war: see below, pp. 118–20, and *Historical*

Discourses upon Several Occasions (London, 1705), pp. 57–72. For his role at Naseby where he acted as Rupert's deputy in command of the reserve line, see below, pp. 164–5.

10. Clarendon, *History of the Rebellion*, IV, para. 77.

11. See below for further discussion of this point.

12. Wiltshire CRO 413/377; C.H. Firth, ed., *Memoirs of William Cavendish, Duke of Newcastle and Margaret his Wife* (2nd edition, London, no date but after 1886), pp. 38–9, 88. Newcastle's cavalry were commanded by a General of Horse, George Goring. Under him in 1644 was a lieutenant general, Sir Charles Lucas, whilst the infantry were commanded in chief by the Scottish professional James King with the rank of lieutenant general.

13. Hopton, 'Bellum Civile', p. 2.

14. Montrose was given a more extensive commission as captain general and deputy governor of Scotland after his victory at Kilsyth in August 1645: see D. Stevenson, *Highland Warrior: Alasdair MacColla and the Civil Wars* (Edinburgh, 1994), p. 204.

15. In some cases they had lieutenant generals serving under them. Hertford, for example, was described as lord general by Sir Ralph Hopton in his account of the campaign in Somerset in June 1643, and his army was commanded by Prince Maurice as lieutenant general: see Young, ed., 'Vindication of Richard Atkyns, p. 12; Hopton, 'Bellum Civile', p. 55.

16. C. Russell, *The Fall of the British Monarchies* (Oxford, 1991), pp. 481–2. See also J. Adamson, *The Noble Revolt: The Overthrow of Charles I* (London, 2007), p. 425n, for a more forthright statement.

17. In the Second Civil War the executive committee was known as the Committee at Derby House and after the proclamation of the Commonwealth as the Council of State.

18. Calendar of State Papers Venetian 1642–3, p. 154; J. Adamson, 'The Baronial Context of the English Civil War', *Transactions of the Royal Historical Society*, 6th series, 40 (1990), pp. 101, 105, 108–9.

19. BL, Additional MSS 18979, f. 129; C. Holmes, *The Eastern Association in the English Civil War* (Cambridge, 1974), pp. 183–5. For Sir William Waller's attempts to free himself from Essex's jurisdiction, see below, pp. 67, 78–9, 115.

20. C. Carlton, 'Sir John Meldrum', *ODNB*, ed. H. Matthew and B. Harrison, vol. 37 (Oxford, 2004), pp. 739–41; CSP Domestic 1644, pp. 207–8, 337, 440, 442; Holmes, *Eastern Association*, p. 74.

21. See R.N. Dore, ed., 'Sir William Brereton's Letter Books', *Lancashire and Cheshire Record Society*, 128 (1990), p. 13, for a convincing argument that he did not hold a major-general's commission. Other colonels who enjoyed enhanced powers within the bounds of a single county for varying periods of time during the First Civil War included Lord Willoughby of Parham in Lincolnshire and Sir John Gell in Derbyshire.

22. He seems at the time to have been on a par with Major General Sydenham Poyntz, commander of Parliament's northern army: see ibid., pp. 240, 263–4, 322.

Chapter 2: The First Campaign of the English Civil War: The Opening Moves

1. George Monck, *Observations upon Political and Military Affairs* (London, 1671), pp. 15–16. These words were written, apparently, at a time when Monck was languishing in the Tower of London after being taken prisoner at the battle of Nantwich in January 1644. Interestingly, he was not drawing on personal experience, as the highest rank he had held up to that date was that of colonel. What he was probably doing was reflecting on the experience of Parliament's first generation of generals, Essex, Manchester and Waller, who Parliament had induced to resign their commissions in March 1645 because they were not winning the war quickly enough.

2. See Peter Edwards's excellent monograph on the supply of military resources in the three kingdoms, *Dealing in Death: The Arms Trade and the British Civil Wars, 1638–1652* (Stroud, 2000).

3. BL, Thomason Tracts, E126 (38).

4. CSP Domestic 1641–3, pp. 371–400.

5. Ibid., pp. 372–3, 379, 384. The behaviour of some of Parliament's regiments at Edgehill suggests a weakness in moral fibre characteristic of men whose principal reason for joining up was not deeply held conviction, though some were there under false pretences having joined the colours to fight the king's enemies in Ireland; see below, Lord Wharton's, p. 242 n.13.

6. BL, Thomason Tracts, E112 (6, 7); R. Codrington, *The Life and Death of the Illustrious Robert, Earl of Essex* (London, 1646), p. 13; V. Snow, *Essex the Rebel: The Life of Robert Devereux, the Third Earl of Essex 1591–1646* (Lincoln, Nebr., 1970), p. 326.

7. J. Morrill, 'Robert Devereux, Third Earl of Essex', *ODNB*, 15, p. 966.

8. Snow, *Essex the Rebel*, p. 300; Morrill, 'Essex', *ODNB*, pp. 962–6.

9. Although sympathy with the difficulties he faced in commanding Parliament's forces seems to be growing, his principal recent biographer can do no better than describe him as 'cautious, slow and very unadventurous': see Snow, *Essex the Rebel*, pp. 498–9.

10. Clarendon, *History of the Rebellion*, II, para. 164.

11. House of Lords Journal, V, p. 206.

12. He is described as such by J. Adamson. See *The Noble Revolt: The Overthrow of Charles I* (London, 2007), p. 64.

13. Morrill, 'Essex', *ODNB*, pp. 962–4.

14. The Venetian ambassador wrote of the camp at Northampton as being 'quarters of idleness': see CSP Venetian 1642–3, p. 169.

15. The letters, written on 6 and 7 September, were concerned with the troops plundering the houses of the gentry without permission, as were those of Nehemiah Wharton: see Bodleian, Tanner MSS lxii, f. 115, 118 lxiii, f. 153; CSP Domestic 1641–3, pp. 387–8.

16. A. Thrush, 'Robert Bertie, First Earl of Lindsey', *ODNB*, 5, pp. 494–5; G. Parker, 'The Limits to Revolutions in Military Affairs', *Journal of Military History* 71-2 (2007), pp. 351–4; D. Lloyd, *Memoirs of the Lives of those Personages that suffered for the Protestant Faith and Allegiance to the Sovereign 1637–1660* (London, 1667).

17. BL, Additional MSS 62084, paras 14, 19; E. Warburton, *Memoirs of Prince Rupert and the Cavaliers* (London, 1849), 3 vols, I, pp. 460–2.

18. The commission sent to Henry Hastings, a Leicestershire commander, authorising him to raise 400 men, type unspecified, on 1 August 1642, stated very clearly that he was only to obey commands issued by the king or by Lord Lindsey; see HMC, R.R. Hastings MSS, II, p. 86.

19. The king's orders to Rupert issued on 27 August, 20–25 September and 23 October are to be found in the Rupert papers: see BL, Additional MSS 62085, ff. 4–5; Warburton, *Memoirs of Prince Rupert*, I, pp. 398–9, II, p. 12.

20. From 5 to 8 September, from 17 to 25 September and from 10 to 18 October: see C.H. Firth, ed., 'A Journal of Prince Rupert's Marches, 5 September 1642–4 July 1646', *English Historical Review* XIII (1898), p. 730.

21. For the allegation, see J. Malcolm, 'A King in Search of Soldiers: Charles I in 1642', *Historical Journal* 21 (1978), pp. 257–68. For a vigorous critique, see M. Wanklyn and P. Young, 'A King in Search of Soldiers: Charles I in 1642. A Rejoinder', *Historical Journal*, 24 (1981), pp. 147–54.

22. The regiment was Sir William Pennyman's. P. Young mentions two regiments, Pennyman's and John Bellasis's: see P. Young, *Edgehill: The Campaign and the Battle* (Kineton, 1967), p. 54; but Bellasis makes it clear that he and his regiment joined the king at Nottingham: see HMC, Ormond MSS, New Series II, p. 379.

23. Clarendon, *History of the Rebellion*, VI, para. 1. The gloomy prognostications of members of the king's entourage at Nottingham described by Clarendon are confirmed by Sir Edward Nicholas in a letter written on 30 August to the marquis of Ormond, the commander of the English troops in Ireland: see Bodleian, Carte MSS 3, f. 474.

24. Young, *Edgehill*, pp. 54–5; Wanklyn and Young, 'A King in Search of Soldiers', p. 153.

25. Clarendon, *History of the Rebellion*, V, paras 372, 374, 445.

26. CSP Domestic 1641–3, p. 389. The King's Lifeguard and Lord Lindsey's from Lincolnshire, John Bellasis's from Yorkshire and Sir Ralph Dutton's from Gloucestershire/Herefordshire: see Young, *Edgehill*, pp. 51–2.

27. Firth, ed., *Memoirs of William Cavendish, Duke of Newcastle*, p. 25. They seem to have reached the king at Chester in late September; see J. Phillips, *Memoirs of the Civil War in Wales and the Marches* (2 vols, London, 1874), II, pp. 11, 17.

28. HMC, Appendix to the 7th Report, p. 191; HMC, Cowper MSS, p. 320; BL, Thomason Tracts, E240 (9); Bulstrode Whitelock, *Memorials of the English Affairs* (London, 1732), p. 124.

29. J. Rushworth, *Historical Collections of Private Passages of State* (7 vols, London, 1721), V, p. 16.

30. Lords Journals, V, pp. 357, 367, 369.

31. BL, Egerton MSS 2541, f. 274.

32. CSP Domestic 1641–3, p. 391; HMC, Appendix to the 5th Report, p. 91; BL, Thomason Tracts, E114 (1, 15).

33. For example, for Castle Morton, see M. Wanklyn, 'Paying for the Sins of our Forefathers', *Midland Catholic History* 12 (2006), p. 37; for Coughton, see BL, Thomason Tracts, E240 (23).

34. This account of the preliminaries to the engagement at Powick Bridge is taken primarily from a detailed description written some weeks later by a cavalryman from Captain Nathaniel Fiennes's troop: see BL, Thomason Tracts, E126 (39). The subtext is that the defeat that followed was entirely due to Colonel Sandys's impetuosity. The tale told has a strong narrative line and is superficially convincing, but it was possibly convenient for the living to load the responsibility on the dead, Sandys having died of his wounds soon after the engagement. Unfortunately, there is no alternative narrative from the perspective of the parliamentary commanders, but Fiennes's account of the various stages in the engagement itself is confirmed by royalist sources.

35. BL, Additional MSS 62084, paras 15–17; 62085, f. 126.

36. Even though it was close to both the Severn and the Teme it was not a meadow. The cavalry in Fiennes's troop described it as a recently ploughed field. Clouds of dust rose up when the horses rode through it, and this impeded their riders' vision: see BL, Thomason Tracts, E126 (39).

37. Sir Philip Warwick, writing well after the Restoration, emphasised the boost that the engagement gave to Prince Rupert's reputation, but he finished with a shrewd comment on Rupert as commanding officer. The heroic style of army generalship where bravery was the touchstone was not the only quality that was required on the mid-seventeenth-century battlefield: Rupert 'put spirit into the king's army', but he lacked prudence: see Sir Philip Warwick, *Memoirs of the Reign of King Charles I* (Edinburgh, 1813), p. 249.

38. There is a partial transcription in J. Webb and T. Webb, *Memorials of the Civil War as it Affected Herefordshire and the Adjacent Counties* (2 vols, London, 1879), I, p. 148. The original is supposed to be in the Carte Manuscript collection in the Bodleian Library, Oxford, but it has not been located.

39. BL, Thomason Tracts, E126 (38, 39).

40. This is the route given in the chronology of Rupert's campaigns usually described as 'Prince Rupert's Marches'. In the diary the prince's amanuensis wrote of his riding from Worcester to Shrewsbury via Bridgnorth. It is possible that he would have gone to Ludlow before Bridgnorth, but it would have been a very roundabout route: see Firth, ed., 'Prince Rupert's Marches', p. 730; BL, Additional MSS 62084, paras 18–19.

41. BL, Thomason Tracts, E127 (12).

42. BL, Thomason Tracts, E240 (40); HMC, Ormond MSS, NS II, p. 381.

43. There was a short-lived panic that the earl had sent another party of horse to capture the king on his way to visit his supporters at Chester, but nothing more: see BL, Additional MSS 62085, ff. 4–5.

44. The movements of Bedford's brigade cannot be traced in their entirety, but Bedford himself was at London on 4 October: see Lords Journals, V, p. 386. Three days before, one of the London journals had reported that his troops were following him, as indeed they were. On 5 October a letter written from Wimborne Minster in Dorset reported that they had just left the town: see HMC, Portland MSS I, p. 62. Soon afterwards they appear to have been redirected towards Worcester, but Essex did not expect them to arrive until 14 October. Bedford himself was there by 18 October, but by then the king's army had been on its march for a week, the

petition had been rejected, and a confrontation of some kind had become inevitable: see BL, Thomason Tracts, E240 (21, 41); Lords Journals, V, p. 412.

45. NAS, D/406/1778; Firth, ed., 'Prince Rupert's Marches', p. 730.

46. See, for example, Young, *Edgehill*, p. 73, for this line of argument.

47. The principal informant was one Blake. *Prima facie* evidence of his activities was discovered amongst Essex's papers that were captured in the royalist pursuit of the parliamentary army as it fell back on Warwick following the battle of Edgehill, and Blake was hanged soon afterwards: see BL, Additional MSS 62084, para. 24; Warburton, *Memoirs of Prince Rupert*, II, p. 47. Another spy had been detected before the army left Shrewsbury: see W. Farrow, *The Great Civil War in Shropshire* (Shrewsbury, 1926), p. 40.

48. HMC, Lord Braye etc. MSS, p. 87; Lords Journals, V, 397.

49. BL, Thomason Tracts, E240 (45, 46). The successive issues of this journal appear to contain precis of Essex's reports to the Committee of Safety which no longer survive.

50. Essex's final communication with London on the day before the battle does seem to contain an element of panic. What forces there were in the vicinity of the capital should rendezvous in a position from which they could hold up the royalists, but this would only have to be for half a day, as his army would be very close behind: see BL, Thomason Tracts, E240 (46).

51. Lords Journals, V, p. 412.

52. BL, Thomason Tracts, E124 (26, 32).

53. BL, Thomason Tracts, E126 (13); E128 (20).

Chapter 3: Over by Winter? Edgehill and Turnham Green

1. NAS, GD406/1/166.

2. Bodleian, English MSS 132, f. 11; BL, Additional MSS 62084, para. 21.

3. Young, *Edgehill*, p. 77.

4. BL, Additional MSS 62084, para. 21.

5. Warburton, *Memoirs of Prince Rupert*, II, p. 12.

6. Essex agreed. His army began deploying on the northern edge of the open land as soon as royalist troops were seen on Edgehill: see BL, Thomason Tracts, E124 (26). The extent of the open ground and the lack of hedges can be seen in a pre-enclosure map of Radley: see Warwickshire CRO, CR 1596.

7. Clarendon, *History of the Rebellion*, VI, para. 90.

8. Ibid., VI, paras 88n, 90. The exact words used by Clarendon were that 'the battle that day was set without advising with him'. 'Set' is slightly ambiguous, but elsewhere he refers to 'the king preferring the prince's opinion in all matters relating to the war before his', and to the prince advising the king at about midnight on 22 October that the rebels' army was at Kineton, that 'it would be in his majesty's power, if he thought fit, to fight a battle the next day, which his majesty liked well and therefore immediately despatched orders to cross the design for Banbury, and that the whole army should rendezvous on the top of Edgehill . . . about two miles from Kineton': see ibid., VI, pp. 357, 367. Scott, Turton and Von Arni suggest that Lindsey may have arrived too late for the Council of War which decided to fight a battle on the 23rd, but the wording of the king's letter to Rupert indicates either that no council had taken place or that the prince had also not been present: see C. Scott, A. Turton and E. Von Arni, *Edgehill: The Battle Reinterpreted* (Barnsley, 2004), p. 35; Warburton, *Memoirs of Prince Rupert*, II, p. 12.

9. Rupert's diary is silent on the matter, whilst other contemporaries or near contemporaries claim that it was not Rupert who was responsible for Lindsey's humiliation. In his memoirs King James II puts words in Lindsey's mouth very similar to those reported by Clarendon, but directed not against Rupert but against Patrick Ruthven, Earl of Forth. John Bellasis and Richard Bulstrode do not say as much, but they do claim that Ruthven favoured the Swedish method of deploying an army for battle. This makes sense as Ruthven had been in Swedish service and was field marshal of the king's army, the officer responsible for putting the various regiments into position prior to the battle. It is also very interesting that Bellasis, who as an infantry brigade commander was likely to

have been better informed about how the foot was deployed than anybody else, maintained that the decision to deploy in the Swedish fashion was not undertaken on the morning of the battle, but some days previously. It is unbelievable that a complete re-formation of the infantry deployment would have taken place on the day of the battle. See J. Clarke, ed., *Life of James II collected out of memoirs written by his own hand* (2 vols, London, 1816), I, p. 10; Bodleian, English MSS 132, ff. 13–14; HMC, Marquis of Ormond MSS, NS II, p. 379; Staffs. CRO, DW 1778/V/1370, a military treatise written by William Legge, *c*.1638. The point about the superiority of the Swedish infantry formation is made in S. Reid, *All the King's Armies: A Military History of the English Civil Wars 1642–1651* (Sevenoaks, 1998), p. 21.

10. Warburton, *Memoirs of Prince Rupert*, II, p. 12. A seventeenth-century abstract of the letter shows that Warburton's transcription was correct: see BL, Additional MSS 62085, f. 5.

11. BL, Thomason Tracts, 669 f6 (88).

12. BL, Thomason Tracts, E124 (26).

13. BL, Thomason Tracts, E126 (38).

14. Ibid. To compensate for moving the horse, Essex may have strengthened the right wing with Sir William Fairfax's regiment of foot, but this is not certain. One source places the regiment there, another to the rear of the middle brigade: see BL, Thomason Tracts, E126 (1), E128 (20); Rushworth, *Historical Collections*, V, pp. 35–9.

15. Edmund Ludlow, *Memoirs 1625–1672*, ed. C.H. Firth (2 vols, Oxford, 1894), I, pp. 40–1.

16. P. Young, 'The Royalist Army at Edgehill', *Journal of the Society for Army Historical Research* XXXIII (1955), p. 61. Bellasis's memoirs give the figure of 1,200 on each wing, but this was before the king's lifeguard joined Prince Rupert on the right (HMC, Ormond MSS, NS II, pp. 379–80).

17. Warwick, *Memoirs*, p. 283.

18. A recent account of Edgehill is very firm on this point: see K. Roberts and J. Tincey, *Edgehill 1642: First Battle of the English Civil War* (Oxford, 2001), p. 56; but the odds of the Royal Lifeguard defeating the enemy reserves would have depended in part on the size of the latter, which, despite Clarendon's description of them as 'that small body' (*History of the Rebellion*, VI, para. 79n), was probably approaching 500 troopers in strength at the start of the day – that is, Essex's lifeguards, 100 strong, and between five and seven troops of Balfour's regiment, only one of which had been at Powick Bridge: see BL, Thomason Tracts, E124 (32) E126 (38); Ludlow, *Memoirs*, I, p. 39.

19. The depiction of Edgehill at Windsor Castle is reproduced in Young's *Edgehill*. Amongst the portfolio of De Gomme's artwork is a depiction of the Battle of the Dunes (1658) in exactly the same format: see BL, Additional MSS 16370.

20. HMC, Ormond MSS, NS II, p. 380; BL, Thomason Tracts, E124 (26).

21. First he listed seventeen royalist infantry regiments when there were at least nineteen and possibly twenty on the battlefield: see Young, *Edgehill*, p. 58. Second, he depicted each brigade as consisting of four units, each containing pike men and musketeers. This, however, makes for difficulties in the case of the three brigades containing either three regiments unless the regiments were disaggregated, and then re-formed with companies from different regiments fighting in the same unit. Yet accounts of the battle make it very clear that the royalist regiments fought as regiments, not as commanded parties: see BL, Thomason Tracts, E124 (32), E126 (38), E128 (20); Clarke, ed., *Life of James II*, I, p. 14.

22. BL, Thomason Tracts, E124 (24).

23. BL, Additional MSS 62084, paras 22–3; Clarendon, *History of the Rebellion*, VI, para. 84.

24. BL, Thomason Tracts, E124 (21), (26); HMC, Ormond MSS, NS II, p. 380; T. Carte, ed., *A Collection of Original Letters and Papers concerning the Affairs of England (1641–1660) found amongst the Duke of Ormonde's Papers* (2 vols, London, 1739), I, p. 10; Bodleian, English MSS 132, f. 13. The claims of a lengthy melee on the parliamentary left made by Scott, Turton and Von Arni (see *Edgehill*, p. 94) are not fully substantiated by any of the accounts of the battle. The Official Royalist Account mentions that the cavalry engagement lasted less than fifteen minutes, but this could as easily refer to Wilmot's fight on the left wing as to Rupert's on the right: see BL, Thomason Tracts, E124 (24).

25. BL, Thomason Tracts, E124 (26).
26. BL, Thomason Tracts, E124 (32), E126 (38). They did not have with them the hammers and nails needed with which to damage the breach mechanisms, or draught horses to drag the cannon back to the parliamentary lines. Even the smallest piece of heavy artillery required at least six horses to move it.
27. Ludlow, *Memoirs*, I, p. 24; BL, Thomason Tracts, E126 (38).
28. BL, Thomason Tracts, E124 (26), (32), E128 (20).
29. Otherwise it is most unlikely that Balfour Force would have been in the right place to deliver such a devastating charge.
30. Ludlow, *Memoirs*, I, 42.
31. Codrington, *Life and Death of Essex*, p. 20; BL, Thomason Tracts, E126 (38), E128 (20).
32. BL, Thomason Tracts, E124 (26), (32), E126 (38), 669 f6 (187).
33. Clarke, ed., *Life of James II*, I, p. 14; BL, Thomason Tracts, E124 (32), E126 (24). There Sir Edward Fitton's regiment joined him, having also suffered few casualties. See J.P. Earwaker, *East Cheshire: Past and Present* (2 vols, London, 1877), II, p. 584n; Staffs CRO, D868 2, f. 67.
34. BL, Thomason Tracts, E126 (38).
35. BL, Thomason Tracts, E124 (26), E126 (24), (38).
36. For critical comment, see Scott, Turton and Van Arni, *Edgehill*, p. 95; P. Young and R. Holmes, *The English Civil Wars* (London, 1974), p. 49; Sir Frank Kitson, *Prince Rupert: Portrait of a Soldier* (London, 1994), p. 99.
37. See below, pp. 104, 106, 163–4, 274 n.72.
38. The cavalry plan of attack can be inferred from the various royalist accounts of the battle: see BL, Thomason Tracts, E53 (10); Clarke, ed., *Life of James II*, I, p. 13; but not so that of the infantry. See below, pp. 30–1.
39. Warwick, *Memoirs*, pp. 252–3; Clarke, ed., *Life of James II*, I, pp. 13–14; BL, Additional MSS 62084, paras 23–4; Bodleian, English MSS 132, f. 13; BL, Harleian MSS 3783, f. 61. Bulstrode describes Lord Caernarvon as being in command of the reserve line, but this seems unlikely as his regiment was in the front line.
40. BL, Additional MSS 62084, para. 23; Wilts. CRO, 413/444Aii, p. 9. Clarendon blamed the charge of the reserves on the indiscipline of the soldiers, who refused to obey their officers' orders to halt: see *History of the Rebellion*, VI, para. 85. He may have obtained this information from Sir John Byron, who provided him with material about what happened at the First Battle of Newbury: see Bodleian, Clarendon MSS 23, piece 1738 (5).
41. BL, Thomason Tracts, E53 (10).
42. Clarendon, *History of the Rebellion*, VI, para. 79n. I prefer the testimony of the author of the life of Sir John Smith who had no reason whatsoever to be hostile towards Digby, as he was his confidential secretary at the time of writing it: see BL, Thomason Tracts, E53 (10); M. Mullett, 'Edward Walsingham', *ODNB*, 57, p. 130. It is also unlikely that Clarendon believed Digby as he commented on the inexperience of the commander of the reserve line.
43. For the other brigades the evidence is exceedingly patchy. The comment made here is based on King James II's account: see Clarke, ed., *Life of James II*, I, pp. 11–12.
44. HMC, Ormond MSS, NS II, p. 380; Sir Henry Ellis, 'The Memoirs of Sir John Hinton', *Original Letters Illustrative of English History 1400–1793* (3 series, 12 vols, London, 1847), III, IV, p. 299.
45. This account of Lindsey's place on the chain of command appears in general terms in Clarendon, *History of the Rebellion*, VI, para. 90. Sir Richard Bulstrode's *Memoirs and Reflections upon the Reign and Government of Charles I and Charles II* (London, 1721), pp. 77–8, and Clarke's, ed., *Life of James II*, I, p. 10, are more specific. My first thought was that both had used Clarendon in their much later accounts. This may be the case with James II, who was Clarendon's son-in-law, but the passage appears in the manuscript of Bulstrode's *Memoirs*, as well as in the printed version, in which the editor did use sections from *History of the Rebellion* to fill in gaps in the manuscript: see Bodleian, English MSS 132, f. 13; C.H. Firth, 'The "Memoirs" of Sir Richard Bulstrode', *English Historical Review* X, 1895.
46. BL, Thomason Tracts, E124 (26).

47. BL, Thomason Tracts, E124 (26).
48. Hence the passage 'had he been with us we should not have presumed to have given you the first advertisement'. The officers were Lieutenant General Sir William Balfour, Thomas Ballard and Sir John Meldrum, commanders of the van and the rear infantry brigade respectively, Colonels Denzil Holles, Sir Philip Stapleton and Charles Pym, a troop commander who was the son of John Pym, chairman of the Committee of Public Safety. They were an ad hoc group. As Meldrum and Ballard were not MPs, the authors were not the committee in the army charged amongst other things with acting as a channel of communication between the army and Westminster: see above, p. 17. Three senior officers were missing apart from Essex himself: the earl of Bedford, the general of artillery the earl of Peterborough, and Sir John Meyrick, the major general of infantry. They had presumably accompanied the lord general to Warwick. Two of the remainder were missing for other reasons. Sir James Ramsey was already in London, whilst the commander of the middle infantry brigade, Charles Essex, had died of his wounds.
49. Clarendon, *History of the Rebellion*, VI, para. 88.
50. Staffs CRO, D868 2, f. 44. The most obvious sign that the letter is a forgery is that the signature is not in Essex's handwriting, but it could have been dictated by the earl to a trusted servant, who then kept a copy for his own private purposes. The process by which the letter found its way into the Leveson archive is potentially less of a problem. The earl's principal seat, Chartley Castle, was in Staffordshire, and it is not impossible that the servant entered the service of the Leveson family after his master's death.
51. BL, Additional MSS 62084, paras 24–5.
52. BL, Additional MSS 11692, ff. 27, 29.
53. Like Rupert, Forth could claim that the failure of the cavalry to secure complete victory for the king was due not to the way in which they had been deployed at the start of the battle but to the mistakes of the commanders of the second line.
54. S. Reid, 'Patrick Ruthven, Earl of Forth and Earl of Brentford', *ODNB*, 48, pp. 410–11.
55. Clarendon, *History of the Rebellion*, VIII, para. 29. Forth's deficiencies in mind and body might have been positively advantageous in the factional infighting at Charles I's court. Clarendon noted the tactical use he made of his deafness, and future blame could be avoided by committing as little as possible to paper. Mental decrepitude, real or assumed, may also have protected him against being dismissed in June 1644 for withdrawing the garrison from Abingdon without waiting for the king's specific order. See below, pp. 95–6.
56. Walker, *Historical Discourses*, pp. 114–15.
57. Warburton, *Memoirs of Prince Rupert*, II, p. 237.
58. See A.H. Burne and P. Young, *The Great Civil War: A Military History of the First Civil War* (London, 1959), pp. 9, 48, 76.
59. This can be inferred from John Hampden's letter reproduced by Lord Nugent: see Lord Nugent, *Memorials of John Hampden, His Party and His Times* (London, 1874), X, p. 323. The instruction cannot be found in the journal of either the Commons or the Lords. It must have been conveyed in a letter to Essex from the Committee of Safety, terrified by the letter from the six officers to the effect that they did not know the general's plans: see BL, Thomason Tracts, E124 (24). In such circumstances there would have been no time to consult Parliament.
60. Nugent, *Some Memorials of John Hampden, His Party and Times* (2 vols, London, 1831), pp. 323–4 (letters written by John Hampden to friends in Buckinghamshire, dated 31 October and 1 November – I have not been able to find the originals); BL, Thomason Tracts, E126 (2), (9), (23); BL, Additional MSS 11692, ff. 25, 27; Firth, ed., 'Prince Rupert's Marches', p. 730.
61. BL, Additional MSS 11692, f. 27. Its significance as a bottleneck or 'pass' (to use the terminology of the time) is apparent from Prince Rupert's 'diary', which describes the royalist army's baggage train as filling the lanes around the bridge: BL, Additional MSS 62084, para. 27.
62. BL, Additional MSS 11692, f. 29.
63. S. Porter, 'The Battle of Turnham Green', *Battlefield* 12.4 (2007), p. 13.
64. John Gwynne, *Military Memoirs: The Civil War*, ed. N. Tucker and P. Young (London, 1967), p. 47.

65. BL, Additional MSS 11692, f. 29.
66. W. Devereux, *Lives and Letters of the Devereux, Earls of Essex* (2 vols, London, 1853), II, p. 362.
67. Codrington, *Life and Death of Essex*, p. 22; Whitelock, *Memorials*, p. 65; G. Davies, 'The Battle of Edgehill', *English Historical Review* XXXVI (1921), pp. 42–3 (transcript of letter written by MS).
68. HMC, Portland MSS III, p. 101; Davies, 'Edgehill', pp. 42–3. Neither regiment took the field again.
69. Whitelock, *Memorials*, p. 65; HMC, Ormond MSS, NS II, p. 381.
70. Whitelock, *Memorials*, p. 66; HMC, Ormond MSS, NS II, p. 381; Davies, 'Edgehill', p. 43.
71. Whitelock, *Memorials*, p. 66; HMC, Ormond MSS, NS II, p. 381; Gwynne, *Military Memoirs*, p. 47; BL, Additional MSS 62084, paras 26–7.
72. Bodleian, Carte MSS 7, f. 423.
73. BL, Thomason Tracts, E242 (17), (19), (37).
74. HMC, Ormond MSS, NS II, pp. 381–2; Warburton, *Memoirs of Prince Rupert*, II, pp. 68–71; W. Phillips, ed., 'The Ottley Papers relating to the Civil War', *Transactions of the Shropshire Archaeological and Natural History Society*, 2nd series, VI (1894), pp. 46–7.
75. M. Wanklyn, 'Royalist Strategy in the South of England 1642–1644', *Southern History* 3 (1981), pp. 66–7; BL, Harleian MSS 6988, ff. 127–8, 130.
76. Journals of the House of Commons, II, p. 860; BL, Additional MSS 11692, f. 35; Rushworth, *Historical Collections*, V, pp. 82–3; BL, Thomason Tracts, E83 (11), E244 (11), (14).
77. J. Washbourne, ed., *Bibliotheca Gloucestrensis* (Gloucester, 1825), pp. 13–15; HMC, Portland MSS III, p. 107.

Chapter 4: Taking Stock, November 1642–April 1643

1. Richard Cust, *Charles I* (Harlow, 2005), pp. 371–9, 418–19.
2. Clarendon, *History of the Rebellion*, VI, para. 97.
3. Ibid., VI, para. 134; Warwick, *Memoirs*, pp. 254–5; BL, Additional MSS 62085a, para. 26; Davies, 'Battle of Edgehill', p. 42 (letter written by MS, Kingston, 14 November 1642).
4. Warwick, *Memoirs*, p. 255.
5. Whitelock, *Memorials*, p. 66.
6. For a description of this type of warfare, see G. Parker, *The Military Revolution: Military Innovation and the Rise of the West 1500–1800* (2nd edn, Cambridge, 1996).
7. BL, Thomason Tracts E19 (14), E90 (27).
8. BL, Harleian MSS 164, f. 243.
9. BL, f. 350.
10. Snow, *Essex the Rebel*, p. 353.
11. BL, Thomason Tracts, E90 (14).
12. BL, Harleian MSS 164, f. 318.
13. Bodleian, Carte MSS 80, f. 176 (Lord Wharton's regiment). However, it is highly doubtful that the promise was met in full, as he had at least seven Edgehill regiments with him in the spring campaign (his own, and those of Lord Robartes, Lord Say and Sele, Lord Rochford, Sir William Constable, Sir Henry Cholmondeley and John Hampden), and possibly nine (those of Francis Martin, formerly Thomas Ballard's, and Henry Bulstrode, formerly Charles Essex's).
14. The term is my own, but the concept is not new. V. Snow in 1970 examined the effect of the demands of the provinces in 1643 on Essex's authority: see *Essex the Rebel*, pp. 361–2, 364. In 1974 C. Holmes looked at the phenomenon from the point of view of the provinces: see *The Eastern Association in the English Civil War*. The argument proposed here, foreshadowed in my 'Royalist Strategy' (1981), is very different to that proposed by R. Hutton, where the emphasis in the discussion of the royalist lieutenant generalships, and by implication of the parliamentary major and lieutenant generalships, is on controlling territory rather than supporting the field armies: see *The Royalist War Effort 1642–1646* (London, 1982), pp. 50–1, 105–9.
15. For example, see below pp. 52–3, 56. Sir William Waller.
16. See above, pp. 14, 21, 237 n.44.

17. Lords Journals, V, pp. 408, 416–17.
18. Commons Journals, III, p. 859.
19. Rushworth, ed., *Historical Collections*, IV, p. 650; Thomas, Lord Fairfax, 'Short Memorials of the Northern Actions', *Select Tracts relating to the Civil Wars in England*, ed. Francis, Lord Maseres (2 vols, London, 1818), I, pp. 415–16.
20. BL, Additional MSS 18978, f. 127 (the Committee of Safety to Lord Fairfax, 21 October 1642).
21. C.H. Firth and R. Rait, eds, *Acts and Ordinances of the Interregnum* (3 vols, London, 1911), pp. 53–8; Lords Journals, V, p. 521; HMC, Appendix to the Sixth Report, pp. 61, 63; HMC, Portland MSS I, pp. 97, 101, 112.
22. Firth and Rait, eds, *Acts and Ordinances of the Interregnum*, I, p. 79.
23. A.J. Hopper, 'Ferdinando, Lord Fairfax', *ODNB*, 18, p. 926.
24. R. Bell, ed., *Memoirs of the Reign of Charles I* (2 vols, London, 1841), I, pp. 43, 49.
25. For example, in the letter written by Lionel Copley to Lord Fairfax on 1 February 1643. See ibid., I, p. 39.
26. BL, Additional MSS 18978, f. 139 (the Committee of Safety to Lord Fairfax, 13 April 1643).
27. Lords Journals, V, p. 643; Bell, ed., *Memoirs*, I, p. 39; BL, Harleian MSS 164, f. 384. It sounds like an attempt to save face, as the commander-in-chief in Lincolnshire, Lord Willoughby of Parham, was a major general at best: see Holmes, *Eastern Association*, p. 105.
28. See below, p. 86.
29. Firth, ed., *Memoirs of the Duke of Newcastle*, p. 10.
30. CSP Domestic 1641–3, p. 371; Rushworth, ed., *Historical Collections*, IV, p. 693.
31. BL, Thomason Tracts, E124 (32), an intercepted letter dated 24 October 1642; Warwick, *Memoirs*, p. 257; Clarendon, *History of the Rebellion*, V, para. 445, VI, para. 261, VIII, para. 84.
32. HMC, Duke of Beaufort MSS, p. 39; Warburton, *Memoirs of Prince Rupert*, II, p. 92. Herbert's authority was subsequently extended to cover the English counties of Monmouthshire and Herefordshire: see Hutton, *Royalist War Effort*, pp. 52–3.
33. Under Sir Edward Stradling, see Wanklyn and Young, 'A King in Search of Soldiers', p. 151 (see below).
34. See pp. 17, 237 n.27.
35. BL, Harleian MSS 6988, ff. 123, 128, 130 (2 November, 24 November, 15 December). Later letters are ambiguous, with the queen's safety in her journey to Oxford and the provision of arms and gunpowder being the principal concerns, and the security of the north also an issue. The nearest to a pre-emptory order is a letter written on 28 April immediately after the fall of Reading, but at that point in the 1643 campaign the context was not an advance on London but the rescue of the king and his beleaguered army from Oxford: ibid., ff. 135, 145.
36. This was also what was expected in London: see BL, Thomason Tracts, E127 (21).
37. Lords Journals, VI, p. 69. Firth, ed., *Memoirs of the Duke of Newcastle*, pp. 190, 193.
38. Cornwall CRO, 1609/11; BL, Thomason Tracts, E100 (6); Wanklyn, 'Royalist Strategy', *Southern History* 3 (1981), pp. 64–8.
39. Hopton, 'Bellum Civile,' pp. 18–19.
40. Washbourne, ed., *Bibliotheca Gloucestrensis*, pp. 26–7.
41. Firth, ed., 'Prince Rupert's Marches', p. 733; W. Hamper, ed., *Life, Diary, and Correspondence of Sir William Dugdale* (London, 1827), p. 46; HMC, Portland MSS I p. 98; Warburton, *Memoirs of Prince Rupert*, I, p. 497, II, pp. 14, 155–6, 159–60.
42. See below, pp. 54–5.
43. Warburton, *Memoirs of Prince Rupert*, II, pp. 82–3; Washbourne, ed., *Bibliotheca Gloucestrensis*, pp. 45, 47.
44. HMC, Beaufort MSS, p. 39.
45. Burne and Young, *The Great Civil War*, p. 34; HMC, Beaufort MSS, p. 39.
46. Lords Journals, V, pp. 475, 488; HMC, Appendix to the Fifth Report, p. 63; BL, Thomason Tracts, E91 (25); Hopton, 'Bellum Civile', p. 30.
47. Washbourne, ed., *Bibliotheca Gloucestrensis*, p. 15; BL, Thomason Tracts, E64 (12).
48. BL, Thomason Tracts, E92 (8). The pay warrants are primarily in National Archives SP28 series.

49. BL, Thomason Tracts, E244 (16); Commons Journals, II, p. 893; Lucy Hutchinson, *Memoirs of the Life of Colonel John Hutchinson* (London, 1808), p. 118; F. Kitson, *Old Ironside: The Military Biography of Oliver Cromwell* (London, 2004), pp. 48–9.
50. BL, Thomason Tracts, E90 (11), E97 (6).
51. See below, pp. 46–7.
52. For example, Charles Gerard's Sir Arthur Aston's and Lord Andover's: see Young, *Edgehill*, pp. 184, 186.
53. Hopton, 'Bellum Civile', pp. 43–5, 86–7; Lords Journals, VI, p.109.
54. R. Sherwood, *Civil Strife in the Midlands 1643–51* (Chichester, 1974), p. 54; A. Hughes, *Politics, Society and the Civil War in Warwickshire 1620–1660* (Cambridge, 1987), pp. 225–33.
55. Holmes, *Eastern Association*, pp. 70–5; BL, Egerton MSS 2646, ff. 209, 257, 269.
56. Adair, *Roundhead General*, pp. 67–8; BL, Thomason Tracts E64 (12), E97 (6); HMC, Portland MSS I, pp. 709, 710, 712, 716–17.
57. Burne and Young, *The Great Civil War*, p. 65.
58. There he remained for some weeks, attracting the hostile attention of some of the London journals, which criticised him for his inactivity: see BL, Thomason Tracts, E90 (24, 28), E91 (5).
59. Young, ed., 'The Vindication of Richard Atkyns', pp. 8–10; Washbourne, ed., *Bibliotheca Gloucestrensis*, pp. 31–5.
60. Washbourne, ed. *Bibliotheca Gloucestrensis*, pp. 28–9; BL, Thomason Tracts, E97 (2).
61. Hopton, 'Bellum Civile', pp. 20–44.
62. M. Wanklyn, 'Landownership and Allegiance in Cheshire and Shropshire at the Outbreak of the First Civil War' (University of Manchester, unpublished Ph.D. thesis, 1976), pp. 203, 242, 251, 255; HMC, Beaufort MSS, pp. 38–9.
63. S. Murdoch and T. Wales, 'James King, Lord Eythin', *ODNB*, 31, p. 630.
64. Prince Maurice and Sir John Berkeley, and at a lower rank Bernard Astley, Walter Slingsby, William Ashburnham and Brutus Buck: see Hopton, 'Bellum Civile', pp. 55–6; Clarendon, *History of the Great Rebellion*, VII, para. 121n.
65. R. Hutton, 'Richard Vaughan, Second Earl of Carbery', *ODNB*, 56, p. 195.

Chapter 5: Parliament's Lost Opportunities, April–July 1643

1. Young and Holmes, *The English Civil Wars*, pp. 105, 113–22; R. Dore, *The Civil War in Cheshire* (Chester, 1966), pp. 26–8.
2. Warburton, *Memoirs of Prince Rupert*, II, p. 159.
3. BL, Additional MSS 18983, f. 3.
4. Young, *Edgehill*, pp. 184, 188.
5. Clarendon, *History of the Rebellion*, VII, para. 38. Unfortunately, the only evidence of this from the parliamentary side is speculation in the London weekly journals, the first English newspapers: see BL, Thomason Tracts, E 94 (29). The committee's minute book no longer survives, and there is no mention of the intended direction of Essex's march in the journals of the two Houses or the House of Lords archives. J.H. Hexter suggests that there is a record in Sir Simon D'Ewes's diary of Essex being ordered to leave his winter quarters and attack the king's forces, but the passage he identifies relates not to the opening of the Thames valley campaign but to a possible attack on Bristol in early March 1643, which was being threatened by Prince Rupert's cavalry: see J.H. Hexter, *Reign of King Pym* (Cambridge, Mass., 1968), p. 114; Lords Journal, V, p. 643; BL, Harleian MSS 164, f. 318.
6. Lords Journals, VI, p. 17.
7. BL, Thomason Tracts, E99 (1).
8. *Mercurius Aulicus*, p. 208; BL, Additional MSS 18983, f. 4; Lords Journals, VI, p. 17.
9. Gwynne, *Military Memoirs*, pp. 49–51.
10. The governor, Sir Arthur Aston, had apparently been struck dumb by a tile that fell on his head early in the siege, but he recovered his voice very soon after the surrender of Reading. Nevertheless he avoided the blame for not having prepared the town to withstand a long siege: see Clarendon, *History of the Rebellion*, VII, para. 42.

11. Gwynne, *Military Memoirs*, pp. 10–11; Young, ed., 'The Vindication of Richard Atkyns,' p. 50: BL, Thomason Tracts, E99 (29); BL, Harleian MSS 164, f. 381.
12. Clarendon, *History of the Rebellion*, VII, paras 36, 39; HMC, Portland MSS I, p. 79; BL, Thomason Tracts, E83 (3, 11). This started a much stronger crescendo of complaints about Essex's generalship, but for Fielding the consequences were more immediate and much more serious. Rumours began to circulate that he had taken a bribe from Essex in return for advocating surrender on terms. In addition, the king was incensed that his honour had been compromised. Men surrendering to Essex who had previously served Parliament were not covered by the terms and could be summarily executed, but this was Charles's mistake for not reading the document more carefully before agreeing to the surrender. The acting governor was court-martialled, condemned to death, and only saved from being hanged by the earnest pleas for mercy from the young Prince of Wales: see Clarendon, *History of the Rebellion*, VIII, paras 39–43; BL, Additional MSS 62085, para. 29.
13. The decision was apparently taken on 1 May, see Firth, ed., 'Prince Rupert's Marches', p. 733. From the fact that Rupert's diary does not claim the prince was responsible for advising the building of the camp, it can be inferred that it was Forth's idea.
14. Lords Journals, VI, p. 43; BL, Harleian MSS 164, f. 389. The spread of disease in the army was not mentioned at all in late April and early May, almost certainly because it had not yet assumed epidemic proportions. The earliest evidence is in a royalist journal, which alleged on 1 June that several boatloads of sick men from Reading had arrived in London: see *Mercurius Aulicus*, p. 307.
15. Sir Samuel Luke, 'Journals', ed. I. Phillip, *Oxfordshire Record Society* 29 (1947), pp. 60, 67, 68.
16. On 27 May Essex wrote to the governor of Bristol as follows demanding the return of four troops of horse: 'our want of horse is so great that they must be forthwith returned to the army': see BL, Additional MSS 18978, f. 137. He is much more specific about the impact of the shortage of cavalry on operations in Oxfordshire in later letters: see HMC, Portland MSS I, pp. 714–15; Lords Journals, VI, p. 127.
17. M.A.E. Green, ed., *Letters of Queen Henrietta Maria* (London, 1857), pp. 193, 197. The approach also ties up with a measure to charge the queen with high treason for bringing in materials of war from abroad, which was also put on ice for the moment. The impeachment charge passed the Commons on about 23 May: see Commons Journals, III, p. 98.
18. It is interesting that when Sir William Waller captured Hereford, allowing the defenders nothing more than a guarantee that he would spare their lives, a London journal explained to its readers that the circumstances were very different from those that had pertained at Reading, suggesting that the writer of the piece knew more than he was allowed to put down on paper: see BL, Thomason Tracts, E100 (7).
19. BL, Harleian MSS 164, f. 384, 389; Lords Journals, VI, p. 43.
20. Warburton, *Memoirs of Prince Rupert*, II, p. 189; *Mercurius Aulicus*, pp. 246, 247, 249, 256; HMC, R.R. Hastings MSS II, pp. 100–1.
21. BL, Harleian MSS 164, f. 384; HMC, Portland MSS I, pp. 706–8; Lords Journals, VI, p. 43.
22. HMC, R.R. Hastings MSS II, p. 101.
23. BL, Harleian MSS 6804, f. 92.
24. Warburton, *Memoirs of Prince Rupert*, II, p.189; *Mercurius Aulicus*, p. 261. Hertford was preceded by a single small infantry regiment, which had been withdrawn from the Malmesbury garrison for the relief of Reading: see J. Bampfield, *Apologie*, ed. J. Loftis and P. Hardacre (Lewisburg, Canada, 1993), p. 39.
25. Clarendon, *History of the Rebellion*, VIII, paras 100, 105, 110; BL, Thomason Tracts, E100 (6, 17).
26. Warburton reproduces two letters from Essex to Waller dated 21 and 27 May, which show very clearly that this was so: see *Memoirs of Prince Rupert*, II, pp. 195n, 195–6.
27. Wanklyn, 'Royalist Strategy', pp. 59–60.
28. Ibid., pp. 62–3; BL, Thomason Tracts, E105 (10); Adair, *Roundhead General*, p. 71.
29. Hopton, 'Bellum Civile', pp. 42, 47.

30. Stamford tried to blame one of his political advisers, Anthony Nicholas, and his infantry commander, George Chudleigh, for issuing the order. Chudleigh changed sides soon afterwards, but there is no evidence that he intended to do so until after he was taken prisoner at Stratton: see ibid., pp. 43, 45; BL, Thomason Tracts, E67 (27).

31. Young, ed., 'The Vindication of Richard Atkyns', pp. 12–13; Hopton, 'Bellum Civile', p. 47, 50; M. Wanklyn, 'The King's Armies in the West of England 1642–46' (University of Manchester, unpublished MA thesis, 1966), pp. 22–3, 35.

32. He was at Bath by 8 June: see Hopton, 'Bellum Civile', p. 91; HMC Portland MSS I, p. 710; Adair, *Roundhead General*, p. 74.

33. BL, Thomason Tracts, E105 (27); Warburton, *Memoirs of Prince Rupert*, II, p. 195n; Bell, ed., *Memoirs*, I, p. 39.

34. Hopton, 'Bellum Civile', pp. 56, 97, 98; BL, Harleian MSS 165, f. 127.

35. See above, pp. 1–5.

36. Wadham College Library, Manuscript Collection, A18.14, f. 63.

37. Hopton, 'Bellum Civile', p. 57.

38. BL, Thomason Tracts, E61 (1, 6, 9); Luke, 'Journals', II, pp. 116–18.

39. BL, Thomason Tracts, E101 (4, 6).

40. Cited in Hexter, *Reign of King Pym*, pp. 111–12.

41. Snow, *Essex the Rebel*, pp. 362, 366, citing BL, Additional MSS 40630 and HMC, Portland MSS I, p. 709.

42. Lords Journals, VI, p. 43; BL, Thomason Tracts, E101 (23), E102 (8).

43. BL, Thomason Tracts, E103 (5).

44. Firth, ed., 'Prince Rupert's Marches', p. 733. The slow and tortuous path it took through the hills was almost certainly a precaution against cavalry attack.

45. Rushworth, ed., *Historical Collections*, V, p. 290; Codrington, *Life and Death of Essex*, p. 22; BL, Thomason Tracts, E71 (7).

46. Lords Journals, VI, pp. 52–3 (18 May 1643); BL, Thomason Tracts, E59 (12).

47. Rushworth, ed., *Historical Collections*, V, p. 290; Snow, *Essex the Rebel*, pp. 366–7.

48. BL, Additional MSS 62085a, para. 31; HMC, Appendix to the Ninth Report, II, pp. 435–6. Unfortunately the writer does not make it clear whether Rupert and Forth made common cause against the civilians as they had done after Edgehill.

49. Hexter saw Hampden's influence on the lord general as crucial in the maintenance of good relations with Parliament and the citizens of London: see *Reign of King Pym*, pp. 115–16.

50. BL, Egerton MSS 2646, f. 293.

51. BL, Harleian MSS 165, ff. 100, 101, 114.

52. Commons Journals, III, p. 160. The letter was read in the Lords the day before: see Lords Journals, VI, p. 127.

53. Hexter, *Reign of King Pym*, pp. 117–18.

54. For this view, see D. Scott, *Politics and War in the Three Stuart Kingdoms* (London, 2004), p. 64, but the only substantive evidence for it is the fact that one of Essex's colonels and one of his ex-colonels acted as tellers for the Commons' motion embodying the Lords' proposal. Even less convincing is the view that his failure to take the field after the First Battle of Newbury is a sign that he was a committed supporter of the 'peace party': see J. Adamson, 'The Triumph of Oligarchy: The Management of War and the Committee of Both Kingdoms, 1644–1645', *Parliament at Work*, ed. C. Kyle and J. Peacey (Woodbridge, 2002), p. 104. In fact Essex was the most likely loser in the event of a negotiated peace. He had stuck his head out further than anybody else and the king saw him as the arch plotter, the traitorous son of a traitorous father: see Snow, *Essex the Rebel*, pp. 322–3.

55. A strong thread of irony runs through Essex's letters at this time as, for example, when he described Sir Henry Vane the younger, one of his leading critics in the House, as 'an intimate friend of mine', and 'if he please, I shall go hand in hand with him to the walls of Oxford': see Bodleian, Tanner MSS 62, f. 166.

56. Hexter thinks the crisis was over by the end of July: see *Reign of King Pym*, pp. 141–7. Adair considers that it lasted well into August: see *Roundhead General*, pp. 106–14.

57. They had occupied Buckingham between 30 June and 6 July.

58. BL, Thomason Tracts, E60 (8, 9); Clarendon, *History of the Rebellion*, VII, para. 122; Luke, 'Journals', I, pp. 105–6; Snow, *Essex the Rebel*, p. 353.

59. Firth, ed., 'Prince Rupert's Marches', pp. 733–4; Lords Journals, VI, p. 127. In a letter to the Norfolk county committee, Essex was reported to have written that 'the king was far stronger in horse than he whereby he [i.e. Essex] was disabled to follow and pursue them': see BL, Thomason Tracts, E59 (12), E60 (17), E71 (7); Snow, *Essex the Rebel*, p. 373.

60. BL, Thomason Tracts, E60 (8); Hutchinson, *Memoirs of John Hutchinson*, pp. 129–31.

61. Bell, ed., *Memoirs*, I, pp. 46–7. Lord Fairfax had conveniently forgotten that the prime purpose of Grey Force was to prevent the convoy leaving the north of England. Interestingly, he soon changed tack. Writing to the House of Commons on 9 June he claimed that his purpose in ordering Cromwell and his fellow commanders into Yorkshire was 'the only means to hinder the queen's convoy coming southwards which she now intends to do'. But this was an after-thought. By then, he already knew that Henrietta Maria had left York for Pontefract on the first leg of her journey. See Lords Journals, VI, pp. 66–7; BL, Harleian MSS 165, f. 112; Hamper, ed., *Diary of Sir William Dugdale*, p. 51.

62. Commons Journals, III, pp. 128–9.

63. Lucy Hutchinson, wife of a leading Nottinghamshire officer, however, saw Grey as being of 'too credulous good nature' and in the past 'too great a favourer of Hotham': see *Memoirs of John Hutchinson*, p. 131. Grey's subsequent career as supporter of Cromwell and regicide does sit well with this assertion.

64. Lords Journals, VI, pp. 66–7; BL, Thomason Tracts, E249 (24); HMC, Appendix to the Ninth Report, II, p. 388.

65. Sherwood, *Civil Strife in the Midlands*, pp. 68–9; Warburton, *Memoirs of Prince Rupert*, II, pp. 226, 242, 243; Rushworth, ed., *Historical Collections*, V, p. 274; Hamper, ed., *Diary of Sir William Dugdale*, pp. 51–2.

66. *Mercurius Aulicus*, pp. 367, 370, 372; BL, Thomason Tracts, E62 (16).

67. Firth, ed., *Memoirs of the Duke of Newcastle*, p. 23.

68. Fairfax, 'Short Memorials', pp. 425–6; Firth, ed., *Memoirs of the Duke of Newcastle*, pp. 22–3.

69. Ibid., pp. 24–5; Fairfax, 'Short Memorials', p. 423; HMC, Portland MSS I, pp. 717–18; Sir Walter Scott, ed., *Original Memoirs, Written during the Great Civil War; being the Life of Sir Henry Slingsby and Memoirs of Captain Hodgson* (Edinburgh, 1806), pp. 96–7. The point about the lack of communication between the two parts of the army is made in Young and Holmes, *The English Civil Wars*, but it is not referenced.

70. T. Wright, ed., *Autobiography of Joseph Lister of Bradford, Yorkshire* (Bradford, 1842), p. 19.

71. Firth, ed., *Memoirs of the Duke of Newcastle*, pp. 24–5; HMC, Portland MSS I, pp. 717–18; Fairfax, 'Short Memorials', pp. 423–4; Sir Henry Slingsby, *Diary*, ed. D. Parsons (London, 1836), pp. 96–7.

72. Hutton, *Royalist War Effort*, pp. 45–6, 82.

73. Instead Essex's intention had been to construct his own camp just to the west of Reading and await the arrival of sufficient resources before advancing: see BL, Thomason Tracts E71 (7).

74. P. Young, ed., 'The Vindication of Richard Atkyns', pp. 26–7; Hopton, 'Bellum Civile', p. 42.

Chapter 6: The King on the Offensive: Bristol, Gloucester and the First Battle of Newbury

1. See above, p. 46.

2. Some cavalry regiments returned north with Sir John Byron, Sir Charles Lucas and Lord Goring between November 1643 and April 1644: see Warburton, *Memoirs of Prince Rupert*, II, pp. 329–30, 356; Slingsby, *Diary*, pp. 102–3; BL, Additional MSS 62984b, f. 71; Hamper, ed., *Diary of Sir William Dugdale*, p. 65.

3. J. Lynch, *For King and Parliament: Bristol and the Civil War* (Stroud, 1999), pp. 22–6, 45–53.

4. A. Warmington, 'Sir Edward Massey', *ODNB*, 37, p. 208. Rupert received several letters from Massey's former colleagues suggesting that they could turn him from his present allegiance: see Warburton, *Memoirs of Prince Rupert*, II, pp. 276, 278.

5. Warburton, *Memoirs of Prince Rupert*, II, p. 235.

6. Clarendon, *History of the Rebellion*, VII, para. 144.

7. Warburton, *Memoirs of Prince Rupert*, II, p. 242.

8. The full text of the king's letter is not in the public domain, but Warburton gives a précis of it and some of the original wording: see ibid., I, p. 497.

9. This brief description of Bristol's defences is taken from the detailed description in Bernard de Gomme's account of the siege, supplemented by some comments in the narrative that Colonel Walter Slingsby wrote for Lord Clarendon: see Warburton, *Memoirs of Prince Rupert*, II, pp. 239–41; Hopton, 'Bellum Civile', pp. 92–3. Hopton's description is only three sentences long and adds nothing of substance that cannot be found elsewhere. It is also totally neutral, neither praising nor condemning Rupert's tactics: see 'Bellum Civile', p. 58.

10. This also made an approach impossible. The idea of digging a zigzag of trenches that would come ever closer to the defences and culminate in an intensive artillery barrage from very close quarters, which would in turn open up a breach through which an assault could be launched into the heart of the town, was clearly unfeasible. A similar survey taken by Hertford's engineers, however, found that geological conditions on the Somerset side made an approach a very practicable proposition: see Hopton, 'Bellum Civile', p. 92.

11. Hertford apparently declared that he could not make a useful contribution to the debate because of his lack of military knowledge: see BL, Additional MSS 62084a, para. 34.

12. Ibid., Thomason Tracts E71 (7); M. Wanklyn and F. Jones, *A Military History of the English Civil Wars* (Harlow, 2004), p. 110; Warburton, *Memoirs of Prince Rupert*, II, p. 242.

13. Hopton, 'Bellum Civile', p. 93.

14. Lynch's estimate of a death toll of 700 in the two royalist armies is probably on the high side, as it is based on figures given by Governor Fiennes in his defence against a charge of treason: see Lynch, *For King and Parliament*, p. 84.

15. Warburton, *Memoirs of Prince Rupert*, II, p. 268. How much was captured was a matter of dispute. A pamphlet printed at Oxford mentioned 60 artillery pieces and 1,700 barrels of gunpowder; de Gomme only mentions 120 barrels of powder in Bristol and other garrisons in the south-west that surrendered in late July or early August 1643: see ibid., II, pp. 264–5, 263.

16. The king mentions this in his letter congratulating Rupert on the capture of Bristol: see Warburton, *Memoirs of Prince Rupert*, II, p. 268. There is no hint in it that the change in army command had anything to do with the unseemly quarrel between the prince and the marquis as to who should be governor of Bristol, as Clarendon implies in his narrative of events in late July and early August 1643: see Clarendon, *History of the Rebellion*, VII, paras 155–6.

17. Clarendon, *History of the Rebellion*, VII, para. 152; Wanklyn and Jones, *A Military History*, pp. 110–11.

18. Hopton, 'Bellum Civile', pp. 59–60, 63–5.

19. See, for example, the narrative given in Kitson, *Prince Rupert*, p. 142.

20. BL, Additional MSS 62084a, para. 35. Although Rupert's diary does not make it completely clear at which of the councils of war he made the suggestion about the advance into East Anglia, Clarendon clearly shows that it was the second: see *History of the Rebellion*, VII, paras 158, 159. This would also help to explain why Clarendon claimed that the prince and the generals alleged at the end of the campaign that they had not advised the siege of Gloucester, putting all the blame on Culpeper: see Clarendon, *History of the Rebellion*, VII, para. 239.

21. This view, which began as speculation in Burne and Young, *The Great Civil War*, is now regarded as fact by many writers on the Civil Wars: see, for example, J. Barratt, *Cavalier Generals: King Charles I and his Commanders in the English Civil Wars 1642–46* (Barnsley, 2004), p. 31; J. Kenyon, *The Civil Wars of England* (London, 1988), p. 81; Kitson, *Prince Rupert*, p. 153; J.S. Wheeler, *The Irish and British Wars 1637–1654: Triumph, Tragedy and Failure* (London, 2002), pp. 83–4. The only person alleged at the time to have thought in

terms of storming Gloucester was King Charles, and he abandoned the idea because 'he feared the loss of the best part of his infantry': see Bulstrode, *Memoirs*, p. 94.

22. Washbourne, ed., *Bibliotheca Gloucestrensis*, p. 46.

23. Clarendon claims that Forth was ordered to leave Oxford and take charge of the siege after the decision was taken. His name is also missing from a list of officers who gave their professional advice to the Council of War: see Clarendon, *History of the Rebellion*, VII, para. 164; Warburton, *Memoirs of Prince Rupert*, II, pp. 280–1. However, in a letter written by Lord Percy, the general of artillery, on 17 August, Forth is described as having been misadvised by the engineers as to the breadth and depth of the moat around Gloucester prior to the meeting of the council, and that his estimate of the length of time it would take to capture the city was based on this information: see W. Day, ed., *The Pythouse Papers* (London, 1879), p. 57.

24. Warburton, *Memoirs of Prince Rupert*, I, p. 497.

25. Ibid., II, pp. 280–2; Washbourne, ed., *Bibliotheca Gloucestrensis*, pp. 43–5, 209–28. King James II, who was present as a nine-year-old boy, criticised Forth in his memoirs for not being ready to explode his mine when Sir Jacob was ready to explode his, but there is no concrete evidence of this in the detailed day-by-day narratives of the siege that were written by officers on both sides: see Clarke, *James II*, I, p. 20.

26. Clarendon claimed that he deliberately distanced himself from the siege as he did not think that it would succeed, but this seems most unlikely. He was only briefly absent and only in the last week. First he accompanied the king on a two-day visit to Oxford to sort out a misunderstanding between Rupert and the queen. He then returned to the siege for a couple of days, after which his services were needed in the Cotswolds as General of Horse. By that time it was known that a relief force was approaching, which might be deterred if it was faced by the massed ranks of the king's cavalry: see Clarendon, *History of the Rebellion*, VII, para. 164; BL, Additional MSS 62084a, para. 38; Firth, ed., 'Prince Rupert's Marches', p. 734.

27. BL, Additional MSS 31116, f. 70. Essex did not mention the expedition in a letter sent to the Speaker of the House of Commons two days earlier: see Bodleian, Tanner MSS 62, f. 284.

28. BL, Thomason Tracts E69 (25), E70 (10); Bodleian, Tanner MSS 62, f. 309.

29. Bodleian, Tanner MSS 62, f. 309; Washbourne, ed., *Bibliotheca Gloucestrensis*, p. 237.

30. BL, Thomason Tracts, E67 (28); Holmes, *Eastern Association*, pp. 95, 114.

31. See Washbourne, ed., *Bibliotheca Gloucestrensis*, p. 56.

32. Ibid., pp. 44–5.

33. S.R. Gardiner, *History of the Great Civil War*, 4 vols (Moreton in the Marsh, 1991), I, p. 208.

34. BL, Thomason Tracts, E69 (15), E70 (10).

35. Bodleian, Clarendon MSS, 1738.5; BL, Additional MSS 62084a, paras 38–9.

36. BL, Thomason Tracts, E70 (10).

37. Firth, ed., 'Prince Rupert's Marches', pp. 734–5; Warburton, *Memoirs of Prince Rupert*, II, pp. 289–90.

38. In the confused fight that followed the king's cavalry regiments suffered higher casualties than Parliament's when they came in range of Essex's musketeers, but things could have been very different to what they had been at Stow-on-the-Wold a fortnight before, as for a time Rupert succeeded in separating enemy horse from foot. The failure to destroy the enemy horse he blamed on other commanders' doubts about the wisdom of becoming involved in a general engagement without infantry support. This led to a blazing row and a lengthy delay, which allowed the enemy horse time to rally under the protection of their foot. Accounts on both sides, however, make it pretty clear that, as at Edgehill, Essex's cavalry regiments were no match for Rupert's in the open field, but at least they had made an orderly retreat instead of flying to all points of the compass: see BL, Thomason Tracts E69 (15, 25), E70 (10); BL, Additional MSS 62084a, para. 39.

39. Warburton, *Memoirs of Prince Rupert*, II, p. 290; Day, ed., *Pythouse Papers*, p. 16; BL, Additional MSS 62084a, paras 38, 40.

40. Warburton, *Memoirs of Prince Rupert*, II, p. 290; Day, ed., *Pythouse Papers*, p. 16.

41. Gwynne, *Military Memoirs*, p. 53; BL, Thomason Tracts, E69 (10).
42. BL, Thomason Tracts, E70 (10); M. Wanklyn, *Decisive Battles of the English Civil Wars* (Barnsley, 2006), pp. 70–1; Wanklyn and Jones, *A Military History*, p. 120.
43. BL, Additional MSS 18980, f. 120; 62084a, paras 40–1.
44. BL, Thomason Tracts E70 (10), E69 (10); BL, Additional MSS 62084a, para. 41.
45. BL, Thomason Tracts E70 (10), E69 (10); BL, Additional MSS 62084a, para. 41.
46. BL, Thomason Tracts, E69 (15).
47. Bodleian, Clarendon MSS, 1738.5; BL, Additional MSS 18980, f. 120.
48. BL, Thomason Tracts, E70 (10); Bodleian, Clarendon MSS, 1738.5.
49. BL, Thomason Tracts, E69 (10); Bodleian, Clarendon MSS 1738.5.
50. Rupert's own regiment lost 300 men and Sir John Byron's 100: see BL, Additional MSS 62084a, para. 41; Bodleian, Clarendon MSS, 1738.5.
51. BL, Thomason Tracts, E70 (10); BL, Additional MSS 62084a paras 41–2; Wilts CRO, 413/444, pp. 4–5 (a twentieth-century copy of contemporary additions to Rupert's diary not in the BL collection).
52. BL, Thomason Tracts, E70 (10).
53. BL, Thomason Tracts, E69 (15), E70 (10).
54. Clarendon does not mention gunpowder at all, whilst the official royalist report of the battle places it second, after heavy casualties in the officers' ranks, amongst the reasons why fighting was not renewed. The official report suggests there were about thirty barrels left, but adds the information that the king's army at Edgehill had consumed only twenty barrels: see ibid., E69 (10); BL, Additional MSS 62084a, para. 42; Clarendon, *History of the Rebellion*, VII, para. 202; BL, Thomason Tracts E69 (10). Reid and Kitson wrongly claim that the king only had ten barrels left: see Reid, *All the King's Armies*, p. 65; Kitson, *Prince Rupert*, p. 151.
55. See BL, Additional MSS 62084a, para. 42; Bodleian, Clarendon MSS, 1738.5.
56. BL, Thomason Tracts, E69 (8), E70 (10); Codrington, *Life of Essex*, pp. 33–4. The Official Account also makes it clear that, although Essex's deputy Major General Phillip Skippon occasionally ventured onto the common, his responsibility was keeping up the bluff in the Kennet valley.

Chapter 7: Odds Even: Fighting in the Provinces, August 1643–April 1644

1. See below, p. 82.
2. Wheeler, *The Irish and British Wars 1637–1654*, pp. 89–90.
3. Day, ed., *Pythouse Papers*, p. 55 (Lord Percy to Rupert, 29 June 1643).
4. Clarendon, *History of the Rebellion*, VI, para. 78, VII, para. 279.
5. However, Sir John Byron's contempt for Prince Rupert, very apparent in the account of the First Battle of Newbury he wrote for Clarendon in 1648, probably did not take firm root until after Marston Moor when the prince tried to unload the blame for the defeat on him: see Bodleian, Clarendon MSS, 1783. 5; BL, Additional MSS 62084b, paras 55–7.
6. There can be little doubt, for example, that Sir John Culpeper subsequently argued that he would not have pushed so strongly for the siege of Gloucester had there existed any prospect of the northern army being brought into the southern theatre of war: see *History of the Rebellion*, VII, paras 181, 239.
7. Young and Holmes, *The English Civil Wars*, p. 356; S.D.M. Carpenter, *Military Leadership in the British Civil Wars 1642–1651: 'The Genius of this Age'* (London, 2005), p. 166.
8. Warwick, *Memoirs*, p. 268; Clarendon, *History of the Rebellion*, VIII, paras. 82–4.
9. The patent is dated 24 October 1643, but the queen addressed Newcastle as marquis in a letter dated 13 August: see Bodleian, Dugdale MSS 19, f. 36; Green, ed., *Letters of Henrietta Maria*, p. 225.
10. BL, Harleian MSS 6988, ff. 71, 74, 75, 127–8; Green, ed., *Letters of Henrietta Maria*, pp. 205–8, 218.
11. Slingsby, *Diary*, p. 95; Firth, ed., *Memoirs of the Duke of Newcastle*, p. 23; Green, ed., *Letters of Henrietta Maria*, p. 218.

12. F. Sunderland reproduces a letter written by Sir Marmaduke Langdale to Sir William Saville in November 1642. In it he states that Newcastle had some hopes of marching southwards 'when he hath settled Yorkshire': see F. Sunderland, *Marmaduke, Lord Langdale* (London, 1926), p. 65.
13. Slingsby, *Diary*, pp. 99–100; BL, Thomason Tracts, E63 (12), E64 (10, 13).
14. Slingsby, *Diary*, p. 99; Clarendon, *History of the Rebellion*, VII, para. 177.
15. This is reasonably clear from the wording of the passage in Clarendon and the lack of a comment to that effect in the letter from the queen described in the next paragraph: see *History of the Rebellion*, VIII, 201n; Green, ed., *Letters of Henrietta Maria*, p. 225.
16. Fairfax, 'Short Memorials', p. 431; Slingsby, *Diary*, p. 99; Firth, ed., *Memoirs of the Duke of Newcastle*, pp. 28–9. The chronology is clear if the later sources are collated with what was printed in the London weekly journals. A major raid on a town in the vicinity of Selby near York took place on about 5 August. Newcastle then left Lincoln on the 7th, spent a fruitless four days trying to browbeat Nottingham into surrender, and was back in Yorkshire by the 13th: see BL, Thomason Tracts, E64 (13), E65 (8, 14); Hutchinson, *Memoirs of Colonel John Hutchinson*, p. 142.
17. Green, ed., *Letters of Henrietta Maria*, p. 225. The idea was apparently first suggested by the marquis himself some months before: see Warwick, *Memoirs*, pp. 267–70.
18. The senior officer with the northern cavalry, Sir Charles Lucas, then at Oxford, was given a commission covering parts of East Anglia: see Bodleian, Dugdale MSS 19, f. 28. Rupert was also interested in campaigning in East Anglia. The prince almost certainly wrote a letter which supported Newcastle's intention to secure Yorkshire first but expressed the hope that they would soon be cooperating with one another. This is implicit in Newcastle's reply written on 29 August: see Warburton, *Memoirs of Prince Rupert*, II, p. 309.
19. Bodleian, Dugdale MSS 19, f. 26. The king also asked him to nominate people for rewards that he as monarch could confer, presumably in the hope that this would help to persuade opponents of the march south to change their minds: see ibid., f. 28.
20. The queen had supported him by writing that she was not in favour of the plan, and that he being on the spot should know best: see Green, ed., *Letters of Henrietta Maria*, p. 225.
21. The letter was written on 3 October: see Warburton, *Memoirs of Prince Rupert*, II, p. 310.
22. For the fullest account of Rupert's plans and how they were frustrated, see M. Wanklyn and F. Jones, *A Military History of the English Civil Wars: Strategy and Tactics* (Harlow, 2004), pp. 128–31.
23. HMC, Portland MSS, I, p. 144; Edward Walsingham, 'Hector Britannicus: The Life of Sir John Digby', ed. G. Bernard, *Camden Society*, 3rd series, 18 (1910), pp. 94–5.
24. The first sign of this was on 12 December when the Committee agreed to meet every day at 2.00 p.m.: see Commons Journals, III, p. 337.
25. Whitelock, *Memorials*, pp. 78, 79.
26. The junta at Edinburgh corresponded not with the earl of Leven but with a subcommittee of its members that accompanied the army: see pp. NAS, PA 11/1, ff. 71, 87, 112, 169, 171.
27. Holmes, *Eastern Association*, pp. 105, 107, 112; Snow, *Essex the Rebel*, pp. 418–20.
28. BL, Harleian MSS 165, ff. 265–6; Bodleian, Tanner MSS 62, f. 619; Lords Journals, VI, p. 494; Adair, *Roundhead General*, pp. 154–7.
29. This is very apparent from letters covering campaigning in the Cotswolds in June: see CSP Domestic 1644, pp. 214, 219.
30. Snow, *Essex the Rebel*, pp. 470–7.
31. He had commanded a regiment at Edgehill but it was one of those that fled the battlefield without coming into contact with the enemy.
32. As Lord Mandeville (his father was still alive), he was one of six parliamentarians the king set out to arrest in January 1642 for treasonable correspondence with the Scots. His political importance in the months and years leading up to the Civil War has at last been acknowledged in J.S. Adamson's *The Noble Revolt*.
33. Clarendon, *History of the Rebellion*, I, para. 247. The others were John Pym, John Hampden, Lord Say and Sele, and the earls of Pembroke and Salisbury.

34. Green, ed., *Letters of Henrietta Maria*, pp. 193–4. See also above p. 53.
35. This allegedly brought an end to the prospect of the northern royalists invading East Anglia: see Young and Holmes, *English Civil Wars*, p. 137; but the chance of it happening had ended when Newcastle learned that he was likely to have to face a Scottish invasion before Christmas: see above, pp. 75–6.
36. Lords Journals, VI, pp. 255–6. See above, p. 32, for the 'evening of the battle' letter.
37. BL, Thomason Tracts, E90 (27). Mark Stoyle claims the speech was delivered in October 1642: see *Soldiers and Strangers: An Ethnic History of the English Civil War* (London, 2005), p. 103; but the open meeting of Brooke with the Warwickshire gentry (not his soldiers) at which officers were elected could not have occurred during the Edgehill campaign. It is popularly believed that such sentiments first emerged from the mouth of Oliver Cromwell in response to the poor performance of the parliamentary cavalry at Edgehill, but we only have Cromwell's word for it and in a speech delivered many years later.
38. It is possible that such questions were put to Manchester prior to his appointment. Waller claims to have been asked similar questions at exactly the same time and upset the radicals by declaring that promoting godly men with no military experience was a recipe for disaster: see Bodleian, Don MSS, d.57.
39. Oliver had more than six months' experience of dealing with the committee structure of the Association and sweet-talking the local taxpayers.
40. Most historians follow Gardiner along the primrose path of hindsight: see *Great Civil War*, I, p. 191. However, the point I have made with regard to 1643 is also made by Alan Marshall, *Oliver Cromwell, Soldier: The Military Life of a Revolutionary at War* (London, 2004), pp. 102, 143.
41. In the first battle the decision to charge was taken by a committee and in the third battle Cromwell provided little leadership as he was unhorsed.
42. It was more polyglot than most, comprising the survivors of Roundway Down, a number of small regiments he had raised for his independent command in the summer, others provided by the Southeast Association who were supposed to be his paymasters, and a brigade of London trained bands: see J. Adair, *Cheriton 1644: The Campaign and the Battle* (Kineton, 1973), pp. 110–16.
43. Adair, *Roundhead General*, pp. 121–2.
44. Hopton, 'Bellum Civile', pp. 61–2; Bodleian, Dugdale MSS 19, f. 33; Clarendon, *History of the Rebellion*, VIII, para. 175.
45. HMC, Portland MSS I, p. 154; Bodleian, Tanner MSS 62, f. 410. He may have been goaded into action by criticism from Essex's supporters in Parliament and in the press.
46. BL, Additional MSS 27402, ff. 14–16; Hopton, 'Bellum Civile', pp. 63, 65–8.
47. Wanklyn and Jones, *A Military History*, pp. 136–80. Dispersal, which had been practicable in Cornwall where movement across country was difficult because of the enclosed landscape, was wrong for chalk down where thin soils and good drainage meant that the reverse was the case.
48. Hopton, 'Bellum Civile', pp. 68–9; Bampfield, *Apologie*, pp. 42–3.
49. BL, Thomason Tracts, E81 (10, 12); BL, Harleian MSS 165, f. 268; Hopton, 'Bellum Civile', pp. 73–6; Bodleian, Tanner MSS 62, ff. 410, 508. The wintry conditions also enabled Hopton to persuade the king that he should remain at Winchester, not withdraw into north Wiltshire where he would be closer to the main field army if Waller advanced towards him: see Hopton, 'Bellum Civile', pp. 73–6; Bodleian, Tanner MSS 62, ff. 497, 508.
50. Bodleian, Firth MSS C6, ff. 132, 133–4, 142; CSP Domestic 1644, p. 33.
51. Bodleian, Dugdale MSS 19, f. 65.
52. Hopton, 'Bellum Civile', p. 77; Hamper, ed., *Diary of Dugdale*, p. 63.
53. Hopton, 'Bellum Civile', pp. 76–7; BL, Additional MSS 18779, f. 87; CSP Domestic 1644, pp. 33–4, 49. This could have caused major problems of command, as Balfour, having a higher rank, was Waller's superior officer, but the two appear to have established a modus vivendi. None of the accounts mention friction between the two commanders as being a cause of wasted opportunities that occurred during the Cheriton campaign.
54. CSP Domestic 1644, p. 71.

55. This can be inferred from Hopton's asides in his account of the run-up to the battle of Cheriton: see Hopton, 'Bellum Civile', pp. 78–81.

56. Henry Roe, 'Military Memoir of Colonel Birch', ed. J. Webb, *Camden Society*, new series, VII (1873), p. 9; Hopton, 'Bellum Civile', pp. 81–2, 101.

57. For a discussion of this hypothesis, see Wanklyn, *Decisive Battles*, pp. 100–2. In his narrative of the battle Walter Slingsby clearly states that the royalist army was ordered to attack on both wings: see 'Bellum Civile', p. 101.

58. Hopton, 'Bellum Civile', pp. 82, 101–2; BL, Thomason Tracts, E40 (13).

59. BL, Additional MSS 18779, f. 87.

60. Lieutenant Harley was apparently in one of the few units not to have been drawn into the melee: see HMC, Portland MSS III, p. 109.

61. Ibid.; Roe, 'Colonel Birch', pp. 9–11; Hopton, 'Bellum Civile', pp. 83–4, 102–3.

62. BL, Additional MSS 27402, f. 23; HMC, Portland MSS III, p. 110.

63. Walker, *Historical Discourses*, pp. 7–8; CSP Domestic 1644, pp. 71, 77, 116; BL, Harleian MSS 986, ff. 79–90.

64. Walker, *Historical Discourses*, p. 7; BL, Additional MSS 27402, ff. 15–16; Hopton, 'Bellum Civile', pp. 63–4.

65. This was not a whim on the prince's part, but the preliminary to a proposal dear to the king's heart for raising yet another army in the West Country under the nominal leadership of the Prince of Wales. This would best be served by eliminating as many parliamentary enclaves there as possible: see Warburton, *Memoirs of Prince Rupert*, II, pp. 132, 134.

66. CSP Domestic 1644, pp. 101, 116–17.

67. T. Carte, *Life of James Butler, Duke of Ormond*, 6 vols (London, 1735), I, pp. 468–9; Bodleian, Dugdale MSS 19, ff. 44, 48; I. Roy, ed., 'Royalist Ordnance Papers', *Oxfordshire Record Society* 49 (1975), p. 312; M. Toynbee, ed., 'The Papers of Captain Stevens, Wagon-master', *Oxfordshire Record Society* 42 (1961), p. 23; BL, Additional MSS 18981, ff. 147, 151; Warburton, *Memoirs*, II, pp. 327–9.

68. Comprising 1,300 horse and 300 foot, principally the regiments of Lord Byron and Lord Molineux: see Carte, *Original Letters and Papers*, I, p. 37; HMC, Portland MSS, I, p. 161; Phillips, ed., *Memoirs of the Civil War in Wales and the Marches*, II, pp. 104–5.

69. His own and Sir Richard Willis's regiments of horse and the Prince of Wales's regiment of foot.

70. Bodleian, Dugdale MSS 19, f. 44.

71. Ibid., Carte MSS 7, ff. 397–8, 492, 513, 592, 8, ff. 27, 48, 63, 9, ff. 3, 19.

72. The commission was issued on 6 January: see Bodleian, Dugdale MSS 19, f. 48. The prince arrived at Shrewsbury on 19 February: see Firth, ed., 'Prince Rupert's Marches', p. 735. The delay was partly due to Rupert's involvement in an attempt to secure the town of Aylesbury by winning over Lieutenant Colonel Moseley, one of the officers of the garrison: see Hamper, ed., *The Diary of Dugdale*, p. 59; HMC, Portland MSS, I, p. 166. The plot did not succeed because Moseley informed his masters.

73. Thomas Malbon, 'Memorial of the Civil War', ed. J. Hall, *Lancashire and Cheshire Record Society* 19 (1889), pp. 82–3, 86–8.

74. Byron received his orders on 7 November and left Oxford on the 21st: see Bodleian, Firth MSS C6, f. 252; Phillips, *Memoirs of the Civil War*, II, p. 105. He was at Shrewsbury on the 26th and at Chester by about 3 December: see HMC, Portland MSS, I, p. 161; Shropshire CRO, Shrewsbury billeting papers, unfol.

75. HMC, Portland MSS, I, pp. 162–3; Malbon, 'Memorial', pp. 96–7.

76. The commission was on its way to Lincolnshire by 14 or 15 December, but Sir Thomas may have delayed his departure until the surrender of Gainsborough, the last royalist garrison in Lincolnshire, on 20 December, though he does not mention this factor: see Gardiner, *Great Civil War*, I, p. 294. In his own account Fairfax claimed that he was waiting for military supplies to arrive before setting out: see Lord Thomas Fairfax, 'Short Memorials of the Northern Actions', *Select Tracts relating to the Civil Wars in England*, 2 vols, ed. Francis, Lord Maseres (London, 1815–18), I, p. 434.

77. Scott, ed., *Original Memoirs*, p. 100; Fairfax, 'Short Memorials', p. 434.

78. It can be argued in mitigation that Byron would have been able to make little use of the cavalry even if they had been where he wanted them to be, on account of the enclosures. Both Byron and Fairfax emphasised this point in their accounts of the battle: see Fairfax, 'Short Memorials', p. 435; Carte, *Original Letters and Papers*, I, pp. 39, 41. However, one contemporary account suggests that Byron being on the wrong side of the river was an important factor in the outcome of the battle given the complicated landscape over which it was fought. If he had been where he should have been, his second-in-command, Major General Gibson, could have taken charge of the infantry at a pass on the Nantwich side of the battleground and insisted on being reinforced, thus making it much more difficult for the garrison to carry out the attack on the rear of the royalist army which almost certainly decided the battle.

79. Fairfax, 'Short Memorials', p. 435.

80. Rushworth, ed., *Historical Collections*, V, p. 302; Fairfax, 'Short Memorials', pp. 435–6; Hodgson, 'Original Memoirs', pp. 101–2; Malbon, 'Memorial', p. 113. The contention that a charge by Fairfax's horse in support of the sally was the really decisive factor is almost certainly an invention by John Vicars, who published his *England's Worthies* as Fairfax was being proposed as General of the New Model Army: see Malbon, 'Memorial', p. 115n. It is not mentioned in Sir Thomas's account: see 'Short Memorials', pp. 435–6.

81. Between 1,000 and 1,300 had rejoined their colours by the following day: see Carte, *Original Letters and Papers*, I, pp. 39, 42.

82. Ibid., I, pp. 39, 42; Malbon, 'Memorial', p. 113. Fighting began at about 3.30 p.m. and finished at 5.00 p.m., by which time it was totally dark. There was no moon that night or it was obscured by clouds. One officer who did not escape was Colonel George Monck, later Cromwell's commander in Scotland and King Charles II's; duke of Albemarle.

83. An intercepted letter shows that Sir Thomas was ordered by his father to join him in Yorkshire in late February, but he did not do so. Instead he then moved into Lancashire and remained there for a month before joining in the reconquest of the west Yorkshire textile towns in late March. This was in defiance of the orders of the Committee of Both Kingdoms that he should join the Scottish army in County Durham, whose operations against the marquis of Newcastle were being hindered by lack of suitable cavalry: see Warburton, *Memoirs of Prince Rupert*, II, pp. 380–1; CSP Domestic 1644, pp. 62, 102. At this point in the war the Scottish army was equipped with small horses and riders armed with lances, which were fit for little more than skirmishing: see BL, Thomason Tracts 811 (2).

84. HMC, Portland MSS, I, pp. 190–1; Malbon, 'Memorial', p. 123; Firth, ed., 'Prince Rupert's Marches', p. 735.

85. Hutton, *Royalist War Effort*, pp. 130–8.

86. CSP Domestic 1644, pp. 23, 33; Hutchinson, *Memoirs of John Hutchinson*, pp. 192–4. The rest of the Eastern Association army under Manchester and Cromwell took up winter quarters in the valley of the Bedfordshire Ouse, where they assumed much of the responsibility for preventing a royalist foray into the Association that had previously been Philip Skippon's: see Sir Samuel Luke, 'Letter Books', ed. H. Tibbutt, *Historical Manuscripts Commission Joint Publications* 4 (1963), pp. 17–18, 351–3; Bodleian, Carte MSS 74, f. 70.

87. *Mercurius Aulicus*, pp. 894–900; Rushworth, ed., *Historical Collections*, V, pp. 306–9; BL, Thomason Tracts, E38 (10), E39 (8); P. Young et al., *Newark on Trent: The Civil War Siegeworks* (London, 1964), p. 19.

88. BL, Harleian MSS 6802, f. 157; Hutton, *Royalist War Effort*, pp. 138–40, 174–5.

89. See below, pp. 130, 144, 151, 155, 167.

90. For example, Kitson, *Prince Rupert*, p. 172; Barratt, *Cavalier Generals*, p. 36; C. Spencer, *Prince Rupert, the Last Cavalier* (London, 2007), pp. 113–14. Burne and Young first drew attention to what was then a neglected battle, but kept their praise within due bounds, largely confining it to the prince's ability to get his cavalry to obey the command to charge, despite being heavily outnumbered: see *The Great Civil War*, pp. 139–43.

91. BL, Additional MSS 18981, ff. 104, 106; Bodleian, Firth MSS C7, f. 10.

92. Bodleian, Firth MSS C7, f. 22.

93. Firth, ed., 'Prince Rupert's Marches', p. 736.

94. BL, Additional MSS 18981, f. 155 (Newcastle to Charles I, 18 April 1644).

Chapter 8: Great Expectations: Selby and Oxford

1. Wanklyn, 'King's Armies in the West', pp. 95–100, 110; Lynch, *For King and Parliament*, pp. 128–37.
2. Wanklyn, *Decisive Battles*, pp. 123–4, 145, 173.
3. See above, p. 84.
4. Firth, ed., *Memoirs of the Duke of Newcastle*, pp. 31–3, 195–8; Slingsby, *Diary*, pp. 105–7. Bellasis's secretary claimed he had 7,000 men at Selby, but this seems unlikely unless the force consisted very largely of cavalry: see HMC, Ormond MSS, NS II, pp. 383–4.
5. BL, Harleian MSS 6988, f. 106; Warburton, *Memoirs of Prince Rupert*, I, p. 504, II, pp. 381, 397, 433–4.
6. Proposals to move Maurice from his command began just before the end of 1643 when an emissary sent by the king to the marquis of Newcastle suggested that Maurice should replace Lieutenant General James King as army commander in the north, with King to replace Forth as lord general of the Oxford army. See Bodleian, Clarendon MSS 1085.
7. M. Coate, *Cornwall in the Civil War and Interregnum 1642–1660* (2nd edn, Truro, 1963), pp. 127–9; E. Andriette, *Devon and Exeter in the Civil War* (Newton Abbot, 1971), p. 97.
8. The best narrative of the royalist conquest of the Devonshire towns is in Andriette, *Devon and Exeter*, pp. 89–101, but apart from Clarendon it is based exclusively on parliamentary sources.
9. Warburton, *Memoirs of Prince Rupert*, II, pp. 410–11. The prince was particularly upset when the king did not consult him when appointing a successor to Lord John Stuart, his lieutenant general of horse, who had been mortally wounded at Cheriton.
10. Ibid., pp. 412–13, 416; BL, Additional MSS 18981, ff. 170, 179.
11. This allegation first appeared in Walker, *Historical Discourses*: see pp. 8, 12.
12. The king did not order his nephew to join him until almost the end of May, and by then it was too late. If he had advanced towards Oxford or even Bristol, he would almost certainly have encountered Sir William Waller commanding a much larger army.
13. See above, pp. 78–80.
14. Holmes, *Eastern Association*, pp. 96–7, 224–5; CSP Domestic 1644, pp. 33, 34, 56, 69, 134.
15. *Mercurius Aulicus*, pp. 912–13; D. Stevenson, *Revolution and Counter-Revolution in Scotland 1644–51* (London, 1977), p. 1. The fullest account of the ten-week campaign is in Reid, *All the King's Armies*, pp. 107–16, but it is too indulgent towards Leven.
16. See below, pp. 97–8.
17. Cust, *Charles I*, pp. 390–1.
18. Even so, responses to changed situations were not always quick enough as, for instance, in the closing stages of the Marston Moor campaign. If Rupert had known that his uncle's army had run rings around Sir William Waller, he might have hesitated about looking for a battle straight after relieving York: see below, p. 100.
19. Walker, *Historical Discourses*, pp. 23–4. At first it had included Lords Hopton and the Second Earl of Lindsey, but the former left for Bristol on 26 May and the latter appears to have remained at Oxford: see ibid., pp. 13–14, 16.
20. The senior secretary, Sir Edward Nicholas, remained at Oxford coordinating amongst other things intelligence reports from around the country.
21. See below, pp. 100–1, for an account of the circumstances under which the royalists withdrew from Abingdon.
22. I. Roy, 'George Digby, Royalist Intrigue and the Collapse of the Cause', in I. Gentles, J. Morrill and B. Worden, eds, *Soldiers, Writers and Statesmen of the English Revolution* (Cambridge, 1998), pp. 83–4; Clarendon, *History of the Rebellion*, VIII, para. 33.
23. I. Roy, 'Why Did Prince Rupert Fight at Marston Moor?', *Journal of the Society for Army Historical Research* 86 (2008), pp. 244–7. However, I cannot agree that Rupert spent a week sulking in Lancashire in mid-June because of his anger over the intriguing against him at Oxford. He had plenty to do in terms of recruiting and arming his troops.
24. Rushworth, ed., *Historical Collections*, V, p. 616.
25. Fairfax, 'Short Memorials', pp. 435–6; HMC, Ormond MSS, NS II, p. 385.
26. BL, Additional MSS 18981, f. 106; Fairfax, 'Short Memorials', p. 436; BL, Thomason Tracts, E42 (29).

27. CSP Domestic 1644, pp. 87–8.
28. Lord Fairfax had 4,000 horse and foot, which included Meldrum's brigade, and Sir Thomas a slightly smaller brigade, which included some Lancashire troops: see BL, Thomason Tracts, 43 (18); H.W. Meikle, ed., 'Correspondence of the Scottish Commissioners in London', *Roxburgh Club* 173 (1917), pp. 7, 15.
29. Lords Journals, VI, pp. 522–3; BL, Thomason Tracts, E43 (14). Wilson was condemned to death. Bellasis suffered sword cuts to his arm and his head but his body armour protected him against pistol balls: see HMC, Ormond MSS, NS II, p. 384.
30. BL, Additional MSS 18981, f. 155. Porter was also held responsible for the failure to evict Lambert from Bradford a month earlier: see HMC, Ormond MSS, NS, II, p. 384.
31. They were mounted on small horses and armed primarily with lances: see BL, Thomason Tracts, E811 (2); Firth, ed., *Memoirs of the Duke of Newcastle*, p. 202, but they were nevertheless blamed for not being sufficiently adventurous: see Meikle, ed., 'Correspondence of the Scottish Commissioners', p. 27.
32. Lords Journals, VI, p. 540; BL, Thomason Tracts, E43 (14).
33. CSP Domestic 1644, p. 153. In May the Committee of Both Kingdoms was inching towards ordering Waller to march to the relief of Lyme, besieged by Prince Maurice since 20 April, but never quite got there: see ibid., pp. 137, 147.
34. CSP Domestic 1644, pp. 195, 214; BL, Harleian MSS 166, f. 83 (Waller to the Committee of Both Kingdoms, 4 June 1644).
35. Holmes, *Eastern Association*, pp. 69–70.
36. It was raised in a letter from the king to Rupert written on 21 April: see Day, ed., *Pythouse Papers*, p. 6; but the prince had received a plea for help from Newark even earlier: see BL, Lansdown MSS 988, f. 204.
37. Firth, ed., 'Prince Rupert's Marches', p. 735.
38. CSP Domestic 1644, p. 141; Lords Journals, VI, p. 540.
39. HMC, Appendix to the Fourth Report, p. 296; Walker, *Historical Discourses*, p. 13.
40. Walker, *Historical Discourses*, p. 11. The earlier decision had been taken at Aldbourne Chase in the second week in April when the king's generals thought they would be facing Waller, Manchester and Essex's armies. Amongst the arguments put forward in May were that it was too late to provision the town adequately and, based on the previous year's experience, that it could not be easily relieved if it was besieged: see ibid; BL, Additional MSS 18981, f. 177 (Digby to Rupert, 11 May 1644).
41. Walker, *Historical Discourses*, p. 10. For the fullest account of the deliberations of the king and his advisers in late May and early June 1644, see Wanklyn and Jones, *A Military History*, pp. 162–5.
42. Walker, *Historical Discourses*, pp. 14–15. Walker's account of the whole episode is odd, in that the field commanders seem to have obeyed their instructions to the letter, as both armies were approaching Abingdon on the west bank of the river. Digby's account is more convincing. The king thought that he had not given a mandatory order, the generals that he had: see BL, Additional MSS 18981, f. 182; Bodleian, Firth MSS C7, f. 117.
43. Richard Symonds, 'Diaries of the Marches of the Royal Army during the Great Civil War', ed. C. Long, *Camden Society* LXXIV (1859), p. 8.
44. BL, Thomason Tracts, E2 (20).
45. Walker, *Historical Discourses*, pp. 19–22; Symonds, 'Diaries', pp. 8, 15.
46. Who ensured that the escape from Oxford was so well executed is a matter of considerable uncertainty. Sir Edward Walker argued that the generals were despondent, and that the king provided the necessary leadership when it was most urgently required, but the operation was no more than a modification of the plan of 26 April to suit the exact circumstances of 3 June. Much of the staff work should therefore have been already in place, possibly on lines laid down by Rupert himself before he left Oxford or else by Lord Wilmot. Neither is likely to have been given the credit for it in Sir Edward's account. He hated the prince and by the time he produced the final draft Wilmot needed to be airbrushed from the narrative: see Cust, *Charles I*, p. 390; M. Toynbee and P. Young, *The Battle of Cropredy Bridge* (Kineton, 1970), pp. 2–3;

Walker, *Historical Discourses,* preface. The only difference from Rupert's plan was the addition of a large body of musketeers. This would have been the responsibility of Sir Jacob Astley as major general of foot, but it is odd that Astley receives scarcely a mention in Walker's description of the events of 3 and 4 June whilst being lavishly praised for his defence of the passes over the Cherwell between 31 May and 2 June: see Walker, *Historical Discourses,* pp. 16–17.

47. CSP Domestic 1644, pp. 206, 211, 214; Walker, *Historical Discourses,* pp. 19–22; Symonds, 'Diaries', p. 8.

48. CSP Domestic 1644, p. 198. The order, agreed in committee on Monday, required the battle to be fought 'this week'.

49. CSP Domestic 1644, p. 234; Lords Journals, VI, pp. 590–1.

50. Clarendon, *History of the Rebellion,* VIII, para. 52.

51. CSP Domestic 1644, pp. 206, 214–15, 219 (Waller to the Committee, 6, 7, 10 June). Only in the final letter of the series did he suggest that his army and Essex's should swop places, as the Committee had now ordered him into the West Country: see ibid., p. 238.

52. CSP Domestic 1644, pp. 226, 238, 246, 247 (letters dated 15–18 June).

53. This letter, signed by Sir William Balfour, Philip Skippon and Lord Robartes, several colonels and one of the commissars, shows very clearly that the decision of the Council of War which agreed to the two armies pursuing the courses that they did had been a unanimous one. As far as Waller's officers were concerned, the deciding factor was probably that the bulk of their troops, who came from London and the counties of Kent, Surrey and Sussex, would be less than keen to be campaigning in the far south-west, leaving their homes and families open to enemy attack: see BL, Harleian MSS 166, f. 86.

54. BL, Harleian MS166, f. 72 BL, Additional MSS 31117, ff. 146–7.

55. Lords Journals, VI, p. 620. The letter would have been much fiercer had Essex's friends in the House of Lords not succeeded in toning down the language. This explains why it was not sent to the earl until 6 July, a month after he had disregarded the Committee's orders. Rushworth reproduces an earlier draft dated 19 June, see *Historical Collections,* V, pp. 683–4.

56. Others have been adamant that it was. See, for example, Young and Holmes, *English Civil Wars,* p. 184.

57. CSP Domestic 1644, pp. 237–8, 238–9, 243, 247; HMC, Appendix to the Fourth Report, p. 267.

58. CSP Domestic, pp. 251, 261–2; Lords Journals, VI, pp. 602–3; BL, Harleian MSS 166, ff. 85, 86. In his replies to the Committee's letters in late June and July, Waller made no mention of Essex's successes in the west, whilst rejoicing in the victory at Marston Moor: see CSP Domestic 1644, p. 324.

Chapter 9: The Marston Moor Campaign

1. P. Wenham, *The Great and Close Siege of York* (Kineton, 1970), p. 12, quoting from a letter of Lord Fairfax written on 20 April. Sir Thomas Fairfax, however, considered that the blockade of the city was not complete even after the arrival of Manchester's infantry: see 'Short Memorials', p. 437.

2. CSP Domestic 1644, p. 202.

3. CSP Domestic 1644, pp. 130, 149; Wenham, *Siege of York,* p. 12 (Lord Fairfax's letter of 24 April 1644); Bodleian, Firth MSS C7, ff. 72, 77.

4. Firth, ed., 'Prince Rupert's Marches', pp. 765–6; Malbon, 'Memorial', p. 126; Commons Journals, III, p. 508. If Rupert had intended to advance on York via Lancashire, his march from Whitchurch would have taken him in a north-easterly direction to the bridge over the Mersey at Stockport. Instead he marched east-south-east to Newcastle-under-Lyme. As the Northern Horse were in the south Pennines rather than the middle Trent valley by that time, it seems likely that the royalist garrison at Sheffield was to act as the rallying point; see Wanklyn and Jones, *A Military History,* pp. 174–5.

5. Warburton, *Memoirs of Prince Rupert,* II, p. 415.

6. Ibid., pp. 438–9.

7. They were caught on the wrong side of the River Ouse and their bridge of boats was in enemy hands: see CSP Domestic 1644, p. 287; BL, Thomason Tracts, E2 (1).

8. CSP Domestic 1644, p. 311; HMC, Appendix to the Fourth Report, p. 268.

9. BL, Additional MSS 62084b, para. 55; Slingsby, *Diary*, pp. 112–13; Sir Hugh Cholmley, 'Memoirs and Memorials', ed. J. Baines, *Yorkshire Archaeological Society, Records Section* CLIII (2000), pp. 135–6.

10. So that the royalist forces were as strong as they could possibly be: see Cholmley, 'Memoirs and Memorials', p. 136.

11. BL, Thomason Tracts, E54 (19).

12. BL, Additional MSS 62084b, para. 55; BL, Thomason Tracts E2 (1), E54 (19); Bodleian, Clarendon MSS 23, 1764.

13. Cholmley, 'Memoirs and Memorials', pp. 136–7; Firth, ed., *Memoirs of the Duke of Newcastle*, p. 40.

14. Cholmley, 'Memoirs and Memorials', p. 137; Shropshire CRO, 455/277.

15. BL, Thomason Tracts, E2 (1); Cholmley, 'Memoirs and Memorials', pp. 136–7.

16. BL, Additional MSS 16370, f. 64.

17. Bodleian, Clarendon MSS 23, 1805 (notes on the war in the north, 1643–4); Cholmley, 'Memoirs and Memorials', pp. 136–7.

18. Although De Gomme's depiction of the way in which the two armies were deployed at the start of the battle shows the ditch as a continuous line, several accounts written straight after the battle show clearly that it was not: see BL, Additional MSS 16370, f. 64; Shropshire CRO, 455/277; BL, Thomason Tracts E2 (1), E54 (19); Bodleian, Clarendon MSS 1764. Nevertheless it is surprising that there was not some kind of barrier between the moorland and the fields to prevent animals grazing on the moor causing damage to the crops growing on the slopes of Braham Hill.

19. BL, Additional MSS 16370, f. 64; Cholmley, 'Memoirs and Memorials', p. 136; Shropshire CRO, 455/277.

20. See, for example, Roberts, *Cromwell's War Machine: The New Model Army 1645–1660* (Barnsley, 2005), pp. 140–3, 152–4.

21. How Rupert intended to respond to an enemy attack is far from certain other than that his cavalry were not to move forward to meet the enemy as they advanced: see BL, Additional MSS 62084b, para. 56. The most likely scenario is that massed ranks of musketeers stationed close to the boundary between the moor and the hill and between the cavalry regiments were intended to slow down the enemy charge. Rupert's cavalry would then presumably counter-attack, chase them from the battlefield, and then turn on the enemy infantry. The role of the cavalry reserve was to attack the enemy infantry or their reserve cavalry depending on which posed the greater threat to the success of the battle plan.

22. P. Newman, *The Battle of Marston Moor 1644* (Chichester, 1981), pp. 47, 49–50, 55.

23. All that Leven had done to offset the inconveniences of the position on Braham Hill was some heavy landscape gardening. The very narrow front that he could present to the enemy at midday was ideal for facing a royalist attack, but it now made for difficulties. With Rupert's forces drawn up in the conventional pattern for a battle fought in open country, with brigades of foot flanked by horse, part of the allied army would need to redeploy once it reached the moor. However, redeployment in the face of an enemy already deployed was highly dangerous. Pioneers were therefore ordered to remove various hedge lines, thus widening the allied frontage on Braham Hill, but they had not done quite enough. Although Cromwell's cavalry on the left wing were able to charge straight down the hill into the ranks of the enemy, Sir Thomas Fairfax's on the other wing would still have to deploy when it reached the moor, and in a place where there were many gorse bushes to impede the redeployment and a heavy concentration of royalist musketeers.

24. At the Tockwith end of the front line were Eastern Association regiments, but it is uncertain whether the next formation was Scottish or Yorkshire foot.

25. P. Young, *Marston Moor 1644* (Kineton, 1970), plate 21; BL, Thomason Tracts, E54 (19). The earl of Manchester's regiment, which he himself commanded, was brigaded with Scottish regiments in the third line: see Rushworth, ed., *Historical Collections*, V, p. 633. This explains why he was not with Major General Crawford and the rest of the Eastern Association infantry.

26. Warwickshire CRO, 2017, C10, f. 135; J. Sanford, ed., Appendix to *The Great Rebellion* (London, 1858), p. 612; Shropshire CRO, 455/277.

27. BL, Thomason Tracts, E2 (1); Young, *Marston Moor 1644*, p. 252.

28. Robert Douglas's diary, an extract from which is reproduced in C. Terry, *Life and Campaigns of Alexander Leslie, Earl of Leven* (London, 1899), p. 282.

29. BL, Harleian MSS 166, ff. 87–8; BL, Thomason Tracts, E2 (1).

30. Sanford, ed., *The Great Rebellion*, p. 612; Shropshire CRO, 445/277.

31. Ibid; J. Thurlow, *A Collection of State Papers of John Thurlow Esquire, Secretary to the Council of State* (London, 1742), I, p. 38; *Mercurius Aulicus*, p. 1,085. The general shape of the battle is reasonably easy to understand, but much of the detail is problematic as some of the evidence is contradictory: see Wanklyn, *Decisive Battles*, chs 10 and 11. More recent interpretations of the archaeological evidence give no grounds for confidence: see P. Newman and P. Roberts, *The Battle of Marston Moor 1644* (2nd edn, Pickering, 2004). Large concentrations of musket balls on Braham Hill are taken as proof of a fire-fight in the closing phase of the battle for which there is no documentary evidence. The musket balls discovered there are likely to be from barrels broken open by royalist cavalry as they pillaged the allied artillery train.

32. Keen-eyed officers of the Northern army saw them fleeing from the moor at the very start of the action and wrote in their memoirs that all Rupert's horse fled immediately after contact with the enemy: see Cholmley, 'Memoirs and Memorials', p. 137; Slingsby, *Diary*, p. 114; Firth, ed., *Memoirs of the Duke of Newcastle*, p. 40; BL, Thomason Tracts, E2 (4). This was an incorrect inference, as is shown by accounts of the fight on the royalist right written by parliamentarian officers immediately after the battle: see Shropshire CRO, 445/277; BL, Harleian MSS 166, ff. 87–8.

33. Marcus Trevor's regiment on the left of the royalist first line probably caught Cromwell's men in the flank. The fact that the Eastern Association horse did not break and run may account for the nickname Ironsides that Rupert gave them after the battle. However, by leaving their position in the battle line Trevor's regiment left a gap which would have given the Eastern Association infantry the opportunity to overlap the flank of the royalist infantry, a point made in one of the Scottish narratives of the battle: see BL, Thomason Tracts, E54 (19). Second, Trevor may have been the man to wound Oliver Cromwell and force him to leave the battlefield, but the provenance of the source cannot be checked as the reference cited by Austin Woolrych is incorrect: see *Battles of the English Civil Wars* (London, 1961), p. 74.

34. There has been enormous debate amongst historians about the progress and length of time of the fight between Cromwell and Rupert's cavalry, and this is not surprising given the discrepancies between the contemporary and near contemporary sources. However, there is little doubt that the melee lasted for quite a time, and that it was resolved by some action on the part of the Scottish cavalry reserves.

35. BL, Thomason Tracts, E54 (19). For the circumstances, see note 33 above.

36. See above, pp. 103–4.

37. Those that managed to break through the enemy lines under Sir Thomas Fairfax's personal command lost contact with the battle altogether as they pursued the royalist regiment that had been denying the flank: see Fairfax, 'Short Memorials', pp. 438–9; Bodleian, Fairfax MSS 36, ff. 15–16.

38. Terry, *Life and Campaigns of Leven*, pp. 282–3; Young, *Marston Moor*, plate 40 (Major General Lumsden's account written at York on 5 July and printed in Edinburgh); BL, Thomason Tracts, E54 (19), E343 (6).

39. BL, Thomason Tracts, E54 (19), E2 (1); Young, *Marston Moor*, plate 40. What was apparently missing, in the final charge at least, was supporting fire from the royalist infantry. This should have been decisive in breaking up the Scottish brigade. Its musketeers could not have met barrage with barrage as the cavalry had forced them to seek shelter within their stand of pikes, and they were unlikely to be able to do anything other than fire at will, a highly ineffective way of delivering a barrage. Possibly the royalist infantry facing Lindsay and Maitland's regiments had already fled from the field by this stage in the battle: see BL, Additional MSS 16370, f. 64.

40. BL, Thomason Tracts, E2 (1).
41. Bodleian, Carte MSS 12, f. 212. John Somerville makes a similar criticism of the prince: see Young, *Marston Moor*, p. 261.
42. Bodleian, Carte MSS 12, f. 212 (Byron to Ormond, Liverpool, 3 August 1644).
43. Firth, ed., *Memoirs of the Marquis of Newcastle*, p. 39.
44. Ibid., pp. 40–1.
45. C.V. Wedgwood, *The King's War* (London, 1958), pp. 338–9.
46. BL, Lansdown MSS 988, f. 205.
47. BL, Lansdown MSS 988, ff. 205–6; CSP Domestic 1644–5, pp. 21, 55, 57, 65, 82.
48. Given the range of reconstructions of the event to be found in recent books on Marston Moor, I have deliberately adopted cautious language. My hunch is that Fairfax was off the field, having sustained several wounds in the cavalry engagement on the other wing, that Leslie and Crawford devised the plan, and that Cromwell accepted it, having returned to the field after treatment to the wound to his neck. This is the only explanation I can give for Somerville's assertion that Cromwell submitted to orders from Leslie: see Young, *Marston Moor*, p. 260.
49. In this they were probably not assisted by what was left of the second line of the Scottish infantry, as these were preoccupied in rescuing Lindsay's brigade from Sir Charles Lucas's regiments of horse.
50. The confused accounts of the last stand of the Whitecoats are to be found in BL, Thomason Tracts E54 (19); Firth, ed., *Memoirs of the Duke of Newcastle*, pp. 40–1; Young, *Marston Moor* (Somerville extract), pp. 261, 137 (testament of William Lilley).
51. Between 3,000 and 4,500, as opposed to about 2,000, captives, see BL, Harleian MSS 166, ff. 87–8; BL, Thomason Tracts E2 (1, 14), E54 (19).
52. Watson's account of a formal action on the same ground as the initial fight between Goring and Sir Thomas Fairfax seems unlikely: see Shropshire CRO 445/277. Watson was a master of spin, which he used to ingratiate himself with Cromwell, as shown by his highly biased account of the Second Battle of Newbury: see CSP Domestic 1644–5, pp. 149–50. Somerville takes a very different line: see Young, *Marston Moor*, p. 261; and other allied accounts are non-committal or too generalised to be of any use in deciding one way or the other. It is, however, odd that they do not mention the episode if it sealed the victory. Also, if things had been as Watson portrays them, it would have been impossible for so many royalist horse to be on the fringes of the battlefield well after the battle had been lost: see Cholmley, 'Memoirs and Memorials', p. 137; BL, Lansdown MSS 988, f. 206; *Mercurius Aulicus*, p. 1,085; Carte, *Original Letters and Papers*, I, pp. 57–8.
53. BL, Lansdown MSS 988, f. 206; Cholmley, 'Memoirs and Memorials', p. 137.
54. Slingsby, *Diary*, p. 120; Cholmley, 'Memoirs and Memorials', p. 139.

Chapter 10: The Generals in Jeopardy: Cropredy Bridge and Lostwithiel

1. CSP Domestic 1644, pp. 235–7, 242, 247; BL, Thomason Tracts, E2 (16).
2. Symonds, 'Diaries', pp. 14–15; Warburton, *Memoirs of Prince Rupert*, II, p. 419; Walker, *Historical Discourses*, pp. 24–5.
3. CSP Domestic 1644, p. 267; Symonds, 'Diaries', p. 18; Walker, *Historical Discourses*, p. 28.
4. CSP Domestic 1644, p. 247.
5. Walker, *Historical Discourses*, pp. 24–5.
6. Warburton, *Memoirs of Prince Rupert*, II, p. 419.
7. CSP Domestic 1644, pp. 247, 252–3, 257, 261–2, 272.
8. CSP Domestic 1644, pp. 253–4, 261–2, 266–7, 267–8, 277, 279.
9. Walker, *Historical Discourses*, pp. 26–8; Warburton, *Memoirs of Prince Rupert*, II, pp. 435–6; CSP Domestic 1644, pp. 279–80.
10. CSP Domestic 1644, p. 290.
11. CSP Domestic 1644, p. 293; Roe, 'Colonel Birch', p. 12; Warburton, *Memoirs of Prince Rupert*, II, pp. 472–3.
12. Roe, 'Colonel Birch', p. 12; CSP Domestic 1644, p. 293.
13. Roe, 'Colonel Birch', p. 12.

14. Walker, *Historical Discourses*, pp. 30–3; Symonds, 'Diaries', pp. 23–4; Roe, 'Colonel Birch', p. 13; CSP Domestic 1644, pp. 293, 316; BL, Thomason Tracts, E2 (16).

15. Roe, 'Colonel Birch', p. 13; CSP Domestic 1644, pp. 293, 298; Warburton, *Memoirs of Prince Rupert*, II, pp. 472–3.

16. Walker, *Historical Discourses*, p. 35.

17. CSP Domestic 1644, pp. 298, 301, 309, 310–11.

18. CSP Domestic 1644, p. 278.

19. BL, Thomason Tracts, E2 (16).

20. CSP Domestic 1644, pp. 301, 310, 324, 326–7.

21. These are the words Gardiner copied down from the Committee's letterbook. The précis given in the Calendar of State Papers domestic is subtly different.

22. The myth was begun by S.R. Gardiner: see *Great Civil War*, II, p. 5.

23. Adair, *Cheriton*, pp. 39–45, 144.

24. CSP Domestic 1644, pp. 333, 357, 365, 370.

25. CSP Domestic 1644, pp. 347, 358, 371, 373.

26. CSP Domestic 1644, p. 380. On 16 July the Committee had recommended that Waller should not be sent into the west, only for the decision to be overruled by Parliament the following day: see ibid., pp. 353, 356.

27. CSP Domestic 1644, p. 373.

28. Ibid., p. 382.

29. Walker, *Historical Discourses*, p. 39. The dispatch no longer survives, though it is possible that the account of the battle in *Mercurius Aulicus* makes use of it. Something may also be gleaned from Lord Digby's reply which shows that Rupert blamed General King for not sending Newcastle's infantry to Marston Moor in time to attack the enemy on 2 July. The report was probably not as positive as that of Sir Richard Byron, the governor of Newark, who wrote of Marston Moor being described by the enemy as an 'Edgehill battle': see *Mercurius Aulicus*, pp. 1,083–6; Warburton, *Memoirs of Prince Rupert*, II, pp. 475, 476; HMC, R.R. Hastings MSS, II, p. 129.

30. Walker, *Historical Discourses*, pp. 26, 35, 37; BL, Additional MSS 18981, f. 203.

31. See above, pp. 53, 245, n.17.

32. Walker, *Historical Discourses*, pp. 37–8, 47; BL, Additional MSS 18981, 203, 208.

33. CSP Domestic 1644, pp. 303, 358. Symonds, 'Diaries', pp. 97–8, reproduces a daily log of the marches of the earl of Essex's army from Beaconsfield to Lostwithiel, which was captured in Cornwall.

34. CSP Domestic 1644, p. 315; BL, Thomason Tracts, E2 (15).

35. M. Stoyle, *From Deliverance and Destruction: Rebellion and Civil War in an English City* (Exeter, 1996), pp. 92–3.

36. Walker, *Historical Discourses*, pp. 41–2; Bampfield, *Apologie*, p. 44. The king had sent messages telling Maurice of his intention to pursue Essex into the West Country from Evesham and from Bath, but the first never reached him and the prince did not receive the second until after returning to Exeter: see Walker, *Historical Discourses*, pp. 37, 39; Bampfield, *Apologie*, p. 44.

37. CSP Domestic 1644, p. 358.

38. Lords Journals, VI, p. 608; CSP Domestic 1644, pp. 288, 304, 351, 420, 437–8, 463–4, 473–4. It was not because distance made operational instructions from the centre out of date or positively dangerous. The Committee had tried to manage operations against Prince Rupert in the north of England during June with some success. Essex in west Somerset and east Devonshire was closer to London, and in the month following the relief of Lyme there would have been no problems in sending him orders that reflected the reality on the ground. For the last six weeks of the campaign, however, the passage of letters back and forth was bound to have been slower, as the final stage of communication was by sea from Weymouth to Plymouth or Fowey.

39. CSP Domestic 1644, pp. 304, 355; Lords Journals, VI, p. 608.

40. This may help to explain Essex's lack of intelligence concerning the movements of the enemy in late July and early August.

41. M. Coate, ed., 'An Original Diary of Colonel Robert Bennett of Hexworthy', *Devon and Cornwall Notes and Queries* 18 (1935), pp. 258–9.
42. CSP Domestic 1644, p. 358.
43. Walker, *Historical Discourses*, p. 42; Bampfield, *Apologie*, p. 44. See also Wanklyn and Jones, *A Military History*, pp. 193–4.
44. In a letter written from Tavistock on 26 July, Essex stated that he had been advised to invade Cornwall: see CSP Domestic 1644, p. 379. This form of words may provide evidence of a major row in the Council of War over whether or not to cross the Tamar, described briefly by Thomas Juxon in his journal: see K. Lindley and D. Scott, eds, 'Thomas Juxon's Journal 1644–47', *Camden Society*, 5th series XIII (1999), p. 56. However, the row may only have been London gossip. There is no record of it in correspondence of the time. In addition, Juxon does not appear to have written up his journal in its final form until some time after the event, see Lindley and Scott, eds, 'Thomas Juxon's Journal', pp. 16–17. He may therefore have been recording the explanations given by Essex's officers and men when they returned to London in late November.
45. Whitelock, *Memorials*, p. 88.
46. Coate, *Cornwall in the Civil War*, p. 139.
47. Ibid., pp. 398–9; BL, Harleian MSS 166, f. 96.
48. CSP Domestic 1644, pp. 379–80, 390, 398–9; BL, Harleian MSS 166, f. 96; CSP Domestic 1644, pp. 398–9. The letter informing the earl that Waller would not be operating at full strength, dated 19 July, is not recorded in the Committee's minute book. It was not received until the very end of the month, by which time Essex's army had reached Bodmin.
49. Coate, *Cornwall in the Civil War*, p. 145.
50. Cornwall CRO, 1/1058; Symonds, 'Diaries', pp. 44–6.
51. CSP Domestic 1644, p. 399.
52. Burne and Young, *The Great Civil War*, p. 173.
53. Ibid., p. 179. Richard Cust is more sanguine, attributing most of the decisions to the advice of the military council: see *Charles I*, p. 390. Sir Richard Cave certainly thought that the old team of Culpeper and Digby dominated the council after Wilmot's dismissal on 8 August, claiming in a letter to Prince Rupert that 'their counsels prevail very much': see Cornwall CRO, 1/1053.
54. Clarendon, *History of the Rebellion*, VIII, paras 93, 103–17.
55. Walker, *Historical Discourses*, pp. 57–8; Warburton, *Memoirs of Prince Rupert*, III, pp. 11–12; Cornwall CRO, 1/1058; Symonds, 'Diaries', p. 58. Nothing was done about closing these conduits until 26 August.
56. Walker, *Historical Discourses*, p. 53; Whitelock, *Memorials*, p. 98; Snow, *Essex the Rebel*, pp. 445–6; *Mercurius Aulicus*, pp. 1,124–6.
57. This was something that Parliament had reserved exclusively to itself from the start of hostilities: see above, p. 9.
58. The dismissal of Wilmot might have occasioned a mutiny but it led to nothing worse than a written protest from the officers of the 'Old Horse', the cavalry who had fought under Wilmot at Edgehill and Newbury. The new cavalry general's interpersonal skills, and the decision to allow Wilmot's own regiment still to be described as such, probably did the trick. It is also possible that the detail of the king's proposals to the earl of Essex, which included a plea for peace signed by the officers of the king's and the western army, suggested to many of those in the know that Charles had taken over the best part of Wilmot's political programme. See Whitelock, *Memorials*, pp. 102–4; Cornwall CRO, 1/1054; Warburton, *Memoirs of Prince Rupert*, III, p. 12; Symonds, 'Diaries', pp. 106–9; Clarendon, *History of the Rebellion*, VIII, para. 96.
59. Warburton, *Memoirs of Prince Rupert*, III, p. 12 (Digby to Rupert, 15 August 1644).
60. The negative effects are described in a letter written to Prince Rupert on 1 September: see Cornwall CRO, 1/1058. It has been alleged that the writer was Lord Hopton, who had recently joined the king's army as general of artillery, but the absence of any reference to Bristol where Rupert was governor and Hopton his deputy makes the attribution unlikely: see pp. 248 n.16, 255 n.19.

61. Coate, *Cornwall in the Civil War*, p. 145.
62. Walker, *Historical Discourses*, pp. 71–2; Symonds, 'Diaries', p. 62; *Mercurius Aulicus*, p. 1,150.
63. A. Miller, ed., 'Joseph Jane's Account of Cornwall during the Civil War', *English Historical Review* XC (1975), p. 101. Sir Lewis Dyve made a similar point in a letter written to Prince Rupert on 4 September in which he referred to 'slackness' in the high command: see Cornwall CRO, 1/1062.
64. Walker, *Historical Discourses*, pp. 69–70; Rushworth, ed., *Historical Collections*, V, pp. 708–9; Whitelock, *Memorials*, pp. 102–3.
65. The day after the surrender, the king wrote as follows: 'had our success been either deferred or of any other kind, only a direct miracle could have saved us': see S.R. Gardiner, ed., 'The Fortescue Papers', *Camden Society*, new series I (1871), pp. 218–19.
66. Rushworth, ed., *Historical Collections*, V, pp. 701–3.
67. *Maseres Tracts*, I, p. 204; Bodleian, Don MSS d.57, ff. 7–8; Whitelock, *Memorials*, pp. 102–3.
68. Rushworth, *Historical Collections*, V, p. 699; Bodleian, Tanner MSS 61, f. 149. However, by late September the honeymoon was over. The failure of some of the promised equipment to arrive saw an indignant Essex reverting to his customary sarcasm in letters to the Committee of Both Kingdoms: see CSP Domestic 1644, pp. 530, 532; 1644–5, pp. 8–9, 26, 35, 45; BL, Harleian MSS 166, f. 133 (Essex to the Committee of Both Kingdoms, 30 September 1644).
69. CSP Domestic 1644, p. 436.
70. See, for example, the contents of successive letters in late July and August (ibid., pp. 420, 437–8, 463, 473, 486).
71. Ibid., pp. 354, 379–80.
72. Whitelock, *Memorials*, p. 103; Lords Journals, VII, p. 25; Symonds, 'Diaries', p. 67.
73. Rushworth, ed., *Historical Collections*, V, p. 702: BL, Thomason Tracts, E8 (22), E21 (34); Whitelock, *Memorials*, p. 105.
74. Snow, *Essex the Rebel*, p. 452; Adamson, 'The Triumph of Oligarchy', in Kyle and Peacey, *Parliament at Work*, eds, pp. 115–21.

Chapter 11: The March to Newbury: Saving the South

1. He was killed at the siege of Lichfield in March 1643: see above, p. 47.
2. Holmes, *Eastern Association*, pp. 177, 197–204.
3. HMC, Appendix to the Eighth Report, pp. 60, 61; W. Abbott, ed., *The Writings and Speeches of Oliver Cromwell* (4 vols, Cambridge, Mass., 1937), I, p. 292. It should, however, be recognised that if resources were in short supply, there were sound military reasons for discriminating against Cromwell's cavalry, which had nothing to do with politics. If the royalist armies were to be brought to battle, it was essential that the infantry regiments in the Eastern Association army remained as strong as possible given the decline in the number of foot soldiers in Essex's and Waller's armies since the end of June. This did not apply to cavalry and dragoons. Parliament's armies in the south had plenty of horse.
4. I have deliberately discounted the evidence given by witnesses against Manchester in the row with Cromwell that began as the campaign ended: see M. Wanklyn, 'A General Much Maligned: The Generalship of the Earl of Manchester, July to November 1644', *War in History* 14:2 (2007), pp. 145–6.
5. CSP Domestic 1644, pp. 282, 396, 405, 414, 428–31, 438–9, 445, 447–8, 481; Commons Journals, III, pp. 582–3.
6. Holmes, *Eastern Association*, p. 198.
7. BL, Thomason Tracts, E22 (10). It is also significant that lack of moral fibre was not a charge levelled against the general in the evidence presented by Cromwell and his allies concerning the earl's conduct at the Second Battle of Newbury. A related argument is that the upsurge in religious conflict in his army produced a mental state verging on despair and with it caution close to paralysis. Manchester was also terrified that if there was no accommodation with the king, anarchy would follow: see Holmes, *Eastern Association*, pp. 198–9. However, the only source is Ashe, and Ashe only went so far as to say that his master worried about the

deleterious effect on the war effort if religious disputes escalated. However, the best remedy for both types of anxiety was a quick and decisive victory on the battlefield, and the least effective was doing nothing.

8. The only evidence of this not tainted by prejudice against the earl is in Ashe's defence of his conduct, but in this case, too, Holmes has misinterpreted the text by taking a passage out of context. The first sentence of the paragraph claims that Manchester was totally lacking in political ambition, stating on several occasions that he would give half of his estates if a godly reformation could be accomplished and with it peace. He would also 'gladly betake himself unto a country life, and leave all other contentments to the world'. This is then followed by the statement 'how frequent, how constant have been his breathings after peace', but that this could only be accomplished 'with the perfection of that Reformation which is hopefully begun'. All he wanted was that the wars would end 'in a comfortable peace'. The word comfortable does not mean exactly what it does today. Instead it means conformable (i.e., in conformity with his war aims, namely the completion of the godly reformation): see Holmes, *Eastern Association*, p. 198; BL, Thomason Tracts, E22 (10).

9. See, for example, P. Gaunt, *Oliver Cromwell* (London, 1996), pp. 58–60, 248–9; S. Robbins, *God's General* (Stroud, 2003), pp. 62–3, 65–7; B. Coward, *Oliver Cromwell* (London, 1991), pp. 95–6.

10. BL, Thomason Tracts, E400 (5).

11. Wanklyn, 'A General Much Maligned', pp. 145–6.

12. A. Cotton, 'Cromwell and the Self-Denying Ordinance', *History* LXII (1977), p. 230.

13. CSP Domestic 1644, p. 359.

14. Juxon, 'Journal', p. 67.

15. See above, pp. 59, 81.

16. HMC, Appendix to the Eighth Report, p. 61 (John Crewe, a civilian member of the Committee of Both Kingdoms to the earl, 9 September 1644).

17. He had even acquired considerable experience of siege warfare at King's Lynn in September 1643, at Lincoln in May 1644, and at York in June and July.

18. CSP Domestic 1644, pp. 223–65, 359–60.

19. These have been taken on board uncritically by twentieth-century writers. Holmes's appraisal of the earl of Manchester, for example, is based almost entirely on what his opponents had to say about him: see *Eastern Association*, pp. 197–8, 226, 281, 289. The same is true of Gentles's assessment in the *ODNB*.

20. The fullest version of his defence delivered in the House of Lords is in the papers of Sir Robert Harley, one of the leaders of the Presbyterian grouping in the Commons: see BL, Loan MSS, 29/123 Misc. 31.

21. Having preserved his reputation as a committed Parliamentarian, he continued to attend the Committee of Both Kingdoms, where he took an active part in planning and resourcing the military operation that ended in victory at Naseby. He also resumed his role as speaker of the House of Lords. Ever his own man, he sided with the army in its confrontation with Parliament in the summer of 1647 and he went on to play a major role in Committee at Derby House, the 'war cabinet' which managed the Second Civil War. See below, pp. 156, 195.

22. CSP Domestic 1644–5, pp. 146–7.

23. See Juxon, 'Journal', p. 59; Robert Baillie, 'Letters and Journals 1637–1662', in D. Laing, ed., *Bannatyne Club* II, p. 229.

24. Baillie, 'Letters and Journals', 1644, pp. 366, 389, 405; Bodleian, Carte MSS 74, ff. 159–60 (journal of the marches of Colonel Edward Montagu's regiment). Only in the case of Tickhill Castle was a junior commander apparently hauled over the coals for showing too much initiative, but we cannot tell the extent to which John Lilburne, the future Leveller, inflated a ticking-off for insubordination into something much more serious in order to assist Cromwell in his case against Manchester: see CSP Domestic 1644–5, pp. 148–9. However, in his letter reporting its capture to the Committee, Manchester made no mention of any misbehaviour on Lilburne's part: see Baillie, 'Letters and Journals', 1644, p. 380.

25. CSP Domestic 1644, pp. 375, 406, 409. Rupert was thought to have at least 7,000 men under his command, and Lord Fairfax was particularly fearful: see Mark, Lord Napier, *Memorials of Montrose and his Times* (2 vols, Maitland Club, Aberdeen, 1848–50), II, p. 140 (Lord Fairfax to the Earl of Leven, 15 August 1644).

26. CSP Domestic 1644, p. 421; J. Bruce and D. Masson, eds, 'Manchester's Quarrel: Documents Relating to the Quarrel between the Earl of Manchester and Oliver Cromwell', *Camden Society*, new series XII, pp. 11–12. The précis in the Calendar have been checked against the full transcripts given by Bruce and Masson. Only when they differ is the Bruce and Masson reference given in the notes.

27. Abbott, ed., *Writings and Speeches*, I, p. 304; CSP Domestic, 1644, pp. 417–18. This group, if it did not include Cromwell (and there is no evidence that he was absent from the army at the time), certainly included his close associates, as the appraisal contained a detailed breakdown of the operational difficulties of managing a large body of horse in enemy quarters, should Rupert send his cavalry into Wales and they were required to follow him: see Bruce and Masson, 'Manchester's Quarrel', p. 9.

28. CSP Domestic 1644, p. 468.

29. CSP Domestic 1644, pp. 459–60, 474.

30. CSP Domestic 1644, pp. 474, 478.

31. Lords Journals, VI, p. 699.

32. Ibid., pp. 699–700.

33. For a full defence of Manchester's behaviour between July and November 1644, see Wanklyn, 'A General Much Maligned', pp. 133–56. The narrative of events presented here has, however, been updated in certain respects. The end result strengthens rather than weakens the original argument.

34. CSP Domestic 1644, pp. 468, 473, 474, 481, 499, 517; Bodleian, Carte MSS 74, f. 160; Lords Journals, VI, pp. 701, 707.

35. Cromwell and Crawford had also been to London, as Manchester mentions that both of them appeared before the Committee of Both Kingdoms to resolve their differences: see BL, Loan MSS 28/123 Misc. 31.

36. CSP Domestic 1644, pp. 504, 505, 521.

37. Commons Journals, III, p. 635; Lords Journals, VI, p. 711; CSP Domestic 1644, pp. 520, 523, 526.

38. CSP Domestic 1644, p. 533.

39. Holmes, *Eastern Association*, pp. 236, 238; CSP Domestic 1644, pp. 539, 540, 542; 1644–5, p. 58; Luke, 'Letter Books', 1644–5, pp. 24, 27, 29, 340, 345, 348. Waller claimed that the royalists were not 10,000 strong, and this probably increased the determination of the Committee that the earl of Manchester should advance into Dorset, but some of the king's brigades were missing and Waller had every reason to underestimate their strength.

40. CSP Domestic 1644, pp. 521, 524, 533, 537, 542, 545. He was right. None fought at Newbury.

41. See above, pp. 70–1, 73.

42. CSP Domestic 1644, p. 545; 1644–5, p. 13.

43. CSP Domestic 1644, pp. 529, 535, 540, 545. The brigade included the two regiments, which had fought so well at the First Battle of Newbury, and the Tower Hamlets' regiment, which had been at Cheriton and defended the bridge at Cropredy: see BL, Thomason Tracts, E40 (1), E69 (15); Roe, 'Colonel Birch', p. 13.

44. CSP Domestic 1644–5, pp. 9, 16, 26.

45. CSP Domestic 1644, pp. 480, 491–2, 497, 501.

46. CSP Domestic 1644, pp. 520, 530; 1644–5, pp. 5, 28–9; BL, Harleian MSS 166, f. 133.

47. CSP Domestic 1644–5, pp. 39–40.

48. The larger figure was Oliver Cromwell's estimation: see Bruce and Masson, 'Manchester's Quarrel', p. 85. Other sources suggest 1,000 fewer horse and just over 1,000 fewer foot: see CSP Domestic 1644–5, p. 56; Holmes, *Eastern Association*, p. 238; S. Peachey and A. Turton, *Old Robin's Foot* (Leigh-on-Sea, 1987), p. 17. The king's generals had about 11,000 troops divided pretty evenly between horse and foot.

Chapter 12: The Second and Third Battles of Newbury

1. Walker, *Historical Discourses*, pp. 86–102; HMC, Hodgkin MSS, pp. 99–103; House of Lords Record Office, 3639, ff. 1–15. Barnstable had surrendered voluntarily in September.
2. Walker, *Historical Discourses*, pp. 98–103.
3. Warburton, *Memoirs of Prince Rupert*, III, p. 27.
4. Walker, *Historical Discourses*, pp. 105–6; BL, Additional MSS 30377, f. 2 (Digby to Rupert, 27 October 1644).
5. Walker, *Historical Discourses*, pp. 108–10; *Mercurius Aulicus*, p. 1,232; Hamper, ed., *Diary of Sir William Dugdale*, p. 74; Luke, 'Letter Books', pp. 671, 673.
6. CSP Domestic 1644–5, pp. 60, 62.
7. CSP Domestic 1644–5, p. 73; HMC, Braye MSS, p. 155; Luke, 'Letter Books', p. 363.
8. Edmund Ludlow, *Memoirs*, I, pp. 102–3; CSP Domestic 1644–5, p. 73.
9. CSP Domestic 1644, pp. 62, 65, 67; HMC, Braye MSS, p. 155.
10. BL, Thomason Tracts, E14 (16); CSP Domestic 1644–5, p. 76; Bruce and Masson, 'Manchester's Quarrel', p. 49; Rushworth, ed., *Historical Collections*, V, p. 722.
11. Bruce and Masson, 'Manchester's Quarrel', p. 63.
12. This is implied in Simeon Ashe's account: see BL, Thomason Tracts, E22 (10).
13. Rushworth, ed., *Historical Collections*, V, pp. 722–3; Luke, 'Letter Books', p. 366.
14. Walker, *Historical Discourses*, pp. 111–12; *Mercurius Aulicus*, p. 1,234; BL, Harleian MSS 166, f. 140; CSP Domestic 1644–5, p. 75.
15. This is very clear from the map that accompanied the Speenhamland enclosure award: see Berkshire CRO, Q/P116B/28/22/1.
16. Rushworth, ed., *Historical Collections*, V, pp. 722–3; Walker, *Historical Discourses*, pp. 111–12; BL, Harleian MSS 166, f. 140.
17. Symonds, 'Diaries', p. 145; Walker, *Historical Discourses*, p. 112.
18. Later than 4.00 p.m.: see BL, Thomason Tracts, E22 (10); half an hour after sunset: see Abbott, ed., *Writings and Speeches*, I, pp. 306–7; about 3.00 p.m.: see Walker, *Historical Discourses*, p. 111.
19. Walker, *Historical Discourses* pp. 113–14.
20. BL, Thomason Tracts E22 (10); CSP Domestic 1644–5, pp. 149, 150, 159.
21. Wanklyn, 'A General Much Maligned', p. 146. See also above, p. 132.
22. Bruce and Masson, 'Manchester's Quarrel', pp. 63–4. For a reconstruction of this part of the battle, see Wanklyn, *Decisive Battles*, II, pp. 153.
23. Walker, *Historical Discourses*, pp. 112–13; *Mercurius Aulicus*, pp. 1,236–7. Sir Richard Bulstrode makes it clear that the charge occurred during Skippon's attack on the barricade defending Speen village, which places it well before dusk: see Bulstrode, *Memoirs*, pp. 117–18.
24. Waller describes himself as being in danger of being killed in a melee at the Second Battle of Newbury 'on Speen field', whilst one of the soldiers in his regiment was wounded in the first engagement on the left wing: see Wadham College Library, MS A18.14, f. 20; CSP Domestic 1645–7, p. 395.
25. There is a possibility that Cromwell did what he could to ensure that the Newbury campaign was indecisive, as a climactic victory at that point in time might kill for good and all the Independents' efforts to secure religious toleration for the Protestant sects: see A. Cotton, 'Cromwell and the Self-Denying Ordinance', *History* 26 (1977), p. 230.
26. Walker, *Historical Discourses*, p. 114.
27. For this reason the king and the Prince of Wales escorted by a party of horse rode off in a different direction before midnight. They met Prince Rupert at Bath late the following afternoon: see ibid., p. 114; Symonds, 'Diaries', p. 146.
28. See *Historical Discourses*, p. 115.
29. Bruce and Masson, 'Manchester's Quarrel', p. 64. Gwynne confirms that only a hedge separated the two armies: see *Military Memoirs*, pp. 58–9.
30. Bodleian, Carte MSS 80, f. 715. See Wanklyn, 'A General Much Maligned', p. 148.
31. BL, Thomason Tracts, E22 (10); Abbott, ed., *Writings and Speeches*, I, p. 310.
32. If this had been the case, the decision not to attack would have been a wise one. With the enemy defensive perimeter restricted still further, the following morning's task would be all the easier.

33. BL, Harleian MSS 166, f. 141. The original is now lost and there is no published copy in the Thomason Tracts in the British Library or in the Wood pamphlets at the Bodleian Library.

34. See above, p. 119, for the escape of Essex's cavalry from Lostwithiel under cover of darkness and for a night attack on a royalist horse quarters near Newbury in late October. Symonds describes an all-night march by the royalist armies in Dorset on 14–15 October: see 'Diaries', p. 128.

35. See above, p. 82. In 1643 Waller's cavalry had attacked the earl of Crawford's brigade near Devizes during the night and captured the ammunition they were escorting: see HMC, Portland MSS III, p. 113.

36. BL, Harleian MSS 166, ff. 141, 160. A letter of intelligence sent by Sir Samuel Luke, Essex's scoutmaster-in-chief, to a friend in the north two days after the battle also described the royalists as retreating through Newbury and past Donnington Castle: see Luke, 'Letter Books', p. 48.

37. Walker, *Historical Discourses*, pp. 114–15; HMC, Appendix to the Fourth Report, p. 297.

38. Abbott, ed., *Writings and Speeches*, I, p. 307; CSP Domestic 1644–5, p. 83. The governor of Abingdon had destroyed New Bridge, the most direct route: see CSP Domestic 1664–5, p. 84.

39. Walker, *Historical Discourses*, pp. 116–17; Symonds, 'Diaries', p. 147.

40. CSP Domestic 1644–5, pp. 83, 85, 86, 96.

41. CSP Domestic 1644–5, p. 96; Warburton, *Memoirs of Prince Rupert*, I, p. 512.

42. Symonds, 'Diaries', pp. 147–8.

43. Walker, *Historical Discourses*, p. 121; Symonds, 'Diaries', p. 147.

44. CSP Domestic 1644–5, pp. 90, 93–4.

45. The departure of Crewe and Johnston did not deliver supreme command to Manchester, as Cromwell claimed in his attack on the earl. This is clear from the correspondence that subsequently passed between London and Newbury: see CSP Domestic 1644–5, pp. 96–139. Most letters written by the Committee of Both Kingdoms are addressed to the earl of Manchester and the commanders-in-chief of the army. Most replies are signed by Manchester, Waller and Balfour. Manchester merely acted as chairman of the Council of War, a task he had probably performed since 25 October when Essex's illness meant that he was the senior general.

46. CSP Domestic 1644–5, pp. 100, 101, 106.

47. BL, Loan MSS 28/123 Misc. 31; Bodleian, Tanner MSS 61, f. 206; Bruce and Masson, 'Manchester's Quarrel', p. 66.

48. Bruce and Masson, 'Manchester's Quarrel', pp. 66–7; Abbott, ed., *Writings and Speeches*, I, p. 309.

49. Walker, *Historical Discourses*, p. 118; BL, Additional MSS 16370, f. 61.

50. Luke, 'Letter Books', pp. 377–8; Rushworth, ed., *Historical Collections*, V, p. 730; Walker, *Historical Discourses*, p. 118; BL, Thomason Tracts, E20 (10).

51. Walker, *Historical Discourses*, p. 118; BL, Thomason Tracts, E20 (10); Abbott, ed., *Writings and Speeches*, I, p. 310; *Mercurius Aulicus*, p. 1,252.

52. Walker, *Historical Discourses*, p. 119; *Mercurius Aulicus*, p. 1,253.

53. Wanklyn, 'A General Much Maligned', pp. 152–4.

54. CSP Domestic 1644–5, p. 117.

55. Commons Journals, III, p. 696; Juxon, 'Journal', p. 66.

56. BL, Thomason Tracts, E17 (4, 8, 11), E18 (6), E19 (1, 4); Juxon, 'Journal', p. 63; Holmes, *Eastern Association*, pp. 206–7.

57. Walker, *Historical Discourses*, pp. 120–2; Luke, 'Letter Books', pp. 399, 400, 402; W.D. Cooper, ed., 'The Trelawney Papers', *Camden Society* LV (1853).

58. Commons Journals, III, p. 704.

59. Luke, 'Letter Books', p. 396.

60. This is implicit in Philip Skippon's reply to a letter from the earl of Essex written on 12 November: see Rushworth, *Historical Collections*, V, p. 731.

61. See above, p. 120.

62. For Cromwell, see above, pp. 123–8.

63. BL, Loan MSS, 29/123, Misc. 31; S.R. Gardiner, ed., 'Manchester's Letter', *Camden Society*, new series, XXXI (1883).

64. Whitelock, *Memorials*, pp. 116–17.

65. Carew was condemned to death on or immediately after 19 November and executed on 23 December, and the Hothams were condemned to death on 7 and 24 December and executed on 1 and 2 January: see S. Wright, 'Sir Alexander Carew', *ODNB*, 10, p. 40; Gardiner, *Great Civil War*, II, pp. 103–4.

Chapter 13: The Reckoning: A New General and a New Army

1. This has been claimed: see Adamson, 'The Triumph of Oligarchy', pp. 116–19, but the steering committee was no more than a device for ensuring that the generals did as the Committee of Both Kingdoms wanted during the Newbury campaign, and it was wound up when the two civilian members, Crewe and Johnston, returned to London on 2 November. It was only revived on a single occasion thereafter when the New Model Army was about to start out on its first campaign. Then it lasted for only two days: see CSP Domestic 1644–5, pp. 438, 441, 445 (28, 29 April).
2. See above, pp. 113–14.
3. See Juxon, 'Journal', pp. 58–68.
4. I do not regard the statement of the Committee of the Eastern Association in a petition delivered to the Commons on the 19th, that it could no longer finance its forces, as of central significance in the formation of the New Model Army. Their army alone could not win the war and the financial problem had been there for months for all to see. See Holmes, *Eastern Association*, pp. 205–6, for an assertion that the two were closely connected.
5. Commons Journals, III, pp. 695, 696, 699; CSP Domestic 1644–5, p. 118. There has been some suggestion that this motion was irrelevant to the formation of the New Model Army, but the breadth of the remit makes it very unlikely that I. Gentles is right in suggesting that the New Model was not on the cards until the plan to purge the generals via the Self-Denying Ordinance was voted down in the Lords on 13 January: see I. Gentles, *The New Model Army in England, Ireland and Scotland 1645–1653* (Oxford, 1992), p. 10.
6. His peerage was a Scottish one and so he did not have a seat in the English House of Lords. However, he sat in the Commons as one of the Members of Parliament for Yorkshire.
7. CSP Domestic 1644–5, pp. 171, 182, 186, 197; Abbott, ed., *Writings and Speeches*, I, pp. 342–4.
8. Whitelock, *Memorials*, p. 120; CSP Domestic 1644–5, pp. 171, 182, 186, 197.
9. CSP Domestic 1644–5, p. 205, 201–21, 230, 232; Commons Journals, III, p. 734.
10. Wanklyn, 'A General Much Maligned', pp. 133–57.
11. Commons Journals, III, pp. 725–6, 728; Lords Journals, VII, p. 135; A. Woolrych, *England in Revolution 1625–1660* (Oxford, 2002), p. 305.
12. See above, pp. 86–7.
13. Politically, he and his father had connections with the Independents through their friendship with Lord Wharton: see I. Gentles, 'Sir Thomas Fairfax', *ODNB*, 18, p. 935.
14. Commons Journals, IV, pp. 16, 18, 21, 26–7, 33.
15. Ibid., IV, pp. 26, 31; Juxon, 'Journal', p. 73. The stock argument is that the intention was that the place was left vacant because it was intended for Oliver Cromwell, who would have been exempted from the ordinance had not the attempt to exclude the earl of Essex almost succeeded. However, it is tinged with hindsight and supported by no more than circumstantial evidence. It also ignores the point that Cromwell was under a cloud because of his poor performance in the Newbury campaign. Possibly, given the absence of an obvious candidate of the right calibre, it was decided to give the various contenders a chance to prove themselves in the winter campaigns. Cromwell's chances were much enhanced by his performance in the short Oxford campaign, by the version of the Self-Denying Ordinance passed in April, which allowed temporary exemptions from the act ironically to satisfy the concerns of the House of Lords, and by Middleton refusing his colonel's commission. The most senior foreign officer in the New Model Army, the Dutchman Bartholomew Vermuyden, probably still rated his chances when put in charge of a force of cavalry and dragoons sent to escort the Scottish army on its march south in mid-May 1645. However, he soon got cold feet. One source claimed that he should be held responsible for the loss of Leicester, and this may have dashed his

hopes even though his force had been outnumbered by three to one and included no infantry or artillery. However, he may have wanted to leave earlier as the earl of Manchester, his former commander, was instructed by the Committee to persuade him not to go before the end of his expedition in search of the Scots: see CSP Domestic 1644–5, p. 563.

16. Fairfax had produced the list of officers, and the initial proposal put before the Commons was that he should appoint all officers of the rank of captain and above apart from the major and the lieutenant general. This proved unacceptable to the Lords, and the ordinance that eventually passed required captains and above to be approved by both Houses of Parliament.

17. Commons Journals, IV, pp. 16, 18, 24, 26–7. The proposal also included a clause that the earl of Essex should be voted an honour for all his services to the people of England.

18. M. Kishlansky, The Rise of the New Model Army (Cambridge, 1979), pp. 36–7. This had been put to Parliament as early as 6 January, with the most intensive debate over finance apparently taking place in the Commons on 12 and 13 January. However, the fine detail was still being worked out in late January: see BL, Additional MSS 31117, f. 186; Commons Journals, IV, p. 28.

19. Firth and Rait, Acts and Ordinances, I, p. 660. The passage reproduced here was from an ordinance strengthening Sir Thomas's powers that passed on 1 April 1645, but in this respect it weakened them by omitting the phrase 'from time to time' between 'and' and 'by', which had been in the ordinance passed on 17 February: see Lords Journals, VII, p. 299.

20. The tendency from Gardiner's days onwards has been to see the formation of the New Model Army as a contentious matter in that it took so long for the Self-Denying Ordinance to pass through both Houses. See Gardiner, Great Civil War, II, pp. 116–19, 128–9, 191; I. Gentles, The English Revolution and the Wars in Three Kingdoms 1638–1652 (Harlow, 2007), pp. 251–3. However, from the perspective of command the Lords and the Commons were largely of one mind. The New Model ordinance was passed by the Commons on 28 January and accepted in principle by the Lords on 4 February with some final concessions by the Commons to satisfy the Lords' concerns about approval of the officers and other matters being agreed on the 7th, 8th and 15th of the month. On the 17th a text acceptable to both Houses was agreed: see Commons Journals, IV, pp. 43–4; Lords Journals, VII, pp. 193, 195–6, 202–3. One of Sir William Brereton's correspondents writing on 4 March described the ordinance for Sir Thomas Fairfax's army as almost all that was visible of God's providence in the reform of the militia: see R. Dore, ed., 'Sir William Brereton, Letter Books I–IV', I, Lancashire and Cheshire Record Society, p. 59.

21. R. Hutton puts a strong argument in favour: see Royalist War Effort, pp. 166–75; but the argument is not convincing. Admittedly there was a precedent for the amalgamation of regiments in what had happened in Worcestershire in July 1644: see ibid., p. 167; but very little evidence of its being followed up. Three cavalry regiments which had fought in different brigades at Marston Moor combined to form the nucleus of the Prince of Wales's new regiment of lifeguards: see HMC, Duke of Beaufort MSS, pp. 43–4. Some amalgamation of the Anglo-Irish regiments may have taken place to form the unit that fought at Naseby as the Shrewsbury Foot, as the officers taken prisoner only came from three of the five regiments that should have been present at the battle, see BL, Additional MSS 16370, f. 63; BL, Thomason Tracts, E288 (28, 38). However, most other regiments that disappeared from the Oxford army and the army of the west between the Second Newbury campaign and the spring of 1645 are known to have been destroyed, for example Sir Henry Vaughan's and Anthony Thelwall's at Bampton Bush: see BL, Thomason Tracts, E281 (55); Wanklyn, 'Landownership and Allegiance', p. 194. Even the smallest cavalry regiments mustered at Aldbourne Chase in April 1644 like Sir George Vaughan's were still discrete units at the battle of Langport fifteen months later: see BL, Harleian MSS 986; BL, Thomason Tracts, E292 (22, 27); Wanklyn, 'The King's Armies', pp. 267–8.

22. See above, p. 139.

23. See below, pp. 151, 159.

24. 'To hinder the levies and contributions in those parts': see CSP Domestic 1644–5, p. 102.

25. HMC, Hodgkin MSS, pp. 101–2; House of Lords MSS 3639, ff. 12, 14; BL, Additional MSS 15752, ff. 24, 26; Bodleian, Firth MSS C7, f. 253. According to Wyndham, he made considerable progress in cutting the town off from the surrounding countryside during October and November, raising hopes that its garrison would shortly be forced to sue for terms because of

lack of provisions: see J. Colemen, ed., 'A Royalist Account of the Withdrawal of the King's Forces from Taunton, 13 December 1644', *English Historical Review*, XIII (1899), pp. 307–9.

26. CSP Domestic 1644–5, pp. 102, 107; Commons Journals, IV, p. 694.

27. CSP Domestic 1644–5, pp. 113, 135, 164, 196; Bodleian, Firth MSS C7, f. 253.

28. CSP Domestic 1644–5, pp. 196, 201, 204. See above, pp. 91, 144, and below, pp. 147–8, for the king's intentions.

29. BL, Thomason Tracts, E24 (24), E25 (17), E26 (9, 12); Clarendon, *History of the Rebellion*, IX, para. 49.

30. Ludlow, *Memoirs*, I, pp. 107–8.

31. See above, pp. 150–2.

32. CSP Domestic 1644, pp. 282, 291, 298; Lords Journals, VII, p. 193; BL, Harleian MSS 166, ff. 185–6; HMC, Portland MSS I, pp. 208–9.

33. Wanklyn, 'The King's Armies', chapters VI, VIII–XI. For Hopton's candidacy, see ibid., pp. 167, 200–1.

34. Ibid., pp. 117–21.

35. BL, Sloane MSS 1519, f. 58.

36. Wanklyn, 'The King's Armies', pp. 136–7, 198–201. In March and April accusations of incompetence flew about, with Goring in particular being blamed. An inquiry of sorts took place but did not apparently come to any firm conclusion. However, there can be little doubt that the principal mistake was not to have broken down the bridge connecting Weymouth and Melcombe. This was clearly the responsibility of the Dorset royalists. See ibid., pp. 119–20, citing Staffordshire County Record Office, Salt MSS 2007 (7 April 1645); Warburton, *Memoirs of Prince Rupert*, III, pp. 66–7; Clarendon, *History of the Rebellion*, IX, para. 8.

37. CSP Domestic 1644–5, p. 334; BL, Harleian MSS 166, f. 187; Luke, 'Letter Books', p. 182.

38. BL, Harleian MSS 166, ff. 188–9.

39. BL, Sloane MSS 1519, f. 66; Washbourne, ed., *Bibliographica Gloucestrensis*, p. 142; Lynch, *For King and Parliament*, p. 135.

40. Bodleian, Tanner MSS 60, f. 15.

41. Bodleian, Clarendon MSS 24, ff. 75, 83, 91, 92, 95, 99; Whitelock, *Memorials*, pp. 140, 141.

42. Bodleian, Clarendon MSS 24, ff. 103–13; Whitelock, *Memorials*, pp. 140, 141.

43. BL, Harleian MSS 166, f. 189 (Cromwell to Sir Thomas Fairfax, 9 April 1645).

44. Wanklyn, 'The King's Armies', pp. 145–51.

45. CSP Domestic 1644–5, p. 415; BL, Additional MSS 31116, f. 205.

46. Bodleian, MSS Don d.57, ff. 8–9.

47. R. Hutton, 'George Goring, Baron Goring', ODNB, 22, pp. 1,006–7.

48. Commons Journals, III, p. 168.

49. Hutton, 'George Goring', p. 1,007; Bodleian, Firth MSS C7, ff. 126, 127.

50. Warburton, *Memoirs of the Cavaliers*, II, pp. 435–6, III, pp. 2–3. See above, pp. 92–3, 95–6, 118–19, for the downfall of Lord Wilmot.

51. See above, p. 134.

52. See above, pp. 106, 134.

53. He worked well with Prince Rupert in June and July 1644 and again in 1645, a difficult task given the ease with which the prince took offence, but he briefly fell foul of him in the autumn of 1644 when he tried to persuade the king that he should receive his orders not from Rupert as lord general but direct from Charles as generalissimo: see Warburton, *Memoirs of Prince Rupert*, III, p. 52: BL, Additional MSS 18982, f. 29.

54. Hutton, 'George Goring', pp. 1,008, 1,009.

55. Clarendon, *History of the Rebellion*, IX, para. 8.

56. Bodleian, Clarendon MSS 24, f. 91; M. Baumber, 'Robert Blake', ODNB, 6, p. 107.

57. He only took a tiny escort with him comprising his regiment of foot, part of his regiment of horse, and his lifeguard of horse, almost certainly fewer than 500 men: see Hamper, ed., *Diary of Sir William Dugdale*, p. 77. Dudley Wyatt, Rupert's commissary general, met Maurice at Evesham on 15 January: see BL, Additional MSS 18982, f. 16; P. Young, *Naseby 1645: The Campaign and the Battle* (London, 1985), p. 2.

58. BL, Additional MSS 18982, f. 27.

59. Shropshire CRO, Ludlow Borough MSS, free quarters discharged by Prince Maurice, unfol.; J. Willis Bund, ed., 'Henry Townshend's Diary', *Worcestershire Historical Society* (1920), pp. 206, 208.

60. See Warburton, *Memoirs of Prince Rupert*, III, pp. 51, 53–4.

61. Malbon, 'Memorial', pp. 155–6; Phillips, *Memoirs*, II, pp. 225–6. Byron was not given a commission as governor of Chester until March: see Dore, ed., 'Brereton, Letter Books', I, p. 141.

62. Malbon, 'Memorial', p. 159; R. Morris, *The Siege of Chester* (Chester, 1924), p. 73, quoting BL, Harleian MSS 2125. In a letter written to the marquis of Ormond from Chester on 30 January, Edmund Verney described His Majesty's affairs as 'going ill in these parts' and said that relief was expected from Maurice, but this was probably commonsense rather than knowledge that help had been promised from Oxford or Worcester: see Bodleian, Carte MSS 13, f. 273.

63. Malbon, 'Memorial', pp. 159–60; Phillips, *Memoirs*, II, pp. 223–4; BL, Additional MSS 18982, f. 9 (Sir John Byron to Prince Rupert, 9 January 1645); Bodleian, Firth MSS C6, f. 316 (Byron to Rupert, 19 January 1645).

64. Hutton, *Royalist War Effort*, p. 153; Dore, ed., 'Brereton, Letter Books', I, pp. 517–30.

65. Malbon, 'Memorial', pp. 161–2; Bodleian, Firth MSS C6, ff. 331, 332; Bodleian, Carte MSS 14, ff. 63, 82 (Maurice to Ormond, 20 February 1645; Sir John Byron to Ormond, 25 February 1645).

66. Phillips, *Memoirs*, II, pp. 235–8; Luke, 'Letter Books', pp. 164–5. There had been four regiments in garrison at Shrewsbury in the autumn, sufficient in the governor's view to defend the town: see BL, Additional MSS 18981, f. 299. On 21 February there were two regiments at most, that of the governor Sir Michael Earnley and that of the townspeople, Sir Francis Ottley's: see Dore, ed., 'Brereton, Letter Books', I, pp. 40–4. However, even the governor's regiment was probably incomplete. In the autumn one of Earnley's companies of foot formed part of the Bridgnorth garrison: see Symonds, 'Diaries', p. 252. Moreover, the town regiment put up little of a fight, probably because its ranks were full of neutrals and malignants.

67. Staffordshire CRO, D1778 Ii, items 41–4; Luke, 'Letter Books', p. 690.

68. Dore, ed., 'Brereton, Letter Books', I, pp. 58, 64, 78.

69. Malbon, 'Memorial', p. 165.

70. Staffordshire CRO, D1778 Ii, item 41.

71. Staffordshire CRO, items 44, 45; Bodleian, Clarendon MSS 28, f. 136; *Mercurius Aulicus*, pp. 1,401–7.

72. Dore, ed., 'Brereton, Letter Books', I, pp. 66, 88–9, 131.

73. A large body of Scottish horse and musketeers led by David Leslie had left Leeds on the 16th and was in the Manchester area three days later, though the princes were not aware of this until the 24th: see ibid., pp. 76–7, 83, 87, 94, 142.

74. Ibid, p. 39 (the Shropshire County Committee to Brereton, 22 February 1645); Staffordshire CRO, D1778, I, i, items 42–4; BL, Additional MSS 18982, f. 46. After capturing it, local parliamentary officials described Shrewsbury variously as 'strong by nature and art' and 'one of the strongest positions in the kingdom': see Dore, ed., 'Brereton, Letter Books', I, pp. 39, 44.

75. Dore, ed., 'Brereton, Letter Books', I, pp. 107–8, 142; Bodleian, Clarendon MSS 28, f. 136.

76. Washbourne, ed., *Bibliotheca Gloucestrensis*, pp. 144–5; *Mercurius Aulicus*, pp. 1,563–4.

77. Hutton, *Royalist War Effort*, pp. 152–3, 174–5; J. Willis Bund, *The Civil War in Worcestershire* (Birmingham, 1905), pp. 156–7. I have not been able to trace the original of the letter from Edward Massey to Speaker Lenthall cited by Willis Bund.

78. Dore, ed., 'Brereton, Letter Books', I, p. 172.

79. Wanklyn and Jones, *A Military History*, p. 222. It is clear from Maurice's letter to his brother that the relief of Chester was not in his original orders, and, given this, that he had less than a fortnight to put together a relief expedition: see Warburton, *Memoirs of Prince Rupert*, III, pp. 51, 53–4.

80. Symonds, 'Diaries', pp. 163–4; Warburton, *Memoirs of Prince Rupert*, III, pp. 80–1; CSP Domestic 1644–5, p. 419; Abbott, ed., *Writings and Speeches*, I, pp. 339–45.

81. Walker, *Historical Discourses*, p. 125; E. Walsingham, 'Hector Britannicus: The Life of Sir John Digby', ed. G. Bernard, *Camden Society*, 3rd series VIII (1910), p. 110; HMC, Appendix to the First Report, pp. 106–7; BL, Additional MSS 18982, f. 44.

Chapter 14: Fairfax, Rupert and the Battle of Naseby

1. CSP Domestic 1644–5, p. 440.
2. Ibid., pp. 459, 476; Rushworth, ed., *Historical Collections*, VI, p. 28. These were the regiments of Ralph Weldon, Richard Ingoldsby, Richard Fortescue, Walter Lloyd and Richard Graves. It is perhaps worth noting that none had formerly been a regiment of the Eastern Association army.
3. CSP Domestic 1644–5, pp. 474, 482, 489.
4. CSP Domestic 1644–5, pp. 488, 493; Commons Journals, IV, pp. 46–7; Lords Journals, VII, p. 379. The original intention had been for Cromwell to command this force, but the Scottish Covenanters' representatives in London demurred: see Meikle, 'Correspondence of the Scottish Commissioners', p. 75.
5. CSP Domestic 1644–5, p. 553; Rushworth, ed., *Historical Collections*, VI, p. 34 (Fairfax to the Committee, 28 May 1645).
6. BL, Harleian MSS 166, f. 191 (Scoutmaster Watson to Speaker Lenthall, 4 June 1645); CSP Domestic 1644–5, p. 580.
7. CSP Domestic 1644–5, pp. 578–9, 580.
8. CSP Domestic 1644–5, p. 491.
9. See below, p. 169.
10. CSP Domestic 1644–5, p. 565; Commons Journals, IV, pp. 165–6, 168; Lords Journals, VII, pp. 393–4.
11. Incoming letters written by Massey to the Committee do not survive, but his account of the first six weeks of his generalship helps to substantiate what can be inferred from letters that the Committee sent him. See Bodleian, Firth MSS C8, f. 301; CSP Domestic 1644–5, pp. 543, 565, 585; Commons Journals, IV, p. 165.
12. Bell, ed., *Memoirs*, I, p. 228.
13. Dore, ed., 'Brereton, Letter Books', I, p. 460.
14. CSP Domestic 1644–5, pp. 580–1.
15. CSP Domestic 1644–5, pp. 492–3, 504.
16. CSP Domestic 1644–5, p. 512; Bodleian, Carte MSS 79, f. 234 (the Commissioners of the Scottish Parliament to the English Parliament, 26 May 1645). Brereton sent him intelligence to this effect: see Dore, ed., 'Brereton, Letter Books', I, pp. 442, 466, 473, 477.
17. CSP Domestic 1644–5, p. 567.
18. Rushworth, ed., *Historical Collections*, VI, p. 38.
19. Abbott, ed., *Writings and Speeches*, I, p. 353.
20. Juxon, 'Journal', p. 79. Sir Thomas was merely commander-in-chief. The title of lord general was not his until Essex was dead (14 September 1646).
21. Commons Journals, IV, p. 163; Lords Journals, VII, pp. 411–12.
22. Commons Journals, IV, p. 166. The Lords received the petition but did not respond to it, the Commons' reply or the Committee's response to the reply.
23. CSP Domestic 1644–5, p. 565.
24. CSP Domestic 1644–5, pp. 578–9. Essex, Manchester and Waller all attended the meeting on that day.
25. Its importance has been grossly overestimated in the past: see Gentles, *New Model Army*, pp. 33–4; Gardiner, *Great Civil War*, II, p. 37.
26. He had been given military command of the Isle of Ely on 27 May: see Commons Journals, IV, p. 155; but the Committee had extended this to the entire Eastern Association before the day on which the petition was presented to Parliament: see CSP Domestic 1644–5, pp. 523, 533, 536, 540. This almost certainly explains why the House of Commons did not mention the Londoners' second demand in its formal reply.

27. He had already been ordered by the Committee to join Fairfax at the rendezvous in north Buckinghamshire with his East Anglian division: see CSP Domestic, 1644–5, p. 533.

28. The petition was not a partisan move on the part of officers who had previously served with Oliver. It was signed by Fairfax, Skippon, five colonels of horse and four of foot, some of whom had previously fought in Manchester's army and some in Essex's.

29. Lords Journals, VII, p. 421; Joshua Sprigg, Anglia Rediviva (2nd edn, Oxford, 1844), p. 32. Sprigg wrote that Vermuyden made his announcement on 8 June, the day on which Fairfax put his proposal to the Council of War, but this was not an example of pique. He had made his intentions clear some days earlier, as on 4 June the Committee of Both Kingdoms asked Manchester, his former general, to persuade him to change his mind: see CSP Domestic 1644–5, p. 563. In fact, Vermuyden did not immediately leave England, as he was shut up in prison for debt until it was discovered that the back-pay he was owed was larger than the amount for which he had been imprisoned: see Lords Journals, VII, pp. 452, 456, 463–4.

30. See above, p. 208 n.15.

31. M. Bennett, Oliver Cromwell (London, 2006), p. 99.

32. Cust, Charles I, pp. 390–91.

33. See HMC, Appendix to the First Report, p. 9; W. Bray, ed., John Evelyn's Diary, 4 vols (Oxford, 1877–9), IV, p. 145.

34. Cust, Charles I, p. 401.

35. See below, pp. 176–7.

36. BL, Sloane MSS 1519, f. 61.

37. CSP Domestic 1644–5, p. 520 (Culpeper to the king, 26 May 1645).

38. Bodleian, Clarendon MSS 24, f. 155.

39. Bray, ed., Evelyn's Diary, IV, pp. 146–50; HMC, Appendix to the First Report, p. 9.

40. BL, Harleian MSS 7379, f. 41.

41. Walker, Historical Discourses, pp. 125–6.

42. Clarendon, History of the Rebellion, IX, para. 30.

43. See pp. 167–8.

44. HMC, Portland MSS I, pp. 224–5.

45. Bodleian, Clarendon MSS 24, f. 167.

46. Clarendon, History of the Rebellion, XI, paras 30–1. In fact, Goring saw Rupert as a trusted confidant in his ongoing struggle with the Prince of Wales's Council over supreme command of the king's forces in the west of England: see Bodleian, Firth MSS C7, ff. 127, 128.

47. For example, Kitson, Prince Rupert, pp. 233–7; Wedgwood, The King's War, pp. 442–51; Cust, Charles I, pp. 400–2; Gardiner, The Great Civil War, II, pp. 234–41. The only piece of personal correspondence to survive for this part of the 1645 campaign, a letter written to Will Legge from Daventry on 8 June, does not make a single substantive point about strategic and operational matters: see Staffordshire CRO, DW 1778, I, i, 54.

48. It is also probably significant that it was the king, not Rupert, who took on the task of persuading the Northern Horse not to ride off north on their own once the move got under way: see BL, Additional MSS 62084b, para. 68; Walker, Historical Discourses, pp. 128–9.

49. Bray, ed., Evelyn's Diary, IV, pp. 150–1; Staffordshire CRO, DW 1778, I, i, 54.

50. Walker, Historical Discourses, p. 129; Wiltshire CRO, 413/444B, para. 37.

51. BL, Additional MSS 18982, ff. 63–7; HMC, Appendix to the First Report, p. 9; Bray, ed., Evelyn's Diary, IV, pp. 150, 152.

52. Luke, 'Letter Books', p. 304.

53. G. Foard, Naseby: The Decisive Campaign (Whitstable, 1995), pp. 199–200.

54. However, the upsurge in activity in the twelve hours before battle was not due to the arrival at army headquarters of an intercepted letter from Goring to Sir Edward Nicholas, which showed that he and his cavalry were still at Taunton. Sprigg shows very clearly that the letter arrived on the evening after the battle: see Sprigg, Anglia Rediviva, pp. 52–3.

55. Rushworth, ed., Historical Collections, VI, pp. 40–2; BL, Harleian MSS 166, f. 190.

56. Rushworth, ed., *Historical Collections*, VI, pp. 41–2; Sprigg, *Anglia Rediviva*, pp. 33, 35, 40. Rushworth's account of the Naseby campaign has an air of authenticity as he was employed as Fairfax's secretary: see J. Raymond, 'John Rushworth', *ODNB*, 48, p. 169.

57. Sir Edward Nicholas had informed him that the rendezvous of parliamentary forces after the withdrawal from Oxford was further to the east: see Wanklyn and Jones, *A Military History*, p. 240.

58. Staffordshire CRO DW 1778, I, i, 56; Walker, *Historical Discourses*, p. 129.

59. Commons Journals, IV, p. 175 (Fairfax to the speaker of the House of Commons, Kislingbury, 13 June 1645).

60. Two copies of what appear to be the pre-battle plan exist. One, which was formerly amongst Prince Rupert's papers, disappeared after the sale of that part of the collection which had been purchased by W. Morrison during the First World War. Fortunately, Warburton included a redrawing of it in volume three of *Memoirs of Prince Rupert and the Cavaliers*. The other is in a volume of manuscripts in the Bodleian Library: see Bodleian, English MSS C51, f. 198. However, the fact that both are headed 'Naseby' shows that they are later redrawings.

61. Symonds, 'Diaries', p. 182; Walker, *Historical Discourses*, p. 131.

62. Woolrych, *Battles of the English Civil War*, p. 125.

63. See Wanklyn and Jones, *A Military History*, p. 248; Wanklyn, *Decisive Battles*, pp. 178–9. The evidence is modest – Sir William Vaughan's surprise at finding infantry blocking the best passage towards the enemy right wing is interesting, as is John Rushworth's assertion that Rupert's cavalry came 'quite behind the rear' of the New Model Army before being halted by the resistance of the train of artillery: see Staffordshire CRO, DW 1778 I, i, item 56; BL, Thomason Tracts, E288 (26). It may also be significant that the royalist right-wing cavalry did not turn on the enemy infantry formations, as Sir Charles Lucas had done at Marston Moor: see above, p. 106.

64. E. Wanty, *L'Art de la Guerre*, 2 vols (Verviers, 1967), I, pp. 242–3.

65. Foard, *Naseby*, pp. 275–87; M. Marix Evans, P. Burton and M. Westaway, *Battlefield Britain: Naseby, June 1645* (Barnsley, 2002), pp. 103–4, 152.

66. BL, Thomason Tracts, E288 (38).

67. Roger Boyle, Earl of Orrery, *A Treatise of the Art of War* (London, 1677), p. 154.

68. Woolrych suggests that Fairfax did not want the sight of the royalist army to scare his greener troops as it advanced towards them: see *Battles of the English Civil War*, p. 123.

69. BL, Thomason Tracts, E288 (22, 25). Stringer's etching of the battle reproduced in *Anglia Rediviva* shows the field artillery in place between the infantry regiments but the heavy guns still limbered up in the artillery park.

70. The criticism originates with Clarendon: see *History of the Rebellion*, IX, paras 39, 42. It is not to be found in Walker, Clarendon's principal source for the Naseby campaign, who shared many of his prejudices. Walker's objection was to Rupert abandoning the position on East Farndon ridge where the royalist army had drawn up first thing in the morning: see *Historical Discourses*, p. 130.

71. Sprigg, *Anglia Rediviva*, p. 42; BL, Thomason Tracts, E288 (26).

72. Slingsby, *Diary*, pp. 151–2. This was probably because the royalist squadrons lost momentum when Cromwell's dragoons fired into their flank. Ireton's men then charged them as they faltered, and a slogging match ensued.

73. Foard, *Naseby*, pp. 409–10; Rushworth, ed., *Historical Collections*, VI, p. 43; Slingsby, *Diary*, p. 152; Sprigg, *Anglia Rediviva*, p. 40.

74. BL, Thomason Tracts, E288 (34). A similar point is made in a marginal note in the 'Diary'. See BL, Additional MSS 62084b, para. 69.

75. The regiment was almost 1,400 strong: see M. Marix Evans, *Naseby 1645: The Triumph of the New Model Army* (Oxford, 2007), p. 61, citing the research of David Blackmore.

76. Walker, *Historical Discourses*, p. 131; BL, Thomason Tracts, E288 (38). According to Rupert, the king's mistake was not to use the infantry reserves to support the attack, see BL, Additional MSS 62084b, para. 69. This had been his intention and it is impossible to fault it, as they could have added firepower to the assault itself and helped parry the threat from Fairfax's regiment. It has recently been suggested that the charge of the lifeguard took place at the end of the

battle after the king and Rupert had assembled their cavalry a mile to the north of the battle-field, but Walker's account makes it very clear that it occurred much earlier in the day: see Marix Evans, *Naseby*, pp. 79–80; Walker, *Historical Discourses*, p. 131.

77. To relieve pressure on one of the New Model infantry regiments, one of Ireton's squadrons charged the enemy but without causing much damage: see Sprigg, *Anglia Rediviva*, pp. 41–3.

78. Foard, *Naseby*, pp. 409–10.

79. BL, Thomason Tracts, E288 (28); Sprigg, *Anglia Rediviva*, p. 41; Rushworth, ed., *Historical Collections*, VI, p. 43. The fact that the second line suffered fewer wounded (27 or 39 as opposed to 241 for the first line) suggests that the royalist musketeers were no longer able to deliver a barrage as the second line approached: see Foard, *Naseby*, pp. 409–10. They were not out of ammunition, having only fired a single volley before engaging the enemy in hand-to-hand combat, but their muskets were probably damaged as a result or their barrels being choked by Northamptonshire mud.

80. Major General Astley appears to have fought with the king's lifeguard of cavalry: see Foard, *Naseby*, p. 276; BL, Thomason Tracts, E290 (11); Symonds, 'Diaries', p. 193.

81. Both seem to have put up a good fight. The first probably fell victim to Fairfax's reckless bravado described below, the second to a cavalry regiment in Cromwell's third line commanded by Colonel John Fiennes: see Sprigg, *Anglia Rediviva*, p. 43; BL, Thomason Tracts, E288 (38), E290 (11).

82. Almost every source states that the royalist infantry surrendered en masse: see, for example, Slingsby, *Diary*, p. 152; Sprigg, *Anglia Rediviva*, p. 43; BL, Thomason Tracts, E288 (32); HMC, Ormond MSS, NS II, p. 366. The only written evidence that may be read as referring to the last stand is a brief passage in an account allegedly written by John Rushworth straight after the battle, but if so the engagement clearly took place much nearer to where the battle had been fought, as Wadborough Hill is a mile beyond the spot where the king and Rupert tried to make a last stand without infantry support. There is without question a large concentration of musket balls on Wadborough Hill, but this is much more likely to represent the last stand of the regiment that defended the artillery train: see Wanklyn, *Decisive Battles*, pp. 182–3.

83. The latest example of this error is in Gentles, *The English Revolution*, p. 268. The mistake is not to be found in Woolrych, *Battles of the English Civil War*, the most insightful of all the modern accounts of the battle.

84. Walker, *Historical Discourses*, p. 131; Slingsby, *Diary*, p. 152; Sprigg, *Anglia Rediviva*, p. 44.

85. See p. 272 n.72 above. It is just possible that the Council of War devised the tactical plan prior to the battle but unlikely, as it was the restricted line of battle that forced Cromwell to have a reserve line.

86. See Sprigg, *Anglia Rediviva*, pp. 47–8; BL, Thomason Tracts, E288 (22, 27, 38).

87. Whitelock, *Memorials*, p. 151. The general may also have assumed a wider responsibility in the closing stages of the battle. He apparently ordered the attack on the king's regiment of foot in the reserve line, and the decision to regroup before advancing to the final attack on the royalist horse a mile to the rear of the battlefield was certainly his: see BL, Thomason Tracts, E290 (11); Sprigg, *Anglia Rediviva*, p. 43; Slingsby, *Diary*, p. 153.

88. It is just possible that D'Oyley's story was an invention. Other sources that seem to describe the same incident maintain that the cavalry attacks failed and that the brigade was finally overcome by an infantry attack: see BL, Thomason Tracts, E288 (26); Sprigg, *Anglia Rediviva*, p. 41.

Chapter 15: Fairfax and Goring

1. Walker, *Historical Discourses*, p. 116; BL, Harleian MSS 6852, f. 275.

2. 'We leave it wholly to you, who are upon the place, to employ the army as you shall judge best': see CSP Domestic 1644–5, p. 611.

3. Sprigg, *Anglia Rediviva*, p. 59; Bodleian, Firth MSS C8, f. 301 (Edward Massey's account of the Langport campaign); CSP Domestic 1644–5, p. 617 (Committee to Fairfax, 26 June 1645); Commons Journals, IV, p. 187; Lords Journals, VII, pp. 263–4 (Fairfax to the Speaker, 26 June 1645). See also Wanklyn and Jones, *A Military History*, p. 255.

4. Sprigg, *Anglia Rediviva*, p. 59; Rushworth, ed., *Historical Collections*, VI, p. 51; Lords Journals, VII, p. 463.

5. CSP Domestic 1644–5, pp. 606, 611, 617; HMC, Portland MSS I, p. 229; Meikle, 'Correspondence of the Scottish Commissioners', p. 89; Bodleian, Tanner MSS 60, ff. 176, 190, 204, 206, 219.

6. CSP Domestic 1645–7, p. 12; Walker, *Historical Discourses*, p. 16; Bodleian, Carte MSS 15, f. 48 (Digby to Ormond, 19 June 1645).

7. Woolrych, *Battles*, pp. 109–10, 125, 138; Young and Holmes, *English Civil Wars*, pp. 245, 249; Reid, *All the King's Armies*, p. 207; Barratt, *Cavalier Generals*, pp. 114–15; Kitson, *Prince Rupert*, pp. 234, 237, 238, 249; Gentles, *New Model Army*, pp. 264–6; Cust, *Charles I*, pp. 401, 403.

8. Bodleian, Clarendon MSS 24, ff. 154–5. For a fuller discussion of the strategic debate, see Wanklyn and Jones, *A Military History*, pp. 233–4, 241–4.

9. This point can be clearly seen in letters that he wrote to Sir Edward Nicholas at Oxford and to the queen in France and in a report in *Mercurius Aulicus* of 7 June: see Bray, ed., *Evelyn's Diary*, IV, pp. 146–51; HMC, Appendix to the First Report, p. 9; BL, Thomason Tracts E292 (27); *Mercurius Aulicus*, p. 1,619. Moreover, the assumption underlying the contents of a letter sent by one of the Prince of Wales's Council to the king on 10 June is that the king had already given permission for Goring to remain in Somerset until Taunton had been captured: see CSP Domestic 1644–5, pp. 581–2.

10. Bodleian, Clarendon MSS 24, f. 130; Bodleian, Firth MSS C7, f. 298.

11. Bodleian, Clarendon MSS 24, f. 136.

12. Sir John Berkeley was originally given the responsibility for conducting the siege as Sir Richard Grenville was still recovering from a wound, but Lord Hopton took over from him and it was he who probably took the decision to rely on the cavaliers at Sherborne. When the New Model Army arrived at Chard, Colonel Bampfield, Berkeley's deputy, was in charge. Hopton's whereabouts are unknown, but he had probably gone to Bristol to consult with the Prince's Council, thinking that nothing was amiss.

13. If the five New Model regiments were at full strength, which seems unlikely, they and their auxiliaries probably numbered between 6,000 and 7,000 men. Goring took about 3,500 to attack Cromwell, which would leave 7,500 in Somerset, assuming that Digby's figure for the rendezvous that took place on the 16 or 17 May is correct: see above, p. 168. Bampfield claimed he only had 1,200 men, the rest being elsewhere. However, he was facing an inquiry and probably hoping to place the real blame on Lord Hopton who he claimed had left him in the lurch: see BL, Clarendon MSS 24, f. 148.

14. CSP Domestic 1644–5, p. 499; Symonds, 'Diaries', p. 166; Bodleian, Firth MSS C7, f. 298.

15. Bodleian, Clarendon MSS 24, f. 49, 26, f. 5; Bodleian, Firth MSS C7, f. 298; CSP Domestic 1644–5, p. 506.

16. CSP Domestic 1644–5, p. 506; Bodleian, Firth MSS C7, f. 298.

17. CSP Domestic 1644–5, p. 512.

18. Wanklyn, 'The King's Armies', pp. 225–6; Bodleian, Clarendon MSS 24, f. 170.

19. Bodleian, Firth MSS C7, f. 308; Bodleian, Clarendon MSS 24, f. 196.

20. Clarendon MSS 24, ff. 196, 200.

21. The letter does not survive, but its contents can be inferred from other pieces of royalist correspondence. As on many previous occasions, the king left the operational details to his generals: see HMC, Portland MSS I, p. 231 (Digby to Goring, 4 July 1645).

22. Sir Edward Nicholas sent such intelligence to Rupert on 25 and 26 June. It seems most unlikely that he did not send something similar to Goring: see BL, Additional MSS 18982, ff. 67–9; Warburton, *Memoirs of the Cavaliers*, III, p. 123.

23. According to Lord Digby, this was the length of time needed to ensure that the royalist forces were strong enough to fight the enemy with a good prospect of winning: see CSP Domestic 1645–7, p. 12.

24. Goring showed no sign of having received a communication to that effect on 30 June, from the text of the letter he sent to the Council on that day: see Bodleian, Clarendon MSS 24, f. 200.

25. Sprigg, *Anglia Rediviva*, pp. 66, 333; BL, Thomason Tracts, E288 (31), E292 (16, 22, 24). A short delay had been caused by the Clubmen, armed neutrals led by local rich yeomen and minor gentry, whom Fairfax encountered on the march in Dorset. Gaining their trust had taken up much of Goring's attention during June, but their activities had no discernible effect on the outcome of the fighting in Somerset. However, if Goring's defensive plan had worked for any length of time, the Clubmen could well have made Fairfax's supply situation very difficult indeed.
26. Sprigg, *Anglia Rediviva*, p. 68.
27. BL, Thomason Tracts, E293 (3, 28); J. Sanford, ed., *The Great Rebellion* (London, 1858), pp. 621, 622–3; Bulstrode, *Memoirs*, p. 120.
28. Bulstrode, *Memoirs*, pp. 136–7; Sprigg, *Anglia Rediviva*, p. 71; Bodleian, Firth MSS C8, ff. 301–2; Bodleian, Wood Pamphlets, 378 (10); BL, Thomason Tracts, E293 (3).
29. Two major sources survive written from a royalist perspective: Goring's letter to Lord Digby of 12 July 1645, and the reminiscences of his chief of staff, Richard Bulstrode: see BL, Additional MSS 18982, f. 70; Bulstrode, *Memoirs*, pp. 137–8. Clarendon, as usual, told his own tale which bore little resemblance to reality.
30. Sprigg, *Anglia Rediviva*, p. 73.
31. Bulstrode, *Memoirs*, p. 138. Whether the rest of the cavalry were supposed to follow or to make their way along the east bank to Burrow is not known.
32. Ibid., pp. 138–40; BL, Additional MSS 18982, f. 70.
33. The regiments of William Slaughter and Matthew Wise: see Bulstrode, *Memoirs*, p. 138. They had probably been raised in the aftermath of General Charles Gerard's victory at Newcastle Emlyn in April, not in early July. The list of colonels who were recruiting in South Wales after Naseby does not include Wise and Slaughter's names, see BL, Harleian MSS 6852, f. 475.
34. Hopton, 'Bellum Civile', p. 84.
35. Bulstrode, *Memoirs*, p. 139.
36. On this occasion Cromwell uniquely claimed the credit for a tactical move on the battlefield that had secured victory. At Marston Moor, Naseby and all engagements in the wars of 1648–1651 he strenuously resisted the temptation to do so. Cromwell's fear was that the Lord would punish generals who were guilty of the sin of pride by not attributing all their successes to God's providence. This was not unique. Waller was firmly convinced that his defeat at Roundway Down was apposite punishment for earlier examples of arrogance. Why did Cromwell break his self-imposed rule at Langport? Possibly worries about his reputation got the better of him. Fairfax had received the full credit for the victory at Naseby when the clinching move had been Cromwell's, and he was determined that the same thing would not happen in the next engagement.
37. Sprigg, *Anglia Rediviva*, pp. 68–73; Bodleian, Wood Pamphlets, 378 (9, 10, 13); Bulstrode, *Memoirs*, pp. 138–9; BL, Additional MSS 18982, f. 70; BL, Thomason Tracts E293 (17, 18). Wise and Slaughter were still in command of a body of 400 men in Hopton's last campaign six months later: see Carte, *Original Letters and Papers*, I, pp. 131–2.
38. Bodleian, Firth MSS C8, ff. 301–2.
39. Sprigg, *Anglia Rediviva*, pp. 72–3.
40. Bodleian, Wood Pamphlets, 378 (9); Sprigg, *Anglia Rediviva*, p. 72; Bulstrode, *Memoirs*, p. 139.
41. BL, Additional MSS 18982, f. 70.
42. BL, Thomason Tracts, E293 (27, 33, 34); Sprigg, *Anglia Rediviva*, p. 81.
43. Sprigg, *Anglia Rediviva*, p. 83; HMC, Portland MSS III, p. 138; Lynch, *For King and Parliament*, p. 144, quoting a pamphlet entitled 'A Great and Glorious Victory'.
44. BL, Harleian MSS 166, f. 220 (21 July 1645). When the king returned to Oxford at the end of August, the Committee of Both Kingdoms refused the temptation to draw regiments from the New Model Army in the south-west to defend East Anglia. Instead it assembled an ad hoc body made up of troops and regiments from many parts of the Midlands and the south-east: see Walker, *Historical Discourses*, p. 136, CSP Domestic 1645–7, pp. 98–103.
45. Sprigg, *Anglia Rediviva*, pp. 83, 84–119; Commons Journals, IV, pp. 278, 279; CSP Domestic 1645–7, p. 153; HMC, Portland MSS I, p. 269.

46. Clarendon, *History of the Rebellion*, IX, para. 133; CSP Domestic 1645–7, pp. 197, 221, 235, 244, 268–9.
47. Sprigg, *Anglia Rediviva*, pp. 146–7.
48. Bell, ed., *Memoirs*, I, p. 239 (Sir Thomas Fairfax to Lord Fairfax, 16 July 1645).
49. Clarendon, *History of the Rebellion*, IX, para. 100.
50. This is what Lord Culpeper recommended in a letter he wrote to Goring on 17 September: see HMC, Portland MSS I, p. 274.
51. Bodleian, Clarendon MSS 25, ff. 21, 31.
52. Wanklyn, 'The King's Armies', pp. 245–6. The king's order that he should advance towards Oxford with his cavalry regiments alone was overtaken by events, as the New Model Army had arrived at Chard on 6 October poised to invade Devonshire: see Bodleian, Clarendon MSS 25, ff. 187, 189, 190, 215; Clarendon, *History of the Rebellion*, IX, para. 96; Bray, ed., *Evelyn's Diary*, IV, p. 162.
53. Firth, ed., 'Prince Rupert's Marches', p. 739; Lynch, *For King and Parliament*, pp. 140–1; Clarendon, *History of the Rebellion*, IX, paras 42, 66–8.
54. Roy, 'George Digby, Royalist Intrigue and the Collapse of the Cause', pp. 86–7.
55. BL, Additional MSS 21506, f. 38 (Digby to Rupert, Cardiff, 25 July 1645); Warburton, *Memoirs of Prince Rupert*, III, p. 152.
56. HMC, Portland MSS I, p. 245. See below, pp. 184–90, for an account of Montrose's progress in Scotland.
57. Kitson, *Prince Rupert*, pp. 252–3; Lynch, *For King and Parliament*, pp. 140–1.
58. Warburton, *Memoirs of Prince Rupert*, III, pp. 149, 154–5; Staffordshire CRO, DW 1778, I, i, 50 (6 August 1645), 57 (29 July 1645). The first of the letters in the Staffordshire CRO is wrongly dated as 6 May in the catalogue of the earl of Dartmouth's manuscripts.
59. Symonds, 'Diaries', pp. 268–72; Warburton, *Memoirs of Prince Rupert*, III, p. 162.
60. Kitson, *Prince Rupert*, pp. 262–8; Whitelock, *Memorials*, p. 195.
61. By then the marquis of Montrose's string of victories in Scotland had come to an end: see below, p. 190.
62. The most authoritative account of Lord Astley's last campaign is to be found in Barratt, *Cavaliers*, pp. 199–205.
63. For example, Gentles, *New Model Army*, pp. 78–81.
64. Sprigg, *Anglia Rediviva*, pp. 250–1, 335–6.
65. Ibid., p. 145; BL, Thomason Tracts, E314 (2, 3); Bodleian, Wood Pamphlets, 378 (41); Carte, *Original Letters and Papers*, I, p. 139.
66. Clarendon, *History of the Rebellion*, IX, paras 103–10, 133–41.
67. Sprigg, *Anglia Rediviva*, pp. 154–7, 171–3, 180–4.
68. Carte, *Original Letters and Papers*, I, pp. 109–10; Clarendon, *History of the Rebellion*, IX, paras 106–7, 117, 139; Bodleian, Clarendon MSS 26, f. 81.
69. Bell, ed., *Memoirs*, I, p. 285; Whitelock, *Memorials*, pp. 192–3; Sprigg, *Anglia Rediviva*, pp. 194–202; Carte, *Original Letters and Papers*, I, pp. 111–14. Wogan's account of the campaign from the parliamentary perspective blamed Fairfax's leisurely campaigning on his lack of cavalry, but it seems an unlikely story given the poor morale of the enemy troops of horse: see Carte, *Original Letters and Papers*, I, pp. 142–3.
70. Carte, *Original Letters and Papers*, I, pp. 120–5, 141–3; Sprigg, *Anglia Rediviva*, pp. 224–37, 239.
71. Andriette, *Devon and Exeter in the Civil War*, pp. 166–7; Coate, *Civil War in Cornwall*, p. 219.
72. Clarendon, *History of the Rebellion*, IX, paras 145–9, X, paras 5–10, 37–47.
73. BL, Additional MSS 18979, f. 207.

Chapter 16: Warfare in Scotland and Ireland 1642–1648

1. Edwards, *Dealing in Death*, pp. 82–3, 119, 126.
2. M. O'Siochru, *Confederate Ireland: A Constitutional and Political Analysis* (Dublin, 1999), pp. 245–7; Stevenson, *Revolution and Counter-Revolution*, chapters 4 to 8.
3. R. Hutton, 'George Monck, First Duke of Albemarle', *ODNB*, 38, p. 582.

4. Baillie, 'Letters and Journals', II, pp. 418–19. Also, see below, pp. 217–19.
5. Wheeler, *Irish and British Wars*, pp. 175–8; J. Wheeler, 'Four Armies in Ireland', in J. Ohlmeyer, ed. *Ireland from Independence to Occupation* (Cambridge, 1995), p. 65.
6. See below, pp. 205–14.
7. P. Lenihan, ' "Celtic Warfare" in the Sixteen-Forties', in J.R. Young, ed. *Celtic Dimensions of the British Civil Wars* (Edinburgh, 1997), pp. 134, 136.
8. A. Clarke, 'Michael Jones', *ODNB*, 30, p. 589; P. Little, 'Murrough O'Brien, Earl of Inchiquin', *ODNB*, 41, p. 367; HMC, Portland MSS I, p. 443–4.
9. For example, J. Buchan, *The Marquis of Montrose* (London, 1928); C.V. Wedgwood, *Montrose* (London, 1952).
10. See below, pp. 185–6. Montrose's principal critics, David Stevenson and Stuart Reid, have a natural desire to question the validity of the traditional interpretation of his generalship. The first has written an excellent biography of Alasdair MacColla, the second intends in part to rescue the Covenanter armies from ridicule: see *Highland Warrior* and *The Campaigns of Montrose: A Military History of the Civil Wars in Scotland* (Edinburgh, 1990).
11. D. Williams, *Montrose, Cavalier in Mourning* (London, 1975), p. 15.
12. D. Stevenson, *The Scottish Revolution 1637–44: The Triumph of the Covenanters* (Newton Abbot, 1973), p. 292; D. Stevenson, 'James Graham, First Marquis of Montrose', *ODNB*, 23, p. 194.
13. Stevenson, *The Scottish Revolution*, pp. 297–8.
14. For Charles's belief that Presbyterianism was incompatible with royal authority see Cust, *Charles I*, pp. 24, 221–2.
15. This is implicit in Williams, *Montrose*, pp. 2–7.
16. Clarendon, *History of the Rebellion*, VII, paras 405, 408; Hamper, ed., *The Diary of Sir William Dugdale*, p. 79.
17. D. Stevenson, 'George Gordon, Second Marquis of Huntly', *ODNB*, 22, pp. 887–90.
18. Turner, *Memoirs*, pp. 35–6; Clarendon, *History of the Rebellion*, VIII, paras 203–7.
19. G. Wishart, *The Memoirs of James, Marquis of Montrose* (London, 1893), pp. 47–50. To make matters worse, the rest, including almost all of Montrose's noble supporters, fell into enemy hands near Preston as they tried to make their way to Oxford: see Rushworth, ed., *Historical Collections*, V, p. 75; M. Napier, ed., *Memorials of Montrose and his Times*, 2 vols (Maitland Club, Edinburgh, 1848–50), II, p. 405.
20. Stevenson, 'Huntly', *ODNB*, pp. 889–90; Williams, *Montrose*, p. 140; Wishart, *Memoirs of Montrose*, pp. 54–6.
21. Stevenson, *Highland Warrior*, pp. 104–8.
22. Ibid., pp. 110–18.
23. This was particularly important as after the embarrassment at Dumfries the king had placed the Irish brigade under the command of the marquis of Huntly: see ibid., p. 115.
24. Wedgwood, *King's War*, pp. 316–17.
25. Stevenson, *Highland Warrior*, pp. 75–84.
26. For example, Napier, ed., *Memorials of Montrose*; Sir John Fortescue, *A History of the British Army* (London, 1910), I, p. 228. John Buchan and C.V. Wedgwood take a similar but less extreme line in their biographies of Montrose, both called *Montrose*, published in 1928 and 1952 respectively.
27. Stevenson, 'Montrose', pp. 191–2, 194–5; Barratt, *Cavalier Generals*, pp. 199, 205.
28. Williams, *Montrose*, pp. 291–4.
29. See below, p. 190.
30. Stevenson, *Highland Warrior*, p. 205.
31. Getting messages across 400 miles of enemy-held territory was a perilous and problematic activity, couriers being frequently intercepted and executed as spies.
32. The principal narrative of Montrose's campaigns was written by George Wishart, his chaplain, and it is hagiography pure and simple. The second, by Patrick Gordon of Ruthven, is a little more critical, but has to be read with caution as it is a deliberate attempt to place the blowing hot and cold by various members of the Gordon family during 1644 and 1645 in the best possible light.

The principal account on the Covenanter side, written by Major General William Baillie, titular commander of the Covenanter forces fighting in Scotland in 1645, is a paean of self-justification, whereas John Spalding's account of the period, though useful for comments on the experience of his native Aberdeen, is in other respects a secondhand reworking of Covenanter propaganda: see Wishart, *Memoirs of Montrose*; Patrick Gordon of Ruthven, 'A Short Abridgement of Britain's Distempers' (Aberdeen, 1844); Baillie, 'Letters and Journals', II, pp. 417–24; John Spalding, 'Memorials of the Troubles in Scotland', II, in J. Stuart, ed., *Spalding Club* (Aberdeen, 1850–51).

33. Gilbert Burnet, *Memoirs of the Lives and Actions of the Dukes of Hamilton* (London, 1677); G. Crawford, ed., *Memoirs of Henry Guthry, Bishop of Dunkeld* (Glasgow, 1702), but circulating in manuscript in the 1670s: see Turner, *Memoirs*, pp. 231–46.

34. This has not, however, prevented squabbles over matters of minor importance affecting Auldearn in particular: see Stevenson, *Highland Warrior*, pp. 173–6, 178–9, 181, 193; Gardiner, *Great Civil War*, II, pp. 223–7; Reid, *Campaigns of Montrose*, pp. 109–16.

35. Wheeler, *The Irish and British Wars 1637–1654*, p. 123; Stevenson, *Highland Warrior*, pp. 127–8.

36. Gordon, 'Short Abridgement', pp. 124, 130, 141.

37. The forces sent back from Ireland and England to hunt down Montrose and bring him to battle, and those raised in Scotland itself in 1645 for that purpose, consisted very largely of infantry.

38. Gordon, 'Short Abridgement', pp. 81, 140.

39. CSP Domestic 1645–7, pp. 68, 85, 90, 94. This came about almost by accident, as Leslie's regiments were already in Yorkshire when the call came. They had left the Scottish army, then besieging Hereford, with the aim of preventing King Charles I raising a new body of infantry in the counties to the north of the Trent. It was only after the king realised that he was not strong enough to face Leslie and Parliament's northern army combined and began his retreat down the Great North Road that it was agreed that Leslie should head north rather than follow the king.

40. See below p. 190.

41. Reid, *Campaigns of Montrose*, p. 186.

42. Wishart, *Memoirs of Montrose*, pp. 98–102, 108–11, 122–5; Gordon, 'Short Abridgement', pp. 121–7, 132–5, 139–45.

43. Stevenson, *Highland Warrior*, p. 262.

44. Ibid., pp. 82–4.

45. Ibid., pp. 106–8.

46. Alasdair's charge broke the enemy body facing him but his men failed to regroup. Instead they set about pillaging Inchiquin's baggage train. Dispersed in this manner, they fell easy victims to a charge from the enemy cavalry reserves: see BL, Thomason Tracts, E418 (6).

47. Gordon, 'Short Abridgement', pp. 82–3.

48. Stevenson, *Highland Warrior*, pp. 182–3.

49. Gordon, 'Short Abridgement', p. 130.

50. Williams, *Montrose*, pp. 187–8.

51. Stevenson, *Highland Warrior*, p. 156; Gordon, 'Short Abridgement', p. 101.

52. At Aberdeen, see Gordon, 'Short Abridgement', pp. 81–2, and at Fyvie, see ibid., p. 85; Wishart, *Memoir of Montrose*, pp. 70–3.

53. Baillie, 'Letters and Journals', II, p. 417.

54. Stevenson, *Revolution and Counter-Revolution*, p. 23.

55. See above, pp. 1, 4, and Williams, *Montrose*, pp. 284–5.

56. Stevenson, *Highland Warrior*, pp. 206–9.

57. Warburton, *Memoirs of Prince Rupert*, III, p. 156; CSP Domestic 1645–7, pp. 160–1; Wedgwood, *King's War*, pp. 500–1.

58. Eight regiments of horse and one of dragoons: see Terry, *Life of Leven*, pp. 375–6.

59. Gordon, 'Short Abridgement', pp. 156–60; Crawford, ed., *Memoirs of Bishop Guthry*, pp. 202–4, Wishart, *Memoirs of Montrose*, pp. 142–8.

60. The Scots were very happy to see him go. The country could not support so large a force of cavalry for long because of the extent to which Montrose's army had plundered it: see Baillie, 'Letters and Journals', II, pp. 315, 323.

Chapter 17: The Second English Civil War

1. Commons Journals, IV, pp. 628–39.
2. Firth and Rait, *Acts and Ordinances*, I, p. 614.
3. Commons Journals, IV, p. 632; BL, Additional MSS 31116, f. 279; M. Steig, ed., 'The Diary of John Harington MP', *Somerset Record Society* 74 (1977), p. 30.
4. Baillie, 'Letters and Journals', III, p. 307; Turner, *Memoirs*, p. 41.
5. Gardiner, *Great Civil War*, III, pp. 112–14.
6. Peter Young has estimated from information given to the House of Lords that Leslie had just over 7,000 men at the siege of Newark in January 1646: see Young et al., *Newark on Trent*, p. 97.
7. See above, p. 122, for the Independents and religious toleration.
8. Sprigg, *Anglia Rediviva*, pp. 310, 320; Woolrych, *Britain in Revolution*, pp. 349–50.
9. J. Kenyon and J. Ohlmeyer, eds, *The Civil Wars: A Military History of England, Scotland and Ireland 1639–1660*, p. 62.
10. Kishlansky, *The Rise of the New Model Army* (Oxford, 1998), pp. 140–2.
11. Commons Journals, V, pp. 90, 91, 106–8.
12. Gentles, *New Model Army*, pp. 88–91, 153; R. Ashton, *Counter Revolution: The Second Civil War and its Origins* (Newhaven, Conn., 1994), pp. 159–65; Whitelock, *Memorials*, pp. 234, 236.
13. Gentles, *English Revolution*, p. 306; Gentles, *New Model Army*, p. 150; Marshall, *Oliver Cromwell: Soldier*, p. 169; Lords Journals, X, p. 410.
14. The text of the 'Declaration of Dislike' is reproduced in Lords Journals, IX, pp. 112–15.
15. Gentles, *New Model Army*, pp. 233–4.
16. Lords Journals, IX, p. 664.
17. The major exception was Major General Edward Massey.
18. CSP Domestic 1648–9, p. 1; Commons Journals, V, pp. 410–12, 416. Early January seems a little premature, the only justification being the king's flight and serious rioting in Canterbury against the banning of Christmas celebrations. The king's supporters had yet to appear in arms, and not surprisingly with little business to do the Committee met very infrequently during the first three months of its existence, seven times in January, nine in February and nine in March, as opposed to sixteen in April and twenty in May: see CSP Domestic 1648–9, pp. 3–89.
19. Manchester presided on most occasions on which the House met between March 1646 and December 1648, as he had done before assuming command of the Eastern Association in 1643. His position was that of acting speaker, as there was no lord chancellor in post to perform the task.
20. He attended on fifty-three out of eighty-five occasions. Sir Gilbert Gerard was present on forty-seven occasions. The only major military or past-military figure other than Manchester on the Committee was Philip Skippon. He attended on seventeen occasions after 1 June, the date on which his name was added: see CSP Domestic 1648–9, pp. 90–261.
21. His function was not merely to report back to the Lords on the business transacted that day. Other members of the Upper House often attended the Committee, but attendance records show very clearly that they did not fill in for Manchester's absences.
22. Ashton, *Counter Revolution*, pp. 449–53, 478.
23. CSP Domestic 1648–9, pp. 52, 56, 58–9, 60, 66, 82, 86–90.
24. Ibid, pp. 62, 66, 67. Sir Arthur Haselrig, the governor of Newcastle, made a plea to this effect to the speaker of the House of Commons: see H. Cary, ed. *Memorials of the Great Civil War in England*, 2 vols (London, 1842), I, pp. 397–8.
25. CSP Domestic 1648–9, pp. 24–5, 27, 57.
26. CSP Domestic 1648–9, pp. 233–4, 245.
27. Ibid., pp. 41–2, 53; Cary, ed., *Memorials*, I, p. 393.
28. CSP Domestic 1648–9, pp. 66, 104, 140, 199; Abbott, ed., *Writings and Speeches*, I, pp. 619–21.
29. CSP Domestic 1648–9, pp. 74–8, 87–8, 116, 138, 140.
30. Bell, ed., *Memoirs*, II, pp. 32–4; Cary, *Memorials*, I, pp. 438–9; Lords Journals, X, p. 301; BL, Thomason Tracts, E445 (36), (40), (42).

31. Bell, ed., *Memoirs*, II, p. 34; Rushworth, ed., *Historical Collections*, VII, pp. 1,136–7.

32. See above, pp. 87, 174–5, 178. [The only argument that can be made in Fairfax's defence is that the force he commanded was smaller than that of the Kentish royalists, but it was not as small as Gentles has claimed: see *New Model Army*, p. 247. It was probably 5,000 strong if an allowance is made for Gentles's underestimate of the size of the contingent Fairfax withdrew from the New Model Army garrison of London. It was also well armed, experienced and highly motivated. On the other hand Alan Everitt's estimate of 8,000 or so is on the high side: see *The Community of Kent and the Great Rebellion* (Leicester, 1966), pp. 260–1.]

33. Gardiner, *Great Civil War*, IV, p. 152.

34. Whitelock, *Memorials*, pp. 331–3.

35. On surrendering in the first war, they had promised not to take up arms again in return.

36. Abbott, ed., *Writings and Speeches*, I, p. 621.

37. Ashton, *Counter Revolution*, pp. 318–35; Scott, *Politics and War*, pp. 164–5, 169–70; Gentles, *English Revolution*, p. 224.

38. On the orders of Fairfax or the Committee at Derby House, Cromwell had to leave behind several regiments that had been with him in Wales, Colonel Ewer's, Colonel Horton's and part of Sir William Constable's: see Gentles, *New Model Army*, pp. 255, 258; CSP Domestic 1648–9, p. 208; Rushworth, ed., *Historical Collections*, VII, p. 1,134.

39. It is generally held that Cromwell ordered Lambert not to fight the enemy until he arrived, but this derives from a comment in a London journal, which Abbott dates at around 6 August: see *Writings and Speeches*, I, p. 626. In fact, Lambert had received instructions from the Committee at Derby House not to engage with the Scots some weeks previously following consultations between them and General Fairfax: see CSP Domestic 1648–9, pp. 134, 139–40, 203–4, 208.

40. See above, p. 235 n.1. The treatise was not published until after Monck's death but under the auspices of the Sidney family who had kept it on their bookshelves for the past twenty-five years.

41. D.N. Farr, 'John Lambert', *ODNB*, 32, pp. 319–20; Bodleian, Fairfax MSS 36, ff. 15–16; R. Hutton, 'George Monck, First Duke of Albemarle', *ODNB*, 38, p. 581.

42. Abbott, ed., *Writings and Speeches*, I, p. 634.

43. Estimates of the size of the army Hamilton commanded vary enormously, largely because it was so scattered when Cromwell attacked. If it had assembled at Preston in its entirety, Cromwell's figure of 22,000 does not seem excessive. If the cavalry at Wigan, two regiments besieging Lancaster and Monro's corps, are deducted, 13,000–14,000 seems a reasonable figure for those involved in the fighting on 17 August, but most of the cavalry were, of course, caught up in the eventual destruction of the army.

44. BL, Thomason Tracts, E460 (35); Wheeler, *Irish and British Wars*, pp. 190–2.

45. Abbott, ed., *Writings and Speeches*, I, p. 634; W. Beamont, ed., 'A Discourse of the Warr in Lancashire', *Chetham Society*, LXII (1864), p. 65; HMC, Portland MSS III, p. 175.

46. Abbott, ed., *Writings and Speeches*, I, pp. 634–5; Turner, *Memoirs*, p. 63. A. Marshall claims that Cromwell was receiving regular and detailed accounts of the progress and condition of Hamilton's army from spies: see *Oliver Cromwell: Soldier*, p. 180, but the source cited describes the intelligence Lambert was receiving at Barnard Castle: see Scott, ed., 'Original Memoirs', p. 112. Moreover, the wording of the passage – that 'we had spies amongst their army daily that brought us true intelligence of their numbers, as near as could be computed, their posture and demeanour' – suggests strongly that the intelligence came from country people and/or longer-distance travellers in transit between County Durham and Carlisle who had to make their way through the army whilst it was quartered in the Vale of Eden.

47. Hamilton did not send the cavalry to Wigan until after Cromwell's Council of War had taken place.

48. Turner, *Memoirs*, p. 63; BL, Thomason Tracts, E467 (21).

49. Bodleian, Clarendon MSS 2862; Turner, *Memoirs*, pp. 248–51. The two versions of Langdale's account of the campaign in print differ slightly from one another: see Carte, *Original Letters and Papers*, I, pp. 159–61; Sunderland, *Lord Langdale*, pp. 133–6. I have therefore used the manuscript version in the Bodleian as it is the earliest extant text. Gilbert Burnet implied that James Livingstone, Earl of Callendar, Hamilton's chief military adviser, knew that Cromwell's army was

approaching Preston along the north bank of the Ribble – see *Dukes of Hamilton*, p. 358 – but chose to keep the information to himself, but there is no confirmation of this in other sources.

50. Clarendon, *History of the Rebellion*, IX, para. 74. The future Lord Clarendon was in France in 1648, but had conversations with Langdale during their exile: see ibid., IX, para. 75.

51. Scott, ed., 'Original Memoirs', pp. 115–17; Abbott, ed., *Writings and Speeches*, I, pp. 634–5; BL, Thomason Tracts, 460 (35). It was even alleged that Hamilton knowingly allowed Langdale to face the brunt of the enemy attack alone so that the whole of the Scottish army could cross the Ribble in safety, but this is suspect as it comes from a parliamentary source: see Beamont, 'Discourse', p. 65. Almost until the enemy breakthrough the Scottish commanders regarded what was happening on the Clitheroe road as a feint which it was appropriate for a flank guard to deal with. The duke may eventually have sent a body of infantry to Langdale's support, but it took no part in the engagement at Ribbleton Moors End. Instead it hung about well to the rear and was presumably destroyed in and around Preston in the same way as the force it was supposed to have reinforced. However, Langdale claimed he received no support apart from a few horse (his description of the Scottish lancers), and so the royalist sources cannot be reconciled on this point: see Turner, *Memoirs*, p. 63; Bodleian, Clarendon MSS 2862; Burnet, *Dukes of Hamilton*, p. 359.

52. Abbott, ed., *Writings and Speeches*, I, p. 635. A slightly different description of the deployment is given in an account of the battle printed in London: see BL, Thomason Tracts, E460 (35). For the parallel with Langport, see Marshall, *Oliver Cromwell: Soldier*, p. 187.

53. Scott, ed., 'Original Memoirs', p. 117; Bodleian, Clarendon MSS, 2862. Both suggest that the Scottish lancers were committed quite late in the engagement at Ribbleton Moors End.

54. This narrative of events is based on the exact words used by Hodgson and Langdale in their accounts of the battle. Hodgson was giving Lambert a warning, not advising him of an opportunity, whereas Sir Marmaduke blamed the Scots for not securing his right flank by mounting a strong guard on the lane that led from Ribbleton Moors End to the bridge over the Ribble: see Scott, ed., 'Original Memoirs', p. 118; Bodleian, Clarendon MSS, 2862.

55. The duke had decided to remain with the rearguard on Preston Moor to the north of the town to await the arrival of stragglers, most unusual behaviour on the part of a commander-in-chief when intelligence strongly suggested that a major engagement was about to take place somewhere to the south of the town.

56. Beamont, ed., 'Discourse', p. 65; Abbott, ed., *Writings and Speeches*, I, p. 636; BL, Thomason Tracts, E460 (35).

57. Most, if not all, of the artillery pieces were either with General Monro or even further north: see BL, Thomason Tracts, E467 (21).

58. HMC, Portland MSS III, p. 175; Scott, ed., 'Original Memoirs', p. 120; BL, Thomason Tracts, E460 (35); Abbott, ed., *Writings and Speeches*, I, p. 635; Turner, *Memoirs*, p. 64.

59. See pp. 213, 277 n.36.

60. Secondary sources claim that Cromwell made his way to Preston from the edge of Preston Moor where we left him at the climax of the first engagement: see Young and Holmes, *English Civil Wars*, pp. 286–7; Marshall, *Oliver Cromwell: Soldier*, p. 183. However, this is based on speculation not on contemporary evidence.

61. He had probably envisaged the final stage of the battle as taking place in Fishwick Bottom, a piece of flat land to the east of the bridge with the royalists having their backs to the river but with no means of crossing it. This can be inferred from the text of Cromwell's letter to the speaker of the House of Commons, see Abbott, ed., *Writings and Speeches*, I, p. 634.

62. HMC, Portland MSS III, p. 175; BL, Thomason Tracts, E460 (35); Abbott, ed., *Writings and Speeches*, I, p. 635.

63. BL, Thomason Tracts, E467 (21); Turner, *Memoirs*, pp. 64–6; Bodleian, Clarendon MSS, 2862; Scott, ed., 'Original Memoirs', pp. 121–2.

64. Abbott, ed., *Writings and Speeches*, I, p. 637.

65. Ibid., I, pp. 639–42; Bodleian, Clarendon MSS 2862; BL, Thomason Tracts, E467 (21). Hamilton was tried for treason and executed early in 1649.

66. Turner, *Memoirs*, p. 68; Abbott, ed., *Writings and Speeches*, I, pp. 641–2; Stevenson, *Revolution and Counter Revolution*, pp. 114–17.

67. Cromwell's other concern was that the politicians at Westminster might think he was exceeding his instructions. This is apparent from his letters to the Committee at Derby House in which he interpreted the order to pursue the enemy 'and not leave them wherever they may go to form a beginning of a new army' as carte blanche to negotiate with Covenanter leaders like the marquis of Argyll who had either opposed the Engagers or refused to join Hamilton's army for the invasion of England. However, the Committee was happy to endorse an initiative that could well bring the war to a speedy end: see CSP Domestic 1648–9, p. 256; Abbott, ed., *Writings and Speeches*, I, pp. 652, 654, 658, 660.

68. Abbott, ed., *Writings and Speeches*, I, pp. 660–2, 663–4, 668–9; HMC, Lord Braye MSS, pp. 168–73; D. Stevenson, *Revolution and Counter Revolution*, pp. 115–18; Lords Journals, X, p. 513; Commons Journals, VI, p. 54; CSP Domestic 1648–9, p. 283; Thurlow, *State Papers*, I, pp. 105–6.

Chapter 18: The British Wars 1649–1652: Ireland

1. Abbott, ed., *Writings and Speeches*, I, pp. 670–4; Bennett, *Oliver Cromwell*, pp. 147–52.
2. This is apparent from a letter he wrote to General Fairfax on the 20th of the month cited by Gardiner: see *Great Civil War*, IV, p. 251.
3. See, for example, a century apart in their dates of publication, Bennett, *Oliver Cromwell*, pp. 150–1, and Gardiner, *Great Civil War*, IV, pp. 247–53. The seriousness of the attempt to get the king to accept a settlement in late December that would have saved his life, and Cromwell's role in that attempt, cannot be tied up one way or the other because of the problematic nature of the source material. Modern opinion would see the attempt as being sincere and driven by concern as to the political consequences of eliminating the king, but this underestimates the moral climate. Righteous indignation motivated many of those who wished Charles to die for having inflicted death on so many others. In addition, stern Providence must not be denied. God had clearly turned his face against the king. To spare his life would therefore be sinful and cause divine wrath to fall on those who had ignored so obvious a sign of divine displeasure.
4. He attended the initial meeting of the court that dealt with preliminaries but never attended again: see Woolrych, *Britain in Revolution*, p. 431.
5. O'Siochru, *Confederate Ireland*, pp. 185, 201–2.
6. Kenyon and Ohlmeyer, eds, *The Civil Wars*, pp. 185–7; CSP Domestic, 1648–9, p. 337.
7. CSP Domestic, 1649, pp. 32, 37, 40; J.S. Wheeler, 'The Logistics of the Cromwellian Conquest of Scotland 1650–1651', *War and Society* 10, p. 41; Gentles, *New Model Army*, pp. 353–4.
8. Gentles, *New Model Army*, pp. 329–48.
9. T.W. Moody, F.X. Martin and F.J. Byrne, eds, *Early Modern Ireland 1534–1691: A New History of Ireland*, 6 vols (Oxford, 1978), III, p. 337.
10. S.R. Gardiner, *The Commonwealth and Protectorate*, 3 vols (London, 1903), I, p. 354; Whitelock, *Memorials*, p. 419; Hutton, 'George Monck', *ODNB*, p. 582. O'Neill's willingness to assist Monck and also Coote, who could not have clung onto Derry without his support, was not simply because he was taken in by lies that the Commonwealth government would look favourably on religious toleration for Irish Catholics. He also acquired some vital military supplies in return, most particularly gunpowder, and this was at the centre of Monck's difficulties with his bosses when he got home to England: see P. Lenihan, *Consolidating Conquest: Ireland 1603–1727* (Harlow, 2007), p. 127; J. Casway, 'Owen Roe O'Neill', *ODNB*, 41, p. 855.
11. Scott, *Politics and War*, p. 196.
12. Marshall, *Oliver Cromwell: Soldier*, p. 199; Cary, *Memorials*, II, pp. 152–3; Wheeler, *Irish and British Wars*, p. 210; Gentles, *English Revolution*, p. 309.
13. P. Morrah, *Prince Rupert of the Rhine* (London, 1976), pp. 240–1.
14. Wheeler, *Irish and British Wars*, p. 211; Moody, Martin and Byrne, eds, *New History of Ireland*, III, p. 211.
15. Carte, *James Butler*, III, pp. 465–6; Whitelock, *Memorials*, p. 211.

16. For example, HMC, Appendix to the 7th Report, p. 55; Cary, *Memorials*, II, pp. 152–3, 160–1. In his memoirs, Colonel Robert Venables, who landed there with his regiment on 22 July, reported on the low state of morale in the Dublin garrison, with 'the soldiers running away to the enemy by hundreds so that they were almost come to a necessity to treat of a surrender': see C.H. Firth, ed., 'The Narrative of General Venables', *Camden Society*, new series, 60 (1900), p. 2.
17. BL, Thomason Tracts, E569 (1); Cary, *Memorials*, II, p. 161.
18. T. Barnard, 'James Butler, Duke of Ormond', *ODNB*, 9, p. 155. Clarendon wrote a glowing character sketch of the marquis, as Ormond was a leading member of his faction in later life: see *History of the Rebellion*, VI, para. 313. However, Cromwell, on seeing a portrait of Ormond for the first time during the campaign in Ireland, declared that he looked 'more huntsman than any way a soldier': see T. Reilly, *Cromwell, An Honourable Enemy* (London, 1999), p. 206.
19. Abbott, ed., *Writings and Speeches*, II, pp. 102–3; BL, Thomason Tracts, E569 (1).
20. Carte, *Life of Ormond*, III, pp. 468–9; BL, Thomason Tracts, E569 (1); Cary, *Memorials*, II, pp. 160–1; Bodleian, Carte MSS 25, f. 132; Ludlow, *Memoirs*, I, p. 230. Carte claimed that Dillon was unaware of what was happening, but it seems highly unlikely that the noise of musket fire would not have carried that far.
21. Cary, *Memorials*, II, p. 161; Bodleian, Carte MSS 25, f. 132; BL, Thomason Tracts, E569 (1).
22. Wheeler is wrong to imply that Jones exaggerated his difficulties as his troops were well equipped, well supplied and well paid: see Wheeler, 'Logistics', p. 42. For Jones to have written as he did when the supply situation was good would have laid him open to a major rebuke, if not worse.
23. Bodleian, Carte MSS 25, ff. 195, 197.
24. Reilly, *Honourable Enemy*, pp. 53, 62.
25. Gentles, *New Model Army*, p. 352.
26. Abbott, ed., *Writings and Speeches*, II, pp. 83–4: T. Barnard, 'Roger Boyle, Earl of Orrery', *ODNB*, 7, pp. 109–10.
27. Marshall, *Oliver Cromwell: Soldier*, pp. 231–3; Lenihan, 'Celtic Warfare', p. 136.
28. This brief narrative is taken primarily from Wheeler, *Irish and British Wars*, pp. 211–20.
29. Moody, Martin and Byrne, eds, *New History of Ireland*, III, p. 339.
30. M. Fissell, *War and Government 1598–1650* (Manchester, 1991), p. 52.
31. This is implicit in most recent narratives, though very often the main thrust is that much remained to be done: see, for example, Gentles, *The English Revolution*, p. 404; Wheeler, *Irish and British Wars*, p. 220; Marshall, *Oliver Cromwell: Soldier*, p. 232. For Coote in 1649, see above, p. 284 n.10.
32. Whitelock, *Memorials*, pp. 463–4; Ludlow, *Memoirs*, I, p. 255; J.S. Wheeler, *Cromwell in Ireland* (London, 1999), p. 172; J. Casway, 'Owen Roe O'Neill', *ODNB*, 41, p. 855.
33. Gentles, *New Model Army*, pp. 368–9. One of Ormond's correspondents summed up Cromwell's expertise as follows: he 'hath used more prudence and policy than ever was practiced by any conqueror whatsoever': see Carte, *Original Letters and Papers*, I, p. 308.
34. His position is made very clear in a long response he wrote to a declaration by the Catholic bishops that the Irish must fight to the end, as no mercy could be expected from Cromwell: see Abbott, ed., *Writings and Speeches*, II, pp. 196–205.
35. Carte, *Life of Ormond*, III, p. 477.
36. Abbott, ed., *Writings and Speeches*, II, pp. 136–8. It is also misconceived to blame Cromwell for losing control of his men at Wexford. Generals found great difficulty in controlling soldiers after a town had been stormed, and it is most interesting that historians do not criticise the duke of Wellington when even worse things happened at Ciudad Rodrigo and Badajoz in the Peninsular campaign. Cromwell, like Wellington, was worried about the impact on discipline in general of troops running amuck, and this rather than politics may explain why indiscriminate slaughter on such a scale did not happen again whilst he was in charge in Ireland: see Marshall, *Oliver Cromwell: Soldier*, p. 233; Cary, *Memorials*, II, p. 179.
37. Abbott, ed., *Writings and Speeches*, II, p. 137. After submitting the manuscript of this book, I heard similar sentiments expressed by Professor Roland Hutton in the television documentary

Cromwell: God's Executioner (2008), part I. Although Hutton did not go as far as I have done in his reading of the text, confining himself simply to the view that Protestant and Catholic soldiers may both have been the subject of Cromwell's remark, it is nonetheless extremely gratifying, as on other occasions in the past, to learn that we think similarly about the wars of the mid seventeenth century.

38. Abbott, ed., *Writings and Speeches*, II, pp. 174, 176.

39. Bennett is wrong to suggest that the first assault at Clonmel having failed, the second might have succeeded if Cromwell had begun it by launching diversionary attacks against another section of the town wall: see *Cromwell*, p. 179. These had not sustained any damage from the artillery barrage of the previous week. It therefore seems unlikely that the governor would have taken any such attacks seriously enough to run down the forces at the breach in order to strengthen the defences elsewhere.

40. Estimates of the size of Cromwell's losses have increased over time. The most modest are 1,000 and 1,500, the first given by an anonymous officer of Sir John Clotworthy's regiment, who was not present at the siege and was writing long after the event, and the second by Sir George Hamilton, who was probably exaggerating in order to impress his superiors: see Reilly, *Honourable Enemy*, pp. 242, 301; Bodleian, Calendar of the Carte Manuscripts, March to July 1650, f. 131. Other more recent estimates vary between 2,000 and 3,000 killed and wounded: see Carte, *Life of Ormond*, III, p. 538; Kenyon and Ohlmeyer, eds, *The Civil Wars*, p. 221; and the television documentary, *Cromwell: God's Executioner*, part II. Henry Ireton, who was present at the siege, apparently referred to losses being higher at Clonmel than in any earlier engagement in England or Ireland in which he had taken part: see Moody, Martin and Byrne, eds, *New History of Ireland*, III, p. 347, reference not supplied, but this is not a telling point, as Ireton had not been at the siege of Colchester (summer 1648). He had been at Naseby where the New Model Army incurred its highest casualties on the battlefield, but it is unlikely from the evidence located by Glenn Foard that more than 200 officers and men were killed there or died of wounds almost immediately afterwards: see Foard, *Naseby*, pp. 405, 406, 409–12. I find two sources particularly convincing as evidence for less than 1,000 Cromwellian dead and wounded at Clonmel. Edmund Ludlow, who took up service in Ireland as lieutenant general of cavalry immediately after Cromwell's departure, and who was not an apologist for the lord lieutenant, made no mention of heavy casualties being incurred: see his *Memoirs*, I, pp. 237–8. Second, at the time the royalists did not see the New Model Army losses at Clonmel as being of major significance. There is nothing in the marquis of Ormond's incoming correspondence in mid- to late May to indicate that the enemy had suffered a major setback. Cromwell was expected to continue his campaign of sieges with Athlone as his next target. There was also no suggestion from his subordinate officers that what had happened at Clonmel had so altered the odds in the royalists' favour that they might or should try their luck against the New Model Army on the battlefield: see Bodleian, Calendar of Carte Manuscripts, April to July 1650, ff. 117, 124, 131.

41. Marshall writes of Cromwell's bullishness, Gentles of his having in mind a quick conquest which he intended to achieve by the application of overwhelming force: see *Oliver Cromwell: Soldier*, p. 233; *New Model Army*, p. 375.

42. See p. 277 n.36. He gave the most explicit account of his theology of providentialism in a letter written after the failure to capture Waterford: see Abbott, ed., *Writings and Speeches*, II, p. 173.

43. Wheeler, *Irish and British Wars*, p. 220; J. Gilbert, ed., *A Contemporary History of Affairs in Ireland from AD 1641–1652*, 3 vols (Dublin, 1880), III, pp. 296–335.

44. Gentles, *English Revolution*, p. 436, citing Lenihan, 'War and Famine 1649–52', *Irish Economic and Social History* 24 (1997).

Chapter 19: The British Wars 1650–1651: Scotland and England

1. Woolrych, *Britain in Revolution*, pp. 480–1. See also p. 284 n.67.

2. Clarendon, *History of the Rebellion*, XII, paras 74, 75, 117, 120.

3. T.F. Henderson, rev. E.M. Furgol, 'David Leslie, First Lord Newark', *ODNB*, 33, pp. 442–3.

4. Whitelock blamed the influence of Fairfax's wife, who was a keen Presbyterian. The lord general stood by his oath and used the word conscience many times in his discussion with other senior officers. He could not regard it as a just war if England was the aggressor. Ill-health was never mentioned. See *Memorials*, pp. 460–2; Commons Journals, VI, pp. 430–2.

5. Sir Thomas Fairfax had initially been described as commander-in-chief, but the title of lord general was revived in 1647 after Essex's death (14 September 1646) and the first army coup.

6. For the best account of the way in which the Council of State supplied the New Model Army during its Scottish campaign, see Wheeler, 'The Logistics of the Cromwellian Conquest of Scotland 1650–1651', pp. 1–18.

7. Stevenson, *Revolution and Counter Revolution*, pp. 170–5: Walker, *Historical Discourses*, pp. 165, 168, 179. The numbers purged were 80 officers and 3,000 rank and file.

8. W. Douglas, *Cromwell's Scotch Campaign* (Edinburgh, 1898), pp. 39–46.

9. Even after occupying Leith and other ports on the south shore of the Firth of Forth in the autumn, the English navy did not have complete control of the sea: see J.D. Grainger, *Cromwell against the Scots: The Last Anglo-Scottish War 1650–1652* (East Linton, 1997), p. 81.

10. Ibid., pp. 96–7; Kenyon and Ohlmeyer, eds, *The Civil Wars*, p. 66. It also had enormous significance for Scots facing an English invasion because below Stirling Castle was the site of the battle of Bannockburn where Robert the Bruce had destroyed the army of King Edward II.

11. Bodleian, Carte MSS 80, f. 734.

12. Abbott, ed., *Writings and Speeches*, II, pp. 314–15, 321–2. Cromwell specifically referred to Lostwithiel in a letter written in September 1650.

13. The evidence is not strong enough to be convincing because it comes from third parties. The most direct evidence suggests that Leslie was happy with the decision to leave Doon Hill. In his own attempt to escape blame after the battle he did not try to shift it onto others. All he was keen to do was to show that he was not solely responsible for decisions taken at Dunbar: see Thurlow, *State Papers*, I, p. 167; D. Laing, ed., 'The Ancram and Lothian Correspondence' (2 vols, Bannatyne Club, 1875), pp. 297–8. In fact, the decision was not inherently disastrous. What was disastrous was the way in which Leslie deployed his army when it got to the low ground by the coast: see below, pp. 218–19.

14. There is some dispute as to the exact time amongst the primary sources: see Carte, *Original Letters and Papers*, I, p. 381 (morning); Abbott, ed., *Writings and Speeches*, II, p. 323 (late afternoon); Scott, ed., *Original Memoirs*, pp. 144–5 (early afternoon implied).

15. Abbott, ed., *Writings and Speeches*, II, p. 323; Scott, ed., *Original Memoirs*, pp. 144–5.

16. Abbott, ed., *Writings and Speeches*, II, p. 324; Carte, *Original Letters and Papers*, I, p. 383; C.H. Firth, 'The Battle of Dunbar', *Transactions of the Royal Historical Society*, new series, 14 (1900), p. 47.

17. Scott, ed., 'Original Memoirs', pp. 146–8. The troops they faced were mainly cavalry, Leslie having massed his horse on the right wing because it was there that the enemy cavalry breakout was most likely to occur, the ground being flatter than elsewhere to the east and south of Dunbar: see Abbott, ed., *Writings and Speeches*, II, p. 323.

18. Scott, ed., *Original Memoirs*, p. 145.

19. Abbott, ed., *Writings and Speeches*, II, p. 324; Scott, ed., *Original Memoirs*, p. 148.

20. Oddly, Cromwell made no mention of the flank attack in any of his accounts of the battle. The only evidence that it took place is in John Hodgson's account printed in Scott, ed., *Original Memoirs*, but the writing is so vivid it is most unlikely that he misremembered. Moreover, the depiction of the battle by Payne Fisher clearly shows the crossing of the Brox Burn close to its mouth and New Model units delivering a flank attack on the enemy right wing: see Firth, 'Dunbar', pp. 20–2. More likely, Cromwell was so personally involved in the flank attack that he did not mention it for fear of attracting God's wrath. See pp. 213, 277 n.36 for Cromwell's fear of committing the sin of pride.

21. Scott, ed., *Original Memoirs*, pp. 147–8; S.R. Gardiner, *Commonwealth and Protectorate*, I, pp. 294–5; Carte, *Original Letters and Papers*, I, pp. 383–4; Abbott, ed., *Writings and Speeches*, II, p. 324.

22. Thurlow, *State Papers*, I, p. 167.

23. See note 13 above.

24. Robert Baillie, 'Letters and Journals', III, p. 111.

25. Laing, ed., 'The Ancram and Lothian Correspondence', II, pp. 297–8; Walker, *Historical Discourses*, p. 180; Robert Baillie, 'Letters and Journals', III, p. 111.

26. Shortcomings in intelligence are mentioned by both Furgol and Carpenter: see Kenyon and Ohlmeyer, eds, *The Civil Wars*, p. 66; *Military Leadership*, p. 150; but as the English troop movements preparatory for the attack across the Brox Burn occurred after dark, intelligence about what was happening could only have come from deserters. However, there is no mention of such in any of the contemporary accounts. In addition, if Leslie had learned anything about enemy plans during the night, the darkness would have made it difficult, if not impossible, to change the deployment of the Scottish army in response without risking great confusion.

27. Firth, 'Dunbar', pp. 144–8; Scott, ed., *Original Memoirs*, pp. 147–8.

28. Carpenter, *Military Leadership*, pp. 145–6.

29. However, Edinburgh Castle was the only gain from what Gentles has described as Cromwell's religious offensive. It must have been disappointing compared with his earlier success in persuading fellow Protestants in Ireland to change sides: see *New Model Army*, pp. 399–400.

30. Bennett, *Cromwell*, pp. 189–91.

31. Grainger, *Cromwell against the Scots*, pp. 58–65, 93–7, 108; Marshall, *Oliver Cromwell: Soldier*, pp. 251–4.

32. Gentles, *English Revolution*, p. 426; Stevenson, *Revolution and Counter Revolution*, pp. 194–202.

33. Gentles, *English Revolution*, p. 432; Cary, *Memorials*, II, p. 292.

34. CSP Domestic 1650, p. 464, 1651, pp. 24, 53, 54. Marshall mentions October – see *Oliver Cromwell: Soldier*, p. 251 – but the origin of his comment is a remark in a London journal, which may have been purely speculation. A descent on the north shore was planned in January 1651, but was not carried through: see J. Akerman, ed., 'Letters from Scotland Addressed to Captain Adam Baynes' (Bannatyne Club, 1856), p. 8. The reason was almost certainly that boats based in the ports and fishing villages along the Firth of Forth which had been seized in September, and English naval vessels operating in Scottish waters, would not have been suitable for transporting either horses or artillery. The number of boats ordered to be built at Newcastle is not known, but they must have been numerous as they required 300 sailors to crew them. Grainger suggests there were fifty: see *Cromwell against the Scots*, p. 98.

35. Marshall, *Oliver Cromwell: Soldier*, pp. 252–4; Wheeler, *Irish and British Wars*, p. 238; Bennett, *Cromwell*, p. 191, citing Grainger, *Cromwell against the Scots*; Gentles, *New Model Army*, p. 403.

36. Stevenson, *Revolution and Counter Revolution*, p. 205.

37. BL, Thomason Tracts, E638 (7), (14); Abbott, ed., *Writings and Speeches*, II, pp. 432–5. The English lost fewer than a hundred men, but mainly in Lambert's regiment of horse: see Akerman, ed., 'Letters from Scotland', p. 36. This explains why I prefer to see the decisive action as being a conventional melee like that at Naseby, and do not rate Carpenter's hypothesis that the English cavalry attack was merely intended to lure the Scots into a killing ground where they could be raked by English cannon and musket fire: see *Military Leadership*, pp. 158–9.

38. D. Farr, *John Lambert: Parliamentary Soldier and Cromwellian Major General* (Woodbridge, 2003), p. 89. This excellent biography puts a convincing case for Lambert's military genius, but it is a little too reliant on the writings of John Hodgson, who hero-worshipped his general and fellow Yorkshireman.

39. Abbott ed., *Writings and Speeches*, II, pp. 434–5, 439–42.

40. Stevenson, *Revolution and Counter Revolution*, p. 207. It is, however, impossible to say how typical was the despair expressed in the duke of Hamilton's letters written in mid-August: see NAS, GD 406/1/5956.

41. For example, Bennett, *Cromwell*, p. 192; Marshall, *Oliver Cromwell: Soldier*, p. 255; J.C. Davis, *Oliver Cromwell* (London, 2001), p. 105.

42. Abbott, ed., *Writings and Speeches*, II, pp. 436, 443, 444; Cary, *Memorials*, II, pp. 288–9.

43. Abbott, ed., *Writings and Speeches*, II, pp. 444–5.

44. Cary, *Memorials*, II, p. 292; Kenyon and Ohlmeyer, eds, *The Civil Wars*, p. 70 (over 13,000); M. Atkin, *Worcestershire under Arms: An English County during the Civil Wars* (Barnsley, 2004), p. 140 (11,000); Clarendon, *History of the Rebellion*, XIII, para. 65 (near 20,000).

45. CSP Domestic 1650–1, pp. 328, 344–5, 354–5.

46. Atkin, *Worcestershire under Arms*, pp. 138–40; Clarendon, *History of the Rebellion*, XIII, paras 64–5; Gardiner, *Commonwealth and Protectorate*, II, p. 40.

47. Turner estimated at least 25,000, but this was either a gross exaggeration or an estimate of the numbers present and on their way to Worcester: see *Memoirs*, p. 95.

48. See above, pp. 19–21.

49. Cary, *Memorials*, II, pp. 353, 355.

50. M. Atkin, *Cromwell's Crowning Mercy: The Battle of Worcester 1651* (Stroud, 1998), pp. 92, 175.

51. Grainger, *Cromwell against the Scots*, p. 142. Clarendon describes him as 'dispirited and confused', giving and revoking orders and resentful of General Middleton, who was optimistic and seemed to enjoy the king's favour: see *History of the Rebellion*, XIII, para. 74; Henderson, rev. Furgol, 'David Lesley, First Lord Newark', *ODNB*, pp. 443–4. Atkin has pointed out that the landscape between the place where the Scottish cavalry were drawn up beside the Severn and Red Hill, where the royalist counter-attack took place, was difficult to negotiate for men on horseback, and that they could well have been intercepted by New Model horse had they begun to move onto the higher ground: see *The Battle of Worcester*, p. 100.

52. Whitelock, *Memorials*, p. 505; Abbott, ed., *Writings and Speeches*, II, p. 445.

53. HMC, Braye MSS, p. 175; Whitelock, *Memorials*, pp. 506–7; Calendar of Clarendon State Papers, 4 vols (Oxford, 1769), II, pp. 559–61; BL, Thomason Tracts, E641 (14, 20); Abbott, ed., *Writings and Speeches*, II, p. 461; Cary, *Memorials*, II, pp. 353–64.

54. HMC, Braye MSS, p. 175; Scott, ed., *Original Memoirs*, pp. 153–4; CSP Domestic 1650–1, pp. 399, 400.

55. F.D. Dow, *Cromwellian Scotland 1651–60* (Edinburgh, 1979), pp. 11–16; Cary, *Memorials*, II, p. 292.

Chapter 20: Generals: The Audit

1. Wanklyn, *Decisive Battles*, pp. 129–30.

2. Reid, *All the King's Armies*, p. 5.

3. Carpenter, *Military Leadership*, p. 166.

Bibliography

Manuscript Primary Sources

National Archives, Scotland
GD406/1/166
PA11/1–4

British Library
Additional MSS 11692, 15752, 16370, 18778–9, 18979–83, 21506, 25708, 27402, 31116–17, 33596, 36913, 40630, 62084–5
Egerton MSS 785, 2541, 2646
Harleian MSS 164–6, 986, 2125, 3783, 6802, 6804, 6852, 6988, 7379
Lansdown MSS 988
Loan MSS 29/123 Misc. 31
Sloane MSS 1519

Bodleian Library, University of Oxford
Carte MSS 6–8, 12–15, 20, 21, 25, 74, 79, 80
Clarendon MSS 21–26, 28
Don MSS d.57
Dugdale MSS 19
English MSS 132, C51
Fairfax MSS 32, 36
Firth MSS C6–8
Rawlinson MSS B200
Tanner MSS 54–5, 60–3

House of Lords
MSS 3639

Wadham College Library, Oxford
MSS A18.14

Berkshire County Record Office
Q/P116B/28/22/1
D/E280/18/1

Cornish County Record Office
R(S) 1/1053–8, 1062

Shropshire County Record Office
455/277, 278
Shrewsbury Borough MSS

Staffordshire County Record Office
D868.2
DW 1778 I i, 40–4, 50–7; DW 1778/V/1370

Warwickshire County Record Office
CR 1596
CR 1998
CR 2017

Wiltshire County Record Office
413/337
413/444A
413/444B

William Salt Library, Stafford
SMS 45
SMS 2007

Printed Primary Sources

Contemporary Biographies, Diaries, Manuals and Memoirs
Atkyns, Richard (1967) 'The Vindication of Richard Atkyns Esquire', published in *Military Memoirs of the English Civil War*, ed. P. Young, London: Longman.
Baillie, Robert (1841) 'Letters and Journals 1637–1662', ed. D. Laing, *Bannatyne Club* 72, 73, 77, Edinburgh.
Bampfield, Colonel Joseph (1993 edn) *Apologie*, ed. J. Loftis and P. Hardacre, Lewisburg, Canada: Bucknell Universities, Associated University Presses.
Bulstrode, Sir Richard (1721) *Memoirs and Reflections upon the Reign and Government of Charles I and Charles II*, London.
Burnet, Gilbert (1677) *Memoirs of the Lives and Actions of the Dukes of Hamilton*, London.
Burnet, Gilbert (1897) *History of My Own Time*, ed. O. Airy, Oxford: Oxford University Press.
Cholmley, Sir Hugh (2000) 'Memoirs and Memorials', ed. J. Baines, *Yorkshire Archaeological Society, Records Section* CLIII.
Codrington, Robert (1646) *The Life and Death of the Illustrious Robert, Earl of Essex*, London.
Corbet, John (1835) 'An Historical Relation of the Military Government of Gloucester from the beginning of the Civil War between King and Parliament and the Removal of Colonel Massey from that Government to the Command of the Western Forces', in *Bibliotheca Gloucestrensis*, ed. J. Washbourn, Gloucester.
Devereux, W. (1853) *Lives and Letters of the Devereux, Earls of Essex*, 2 vols, London.
Drake, Nathan (1860) 'A Journal of the First and Second Sieges of Pontefract', *Surtees Society* XXXVII.
Fairfax, Lord Thomas (1815–18) 'Short Memorials of the Northern Actions', *Select Tracts relating to the Civil Wars in England* (2 vols), ed. Francis, Lord Maseres, London: R. Wilkes.
Gordon, Patrick, of Ruthven (1844) 'A Short Abridgement of Britain's Distempers', *Spalding Club*, Aberdeen.
Guthry, Henry (1702) *Memoirs of Henry Guthry, Late Bishop of Dunkel in Scotland*, ed. G. Crawford, Glasgow.
Gwynne, John (1967) *Military Memoirs: The Civil War*, ed. N. Tucker and P. Young, London: Longman.
Holles, Denzil (1815) 'Memoirs of Denzil Lord Holles from 1641 to 1648', *Select Tracts relating to the Civil Wars in England*, (2 vols) ed. Francis, Lord Maseres, vol. I, London: R. Wilkes.
Hopton, Lord Ralph (1902) 'Bellum Civile', ed. C. Chadwyck-Healey, *Somerset Record Society* 18.
Hutchinson, Lucy (1808) *Memoirs of the Life of Colonel John Hutchinson*, London: Longman.

Hyde, Edward, Lord Clarendon (1888) *The History of the Rebellion and Civil Wars in England*, 6 vols, ed. W. Macray, Oxford: Oxford University Press.

Jane, Joseph (1975) 'Joseph Jane's Account of Cornwall during the Civil War', ed. A. Miller, *English Historical Review* XC.

Juxon, Thomas (1999) 'Thomas Juxon's Journal 1644–47', ed. K. Lindley and D. Scott, *Camden Society*, 5th series XIII.

Lloyd, David (1667) *Memoirs of the Lives of those Personages that suffered for the Protestant Faith and Allegiance to the Sovereign 1637–1660*, London.

Ludlow, Edmund (1894) *Memoirs 1625–1672*, 2 vols, ed. C.H. Firth, Oxford: Oxford University Press.

Luke, Sir Samuel (1947, 1950, 1952–3) 'Journals', 3 vols, ed. I. Phillip, *Oxfordshire Record Society* 29, 31, 33.

Luke, Sir Samuel (1963) 'Letter Books', ed. H. Tibbutt, *Historical Manuscripts Commission Joint Publications* 4, HMSO.

Malbon, Thomas (1889) 'Memorial', ed. J. Hall, *Lancashire and Cheshire Record Society* 19.

Monck, George, Duke of Albemarle (1671) *Observations upon Political and Military Affairs*, London.

Orrery, Roger Boyle, Earl of (1677) *A Treatise of the Art of War*, London.

Roe, Henry (1873) 'Military Memoir of Colonel Birch', ed. J. Webb, *Camden Society*, new series, VII.

Rohan, Henri, Duc de (1640) *The Complete Captain III: A Particular Treatise of Modern War*, trans. Captain John Cruso, Cambridge: Cambridge University Press.

Slingsby, Sir Henry (1836) *Diary*, ed. D. Parsons, London: Longman.

Slingsby, Walter (1902) 'Accounts of the Campaigns in the South of England 1643–44', *Somerset Record Society* 18.

Spalding, John (1850–51) 'Memorials of the Trubles in Scotland', 2 vols, ed. J. Stuart, Aberdeen: Spalding Club.

Sprigg, Joshua (1844 edn) *Anglia Rediviva*, Oxford: Oxford University Press.

Symonds, Richard (1859) 'Diaries of the Marches of the Royal Army during the Great Civil War', ed. C. Long, *Camden Society* LXXIV.

Townshend, Henry (1920) 'Diary', ed. J. Willis Bund, *Worcestershire Historical Society*.

Turner, Sir James (1829) *Memoirs of His Own Life and Times*, Edinburgh: Bannatyne Club.

Vicars, John (1647) *England's Worthies under whom all the Civill and Bloedy Warrs 1642 to 1647 are related*, London.

Walker, Sir Edward (1705) *Historical Discourses upon Several Occasions*, London: S. Keble.

Walsingham, Edward (1910) 'Hector Britannicus: The Life of Sir John Digby', ed. G. Bernard, *Camden Society*, 3rd series, 18.

Warwick, Sir Philip (1813) *Memoirs of the Reign of King Charles I etc.*, Edinburgh: Bannatyne.

Whitelock, Bulstrode (1732) *Memorials of the English Affairs etc.*, London: J. Tonson.

Wishart, George (1893) *The Memoirs of James, Marquis of Montrose*, ed. A.S. Murdoch and H.M.F. Simpson, London: Longman's, Green.

Collections of Primary Sources

Abbott, W. ed. (1937) *The Writings and Speeches of Oliver Cromwell*, 4 vols, vol. 1, Cambridge, Mass.: Harvard University Press.

Akerman, J. ed. (1856) 'Letters from Scotland Addressed to Captain Adam Baynes', Bannatyne Club.

Beamont, W. ed. (1864) 'A Discourse of the War in Lancashire', *Chetham Society* LXII.

Bell, R. ed. (1841) *Memoirs of the Reign of Charles I*, 2 vols, London: Richard Bentley.

Bray, W. ed. (1877–9) *John Evelyn's Diary*, 4 vols, IV, Oxford: Oxford University Press.

Bruce, J. and Masson, D. eds (1875) 'Manchester's Quarrel: Documents Relating to the Quarrel between the Earl of Manchester and Oliver Cromwell', *Camden Society*, new series XII.

Calendar of the Clarendon State Papers (1869), Oxford: Oxford University Press.

Calendar of State Papers Domestic 1644, 1644–5, 1645–7, 1648–9, 1650–51, 1625–49 addenda, London: HMSO.

Calendar of State Papers Ireland.

Calendar of State Papers Venetian, 1642–3.

Carlyle, T. ed. (1846) *Letters and Speeches of Oliver Cromwell*, vols I and II, London: Chapman & Hall.

Carte, T. (1735) *Life of James Butler, Duke of Ormond*, 6 vols, London.

Carte, T. ed. (1739) *A Collection of Original Letters and Papers concerning the Affairs of England (1641–1660) found amongst the Duke of Ormonde's Papers*, 2 vols, London: J. Buttenham.

Carte, T. ed. (1851) *The Life of James Butler, Duke of Ormond*, 6 vols, Oxford: Oxford University Press.

Cary, H. ed. (1842) *Memorials of the Great Civil War in England*, 2 vols, vol. II, London: Henry Colburn.

Clarke, J. ed. (1816) *Life of James II collected out of memoirs written by his own hand*, 2 vols, vol. 1, London: Longman.

Coleman, J. ed. (1898) 'A Royalist Account of the withdrawal of the King's Forces from Taunton, 13 December 1644' (Wyndham's letter), *English Historical Review* XIII.

Cooper, W.D. ed. (1853), 'The Trelawney Papers', *Camden Society* LV.

Day, W. ed. (1879) *The Pythouse Papers*, London: Bickers & Son.

Dore, R. ed. (1983–4 and 1990) 'Sir William Brereton, Letter Books I–IV', *Lancashire and Cheshire Record Society* 123 and 128.

Ellis, Sir Henry ed. (1847) *Original Letters Illustrative of English History 1400–1793*, 3rd series, 12 vols, London: Richard Bentley.

Firth, C.H. ed. (no date, but after 1886) *Memoirs of William Cavendish, Duke of Newcastle and Margaret his Wife*, London: Routledge.

Firth, C.H. ed. (1898) 'Prince Rupert's Marches', *English Historical Review* XIII.

Firth, C.H. ed. (1900) 'The Narrative of General Venables', *Camden Society*, new series 60.

Firth, C.H. ed. (1903) *Stuart Tracts*, Westminster: Archibald Constable.

Firth, C.H. and Rait, R. eds (1911) *Acts and Ordinances of the Interregnum 1642–1660*, 3 vols, London: HMSO.

Gardiner, S.R. ed. (1871) 'The Fortescue Papers', *Camden Society*, new series, I.

Gardiner, S.R. ed. (1883) 'Manchester's Letter', *Camden Society*, new series, XXXI.

Gilbert, J. ed. (1879) *A Contemporary History of Affairs in Ireland from AD 1641–1652*, 3 vols, Dublin: Irish Academic Press.

Gilbert, J. ed. (1882) *The Irish Confederation and War in Ireland 1641–9*, 7 vols, Dublin: M.M. Gill.

Green, M.A.E. ed. (1857) *Letters of Queen Henrietta Maria*, London: Richard Bentley.

Hamper, W. ed. (1827) *Life, Diary, and Correspondence of Sir William Dugdale*, London: Harding, Lepard.

Historical Manuscripts Commission (HMC), London: HMSO. Appendixes to the 1st Report (House of Lords), 4th Report (Earl de la Warre, Earl of Denbigh), 5th Report (Duke of Sutherland), 6th Report (House of Lords), 7th Report (Verney), 8th Report part II (Duke of Manchester), 9th Report part II (A. Morrison), 10th Report VI (Lord Braye), 12th Report II (Earl Cowper), 12th Report IX (Duke of Beaufort), 13th Report I, III (Duke of Portland), 14th Report VII (Marquis of Ormond), 15th Report II (Hodgkin), 16th Report (R.R. Hastings II).

House of Commons Journals II, III, IV, V, VI.

House of Lords Journals V, VI, VII, VIII, IX, X.

Laing, D. ed. (1875) 'The Ancram and Lothian Correspondence', II, *Bannatyne Club*.

Meikle, H.W. ed. (1917) 'Correspondence of the Scottish Commissioners in London', *Roxburgh Club*.

Napier, M. ed. (1848–50) *Memorials of Montrose and his Times*, 2 vols, *Maitland Club*, Edinburgh.

Peachey, S. and Turton, A. (1987) *Old Robin's Foot*, Leigh-on-Sea: Partizan Press.

Petrie, Sir Charles ed. (1935) *The Letters of King Charles I*, London: Cassell.

Petrie, Sir Charles ed. (1974) *Charles I, Prince Rupert and the Civil War*, London: Routledge & Kegan Paul.

Phillips, J. ed. (1874) *Memoirs of the Civil War in Wales and the Marches*, 2 vols, vol. 2, London: Longman.

Phillips, W. ed. (1894–6) 'The Ottley Papers relating to the Civil War', *Transactions of the Shropshire Archaeological and Natural History Society*, 2nd series, 6–8.

Roy, I. ed. (1964 and 1975) 'Royalist Ordnance Papers', *Oxfordshire Record Society* 43 and 49.

Rushworth, J. ed. (1721) *Historical Collections of Private Passages of State*, 7 vols, vols V and VI, London: D. Browne.

Sanford, J. ed. (1858) Appendix to *The Great Rebellion*, London: Bickers & Son.

Scott, Sir Walter ed. (1806) *Original Memoirs, Written during the Great Civil War; being the Life of Sir Henry Slingsby and Memoirs of Captain Hodgson*, Edinburgh.

Scott, Sir Walter ed. (1809–15) Somers Tracts, IV.

Somerville, J. (1815) *Memorie of the Somervilles; being a History of the Baronial House of Somerville*, ed. Sir Walter Scott, Edinburgh: A. Constable.

Steig, M. ed. (1977) 'The Diary of John Harington MP', *Somerset Record Society* 74.

Thurlow, John (1742) *A Collection of State Papers of John Thurlow Esquire, Secretary to the Council of State*, ed. T. Birch, London, 7 vols,

Toynbee, M. ed. (1961) 'The Papers of Captain Stevens, Wagon-master', *Oxfordshire Record Society* 42.

Trevelyan, Sir Walter and Sir Charles eds (1872) 'The Trevelyan Papers', *Camden Society* CV.

Warburton, E. (1849) *Memoirs of Prince Rupert and the Cavaliers*, 3 vols, London: Richard Bentley.

Washbourne, J. ed. (1825) *Bibliotheca Gloucestrensis*, Gloucester.

Wright, T. ed. (1842) *Autobiography of Joseph Lister of Bradford, Yorkshire*, Bradford.

Young, P. ed. (1953) 'Sir John Byron's Relation of the Late Western Action', *Journal of the Society for Army Historical Research XXXI*.

Collections of Newspapers and Pamphlets

Bodleian Library, Wood Pamphlets

British Library, Thomason Tracts

Mercurius Aulicus

Printed Secondary Sources

Books

Adair, J. (1973) *Cheriton 1644: The Campaign and the Battle*, Kineton: Roundwood Press.

Adair, J. (1976) *John Hampden the Patriot*, London: MacDonald and Jane's.

Adair, J. (1997) *Roundhead General: The Campaigns of Sir William Waller*, Stroud: Sutton.

Adamson, J.S.A. (2007) *The Noble Revolt: The Overthrow of Charles I*, London: Weidenfeld & Nicolson.

Andriette, E. (1971) *Devon and Exeter in the Civil War*, Newton Abbot: David & Charles.

Ashley, M. (1957) *The Greatness of Oliver Cromwell*, London: Hodder & Stoughton.

Ashley, M. (1975) *The English Civil War*, London: Thames & Hudson.

Ashton, R. (1994) *Counter Revolution: The Second Civil War and its Origins*, Newhaven, Conn.: Yale University Press.

Atkin, M. (1998) *Cromwell's Crowning Mercy: The Battle of Worcester 1651*, Stroud: Sutton.

Atkin, M. (2004) *Worcestershire under Arms: An English County during the Civil Wars*, Barnsley: Pen and Sword.

Barker, T.M. (1975) *The Military Intellectual and Battle: Raimondo Montecuccoli and the Thirty Years War*, Albany, NY: State University of New York Press.

Barratt, J. (2000) *Cavaliers: The Royalist Army at War 1642–46*, Stroud: Alan Sutton.

Barratt, J. (2003) *The Battle for York: Marston Moor 1644*, Stroud: Tempus.

Barratt, J. (2004) *Cavalier Generals: King Charles I and his Commanders in the English Civil Wars 1642–46*, Barnsley: Pen and Sword.

Barratt, J. (2005) *The First Battle of Newbury 1643*, Stroud: Tempus.

Bartlett, T. and Jeffrey, K. eds (1996) *A Military History of Ireland*, Cambridge: Cambridge University Press.

Bennett, M. (1995) *The English Civil War*, London: Longman.

Bennett, M. (1997) *The Civil Wars in Britain and Ireland 1638–1651*, Oxford: Blackwell.

Bennett, M. (2006) *Oliver Cromwell*, London: Routledge.

Black, J. (2000) *War – Past, Present and Future*, Stroud: Sutton.

Black, J. (2004) *Rethinking Military History*, London: Routledge.

Buchan, J. (1928) *Montrose*, London: Nelson.

Burne, A.H. (1996 edn) *Battlefields of England*, London: Penguin.

Burne, A.H. and Young, P. (1959) *The Great Civil War: A Military History of the First Civil War*, London: Eyre & Spottiswoode.

Carlton, C. (1992) *Going to the Wars: The Experience of the British Civil Wars 1638–1651*, London: Routledge.

Carpenter, S.D.M. (2005) *Military Leadership in the British Civil Wars, 1642–1651: 'The Genius of this Age'*, London: Frank Cass.

Carte, T. (1851) *Life of the First Duke of Ormond*, Oxford: Oxford University Press.

Childs, J. (2001) *Warfare in the Seventeenth Century*, London: Cassell.

Coate, M. (1963) *Cornwall in the Civil War and Interregnum 1642–1660*, 2nd edn, Truro: Bradford Barton.

Coward, B. (1991) *Oliver Cromwell*, London: Longman.

Coward, B. (1994) *The Stuart Age: England 1603–1714*, London: Longman.

Cust, Richard (2005) *Charles I*, Harlow: Pearson/Longman.

Davis, J.C. (2001) *Oliver Cromwell*, London: Arnold.

Devereux, W. (1853) *Lives and Letters of the Devereux, Earls of Essex*, vol. II, London: John Murray.

Dore, R. (1966) *The Civil War in Cheshire*, Chester: Cheshire Community Council.

Douglas, W. (1898) *Cromwell's Scotch Campaign 1650–51*, London: Elliot Stock.

Dow, F. (1979) *Cromwellian Scotland 1651–1660*, Edinburgh: John Donald.

Earwaker, J.P. (1877) *East Cheshire: Past and Present*, 2 vols, London: privately printed.

Ede-Borrett, S. (2004) *Lostwithiel 1644: The Campaigns and the Battles*, Farnham: Pike and Shot Society Publication.

Edgar, F. (1968) *Sir Ralph Hopton*, Oxford: Oxford University Press.

Edwards, P. (2000) *Dealing in Death: The Arms Trade and the British Civil Wars, 1638–1652*, Stroud: Sutton.

Everitt, A. (1966) *The Community of Kent and the Great Rebellion 1640–60*, Leicester: Leicester University Press.

Farr, D. (2003) *John Lambert: Parliamentary Soldier and Cromwellian Major General*, Woodbridge, Suffolk: Boydell & Brewer.

Farrow, W. (1926) *The Great Civil War in Shropshire*, Shrewsbury: Wilding.

Firth, C.H. (1904) *Cromwell*, London: Putnam's.

Firth, C.H. (1962 edn) *Cromwell's Army*, London: Methuen.

Fissell, M. (1991) *War and Government 1598–1650*, Manchester: Manchester University Press.

Fissell, M. (1994) *The Bishops' Wars: Charles I's Campaigns against Scotland 1638–40*, Cambridge: Cambridge University Press.

Fletcher, A. (1981) *The Outbreak of the English Civil War*, Edward Arnold; London.

Foard, G. (1995) *Naseby: The Decisive Campaign*, Whitstable: Prior Publications.

Fortescue, Sir John (1910) *A History of the British Army*, 13 vols, vol. 1, London: Macmillan.

Fuller, J.F.C. (1933) *Generalship: Its Diseases and their Cure*, London: Faber and Faber.

Gardiner, S.R. (1901) *Oliver Cromwell*, London: Longman.

Gardiner, S.R. (1903) *The Commonwealth and the Protectorate*, 3 vols, London: Longman.

Gardiner, S.R. (1991 edn) *History of the Great Civil War*, 4 vols, Moreton in the Marsh: Windrush Press.

Gaunt, P. (1996) *Oliver Cromwell*, Oxford: Blackwell.

Gaunt, P. (1997) *The British Wars*, London: Routledge.

Gaunt, P. ed. (2000) *The English Civil War*, Oxford: Blackwell.

Gentles, I. (1992) *The New Model Army in England, Ireland and Scotland 1645–1653*, Oxford: Blackwell.

Gentles, I. (2007) *The English Revolution and the Wars in Three Kingdoms 1638–1652*, Harlow: Longman, Pearson.

Grainger, J.D. (1997) *Cromwell against the Scots: The Last Anglo-Scottish War 1650–1652*, East Linton, East Lothian: Tuckwell Press.

Hayes-McCoy, G. (1989) *Irish Battles: A Military History of Ireland*, Belfast: Appletree Press.

Hexter, J.H. (1968 edn) *The Reign of King Pym*, Cambridge, MA: Harvard University Press.

Hill, J.E.C. (1961) *The Century of Revolution*, Edinburgh: Nelson.

Hirst, D. (1999) *England in Conflict 1603–1660*, London: Arnold.

Holmes, C. (1974) *The Eastern Association in the English Civil War*, Cambridge: Cambridge University Press.

Holmes, R. ed. (2001) *The Oxford Companion to Military History*, Oxford: Oxford University Press.

Hughes, A. (1987) *Politics, Society and Civil War in Warwickshire, 1620–1660*, Cambridge: Cambridge University Press.

Hutton, R. (1982) *The Royalist War Effort 1642–1646*, London: Longman.

Hutton, R. (2004) *Debates in Stuart History*, London: Palgrave.

Jones, A. (1987) *The Art of War in the Western World*, Oxford: Oxford University Press.

Kaufman, H. (1962) *Conscientious Cavalier: Colonel Bullen Reymes MP, FRS 1613–1672*, London: Jonathan Cape.

Keegan, J. (1976) *The Face of Battle*, London: Jonathan Cape.

Keegan, J. (1987) *The Mask of Command*, London: Jonathan Cape.

Kenyon, J. (1988) *The Civil Wars of England*, London: Weidenfeld & Nicolson.

Kenyon, J. and Ohlmeyer, J. eds (1998) *The Civil Wars: A Military History of England, Scotland and Ireland 1639–1660*, Oxford: Oxford University Press.

Kishlansky, M. (1979) *The Rise of the New Model Army*, Cambridge: Cambridge University Press.

Kitson, Sir Frank (1994) *Prince Rupert: Portrait of a Soldier*, London: Constable.

Kitson, Sir Frank (2004) *Old Ironside: The Military Biography of Oliver Cromwell*, London: Weidenfeld & Nicolson.

Lee, jun., M. (1985) *The Road to Revolution: Scotland under Charles I 1625–37*, Urbana, Ill.: Illinois University Press.

Lenihan, P. ed. (2001) *Conquest and Resistance: War in Seventeenth-Century Ireland*, Leyden: Brill Academic Publishing.

Lenihan, P. (2007) *Consolidating Conquest: Ireland 1603–1727*, Harlow: Pearson/Longman.

Lynch, J. (1999) *For King and Parliament: Bristol and the Civil War*, Stroud: Sutton.

MacInnes, A. (1991) *Charles I and the Making of the Covenanting Movement*, Edinburgh: John Donald.

Mackay, W. (1939) *Little Madam: A Life of Queen Henrietta Maria*, London: Bell.

Malcolm, J. (1983) *Caesar's Due: Loyalty and King Charles I*, London: Royal Historical Society.

Marix Evans, M. (2007) *Naseby 1645, the Triumph of the New Model Army*, Oxford: Osprey

Marix Evans, M., Burton, P. and Westaway, M. (2002) *Battlefield Britain: Naseby, June 1645*, Barnsley: Leo Cooper.

Markham, Sir Clement (1870) *The Great Lord Fairfax*, London: Macmillan.

Marshall, A. (2004) *Oliver Cromwell: Soldier – The Military Life of a Revolutionary at War*, London: Brasseys.

Matthew, H. and Harrison, B. eds (2004) *Oxford Dictionary of National Biography*, Oxford: Oxford University Press.

Miller, A. (1979) *Sir Richard Grenville of the Civil War*, Chichester: Phillimore.

Moody, T.W., Martin, F.X. and Byrne, F.J. eds (1978) *Early Modern Ireland 1534–1691: A New History of Ireland*, 6 vols, vol. III, Oxford: Oxford University Press.

Morrah, P. (1976) *Prince Rupert of the Rhine*, London: Constable.

Morrill, J. (1973) *Cheshire 1630–60*, Oxford: Oxford University Press.

Morrill, J. (1980) *Seventeenth-Century Britain*, Folkestone: Dawson.

Morrill, J. ed. (1990) *Oliver Cromwell and the English Revolution*, London: Longman.

Morrill, J. ed. (1990) *The Scottish National Covenant in its British Context*, Edinburgh: Edinburgh University Press.

Morris, R. (1924) *The Siege of Chester*, Chester: Cheshire Archaeological Society.

Napier, Mark, Lord ed. (1848–50) *Memorials of Montrose and his Times*, 2 vols, Aberdeen: Maitland Club.

Newman, P. (1981) *The Battle of Marston Moor 1644*, Chichester: Phillimore.

Newman, P. and Roberts, P. (2003) *The Battle of Marston Moor 1644*, 2nd edn, Pickering: Blackthorn Press.

Nugent, George Grenville, Lord (1874) *Memorials of John Hampden, His Party and His Times*, 2 vols, 5th edn, London: Bell.

Ohlmeyer, J. ed. (1995) *Ireland from Independence to Occupation*, Cambridge: Cambridge University Press.

Ollard, R. (1976) *This War without an Enemy: A History of the English Civil Wars*, London: Hodder & Stoughton.

O'Siochru, M. (1999) *Confederate Ireland: A Constitutional and Political Analysis*, Dublin: Four Courts Press.

Paret, P. (1986) *Makers of Modern Strategy: From Machiavelli to the Nuclear Age*, Princeton, NJ: Princeton University Press.

Parker, G. (1996) *The Military Revolution: Military Innovation and the Rise of the West 1500–1800*, 2nd edn, Cambridge: Cambridge University Press.

Phillips, J. (1874) *Memoirs of the Civil Wars in Wales and the Marches*, vol. 2, London: Longman.

Porter, S. ed. (1996) *London and the Civil War*, London: Macmillan.

Powell, J.R. (1972) *Robert Blake: General-at-Sea*, London: Collins.

Reid, S. (1990) *The Campaigns of Montrose: A Military History of the Civil Wars in Scotland*, Edinburgh: Mercat Press.

Reid, S. (1998) *All the King's Armies: A Military History of the English Civil Wars 1642–1651*, Sevenoaks: Spellmount.

Reilly, T. (1999) *Cromwell, an Honourable Enemy*, London: Phoenix Press.

Robbins, S. (2003) *God's General: Cromwell the Soldier*, Stroud: Alan Sutton.

Roberts, K. (2003) *First Newbury 1643: The Turning Point*, Oxford: Osprey Publishing.

Roberts, K. (2005) *Cromwell's War Machine: The New Model Army 1645–1660*, Barnsley: Pen and Sword.

Roberts, K. and Tincey, J. (2001) *Edgehill 1642: The First Battle of the English Civil War*, Oxford: Osprey.

Rogers, C.J. ed. (1995) *The Military Revolution Debate: Readings in the Military Thought of Early Modern Europe*, Boulder, Colo.: Westview Press.

Rogers, H. (1968) *Battles and Generals of the English Civil War*, London: Seeley Press.

Russell, C. (1991) *The Fall of the British Monarchies*, Oxford: Oxford University Press.

Scott, C., Turton, A. and Von Arni, E. (2004) *Edgehill: The Battle Reinterpreted*, Barnsley: Pen and Sword.

Scott, D. (2004) *Politics and War in the Three Stuart Kingdoms*, London: Palgrave.

Seel, G. (1996) *The English Civil Wars and Republic 1637–60*, London: Routledge.

Seymour, W. (1975) *Battles in Britain 1642–1746*, London: Sidgwick & Jackson.

Sherwood, R.L. (1974) *Civil Strife in the Midlands 1642–1651*, Chichester: Phillimore.

Smith, D. (1998) *A History of the Modern British Isles 1603–1707*, Oxford: Blackwell.

Snow, V. (1970) *Essex the Rebel: The Life of Robert Devereux, the Third Earl of Essex 1591–1646*, Lincoln, Nebr.: University of Nebraska Press.

Spencer, C. (2007) *Prince Rupert, the Last Cavalier*, London: Weidenfeld & Nicolson.

Stevenson, D. (1973) *The Scottish Revolution 1637–44: The Triumph of the Covenanters*, Newton Abbot: David & Charles.

Stevenson, D. (1977) *Revolution and Counter-Revolution in Scotland 1644–51*, London: Royal Historical Association.

Stevenson, D. (1994) *Highland Warrior: Alasdair MacColla and the Civil Wars*, Edinburgh: The Saltaire Society.

Stoyle, M. (1996) *From Deliverance to Destruction: Rebellion and Civil War in an English City*, Exeter: University of Exeter Press.

Stoyle, M. (2005) *Soldiers and Strangers: An Ethnic History of the English Civil War*, London: Yale University Press.

Sunderland, F. (1926) *Marmaduke, Lord Langdale*, London: Jenkins.

Terry, C. (1899) *Life and Campaigns of Alexander Leslie, Earl of Leven*, London: Longman, Green.

Tincey, J. (2003) *Marston Moor 1644: The Beginning of the End*, Oxford: Osprey.

Toynbee, M. and Young, P. (1970) *The Battle of Cropredy Bridge*, Kineton: Roundwood Press.

Underdown, D. (1973) *Somerset in the Civil War and Interregnum*, Newton Abbot: David & Charles.

Van Crefeld, M. (1985) *Command in War*, Cambridge, Mass.: Harvard University Press.

Van Crefeld, M. (2000) *The Art of War: War and the Military Mind*, London: Cassell.

Wanklyn, M. (2006) *Decisive Battles of the English Civil Wars*, Barnsley: Pen and Sword.

Wanklyn, M. and Jones, F. (2004) *A Military History of the English Civil Wars: Strategy and Tactics*, Harlow: Pearson/Longman.

Wanty, E. (1967) *L'Art de la Guerre*, 2 vols, vol. I (*Marabout Université 142*), Verviers: Les Editions Gérard.

Wavell, Archibald, Lord (1941) *Generals and Generalship*, London: Penguin.

Webb, J. and Webb, T.W. (1879) *Memorials of the Civil War as it Affected Herefordshire and the Adjacent Counties*, 2 vols, London: Longman.

Wedgwood, C.V. (1952) *Montrose*, London: Collins.

Wedgwood, C.V. (1958) *The King's War*, London: Collins.

Weigley, R. (1993) *The Age of Battles*, London: Pimlico.

Wenham, P. (1970) *The Great and Close Siege of York*, Kineton: Roundwood Press.

Wheeler, J.S. (1999) *Cromwell in Ireland*, London: Gill and Macmillan.

Wheeler, J.S. (1999) *The Making of a World Power: War and Military Revolution in the Seventeenth Century*, Stroud: Sutton.

Wheeler, J.S. (2002) *The Irish and British Wars 1637–1654: Triumph, Tragedy and Failure*, London: Routledge.

Willan, T.S. (1938) *The English Coastal Trade 1600–1750*, Manchester: Manchester University Press.

Williams, D. (1975) *Montrose, Cavalier in Mourning*, London: Barrie and Jenkins.

Willis Bund, J. (1905) *The Civil War in Worcestershire*, Birmingham: The Midland Educational Committee.

Woolrych, A. (1961) *Battles of the English Civil War*, London: Batsford.

Woolrych, A. (2002) *Britain in Revolution 1625–1660*, Oxford: Oxford University Press.

Young, M. (1997) *Charles I*, London: Macmillan.

Young, P. (1967) *Edgehill: The Campaign and the Battle*, Kineton: Roundwood Press.

Young, P. (1970) *Marston Moor 1644*, Kineton: Roundwood Press.

Young, P. (1985) *Naseby 1645: The Campaign and the Battle*, London: Century Press.

Young, P. and Holmes, R. (1974) *The English Civil Wars*, London: Eyre Methuen.

Young, P. et al. (1964) *Newark on Trent: The Civil War Siegeworks*, London: HMSO.

Essays and Journal Articles

Adamson, J.S.A. (1990) 'The Baronial Context of the English Civil War', *Transactions of the Royal Historical Society*, 6th series, 40.

Adamson, J.S.A. (2002) 'The Triumph of Oligarchy: The Management of War and the Committee of Both Kingdoms, 1644–1645', C. Kyle and J. Peacey, eds, *Parliament at Work*, Woodbridge: Boydell Press.

Beats, L. (1977–8) 'The East Midlands Association 1642–1644', *Midland History* IV.

Bennett, M. (1986) 'Contribution and Assessment: Financial Exactions in the English Civil War, 1642–1646', *War and Society* 4.

Burke, J. (1990) 'The New Model Army and the Problems of Siege Warfare, 1648–51', *Irish Historical Studies*, XXVII.

Burne, A.H. (1951) 'Generalship in the First Civil War 1642–1644', *History Today*, April issue, pp. 63–9.

Coate, M. (1935) 'An Original Diary of Colonel Robert Bennett', *Devon and Cornwall Notes and Queries* 18.

Cotton, A. (1977) 'Cromwell and the Self-Denying Ordinance', *History* LXII.

Crawford, L. (1975) 'The Savile Affair', *English Historical Review* XC.

Davies, G. (1921) 'The Battle of Edgehill', *English Historical Review* XXXVI.

Davies, G. (1934) 'The Parliamentary Army under the Earl of Essex 1642–1645', *English Historical Review* XXXIX.

Firth, C.H. (1895) 'The "Memoirs" of Sir Richard Bulstrode', *English Historical Review* X.

Firth, C.H. (1899) 'The Raising of the Ironsides', *Transactions of the Royal Historical Society* XIII.

Firth, C.H. (1900) 'The Battle of Dunbar', *Transactions of the Royal Historical Society*, new series, 14.

Firth, C.H. (1904) 'Clarendon's History of the Great Rebellion', *English Historical Review* XIX.

Gilbert, C.D. (1993) 'Clubmen in Southwest Shropshire, 1644–5', *Transactions of the Shropshire Archaeological and Natural History Society* LXXVII.

Gladwish, P. (1985) 'The Herefordshire Clubmen: A Reassessment', *Midland History* X.

Lenihan, P. (1997) ' "Celtic Warfare" in the Sixteen-Forties', in J.R. Young, ed., *Celtic Dimensions of the British Civil Wars*, Edinburgh: Edinburgh University Press.

Lenihan, P. (1997) 'War and Famine 1649–52', *Irish Economic and Social History* 24.

Malcolm, J. (1978) 'A King in Search of Soldiers: Charles I in 1642', *Historical Journal* 21.

Malcolm, J. (1979) 'All the King's Men: The Impact on the Crown of Irish Soldiers in the English Civil War', *Irish Historical Review* XVI.

Parker, G. (2007) 'The Limits to Revolutions in Military Affairs', *Journal of Military History* 71.2.

Parrott, D. (1992) 'The Military Revolution in Seventeenth-Century Europe', *History Today*.

Phillips, C. (1978) 'The Royalist North: The Cumberland and Westmorland Gentry 1642–1660', *Northern History* XIV.

Porter S. (2007) 'The Battle of Turnham Green', *Battlefield* 12.4.

Roy, I. (1962) 'The Royalist Council of War, 1642–46', *Bulletin of the Institute of Historical Research* 35.

Roy, I. (1975) 'The English Civil War and English Society', in B. Bond and I. Roy, eds, *War and Society: Military History Yearbook 1*, London: Croom Helm.

Roy, I. (1978) 'England Turned Germany? The Aftermath of the Civil War in its European Context', *Transactions of the Royal Historical Society*, 6th series, 28.

Roy, I. (1998) 'George Digby, Royalist Intrigue and the Collapse of the Cause', in I. Gentles, J. Morrill and B. Worden, eds, *Writers and Statesmen of the English Revolution*, Cambridge: University Press.

Roy, I. (2008) 'Why Did Prince Rupert Fight at Marston Moor?', *Journal of the Society for Army Historical Research* 86.

Russell, C. (2003) 'James VI and I's Rule over Two Kingdoms: An English View', *Historical Research* LXXVI.

Stoyle, M. (1996) ' "Sir Richard Grenville's Creatures": The New Cornish Tertia, 1644–46', *Cornish Studies* 4.

Tibbutt, H. (1948) 'The Life and Letters of Sir Lewis Dyve', *Bedfordshire Record Society* 22.

Wanklyn, M. (1968) 'The Royalist Campaign in Somerset in July 1645', *Journal of the Society for Army Historical Research* 46.

Wanklyn, M. (1981) 'Royalist Strategy in the South of England 1642–1644', *Southern History* 3.

Wanklyn, M. (2006) 'Paying for the Sins of our Forefathers: Catholic Loyalism in the Midlands in the Great Civil War', *Midland Catholic History* 12.

Wanklyn, M. (2007) 'A General Much Maligned: The Generalship of the Earl of Manchester, July to November 1644', *War in History* 14.2.

Wanklyn, M. and Young, P. (1981) 'A King in Search of Soldiers: A Rejoinder', *Historical Journal* 24.

Wheeler, J.S. (1992) 'The Logistics of the Cromwellian Conquest of Scotland 1650–1651', *War and Society* 10.

Young, P. (1953) 'The Royalist Army at the Battle of Roundway Down', *Journal of the Society for Army Historical Research* XXXI.

Young, P. (1955) 'The Royalist Army at Edgehill', *Journal of the Society of Army Historical Research* XXXIII.

Theses

Jones, F. (2000) 'The Role and Effectiveness of Cavalry in the English Civil War', M.Phil., Wolverhampton.

Roy, I. (1963) 'The Royalist Army in the First Civil War', Ph.D., Oxford.

Wanklyn, M. (1966) 'The King's Armies in the West of England 1642–46', MA., Manchester.

Wanklyn, M. (1976) 'Landownership and Allegiance in Cheshire and Shropshire at the Outbreak of the First Civil War', Ph.D., Manchester.

Film Made for Television

Cromwell: God's Executioner (2008) Documentary, History Channel.

Index